CAPITAL MARKETS AND CORPORATE GOVERNANCE

Capital Markets and Corporate Governance

NICHOLAS DIMSDALE

AND

MARTHA PREVEZER

CLARENDON PRESS · OXFORD

Oxford University Press, Great Clarendon Street, Oxford OX2 6DP
Oxford New York
Athens Auckland Bangkok Bogota Bombay
Buenos Aires Calcutta Cape Town Dar es Salaam
Delhi Florence Hong Kong Istanbul Karachi
Kuala Lumpur Madras Madrid Melbourne
Mexico City Nairobi Paris Singapore
Taipei Tokyo Toronto Warsaw
and associated companies in
Berlin Ibadan

Oxford is a registered trade mark of Oxford University Press

Published in the United States by
Oxford University Press Inc., New York

First published 1994
Reprinted 1995, 1998

British Library Cataloguing in Publication Data
Data available
ISBN 0-19-828788-7

Library of Congress Cataloging in Publication Data
Capital markets and corporate governance / [edited by] Nicholas
Dimsdale and Martha Prevezer.
p. cm.
Papers presented at a conference organized by the National
Economic Development Office in Nov. 1991.
Includes bibliographical references.
1. Corporations—Great Britain—Finance—Congresses. 2. Corporate
governance—Great Britain—Congresses. 3. Capital market—Great
Britain—Congresses. 4. Corporations—Germany—Finance—Congresses.
5. Corporate governance—Germany—Congresses. 6. Capital market—
Germany—Congresses. 7. Corporations—Japan—Finance—Congresses.
8. Corporate governance—Japan—Congresses. 9. Capital market—
Japan—Congresses. I. Dimsdale, Nicholas. II. Prevezer, Martha.
HG4135.C36 1994 658.15—dc20 93-27107
ISBN 0-19-828788-7

3 5 7 9 10 8 6 4

Printed in Great Britain on acid-free paper by
Antony Rowe Ltd., Chippenham, Wilts

PREFACE

CORPORATE governance is concerned with the way in which corporations are governed and in particular in the United Kingdom the relationship between the management of a company and its shareholders. There has been a rapid growth of interest in this area recently in the United States which is now spreading to the UK.

This follows the development of an active market for corporate control in the 1980s. Contested takeover bids illustrate in a dramatic way the consequences of an underlying difference of interest between management and shareholders. In a successful company such differences are less acute, since the market valuation of the firm is not depressed so as to invite a bid to challenge the incumbent management team. Nevertheless differences do exist as current controversies over the determination of the remuneration of senior executives in major corporations demonstrate.

In Britain there are serious difficulties of enforcing accountability of management to shareholders because of the predominance of directors with executive responsibilities on company boards. Shareholders, whether institutional or private, are frequently not in a good position to enforce accountability of management through representation on boards or by exercise of voting rights at AGMs.

The situation is made worse if the manager's competence is called into question. The remedy in such circumstances has been the development of an active market for corporate control, but unease has been expressed about the takeover mechanism. This leads back to the need to improve the internal operation of the system of corporate governance. Such concerns have been expressed in the British and US context.

The backdrop to this debate has been the growing demand during the 1980s for openness and accountability, and the dismantling of exclusive networks in favour of more competitive markets. In the context of UK corporate governance this has meant accountability to shareholders, subject to legal constraints. Implicit corporatist social responsibilities have diminished in the sharper, more legalistic climate of the 1980s. Elsewhere social responsibilities have survived.

Accountability in Germany and Japan, for instance, means not just accountability to shareholders but to a range of interested parties. These include employees, suppliers and creditors, as well as shareholders. The unique role of the shareholder as the holder of residual income, and the presumption that risk is borne by the holder of residual income, have not prevailed in Germany and Japan in the 1980s.

One may characterize these differences between systems in various ways. The German and Japanese system of allying decision-making power and availability of information with interested parties has been described as an insider system. This contrasts with that in the UK and the USA where those in whom ultimate sanction resides are outsiders, divorced from those who are interested parties in the business. In an insider system the powers of the shareholder are diluted and those of the banks, suppliers and employees are increased. The role of the banks is more prominent in disciplining company managements, while that of the stock market is reduced.

The Cadbury Committee has focused on the accounting aspects of corporate governance with the aim of making the existing UK system function more effectively. It has made a useful contribution to the debate on the role of the board of directors in the running of companies. The details of the draft report are discussed by Dimsdale in this volume. The consideration of corporate governance by the Cadbury Committee does not extend to the benefits and drawbacks of insider and outsider systems, more widely defined. This book includes surveys of German and Japanese relationships between their capital markets and companies to begin to assess these questions.

The book stems from a conference organized by the National Economic Development Office in November 1991. We would like to thank all the participants at the conference as well as the contributors of the papers. Also the following people who contributed enormously in helping us to focus on the issues, organize the conference, and edit the book: Alex Bowen, Alan Cawkwell, Walter Eltis, Julian Franks, John Kay, Colin Mayer, and Ken Mayhew.

The editors would like to express their gratitude to the staff of Oxford University Press for their unfailing assistance in the production of this volume. Their special thanks are due to Andrew Schuller and Tracy Mawson for patience and encouragement.

N.H.D. and M.P.

CONTENTS

Contents

II
GERMANY AND JAPAN

ABBREVIATIONS

ABI	Association of British Insurers
ACOST	Advisory Council on Science and Technology
AGM	Annual General Meeting
BEQB	Bank of England Quarterly Bulletin
BIS	Bank for International Settlements
BVCA	British Venture Capital Association
CAPM	Capital Asset Pricing Model
CCA	Current Cost Accounting
CEO	Chief Executive Officer
CP	Commercial Paper
EC	European Community
EPS	Earnings Per Share
ERISA	Employee Retirement Income Security Act
EVCA	European Venture Capital Association
HMSO	Her Majesty's Stationery Office
LBO	Leveraged Buy-Out
MBAR	Market-Based Accounting Research
MBO	Management Buy-Out
MGS	Mutual Guarantee Schemes
MITI	Ministry of International Trade and Industry
NASDAQ	National Association of Securities Dealers Automated Quotations
NED	Non-executive Director
NPV	Net Present Value
NRI	Nomura Research Institute
NVCA	National Venture Capital Association
NYSE	New York Stock Exchange
OECD	Organization for European Co-operation and Development
OTC	Over the Counter
PEP	Personal Equity Plan
PRH	Private Rented Housing
PRONED	Promotion of Non-executive Directors
ROE	Return on Equity

RONA	Return On Net Assets
ROTA	Return On Total Assets
S & P	Standard and Poors
SEAQ	Stock Exchange Automatic Quotation
SFIC	Small Firms Investment Company
SMART	Special Merit Award for Research and Technology
SME	Small and Medium-sized Enterprises
SPUR	Support to Projects Under Research
WRA	Weighted Risk Asset

PART 1
United Kingdom

Introduction

Reading the chapters contributed to this book, I was struck by the extent to which the writers had seen the benefit of a close relationship between all those involved in making a success of business and industry in this country. At one level the concern was to secure better control of companies, and greater accountability, so as to ensure both that business performed more effectively and that unexpected surprises were so far as possible avoided. Another strand was the importance of banks getting closer to their customers and developing a stronger involvement with industry such as through venture capital investment. We at National Westminster support the emphasis that has recently been given to improve corporate governance.

To some extent the debate has been promoted by a belief that hostile takeovers are but a blunt instrument to secure more effective management of a company, and may have wasteful consequences. Such concerns have partially been the result of a number of high-profile corporate failures which have occurred without any apparent warning in prior accounts. The purpose of this scrutiny of our corporate governance structure must be to secure, through proper performance of the board and management, a greater efficiency in our industry. All this must be welcome to the banks, whose progress reflects both the success of the economy and that of the individual businesses to whom they lend. I also strongly support those who express the view that banks ought to acquire increasingly detailed knowledge about the companies to whom they lend. I believe that, certainly within our own bank, this is happening as we focus in greater depth on the needs of our customers and build ever closer relationships with them. I believe strongly in a relationship banking approach.

As to equity investment, we cannot simply leap into the position in which the German banks now find themselves. Their involvement as investors in companies reflects the history of the German economy over the last hundred years. Corporate failures between the wars, and after the last war in some cases, gave the banks no choice but to become shareholders if they were to have any prospect of recovering their investment. However, such has been the success of the Germany economy over the last forty years that such investments have since served them well.

THE BRITISH ECONOMY

I should like first to stand back from the debate in these chapters and say a few words about what seems to me to be at the heart of many of the concerns that have been expressed. This is, quite simply, the economic background against which we have had, for so long in this country, to conduct our activities. At the moment, we are all searching and hoping for signs of a recovery in the economy. We look forward to increased output, lower levels of unemployment, and higher profitability. But surely we must also look forward to freedom from the devastating economic swings which have been the burden of industry over the last two decades. The 'boom and bust' pattern of the economy must be stopped.

It has been remarked, accurately, that a recession finds out companies that are weak whether in balance sheet structure, strategically, ethically, or in corporate structure and governance. Mistakes are brought to the surface at such times. Everyone in industry and commerce makes errors of judgement from time to time, and for these a price has to be paid. But it is quite a leap of imagination to claim that factory closures, job losses, and credit losses at the present time are therefore the fault of management in industry, commerce, and finance.

It is much more the volatility of the economic environment that significantly increases the risks faced by the private sector. Irrespective of how the private sector behaves, a more volatile environment will damage companies, employment, and credit. In the UK the private sector has been subject to very high economic volatility, such as inflation of 11 per cent in one year, followed by a fall in GNP of 2 per cent the next. It would therefore be of considerable benefit to industry and commerce if the external risk to which they were subject were diminished as much as possible.

In a future environment of price stability we shall also be dependent for our success and international competitiveness upon fundamentals such as the productivity of our manufacturing and service industries and the disciplines imposed upon our wage negotiations, the quality of our education and training, and the efficiency of our infrastructure.

These are all challenges, and painful ones. I believe the strenuous efforts called for in all these areas are infinitely preferable to the uncertainty and instability inherent in the UK's 'stop-go' economy over the last two decades. The benefits to be gained from operating in a more predictable environment will be well worth the effort. To begin with, lower public spending and a low rate of inflation should encourage more private sector savings. Industry will also have greater confidence to invest in the new technology and research and development that are so necessary to our future. Indeed, companies will be able to spend less time worrying about how to react to a seemingly ever-changing financial environment, and more on proactively developing the business for the long term. This shift in priorities from day-to-day finance to production and investment may lead to a welcome change in the trend highlighted by Walter Eltis and his colleagues in their excellent paper 'The Lessons for Britain from the Superior Economic Performances of Germany and Japan', *National Westminster Bank Quarterly Review* (February 1992).

The paper notes:

Given the sharp difference in macroeconomic environments, it is not surprising that accountants and auditors so often reach the top in Britain, while engineers, technologists and scientists get so much further in Germany and Japan.

If we do achieve a more stable economic environment, it must also be to the benefit of the financial sector. The greater freedom of companies to pursue long-term goals will mean that bankers will have more confidence in the future performance of their corporate customers, and thus feel more inclined to lend for longer periods.

Such a strict economic and monetary discipline will ensure that companies are forced to focus on productivity and output per person, rather than rely on economic booms, inflationary adjustments, or exchange rate fluctuations, to conceal weak management. A stabler economic climate, and a greater concentration on fundamentals, may serve to discourage short-termism.

SHORT-TERM PRESSURES

The pressures for short-term performance in this country in recent years have not served long-term needs. Lord Benson, with his immense City experience, recently warned: 'predators lurk in the City, seeking to snap up companies which in their opinion have not distributed sufficient profits or which have accumulated a fund of liquid assets' (*Hansard, House of Lords* (19 June 1991), 180).

The increase in productivity in the 1980s led to higher wages, higher dividends, and this was coupled with over-gearing and a level of investment which our continental competitors would not regard as satisfactory. It is a stark reminder to us that our productivity level is still so much lower than that in Germany.

So perhaps, if we can achieve steady low inflation and more effective long-term planning, we may hear fewer accusations and counter-accusations about short-termism, so that the City and industry will be able, as Alan Clements hopes, to 'stop blaming each other' (*Financial Times*, 22 July 1991).

CORPORATE GOVERNANCE

The chapters in this book provide food for thought on the issue of corporate governance in the UK. They debate the pertinent issues more thoroughly than I have seen in any previous group of papers. Indeed, the view now seems to be polarizing into two schools of thought, both of which need to be taken seriously and which should form the basis of public debate.

The first school of thought is that we should be able to do everything better; to improve relations between companies and their shareholders; to improve the quality of outside directors; to encourage people to think longer term; to ensure that the stock-market values shares properly; to ensure that executive management is monitored properly in the interests of shareholders, such as through audit and other committees, and so on. The view of this school is that there is nothing intrinsically wrong with the British system of corporate governance, the issue is simply one of execution.

The other school of thought is that the British system has a fundamental flaw, and that it is a mistake to have such an efficient market in corporate control. If one allies the ease of transfer of ownership of companies with a financial services industry which benefits from buying and selling companies, then it is difficult to withstand the pressures to trade in company ownership. Companies will, therefore, forever be casting one eye over their shoulder at the stock-market. Long-term thinking gets driven out steadily. The management of companies comes under increasing and at times crushing pressure. The only solution is to change the system for achieving a change in corporate control.

It seems generally to be agreed that it would be impossible to deal with the second view simply by appealing to people's better nature and asking them to act on a longer-term perspective. The incentive to 'free-ride' on the self-restraint of others would prove irresistible.

If we are to see a greater degree of long-termism in corporate policy making it is argued that a longer-term relationship between investors and companies is essential. In turn this could mean that at least some investors might have to forego their right to sell at any moment when the rate of return calculations made it most convenient. This argument is developed in more detail by Allen Sykes in Chapter 5. Whether his ideas are practical or not would depend on the views of the investment institutions. One can see many difficulties in their way. The chapter presents an interesting argument, and puts forward most clearly the case at one end of the spectrum of opinion.

Most other suggestions for changing the system of corporate governance, so as to remove the short-term threat managements perceive, would require changes in the law. This is a severe handicap, since at present there is no consensus among industry and commerce as to what the preferred legal changes should be.

The contrary argument is that the present system of having a very efficient market in corporate control is essential as a means of keeping corporate management on its toes. If there were no such sanction then companies might become sluggish.

In principle there seems no reason why that need be the case. Companies would still have to compete in product and service markets, as long as those markets are fully competitive. Any loss of profitability or of sales would be noted within the company. The shareholder interest would be made clear to the company. Looking elsewhere German, Italian, French, Belgian, and Dutch companies, to name those from but a few countries, are often extremely efficient in the product and service markets. There are many arguments on both sides and this debate needs to be pursued with vigour.

TRAINING

We cannot exploit our opportunities nor compete effectively in Europe's increasingly unfettered market-place, without tackling a number of fundamental weak links in our economic system. The low availability of skilled and well-educated labour will be a particularly effective brake on future performance. A recent article in the *Financial Times* (6 September 1991), comparing the German and British education systems, opens with the quotation:

We have to face the fact that it will take us, under the best conditions, between 20 and 30 years . . . to remodel our secondary and higher education, and to put ourselves on a level with the Germans. During that period Germany herself is not likely to be idle.

Those words were written by the Board of Education in 1902. I do not know whether the time scale for Britain to catch up is the same ninety years on—I would hope it would be shorter. But I would say that the country still appears to be struggling to develop the skills and level of experience which are the bedrock of our future industrial success. However, I think we can take some heart from the Government's White Papers on Education and Training, which include the proposal to develop National Vocational Qualifications.

The fact that these NVQs will be recognized nationally, and are intended to have equal standing with academic qualifications at the same level, may help to encourage more young people to seek out training, and thus help to raise the level and standard of vocational training in this country.

Even those companies which have already trained their work force to a high level need to recognize that the skills they require are changing all the time. Many skills, such as general managerial ability, are easily transferable between different posts, but others required for specific tasks may not be. In many cases, it has become much more difficult to match a company's skills requirements with the particular staff complement on hand. The solution is a choice between further in-house training, or skills recruitment from outside. In some cases, both steps may be necessary. Whichever solution is chosen will be expensive—but such flexibility is vital if British industry is to improve its competitiveness.

SMALL BUSINESSES

The availability of a skilled work force is of particular importance to small businesses—especially to those businesses which want to expand. A recent study carried out by Aston Business School (Constraints on the Growth of Small Firms (Aston Business School, 1991)) found that the main problem experienced by firms considering growth was the low availability of skilled labour. (By comparison, only 19 per cent of such firms reported that obtaining finance had been—or was expected to be—difficult). Furthermore, a related survey found that a lack of management ability is the most pervasive and significant constraint on the growth of small firms. Such findings should be of concern to all of us. The health of the small firms sector, and the ability of this sector to produce sound, medium-sized companies, is fundamental to the future of our economy. Small businesses account for something like 35 per cent of private sector employment, and contribute around 25 per cent of GDP.

In addition, in the words of the economist Alfred Marshall from over seventy years ago: 'small businesses are, on the whole, the best educators of the initiative and versatility which are the chief sources of industrial progress' (Small Business Policy in Europe, Britain, Germany, and the European Commission (Anglo-German Foundation, 1991)).

We are all aware of the recent strains in the relationship between small businesses and their bankers. This is not the place to discuss in detail the points made in Chapter 7, but, as a banker, I am conscious that the sentiments expressed there are held by a number of small businesses. We, at NatWest, are determined to maintain our presence in the small business market, supporting that sector. There have been criticisms, sometimes justified, of the standard of service or of treatment in particular cases. We intend to improve our service quality on a continuing basis. We hope that the clear evidence of our continuing commitment to that sector, and also our commitment to improved service, such as for example through the various banks' codes for small business customers, will build up and improve relationships.

Both the City and industry have a role to play in encouraging small businesses to grow further. The banks are already providing some £45 b. of funding for small firms. But they cannot simply make this financing cheaper, or ignore the risks involved.

Perhaps the optimum way for banks to support innovative business in small firms is to develop a more flexible approach to traditional funding, and provide tailored financial packages to meet the quite diverse needs of the sector. Technology-based businesses in particular have specific financing needs, not least because of the longer than usual lead-time before income starts to flow, and profits can be made.

Another valuable role to be played by banks is in the provision of business advice and guidance, such as on national and regional grants and schemes, training initiatives, and government and European Community legislation. In addition, the seconding of managers to small business organizations, such as Local Enterprise Agencies—an initiative carried out by each of the major banks—presents an excellent opportunity to offer professional business counselling and encouragement. NatWest currently seconds around 30 managers to such organizations throughout the country, for periods of between 18 months and 2 years, and 120 of our current managers have now had that experience.

The banks obviously benefit from such attachments, through the increased experience and broader outlook of the secondee, together with the many contacts made in the small business community. But the principal rationale behind this practice must be to ensure that the entrepreneurial spirit which drives so many small business men and women is complemented by sound business management and planning.

CAPITAL AND CREDIT

The principal constraint on banks throughout the world will be the importance of sensible use of their capital. In many countries, including the United States and the United Kingdom, they are badly bruised by the experience of commercial bad debts. In large measure, as my colleague David Lomax mentions in Chapter 8, these were caused by the recession. We are inevitably exposed to the fortunes of our customers. If wide swings in the economic cycle are forever proving companies' business forecasts false, it is little surprise that lending banks will incur losses. But there were other problems. In the intense competition to lend in the successful years of the mid-1980s, banks were forced to reduce their margins and, in some cases, to increase their risk profile. The consequences are being felt in the current unprecedented level of provisioning.

The fact that there is now a discipline on the required level of capital support, and that banks will naturally seek to improve the quality of their assets and readjust their risk–reward ratio to a sustainable level, does not mean that they will be unwilling to back the recovery when it comes. Bank lending was relatively low in 1991. One reason for this is that the customers, who became too heavily exposed in the past, have been rightly cautious about borrowing. Another reason is that there has been a relative shortage of sound borrowing propositions.

I do not personally see a 'credit crunch' developing in the United Kingdom. Technically, I suppose, a credit crunch means that someone is unable to borrow funds at any price. But in practice most people would regard it as an inability to borrow money except at a wholly unrealistic margin above base rate.

In the UK, there will be competition between banks as the recovery comes. However, I believe that banks will not be able to afford to 'buy' market share through subsidizing underperforming businesses from profits made elsewhere. This will mean that banks will have to seek margins which enable each business to be conducted on a profitable basis. What we must give in return for this is a quality service. We must also seek to be rigorous about our own cost control. We are justified in seeking reasonable profit margins from our customers, but we would not be entitled to increase those margins to sustain an inefficiently managed business.

Banks recently came under some pressure externally, both from the media and from some within politics. They wished to discourage banks from increasing their margins on small business lending, despite the fact that such increases reflected the greater risks of that business sector as a result of the recession. I would very much hope we shall not come under any similar pressure to fuel the recovery by lending either contrary to our own best judgement of risk, or at margins which give neither a proper return on capital nor reflect the risks which the bank, as intermediator, is accepting. Any such approach, given the problems the banking industry has had in recent years, could lead to systemic fragility.

CONCLUSION

Our industrial base will need to be strengthened by developing small businesses into a solid tier of medium-sized companies, which will be better able to withstand future economic downturns. The Government, the banking profession, and industry all have a role to play in this endeavour. The economic upswing may lead to an increase in demand for banking facilities, but such an increase should not preclude the desire to provide customers with the best possible service.

The intense competition we shall see within Europe makes it even more important that British policy making is guided towards fundamental factors and not towards thought of gimmicks or financial manipulation. Our infrastructure needs to be of the best: our education and training need to be of the best; our structure of taxation needs to encourage economic and business activity. We need to address seriously, and with an open mind, the issue of the best structure of corporate governance in the UK.

1

The Need to Restore Corporate Accountability: An Agenda for Reform

N. H. DIMSDALE

1.1 INTRODUCTION

Corporate governance has become a highly topical issue as indicated by the extensive recent discussion in the financial press and the appointment of the Cadbury Committee. The way in which managers are made responsible to boards of directors and they in turn to shareholders is an important aspect of the functioning of a free enterprise economy.

Decision takers must ultimately be accountable to someone for their decisions. In the British system it is quite clear that accountability is to the shareholders as owners of the company. Boards of directors are appointed to represent the interests of shareholders, while managers report to the board. However clear in principle, shareholder supremacy has hardly been a conspicuous feature of the British corporate scene in much of the postwar period. Managers have enjoyed a measure of discretion to pursue their own objectives without the need to consider seriously the interests of shareholders. This situation has led to the criticism that managers of large corporations exercise power without responsibility and that company boards are self-perpetuating oligarchies. Such a situation is far removed from the theory underlying the system. Now that the need for accountability of decision takers is being emphasized as a means of achieving good company performance, there is a strong case for reviving the traditional system of corporate governance in the form of clearer responsibility of boards and managers to shareholders.

One result of the lack of communication and diverging interests between shareholders and management has been the growth of contested takeover bids. Such bids are a costly, but necessary, method of disciplining managements. The role of the market for corporate control needs consideration since it has been such a prominent feature of the corporate sector during the 1980s. Views have been expressed that there are too many hostile takeovers and that their disruptive effects and high costs make them undesirable. Against this it has been claimed that such takeovers have an essential role in view of the lack of accountability of management to shareholders under current conditions.

There are major differences in the operation of management accountability in Britain and the United States, and that observed in Germany and Japan. In the last two economies contested takeover bids are virtually unknown. Accountability of the management to shareholders appears to be achieved by closer collaboration between the suppliers and users of capital. The USA and the UK can be classified as predominantly market-based systems in contrast to the bank-based systems of Germany and Japan. Such categories can of course be misleading and it must be recognized that there are wide differences between the German and Japanese financial systems. In bank-based systems, shareholders and lenders have close contacts with management through a variety of channels, hence the division between ownership and control, which is such a feature of the UK and USA market-based systems, is less of a problem. Where market forces predominate in the capital market, shareholders can conveniently trade titles to ownership of a fraction of a company, while hardly being aware of their role as its owners. This contrasts with the long-term commitment and greater knowledge built up by banks in the German and Japanese systems. Bank-based systems do not appear to suffer from the same problems of recognizing and enforcing accountability to shareholders and lenders.

Furthermore the economic performance of both Germany and Japan has comfortably exceeded that of both the UK and the USA in the post-war period. This prompts the question whether the superior achievements of these economies can be partly attributed to differences in their system of corporate governance.

The British system of corporate organization is the outcome of a long process of historical evolution which will be briefly outlined in the next section. Similarly, the German and Japanese systems are the outcome of different institutional and historical backgrounds. Even if bank-based systems were judged to be more effective than market-based systems, it is not obvious that a general transfer to the UK of institutional arrangements developed overseas would be feasible or even desirable. It may, however, be useful to consider what can be learned from systems practised in other countries which seem to avoid the problems which are causing us concern.

The next section of this chapter reviews the development of company organization in Britain, and in particular the widening gap between ownership and control of companies. This situation has given rise to problems which are reviewed in section 1.3 followed by a consideration of possible remedies in section 1.4. The postscript to the chapter examines the proposals of the Cadbury Committee on the financial aspects of corporate governance.

1.2 THE SEPARATION OF OWNERSHIP FROM CONTROL

The modern British corporation is characterized by a separation of owner-ship from control, in that the shareholders have little influence on the day-to-day running of a company. This is in contrast to the earlier forms of capitalism in which the entrepreneur who ran the business also owned it through his own or his family's shareholdings. The change in the structure of firms has been the result of a gradual process of historical evolution. During much of the nineteenth century the predominant form of business unit was the partnership, where partners accepted unlimited liability for losses. Major undertakings, such as railways, were operated by joint stock companies with transferable shares, and were granted corporate status by Act of Parliament. This was a costly procedure and was not therefore open to firms in manufacturing industry. Whereas railway companies needed to mobilize the savings of large numbers of small investors to create the capi-tal needed for their construction, firms in manufacturing could finance themselves largely from retained profits and the resources of a small group of partners (Payne 1974).

The Joint Stock Companies Acts of 1856 and 1862 enabled firms to become joint stock companies with limited liability. At the time of this leg-islation pressure came from those seeking to provide new outlets for the savings of small investors rather than from businessmen who found the tra-ditional form of business organization unduly constricting. The experience of the first public companies with limited liability floated in the years fol-lowing 1862 was not encouraging. Many ventures ended in insolvency and blame was placed on company promoters taking advantage of the igno-rance of the public (Hannah 1983).

During the remainder of the nineteenth century there was a growth in publicly-quoted companies among large firms in major industries, such as cotton, shipbuilding and iron and steel, where the former family owners generally remained in control of the company. More commonly, family-owned concerns chose to register as private companies, so obtaining the benefits of limited liability, while retaining privacy in the conduct of their affairs and keeping control of the business within the family. By 1914, 80 per cent of registered companies were private companies. There was, how-ever, a marked increase in the number of companies quoted on the London Stock Exchange, rising from about 60 to 600 between 1885 and 1907 (Hannah 1983). This reflected in part an early merger movement in which groups of family firms formed amalgamations which were floated as public companies. The merged enterprises frequently retained many of the former directors and old family influences tended to persist.

The inter-war period witnessed major changes on the corporate scene.

The movement towards public quotations for family-owned businesses gathered pace and was particularly strong in the stock-market booms of 1919–20 and the later 1920s. Established firms tended to go public or merge with an already quoted company. Merger activity was high in the 1920s and the new issue market reached a peak in 1928.

Company promoters advised the owners of firms on how best to market their businesses to take advantage of bullish sentiment on the stock-market. Wealthy families tended to diversify their portfolios by holding a range of stocks rather than having a large, concentrated holding in the family business. The result of this tendency towards a more dispersed ownership of shares was some weakening of the link between the ownership and control of companies. This divorce of control from ownership was illustrated most clearly in the formation of giant companies, such as ICI and Unilever, where the size of the firm dwarfed the shareholding of even the wealthiest individual. Here the amount of share capital controlled by the board was negligible. Such giant companies were not, however, typical of British industry. In large companies, family interests frequently retained about 20 per cent of the equity which, when combined with representation on the board, was sufficient to give them control of the company. In his study of the ownership of the 82 largest British companies in 1935, Florence (1953) found that in 58 per cent there was a dominant ownership interest and in only 9 per cent was ownership widely dispersed. Hence it is premature to speak of a managerial revolution in Britain in the 1930s. At most there was a partial separation of ownership from control (Payne 1978).

Among giant companies formed by amalgamation a modern corporate structure was evolved. Management decisions became the responsibility of a new profession of managers, frequently with qualifications as accountants, engineers or scientists. The new managers did not typically come from a propertied background and depended upon their salaries rather than *rentier* income.

The growth of company quotations was rapid in the early twentieth century as indicated by the rise in quoted firms in manufacturing and distribution from 570 in 1907 to 1,700 in 1939. The rise in the number of quoted companies and the dispersion of share ownership opened up the way for a market in corporate control. Shareholders were content to accept the recommendations of their boards on whether to accept merger proposals, and it was widely accepted that only directors were competent in assessing such issues and had access to the relevant information. Directors could, on occasion, reject proposals which were in the interests of shareholders and demand compensation in the event of a merger going ahead. Contested takeover bids, in which bidders appealed to shareholders over the heads of the incumbent board, were unknown before 1950 (Hannah 1983).

During the post-war period there has been a continuing erosion of family ownership of large companies. By 1968–9 the boards of the 100 largest British companies controlled only 7½ per cent of the equity. This trend reflected the growing predominance of professional directors and managers and the gradual displacement of owner–managers. The weakening of family ownership reflected the sale of shares to meet payments of estate duty and the dilution of concentrated ownership due to the renewed merger movement of the 1960s. Companies with continuing close family links have frequently put the control of the company in the hands of employed executives without family connections. This has been necessary to ensure that the company is controlled by professionally competent management, even though this is drawn from outside the family.

The sale of equities by private shareholders during much of the post-war period has been offset by the growth in shares owned by pension funds and, later, life insurance companies. The change in the distribution of income has encouraged the growth of savings by wage and salary earners which have been largely channelled through institutional funds. The trend towards investment through institutions rather than by direct ownership of shares has been reinforced by fiscal incentives. As a result, the proportion of ordinary shares of British quoted industrial companies held by financial institutions rose from 18 per cent to 41 per cent from 1957 to 1973. This trend has continued into the 1980s, so that the institutions now own more than 60 per cent of ordinary shares in quoted British companies. The erosion of share ownership by boards of directors has continued so that by 1973 the boards of the largest 100 manufacturing companies owned only ½ per cent of the ordinary shares (Prais 1976; Cosh and Hughes 1987).

The widening gap between ownership and control in major companies has, it is claimed, led to the emergence of separate objectives of management and shareholders. Whereas shareholders are primarily concerned with financial returns from an investment, managers are concerned with a broader range of factors, such as the size and growth of the company and other measures of professional prestige. These arguments are evaluated in Hay and Morris (1991). In Britain the rise of the corporate economy led to greater emphasis on company growth through retained earnings and less on dividend payments in the early post-war period. Institutional investors, like the highly dispersed private shareholder whom they have increasingly displaced, have tended to be relatively passive. Hence management-dominated boards have enjoyed a substantial element of autonomy, which has recently been checked by growth of an active market for corporate control via contested takeover bids.

The 1948 Companies Act has facilitated the process of bidding for companies, since boards are required to publish more information about their profits and balance sheets. This has improved the information available to both bidders and shareholders, and enabled them to assess the performance of a company and the competence of the board of directors. Takeover bids were encouraged by the depression of market valuation of assets due to dividend restraint in the 1940s and 1950s. Such bids could be mounted more easily when companies were quoted but not family controlled. The initial post-war takeover boom occurred in the 1960s, and resulted in 38 per cent of quoted companies being acquired by other quoted companies in the period from 1957 to 1967 (Hannah 1983). Activity in this area continued to rise reaching a peak in the early 1970s, when the number of acquisitions in the UK reached 1,212, exceeding the previous peak of 1,000 recorded in 1965 (Bannock 1990). The renewed growth of acquisitions in the 1980s reached and exceeded the previous peak in 1988. The majority of acquisitions have not involved a contest between the bidder and the acquired company. According to Bannock (1990) 30–40 per cent of bids for UK quoted companies were contested in the period 1984–8. A market for corporate control has, therefore, emerged which is putting greater pressure on incumbent managements to achieve satisfactory results, despite a widening gap between shareholders and management in the period since the Second World War.

1.3   THE PROBLEMS OF GOVERNANCE OF BRITISH COMPANIES

The failure to enforce accountability to shareholders has been a characteristic of large companies for much of the post-war period. The system which has evolved can be considered in its various components. These include the composition and operation of company boards, the role of the shareholder, both institutional and private, the role of the banks, and the impact of the capital market on the ownership of companies. Each of these will be considered in turn. Much of what follows has been influenced by the stimulating papers on corporate governance by Charkham (1989*a*; 1989*b*) and Sykes (1990).

1.3.1.   *The Composition and Structure of Company Boards*

The British system of corporate control has moved in the direction of concentrating authority in larger companies on the board of directors with whom the shareholders have little direct contact. There has been a tendency to increase the proportion of executive directors, who combine the role of director with responsibility for management within the company. Thus the distinction between directors who are representatives of shareholder interests and management has tended to become obscured. Where the board is dominated by executive directors the difference between the board and the higher management of the company largely disappears.

The lack of effective shareholder representation is of some importance since there are major areas where the interests of managers and shareholders do not coincide. These include a wide range of issues, such as for example, the level and structure of executive pay, the allocation of funds between dividends and retentions, and the priority to be accorded to growth in relation to profitability.

A preponderance of executive directors could be corrected if the number of non-executive directors was increased, as the latter could be expected to attach a greater weight to the interests of shareholders. Measure are being taken to increase the numbers of non-executive directors on British' company boards as a result of the activities of PRONED. However, the British system of a unitary board and widely varying numbers of non-executive directors contrasts with the US practice where the majority of directors do not have executive responsibilities. In Britain all directors bear equal responsibility for the operation of the company, although the knowledge and specific skills of the executive directors are likely to be greater than those of the non-executive directors. Given this situation, it is difficult for a non-executive director to monitor effectively the activities of the executive directors, particularly when he is bearing joint responsibility for boardroom decisions.

One advantage of the more formalized German structure of separate management and supervisory boards is that it recognizes the difference in the position of executive and non-executive directors. The supervisory board can monitor the decisions of the management board and ensure that these decisions are in the best interests of the shareholders, without requiring non-executives to accept responsibility for executive-level decisions. Charkham correctly points out that the British system of unitary boards depends for its successful operation on a measure of self-discipline by members of the board since this is not provided for by the structure itself.

The conflict of functions on a unitary board may be increased where the roles of chief executive and chairman are combined. The individual who holds both offices is subject to a measure of conflict between his commitment to management and the need for a balanced view of the interests of shareholders. Individuals may be found who can cope with this situation in a satisfactory way, but they are likely to be rare. There is a danger that the interests of shareholders will be subordinated to the priorities of management. Shareholders are deprived of a safeguard, in that one of the functions of the chairman is to dismiss the chief executive should that be necessary. The removal of the chief executive becomes considerably more difficult if the office is combined with the chairmanship of the company. Where there is a combined chairman/chief executive the need for strongly independent non-executive directors is even more pressing.

1.3.2   *The Role of Shareholders*

Shareholders are entitled to attend the Annual General Meeting (AGM) of a company at which they approve the accounts and the annual report. They elect new board members proposed by the current directors and re-elect board members offering themselves for re-election by rotation. Small shareholders who are dissatisfied with the results of a company cannot generally expect to make much impact on the board at a formally constituted AGM. A well-informed small investor could, however, cause some discomfort to a board by posing searching questions. Few small investors behave in this way, leaving the dissatisfied private shareholder with the option of selling his holding if his disappointment with the company continues.

For larger institutional investors, the option is open of holding discussions with the board of a company producing unsatisfactory financial results. Institutions do not generally intervene at AGMs to express their dissatisfaction, but other channels of complaint are open to them. It is perhaps surprising that major financial institutions have not, until recently, put greater pressure on boards, when they are concerned about the fortunes of a company. These institutions could bring about changes in a board and possibly displace a chief executive. Frequently this has not happened and institutions have signalled their disappointment by disposing of their shareholding. Using the distinction due to Hirschman (1970), 'Exit' has frequently been preferred to 'Voice'.

There are good reasons why fund managers have commonly sought the convenient escape route of selling stock. As investment managers they do not wish to become involved in sorting out the problems of company management and do not have any special expertise in this area. Since they generally hold no more than 5 per cent of a diversified portfolio in a single holding, it may not be worth their while attempting to remedy the deep-seated problems affecting an unsuccessful company. If the holding in the company is relatively large and the shares are not easily marketable, the case for a more patient policy is strengthened.

A single institution acting independently might encounter considerable difficulty in seeking to bring about changes in management in a major public company. Substantial results would be unlikely to be achieved without concerted action by all institutions involved with the company. Such collective action is not readily achieved by financial institutions which are actively engaged in competing with each other.

Detailed discussions between one or more institutional shareholders and the management of an ailing company runs into the issue of inequality of treatment of shareholders. The special knowledge gained by those participating in the discussions makes them insiders, who are in a position to take advantage of the ignorance of other shareholders who have been denied this relevant information. Thus the principle of equal treatment of shareholders may be compromised. There are therefore objections to 'Voice' which go some way to account for the unwillingness of institutions to become involved directly in the management problems of companies.

In Germany there appears to be more informal dialogue between the owners of a company and its management. There is an ongoing discussion of the company's progress on the supervisory board and major shareholders can express their views to management although such discussion is not open to small shareholders. Similar opportunities for discussion of management problems occur in the Japanese keiretsu system of family-related companies (Charkham 1989*a*).

1.3.3   *The Role of the Banking System*

Reference to corporate governance in Germany and Japan leads naturally to a consideration of the role of banks in influencing management. In both countries, banks have historically played a larger part in financing industrial investment than in countries with relatively well-developed capital markets, such as Britain and the United States.

Although in Britain, banks are an important source of finance for industry, particularly for small and medium-sized companies, they do not seek to become involved directly in the provision of long-term capital. They may provide finance for companies over a considerable period by rolling over short-term loans. They have sought to avoid a deep long-term commitment to borrowers, but in some circumstances it has been thrust upon them. A conspicuous example of this occurred in the inter-war period when the effective freezing of bank loans to both the cotton and steel industries due to prolonged depression of demand forced on the banks a more active role. They brought about the restructuring of companies which would otherwise have been forced into liquidation with consequent losses to the banks. The Lancashire Cotton Corporation was formed partly as a result of pressure from the banks and similar pressures led to major amalgamations in the steel industry. Perhaps this experience confirmed the banks' traditional preference for short-term lending.

British banks have sought to provide assistance to smaller companies following the identification of the Macmillan Gap[1] in 1931. Longer-term loans were made to small firms through subsidiaries, such as the United Dominion Trust, set up by the banks in the 1930s. The Industrial and Commercial Finance Corporation (ICFC) was founded in 1945 to hold

---

[1] The Macmillan Committee referred to the inadequate provision of long-term finance to medium-sized and small companies by the British capital market. It collected evidence on the high cost of making relatively small public issues and recommended that measures be taken to close what became known as the Macmillan Gap Report of the Committee on Finance and Industry(1931).

securities in unquoted companies, and received financial support from the banks. More recently banks have held shares in smaller companies through venture capital subsidiaries and affiliated institutions, such as *3i*, the successor to ICFC. Although British banks have not confined themselves to traditional short-term lending, they have not accepted a commitment to provide long-term finance as in Germany and Japan nor have they become involved in management problems through representation on company boards.

Unlike British banks, the German banking system has participated in long-term lending to industry and has some equity holdings. In addition, German banks hold bearer shares which are deposited with them on behalf of shareholders and can exercise proxy votes at company meetings. They provide a wide range of financial services to companies and frequently hold the chairmanship or deputy chairmanship of the supervisory board of major companies. German banks have become closely associated with some companies and have built up detailed knowledge about the nature of their business and future prospects. They are, therefore, in a good position to assess, on the basis of their own experience, the risks involved in industrial projects. 'Exit', through disposing of shares and calling in loans, is hardly an option for them, should financial results be disappointing. Management changes can, if required, be brought about through extensive internal discussion. In extreme cases a bank may find itself as manager of a struggling business but this is not a situation which is normal or intended.

Historically, German banks played a major role in the finance of technologically-advanced industries, such as the steel and electrical industries, in the late nineteenth century. They helped to finance the technology which was at the forefront of Germany's drive to industrialize at a time when the resources of the capital market were very limited, Milward and Saul (1977).

Today the situation has changed in that dependence upon bank finance is more important for medium-sized companies than for large corporations (Mayer and Alexander 1990). For larger companies banks are still important on account of their holdings of bearer shares and their powerful representation on supervisory boards. Banks' relationships with companies remain close, even when companies are large and can finance themselves through retained earnings without heavy reliance upon bank lending.

External pressures can be brought to bear more readily on companies in the more bank-dependent systems of Germany and Japan than in the more market-orientated British and US systems. In Britain large financial institutions, despite their growing preponderance in share ownership, have not sought to intervene in the running of companies. In the USA where a larger proportion of shares is held by households than by financial institutions, it may be more difficult to exert external influences on company boards.

1.3.4. *The Capital Market and the Threat of Takeover*

The capital market has traditionally been seen as a primary market in which new capital can be raised by companies. It is also a secondary market in which existing shares and bonds are valued and can be traded. In more recent years it has become a market for companies in which the control of a company can be acquired by a bidder who is willing to pay a sufficient premium over the prevailing level of market prices.

During the 1970s there was concern about the willingness of financial institutions to finance British industry. The Wilson Committee (1980) looked into this question and proposals were made for a new investment institution which would be primarily concerned with meeting the financial needs of industry. In the 1980s there was little scope for the capital market as a market for primary securities, since industry financed itself largely from retained earnings and from bank borrowing. Dependence on the capital market for raising new funds was slight, although the revival of rights issues in the early 1990s points to the role of capital raising as still being of importance. The 1980s saw the market focus on merger and takeover activity, and the market for corporate control has been extremely active.

The main day-to-day business of the equity market is the valuation of the existing stock of shares. The case of share dealing and reduced transaction costs as a result of deregulation of the stock-market have served to reinforce the idea of shares as trading chips rather than as claims with ownership obligations. Share prices are subject to wide short-term fluctuations. Yet financial theory claims that capital markets are generally efficient. This does not imply that the market valuation of companies is always correct. In an efficient market the price of a share incorporates all known information about the company. The valuation should be unbiased being neither persistently above or below the true value.

Efficient market theory has been stated in a variety of forms, strong, semi-strong and weak. Much of the evidence in its favour was set out by Fama (1970) and market efficiency has been vigorously asserted by Marsh (1990). There are, however, some notable dissenters. Shiller (1981) argues that share prices are more volatile than can be justified by market fundamentals. De Bondt and Thaler (1985) provide evidence of the market's over-reaction to new information and Summers (1986) argues that share prices can differ persistently from correct values. It would appear that while market valuations reflect fundamental values they may also include a variable premium or discount in the light of the previously cited studies.

There is a difference in the value of a company derived from marginal trading of shares on the stock-market and the total value of the company as a going concern. The difference is the market premium required for buying all the stock necessary to secure control of the company. By acquiring corporate control, a takeover bidder has a wider range of opportunities than the right to an income-stream from the purchase of one or more units of equity. This difference is reflected in the bid premium which emerges as soon as a takeover bid seems likely to occur. In the absence of information about a prospective bid, the equity market would not be justified in including the bid premium in the share price. When a bid is announced, the new information is reflected in the emergence of the premium element in the share price. The upsurge in the price which can occur, if the bid is unexpected by the market, is not incompatible with the notion of market efficiency.[2]

Grossman and Hart (1980) have pointed out that shareholders in a company subject to a hostile takeover bid have an incentive not to accept the bid and will hope that others will sell out. Should the bid succeed the resistant shareholder can reap the full value of the equity arising from the reorganization of the company, which may exceed the value of the bid. The shareholder will free-ride on the eventual returns to the bidder. If all shareholders behaved in this way a bid would fail which everyone agreed should succeed. The free-rider problem would imply that the number of takeover bids would be too small because the chances of success would be low. This hardly seems relevant to recent British experience where many observers consider that takeover activity during the last decade has been excessive.

Institutional investors face a test of loyalty when confronted with a takeover bid. They may remain loyal to the incumbent management or accept the offer of the bidder. Their duty as managers of funds is to those for whom they act, that is policy holders for an insurance company, and

[2] The argument about the existence of a bid premium may be illustrated more formally. It is assumed for convenience that dividends are paid and discounted continuously. The initial dividend paid by the firm is D_0 and it is expected to grow continuously at the rate g. It is discounted by the market at the rate of discount r where $r > g$. The dividend in year t is $D_t = D_0 e^{gt}$. The valuation of the firm is assumed to be equal to the present value of the expected future dividends so that:

$$PVF_0 = \int_0^\infty D_0 e^{(g-r)t} dt = \frac{D_0}{r-g}$$

A takeover bidder who acquires the firm will receive its total earnings which are generally greater than total dividends paid out so that $\pi_0 \geq D_0$. This should not raise the value of the company if an optimum dividend policy is being followed. In addition under a new management the growth of earnings k will be expected to exceed the growth of dividends under the present management so that $k > g$ but $k < r$. The new valuation of the firm upon takeover is therefore:

$$PVT_0 = \int_0^\infty \pi_0 e^{(k-r)t} dt = \frac{\pi_0}{r-k}$$

The present value of the firm as a takeover target exceeds the present value of expected future dividends, the difference being its maximum premium which a bidder would pay to acquire control of the company, that is:

$$BP_0 = PVT_0 - PVF_0 = \frac{\pi_0}{r-k} - \frac{D_0}{r-g}$$

members of a pension scheme for a pension fund. The need to act in accordance with these interests was confirmed in the Megarry judgment of 1984, but it is not clear if this implies that the short-term financial interests of members and policyholders are the paramount consideration. If they were, a financial institution would have no alternative but to accept the bid on the most favourable terms. In practice, major institutions attempt to balance the position of the incumbent management and the long-run prospects for the company against the value of the bid. Artus (1990) explains the policy of the Prudential in a bid situation in these terms.

There must be a presumption that shareholders will take advantage of a generous premium offered by a bidder and that a bid will, in these circumstances, generally succeed. In the British system of corporate governance hostile bids play an important role in disciplining boards of unsuccessful companies. The failure of shareholders to hold company boards accountable for a weak financial performance means that this role is taken on by the hostile bidder. The rationale for this process is that the bid transfers resources tied up in the company to a new management group which places a higher value on the assets. Provided such a transfer of ownership does not involve an undermining of competition, it should lead to an improvement in resource allocation. Jensen (1988) puts the case for an active market in corporate control. He argues that it is a way of restructuring large corporations through the capital market, when the internal pace of change is being obstructed by the incumbent management and claims:

The takeover market serves as an important source of protection for investors in these situations. Other management teams that recognize an opportunity to reorganize or redeploy an organization's assets and thereby create new value can bid for control rights in the takeover market. To be successful such bids must give investors an opportunity to realize part of the gains from reorganization and redeployment of assets.

The upsurge in takeover activity during the 1980s while welcome in bringing pressure to bear on managements to take heed to the interests of shareholders, has not been wholly beneficial. Acquisitions can result in excessive concentration upon putting deals together. Managerial effort is directed to immediate financial operations and away from the longer-term objectives of organizing production and growth. The costs of takeovers are considerable and concentrate benefits upon certain sections of the financial services industry.

The threat of takeover places managements in a situation where priority is given to survival and there is concentration upon short-term objectives. Boards have an incentive to raise dividends at the expense of longer-term objectives, such as investment in fixed assets and expenditure upon research and development. This leads to the criticism of short-termism. Defenders of efficient markets can respond that share prices include the capital market's valuation of the future benefit of long-term corporate programmes. Hence a rise in dividends which damages a company's long-run prospects should lead to a decline in the share price rather than a rise. Nevertheless, the criticism persists that a capital market which can put companies into play at short notice does not create an environment in which managements can plan sensibly for the long-term development of a business. Some evidence of short-termism in share pricing is claimed in Miles (1991).

There have been numerous studies of the effects of mergers and takeovers on economic performance. A detailed survey of this work is provided in Hughes (1989) and Peacock and Bannock (1991). Studies which seek to measure changes in the accounting rate of return of companies following an acquisition are subject to qualification because of differences in accounting practices between firms and other problems associated with consolidating accounts. Researchers have resolved these problems as best they can and derived measures of normalized profitability after mergers. In the studies cited by Hughes there is little evidence that mergers increase profitability, if anything there is a small negative effect on the profitability of the acquiring company. However, negative financial effects were not found for acquirers who had a preponderance of institutional investors. There was also some evidence that the post-merger financial results were more favourable for non-horizontal than for horizontal mergers.

A more relevant test from the point of view of the shareholder is the impact of takeovers on share values of both acquired and acquiring companies. Franks and Harris (1989) report the results of examining 1,900 mergers in the UK and find that there is an average gain of 22 per cent to shareholders in the target company in the month of the bid. Over the six months beginning four months before the bid, the gain is 30 per cent, which may include the market's anticipation of the bid. By contrast, the gains of the shareholders in the acquirer are slight; only 1 per cent in the month of the bid and 7 per cent over the six-month period previously defined. These results should be qualified by noting the larger average size of the acquirer. Returns to shareholders in the acquirer for two years after the merger are approximately in line with those of the market. The result is consistent with an efficient stock-market where abnormal returns should not persist. Hughes (1989) cites the results of other studies of the financial returns from mergers which suggest that the main beneficiaries are the shareholders of the acquired company at the time of the bid.

Shareholders in bidding companies are bearing a considerable risk when their board decides to launch a bid for another company, but the expected returns from such a venture are meagre. There could well be a conflict of interest in this situation, as pointed out by Davis and Kay (1990). Managements stand to benefit from mergers in that the size of the merged firm will rise after a bid, enlarging the resources which managers can organize. On conventional management criteria both remuneration and prestige will be enhanced for executives in the successful bidder. The longer-term benefits of a takeover bid for the shareholder in the acquirer are more problematic. If there are benefits from synergy, they appear to be largely anticipated by the capital market and are reflected in the bid premium to the benefit of shareholders in the acquired company.

In contrast with Britain and the United States a market for corporate control hardly exists in Germany and Japan. Although mergers do take place they are generally agreed and contested takeovers are rare. The predominance of takeovers in the UK and the USA, and their rarity in Japan and Germany is documented by Bannock (1990) in his study of the international incidence of bids.

The observed difference reflects the contrasting systems of corporate governance in two groups of countries and in particular the differing role of the banks. In Britain and the United States the banking system has provided much of the finance for takeovers, so making possible an active market for corporate control. In Germany the close connection between banks and companies acts as a protective influence against hostile bids. A bank or group of banks will frequently control a major block of voting rights in a major company through exercising proxies for the bearer shares deposited with it. They are, therefore, able to shield a company from a predator. Banks can also exercise influence over large companies through representation on the supervisory board and are in a good position to monitor company performance. Medium-sized German companies are protected against bids because of their greater dependence on long-term bank finance and lower incidence of stock-market quotation than in the UK. This also explains the smaller number of quoted companies in Germany and more limited scope for a market in corporate control.

1.4 SOME REMEDIES FOR THE PROBLEMS OF CORPORATE GOVERNANCE

In Britain there has been a lack of a continuous way of making managements responsible to shareholders. The threat of a hostile takeover provides, in the last resort, a way of disciplining boards of underperforming companies. The bid itself is a costly and disturbing process. It provides too drastic a solution to the problem of ineffective management, in that what is required is a change of management, but the change in ownership associated with the bid may be strictly unnecessary. If boards could be made more responsible to shareholders, then changes in management could be brought about without any change in ownership. Such a system requires that shareholders should fulfil their responsibilities as owners and not act as transitory holders of share certificates. Shareholders should ensure that

boards communicate with them and that managements are made accountable for their actions. Such a system is far removed from the way in which
corporate governance has evolved in much of the post-war period. It is now
time to consider how the present system might be improved.

1.4.1 *The Structure of Company Boards*

A major cause of the present difficulties of controlling companies is the
excessive weight of managerial—as opposed to shareholder—interests on
the board. The most direct way of redressing the balance is to augment the
role of non-executive directors and this proposal has been supported by a
number of commentators. One of the problems arising here is that non-
executive directors tend to be selected initially by the chief executive and
have their appointment endorsed by the board. This process leads to individuals being selected who may be too close in attitude to the executive
directors, and not sufficiently independent to represent effectively the interests of shareholders. It is to meet this criticism that the chairman of
PRONED has called for non-executives to be known in future as independent directors. Currently many non-executive directors are former executive
directors or chief executives of other companies. In neither case does their
background suggest that they are likely to be truly independent.

There is, as Davis and Kay (1990) point out, an ambiguity about the
duties of non-executive directors which include roles as adviser, decision
taker, and monitor of management. These roles may well conflict and some
clarification seems desirable. If, as under the present British system, all
directors bear equal joint responsibility for the affairs of a company, it is
difficult to see how one group of directors can effectively monitor another
group. The roles of each type of director should be defined more closely
and external directors should be drawn from a wider range of backgrounds
than currently. Major shareholders could perhaps play a greater role in the
selection of non-executive directors.

A suggestion has been made that there should be a proportion of external directors, determined by statute, on company boards (Ball 1990). This
would ensure that the wide variation currently observed in numbers of non-
executives on boards of different companies would be reduced. Norms
might be set for the numbers of non-executive directors required to give
adequate representation of independent views on a board. Such norms
could be set by major institutional shareholders and this would not require
statutory enforcement.

A more rigid distinction between the roles of executive and non-executive
directors is called for by Gilson and Kraakman (1990). They recommend
the creation of a new class of professional outside director who would have
the knowledge and time to monitor management in the interests of share-

holders. Such professional non-executive directors would be specialists in ensuring accountability of managements, but they would not share responsibility for management decisions. They would be a potentially divisive factor within the unitary board structure of a British company.

Once the basic difference in functions of external and executive directors is recognized, the question arises whether the board should not be divided into two sections on the German pattern. In such a system the monitoring and decision-making roles of directors can be clearly separated. Some doubts have, however, been expressed about the two-tier system in Germany because of the distance of the supervisory board from the day-to-day conduct of business (Edwards and Fischer 1990). Non-executive directors placed on a separate board might be more remote and less well-informed than under the unitary board system, which Charkham (1989*a*) favours retaining on balance.

There appears to be a wide measure of agreement on the undesirability of combining the roles of chief executive and chairman of the company. The potential conflict of interest involved in this situation should make the combination of the offices unacceptable in a large public company. The combination might, however, be more acceptable in a small company, where the chairman/chief executive was a major shareholder, providing an essential element of leadership to the company. In such circumstances the owner-manager pattern of capitalism should be permitted to flourish. There will need to be a division of functions as the company grows and seeks to attract financial support from major institutional investors.

One of the major disadvantages of external directors is their lack of knowledge about the current state of a company. This ignorance could be aggravated if they were confined to supervisory boards with infrequent and formalized meetings. The American system of audit committees on which external directors serve could assist in rectifying this problem. It would ensure that non-executives were well informed about the financial state of the company and could provide auditors with direct access to those representing the interests of shareholders. Audit committees could also provide an additional channel for detecting cases of fraud. Such reinforcement is necessary, as shown by the cases of Polly Peck and Ferranti International, where non-executive directors could be criticized for failing to protect adequately the interests of shareholders.

Management remuneration is an area where non-executives should bear important responsibility. It is desirable that the remuneration committees of major companies should not be dominated by the interests of the executive directors of the company. Independent non-executives are needed to assess both the level and structure of management remuneration. The design of pay packages should encourage managers to promote the interests of shareholders. An obvious example is the relating of pay to profitability rather than to volume of sales or other measures of company size. As shareholders benefit from greater profitability so should management. Hence stock options and bonuses should be provided as well as salary, to make executive rewards vary directly with the fortunes of the company.

The position of non-executive directors is also critical where the executive directors embark on a management buy-out. Non-executives have a duty to protect the interests of shareholders in this situation, where there will be a direct conflict between the need to obtain a fair price for the company and the interest of the management in acquiring assets as cheaply as possible.

1.4.2   *The Role of Shareholders*

Now that the institutions hold more than 60 per cent of the shares in British listed companies, they must play the dominant part in any revival of shareholder activity in corporate governance. In the past the institutions have not generally played an active part in putting pressure on company managements with poor records. Unsatisfactory companies such as British Leyland, Distillers, and Dunlop have continued on a downward path without provoking a revolt among financial institutions and demands for replacement of the management.

This attitude reflects the ability of pension funds and insurance companies to spread their investments over a wide range of investments. In a highly diversified portfolio, some problem shares are to be expected. Institutions may either sell the shares of a poorly performing company on a rising market or wait for a hostile takeover bid.

The growing predominance of the institutions makes it more difficult for them to dispose of holdings. One institution may succeed in selling its shares, but institutions as a whole, as dominant shareholders, cannot sell out and so escape responsibilities as owners. Most major companies are now effectively owned by twenty-five to thirty institutions. Collective action by institutions may be the only way of dealing with an unsatisfactory management, the action being aimed at improving company performance with the prospect of benefiting all shareholders. The difficulty with organizing such collective action is that individual institutions have an incentive to act independently and to free-ride on the efforts of those struggling to bring about management changes.

In practice there may be difficulties in achieving collaboration among different institutions. This is likely to be increased if there is a move towards indexed funds, where each portfolio aims to be a close replica of the market as a whole and institutions follow a passive investment policy. Similarly, a highly active portfolio where stocks are turned over at a rapid rate can hardly justify efforts to change the management of a company in what is likely to be a temporary holding.

A more appropriate investment policy for effective corporate governance would be for portfolios to be concentrated upon a relatively narrow range of investments with a reduced rate of turnover of shares. In this way institutions could accumulate information about the companies in which they are invested and build up communications with the management. Efforts made to rectify management difficulties could then yield substantial benefits to an institution, so internalizing returns which would otherwise be external and create opportunities for free-riding by other investors. Such a directed investment policy would be at the cost of portfolio diversification but could have its advantages, particularly if a small group of institutional investors could continue to act in concert in putting pressure on company management. This policy is similar to the active shareholder policy advocated by Charkham (1989b). In effect, major institutional investors would be moving some way towards the position of German banks who exercise some measure of control over companies through the proxy voting rights of bearer shares deposited with them. A further step in this direction would be the appointment of non-executive directors to represent the interests of major shareholders, which would approximate to the representation of the interests of banks on the supervisory board in the German system.

Recently, rights issues have opened up a new path for institutions to call failing managements to account. Several of the rights issues are required to provide longer-term funding for expansion schemes initiated in the boom of the 1980s, which subsequently ran into difficulties. In such circumstances institutions have made it clear that they will not provide the finance which is being sought, unless they are assured that past mistakes will not be repeated. This may involve management changes as the prominent examples of Asda and British Aerospace have shown. In the recent severe recession institutions have become more active in seeking changes in management, either acting alone or, more frequently, in concert. The cases of Tace, Bunzl, and Budgens illustrate this type of action.

The question arises whether this behaviour is merely a result of the current phase of the trade cycle or whether it marks a sea change in the attitude of institutions to the companies in which they invest. What has been demonstrated is that the conventional primary function of the capital market, the provision of new capital, provides a powerful case of enforcing accountability of managements to shareholders. It provides an alternative path to the threat of takeover which is likely to be more effective when economic conditions are favourable and bidders have ready access to finance.

Institutional pressure can achieve several of the objectives discussed in the previous section on the structure of company boards. Institutions can let it be known that they favour a strong representation of independent non-executive directors on boards and that they do not generally approve of the offices of chief executive and chairman being combined. They may also express views on management remuneration, including incentive schemes and compensation for ousted directors.

There could, however, be a danger of increased institutional involvement creating undue pressures on company boards and giving rise to renewed charges of short-termism. This problem could be overcome by institutions making clear that they are primarily concerned with the long-run success of companies. Institutions should also take care that their current preference for dividends does not put too much pressure on company cash flows, particularly during periods of recession. In Germany companies rely to a greater extent upon retentions and are not under such pressure to maintain high dividend payments. Similarly in Japan, the dividends paid by companies are hardly burdensome. There may be advantages in the British system of high dividends and greater reliance upon external finance, but the low dividend pattern of German and Japanese finance has produced good results. Institutions should consider whether maintaining a high rate of dividend payment is in the best interests of the companies to which they have a long-term commitment.

Monitoring of company performance by shareholders is unlikely to be effective unless appropriate standards are observed in reporting financial results. The proposals of the Accounting Standards Board for clarifying the components of the profit and loss account are most welcome for this reason. The proposed reforms, which seek to separate ongoing revenues and costs from those classified as exceptional and extraordinary, should make profit and loss statements more useful to both investors and creditors. There should be reduced scope for giving a misleading impression of profits through reductions in discretionary expenditure, which includes spending on research and development. The identification of movements in reserves will also serve to correct the potentially distorting effects of such movements on profits. In short, the proposals of the Account Standards Board accord with the need to inform shareholders who are bearing the responsibility of making managements properly accountable.

A related issue arises from the responsibilities of auditors. There are complaints that auditors' relationships with managements are too close. Conflicts of interest can arise when accounting firms use auditing services as a loss-leader to obtain more lucrative consultancy work from their corporate clients. This situation is anomalous since auditors are responsible to shareholders rather than to managers and should be reminded of this. They should not agree to settle points of detail in favour of management. Financial institutions should be in a position to establish the accountability of auditors and to agree an appropriate scale of fees for their services. The role of auditors will need to be enhanced as part of a general scheme of improving accountability and institutional investors could ensure that shareholders obtain the appropriate standard of reporting from their auditors.

This discussion has focused entirely upon institutional shareholders to the exclusion of private shareholders, who are a diminishing force in share ownership. There have been proposals notably from the Wider Share Ownership Task Force of the CBI to promote private shareholding. The popularity of private shareholders among industrial leaders is attributed to the claimed greater loyalty of small shareholders compared with the institutions, when firms are subject to hostile takeover bids. However, the trend towards institutional ownership of shares is now running so strongly that it can hardly be reversed; even privatization, while making share ownership more widespread, has not affected the overall position.

The growth of shareholding by financial institutions reflects a desire on the part of the public for well-diversified and professionally managed portfolios which is entirely justifiable. Where the investing institutions owe their predominance to favourable tax treatment the issue is not so straightforward. As a long-term objective the aim might be a level playing field, enabling all types of savings to enjoy the same fiscal incentives. A move is taking place in this direction as the tax benefits of saving through pension funds and life assurance policies have been reduced and concessions made available to savings in other media, such as PEPs in unit and investment trusts. Changes of this kind are not, however, likely to reduce the growing preponderance of the institutional shareholder, although they may affect the relative attractions of different forms of saving.

1.4.3 *The Position of the Banks*

The role of the banking system could be important in improving corporate governance in Britain. Banks have provided much of the external finance for British industry in the 1980s at a time when the contribution of organized capital markets has been small. Historically the banks have seen themselves as providers of short-term finance even though in practice their commitments have frequently been considerably longer. More than half of the increase in lending by the National Westminster Bank between 1985 and 1990 was for loans of less than a year in duration. This pattern of lending contrasts with the much greater involvement of German banks with longer-term loans, for example in the case of the Deutsche Bank, more than half of its loans are typically for a term of four years or longer.

Heavy dependence upon short-term borrowing will tend to favour the acceptance by firms of projects which will generate cash relatively quickly. Marsh (1990) reports that British companies have continued to use crude pay-back methods of investment appraisal rather than theoretically superior discounted cash flow techniques. The resulting bias towards projects

yielding quick returns could partly reflect the priority accorded by management to cash flows arising in the near future. These cash flows would help
to ensure that short-term loans can be repaid without difficulty.

The recent experience of bank lending in Britain has not been happy.
The feast of loans in the mid-1980s has been followed by stringency in
lending in the early 1990s, leading to vigorous complaints, particularly from
smaller companies. The present difficulties are not unprecedented as
observers of the over-extension of credit by secondary banks in the early
1970s, following the first wave of deregulation, will remember.

Now that banks are being more cautious in their lending policies than in
the period of deregulation in the mid-1980s, it would be in their interests to
acquire greater knowledge about the companies to which they lend. A move
in this direction of a greater commitment to industrial borrowers could also
help to improve corporate governance. It could be accompanied by a willingness to extend a higher proportion of longer-term loans and a closer
monitoring of the progress of companies.

Mayer and Alexander (1990) have shown that German banks make a
valuable contribution towards the finance of small and medium-sized firms
through offering longer-term loans. Such firms can retain a higher proportion of their earnings than their British counterparts, who may have little
alternative to seeking a stock-market quotation at a relatively early stage in
their development. While it is not possible to judge whether the British
market-based pattern is superior to the German bank-based approach there
seems to be a case for allowing British firms to opt for the route of using
long-term bank finance. This would enable managements who were concerned about the short-term pressures associated with a market quotation,
to follow an alternative path of development on the German model. Such
an alternative would, however, call for a greater commitment to the internal affairs of borrowing companies than British banks have been willing to
make in the past.

Closer association between banks and borrowing companies could give
rise to problems, since under the Insolvency Act 1986 a bank could run the
risk of being deemed to be a shadow director of a company experiencing
trading difficulties. The bank could in these circumstances be liable to
severe penalties. To avoid such problems banks have given advice to customers as outsiders rather than insiders, and have tended to distance themselves from boards encountering severe financial pressures. Such behaviour
is not conducive to long-term trust between banks and commercial borrowers. There would seem to be a case for reconsidering the risks which banks
run in such circumstances under current legislation. This should ensure that
banks are adequately equipped to bring about the necessary changes in
management, where a failing company is worth salvaging. The ability of
banks to insist upon major boardroom changes as a condition of a renewal

of borrowing is illustrated in the case of Dicht Walker. Further examples of this type of intervention may be needed if banks are to monitor their borrowers effectively.

There may be a danger that a bank will be tempted to use its position as a privileged creditor, due to its possession of collateral, to force a company into premature liquidation. This would safeguard the position of the bank but inflict, possibly unnecessary, losses upon other creditors. Hence it has been proposed that a bank should rank with all other creditors in a bankruptcy and should not be accorded any priority on account of the holding of collateral. This would create incentives for banks to examine the credentials of potential borrowers more carefully and to monitor more closely the progress of the companies to whom they lend. There is, however, a danger that the ending of collateral would raise the risks faced by banks leading to a higher risk premium. Banks should be encouraged to nurse stricken companies, promoting management changes and seeking their liquidation only as a last resort.

The 1980s have seen rapid growth of venture capital funds which have taken up the equity of small companies, sometimes operating in technically advanced areas. Banks should be encouraged to join with other institutions in contributing to the finance of venture capital funds. Such has been the success of venture capital funds that Sykes (1991) has recently suggested that the venture capital model could be applied more widely to the provision of equity to larger firms. This proposal certainly merits discussion as it suggests building upon the success which has already been achieved. There may be a danger that, following the proposed flotation of *3i*, bank support for the equity funding of smaller companies would be reduced. Fears have been expressed that the emergence of *3i* as an investment trust could be associated with a greater concern for short-term considerations than have characterized it in the past. The extension of venture capital schemes could make good any short-fall in the provision of equity finance which might arise for this reason.

1.4.4   *Takeover Bids and the Capital Market*

Even if measures are taken to improve corporate governance through adopting some of the proposals outlined in the previous three sections of the paper, there is still likely to be a need for the contested takeover bid. Hostile bids are the ultimate sanction against company boards which do not achieve satisfactory financial results and fail to make the best use of the resources at their disposal. While such bids play a negligible part in the German and Japanese systems of corporate governance, they are likely to be of continuing importance in both the British and US systems. During the 1990s, the focus of takeovers may be less on rectifying weaknesses in management, and more on building up corporations which are capable of operating on a global scale to take advantage of the growing integration of world markets.

The upsurge of takeover activity in Britain and the United States in the 1980s has prompted a number of proposals for reforming the takeover mechanism. A fundamental issue has been raised by Schliefer and Summers (1988) who question whether takeovers are in the public interest. They argue that shareholders are not alone in bearing residual risk in a company. Other participants, such as workers and executives, are also stakeholders with long-term commitments which could be damaged as a result of a takeover. An example of this would be workers who have built up jobs with specific skills which are not readily transferable. They are employed on implied contracts which offer continuing employment as an inducement to the acquisition of such skills. A new management, following a successful takeover bid, may reduce costs through reneging on implied contracts involving other stakeholders. Short-term gains to shareholders may have damaging long-run effects on the company, if the incentives for workers to acquire non-transferable skills is diminished. This general argument can be used to support measures which will restrain the takeover process, such as 'poison pill' strategies. These could include generous redundancy payments to existing employees and full compensation to managements for loss of office.

A more concrete proposal for making the process of takeover more orderly has been put forward by Lipton and Rosenbaum (1991). They recommend a framework for assessing the achievements of the incumbent management at regular intervals, while granting them immunity from takeover between quinquennial reviews. Boards of public companies would have the opportunity to offer themselves for re-election on the basis of their conduct of management since their last assessment and their proposals for the next five years. Bids from other groups of managers could be considered at the same meeting of shareholders. The proposal meets the criticism that managers should not be assessed on the basis of short-term results without granting total security to the incumbent management. The achievements and plans of managers could be more openly discussed than at present as also would be the arguments for accepting a takeover bid. The recommended procedure of five-yearly plans and assessments is rather inflexible. It is questionable whether any management could be fairly judged against plans drawn up as long as five years ago. A period of grace running for a quinquennium seems rather long in view of the pace of change in modern business.

Proposals for restraining the takeover process through offering increased protection to managements are naturally popular among incumbent managers. They have recently been canvassed by Plender (1990) who favours the use of competition policy to discourage hostile bids. All takeovers above a specified size would be referred to the Monopolies and Mergers Commission and the onus of proof that the bid is in the public interest would be placed on the bidder. The public interest would, however, be defined narrowly to include only the criteria of competition and efficiency. The threshold at which a predator would be obliged to make a general offer to all shareholders would be reduced from 30 per cent as at present to 15 per cent, so reducing the scope for building up a substantial minority holding in a target company before launching a contested bid. An alternative idea is to raise the threshold at which a full bid must be launched, since the compulsion to launch full bids at 30 per cent of holdings may have stimulated the takeover market at the expense of other methods of transferring ownership and control (Franks and Mayer 1990).

The effect of the proposed changes to the rules governing takeovers could be to slow down the operation of the market in corporate control. The increased security offered to established managements would mean that greater priority would have to be placed on other ways of strengthening corporate governance as the takeover process would be retarded, if not eliminated.

The major defect in the takeover process which has been identified in the previous discussion is that emphasized by Davis and Kay (1990), namely the damage which a successful bid may do to the interests of shareholders in the bidding company. In view of the risks to which shareholders are exposed, it would be appropriate that their consent should normally be sought before a bidder sets out on the takeover path. There appears to be a certain reluctance to inform shareholders about the costs which are being incurred by management on their behalf. Managements involved in takeover bids should endeavour to keep their shareholders informed in these matters. The information itself should not become an issue in the takeover contest, but there seems no reason why the relevant costs should not be disclosed. If such disclosure were to discourage takeovers, this would be entirely consistent with the responsibilities of acquiring companies to their shareholders.

CONCLUSION

This chapter have surveyed the problems arising from a lack of governance in British industry for much of the post-war period. The proposals which have been discussed in this chapter are summarized in the following tables. They relate to the structure of company banks, the role of shareholders, the role of the banks and the contribution of takeovers. Problems have been identified in the composition of company boards, which are closely associated with the interests of the management rather than those of the shareholders.

These themes are developed at greater length in the chapters which follow. The composition of boards of directors and the role of the institutional investor are discussed by Charkham and Sykes in Chapters 4 and 5. The pricing of equities and the operation of the capital market are examined in Chapters 3 and 9 by Marsh and Mayer, and the contribution of banks to industrial finance is discussed in Chapters 6 and 8. The problems raised by the financial needs of smaller companies are reviewed in Chapters 7 and 11, and the provision of venture capital is discussed in Chapter 10. Chapter 12 provides a summary of theoretical issues and a review of international trends in the sources and uses of capital; Chapters 13 and 14 examine the role of the banks in the German financial system; and Chapters 15 and 16 review the main features of the Japanese financial system.

Table 1.1. *Summary of proposals for consideration*

Problems in UK	Proposals	Chapters addressing these issues
Structure of company boards Lack of accountability to shareholders. Difficulties where chairman is also chief executive—lack of independence of non-executive directors. Too little reliable information for shareholders.	Roles of each type of director to be more closely defined. External directors from a wider range of backgrounds Proportion of external directors on boards to be determined by statute. or Norms set by institutions for numbers of NEDs. New class of professional outside director. Separation of roles of chief executive and chairman. NEDs to serve on audit committees—giving information to NEDs and access for auditors to shareholders' representatives. Relate executive pay to profitability rather than volume of sales or company size.	Charkham (4) Edwards (13) Marsh (3) Schneider-Lenné (14) Sykes (5)
Role of shareholders Role of institutions—too passive, too much turnover, too widely diversified portfolios, too little knowledge of company managements.	Collective action by institutions to deal with unsatisfactory management. Institutions to concentrate portfolios on narrower range of investments with reduced turnover (i.e. directed investment). Accumulate information about companies and managements in which they have holdings. Appointment of NEDs to represent interests of shareholders. Put pressure for needed management changes when companies make rights issues.	Charkham (4) Marsh (3) Masuyama (16) Mayer (3) Sykes (5)

Table 1.1. Summary of proposals for consideration (*cont.*)

	Institutions to effect separation of chairman and chief executive and structure of management remuneration.	Beecroft (10)
	Institutions to review whether it is right to maintain dividends in recession.	Corbett (15)
	Companies to clarify components of profit and loss accounts—to separate ongoing revenues and costs from exceptional expenditure.	Edwards and Fischer (13)
	Companies to identify movements in reserves to make profit and loss statements more useful to investors and creditors.	Hughes (11)
	Institutions to make auditors accountable to shareholders in practice.	McWilliams & Sentance (6)
	Role of auditors to be enhanced.	Mayer (9)
		Middleton (7)
		Schneider-Lenné (14)
Role of banks		
Too much short-term lending—leading to favouring of short-term projects. Pay-back methods of investment appraisal increase bias towards short-term projects.	More loans of up to four years to companies instead of for less than a year.	
	Use of discounted cash flow techniques by companies instead of pay-back methods of investment appraisal.	
	Closer monitoring of companies' progress.	
	Encourage medium-sized companies to opt for long-term bank finance as alternative to equity market.	
Banks maintain themselves as outsiders to prevent being deemed shadow directors under Insolvency Act.	Reconsider risks of banks under current legislation.	
	Banks to bring about management changes if worthwhile and necessary as a condition of renewed borrowing.	

Banks bring about premature liquidation because of position as privileged creditors with collateral.

Banks to check credentials of borrowers more carefully and to monitor their progress more closely.
Banks to be discouraged from calling in loans prematurely, forcing borrowers into liquidation, which could be avoided with greater patience.
Banks to contribute to venture capital funds.
Banks to provide longer-term loans to medium-sized firms.

Kay (2)
Marsh (3)
Mayer (9)
Sykes (5)

Damage of takeovers
Damage to interests of shareholders in bidding company.
Reneging on implied contracts of stakeholders—disincentives for workers to acquire non-transferable skills.

Consent for bid to be obtained from shareholders of acquiring company with disclosure of relevant costs.

Other issues discussed
Restrain takeover process—assess achievements of management in quinquennial reviews with immunity from takeover in the interval. Use of competition policy to discourage hostile bids—refer bids to MMC—onus of proof that bid is in public interest placed on bidder. Threshold for launching full bids lowered to 15 per cent from 30 per cent—reduce scope for building up minority holdings.
or
Threshold for launching full bids to be raised above 30 per cent to allow stakeholds to be built up without inducing a bid.

A Postscript on the Draft Report of the Cadbury Committee

N. H. DIMSDALE

In its Draft Report[1] the Committee on the Financial Aspects of Corporate Governance (1992), known as the Cadbury Committee, reviews many of the problems of corporate governance concentrating upon the composition of boardrooms, the responsibility of non-executive directors, and the role of auditors. The Report is primarily concerned with the boardroom and accounting aspects of governance rather than the operation of the capital market and the role of takeovers in disciplining managements. It does, however, adopt a similar view to this chapter on the basic issue which is seen as the need to ensure the accountability of boards of directors to shareholders. The shareholders elect the board who report on their stewardship in financial statements which are subject to external checks through the company's auditors. The Report places particular emphasis on the need for fair and accurate reporting of a company's progress to its shareholders, which is the responsibility of the board, and is subject to confirmation by its auditors.

The major recommendation of the Report is the defining of a Code of Best Practice for companies. The Committee proposes that all listed companies should comply with the Code and that the Stock Exchange should require the annual report of all listed companies to include a statement about the extent of compliance (para. 3.7). Should a board not comply with the Code's provisions it would have to provide reasons for its behaviour. This essentially voluntary code of practice is preferred to an extensive reform of Company Law.

The Committee favours the separation of the offices of chairman and chief executive to prevent excessive concentration of power in boardrooms. Where the offices are combined, there should be a strong group of non-executive directors with an appointed leader to counterbalance the power of the executive (para. 4.6.). The Committee seeks to promote the power and influence of non-executive directors who should be independent and of high calibre, so that their views will carry weight in board discussions (para. 4.8). They should be able to seek independent professional advice at the company's expense. While the principle that all directors are equally responsible for the board's decisions is retained, non-executives are seen as being in the best position to monitor the performance of the company and

[1] Committee on the Financial Aspects of Corporate Governance, *Draft Report (Cadbury Committee)* (1992).

of the executive directors. The Report does not recognize the potential conflicts of interest which could arise in this situation where non-executives are actively participating in board decision making and also acting as monitors of the board.

Non-executives are to be in a majority on the nominating committee which is responsible for making recommendations for board membership. This provision is intended to ensure that candidates are judged on their merits and not according to their standing with the chief executive. Whether it will suffice to ensure the appointment of truly independent and forceful non-executives remains to be seen. At least the Committee has recognized the danger of having ineffectual non-executive directors as at Polly Peck and the Mirror Group, and has made recommendations which are intended to prevent such situations recurring.

Companies are to set up audit committees whose membership should be confined to non-executive directors (para. 4.29). The function of the audit committee is to advise on the appointment of auditors, to ensure the integrity of the company's financial statements and to discuss with the auditor any problems arising during the course of the audit. The Committee sees the audit committee as playing a major role in improving standards of corporate governance.

Board remuneration is a controversial issue following the recent massive increases in salaries of chief executives and other senior executives in major companies. The Committee proposes that companies should set up remuneration committees consisting wholly or mainly of non-executive directors who should make recommendations to the board on the pay of executive directors (para. 4.34). This is despite recent experience in Britain and the US that remuneration committees staffed by non-executive directors do not prevent massive pay increases for executive directors. The Committee recommends that directors' total emoluments and those of the chairman and highest paid directors should be disclosed in the company's report, including a breakdown between salary and performance related pay. It can be argued that Cadbury's recommendations for disclosure in this area do not go far enough. What is needed is a fine breakdown of the remuneration package of the five highest paid directors, giving full details of stock options, as required by the Securities and Exchange Commission. Furthermore, the ability of shareholders at the Annual General Meeting to challenge companies on directors' pay should be increased in contrast to Cadbury's attempt to skirt this issue.

The Report recommends improvements in the reporting of financial information which are to be welcomed. It emphasizes the responsibility of boards to present a balanced and understandable assessment of their company's position (para. 4.41). It recognizes that because of the varying nature of accounting practices there is scope for uncertainty and even manipulation in the presentation of a company's results. In these circumstances the need for 'true and fair' financial reporting is emphasized. Specific improvements are recommended in that interim reports should include balance sheet information. They should be reviewed by its auditors and discussed with the audit committee. They should also provide information on cash flow, which is needed to assess whether the company is a continuing enterprise (para. 4.4). This is an issue on which directors are to be required to give specific assurances and on which auditors must comment. Following the Maxwell affair the Committee recommends that good corporate governance requires that the control of the company's pension fund should be separated from the rest of the company. This is intended to safeguard the assets of pension funds whatever the fate of a company (para. 4.51).

The Report recognizes that there is a conflict of interest between auditors who are appointed by managers and yet are responsible for the interests of shareholders. Accounting practices allow considerable scope for presenting information in a variety of ways which could favour the interests of the management rather than the shareholder. One solution to this problem would be to make the appointment of auditors by shareholders more than a formality and so to strengthen the connection between auditors and shareholders. The Cadbury Report rejects this approach and calls for a professional and objective relationship between boards of directors and auditors (para. 5.7). It puts its faith in a general improvement in accounting standards and in providing the auditors with access to non-executive directors on audit committees.

Auditors may well be tempted to accede to management pressures on auditing issues in order to secure remunerative consulting work. The proposal that auditors should not provide consulting and other services to managements, so-called quarantining, was rejected by the Committee although it does recommend disclosure of payments by companies to auditors for non-audit work (para. 5.11). Such a recommendation seems rather feeble in view of the presence of conflicts of interests in this area, which could well not be resolved to the advantage of shareholders.

The Report recommends that there be a regular rotation of partners in auditing firms so that auditors and management do not build up too close a relationship during the course of time (para. 5.12). It does not go so far as to suggest regular changes in accounting firms, but only in personnel.

The Committee has recognized the existence of an 'expectations gap' between what is commonly expected of auditors and what they see themselves as doing (para. 5.13). Auditors are seen as failing when a company fails or when the management are found to be incompetent and possibly fraudulent. Cadbury does not question the decision of the House of Lords in the *Caparo* case which limits the responsibility of auditors to a duty of care to shareholders in general. This responsibility does not extend to the interests of individual shareholders or of prospective purchasers of the company's stock (paras. 5.31–5.33). It could be argued that this approach is rather restrictive and shelters the auditors. If their responsibilities were more widely defined, they would have a greater incentive to qualify accounts, should they be dissatisfied with either the state of a company's accounts or its internal control systems. More frequent qualifications of accounts by auditors would provide the shareholders and the capital market with valuable information about the difficulties being encountered by companies.

The Report does, however, recommend a change in legislation which would protect auditors against charges of breach of client confidence if they report cases of suspected fraud to the investigating authorities (para. 5.28). It could be argued, in the light of recent British experience, that the recommendation should have been stronger, making the reporting of such suspicions mandatory.

The Committee naturally wishes to strengthen the accountability of company boards to their shareholders. The chief way of achieving this objective is through securing general compliance with the proposed Code of Conduct (para. 6.3). Other suggestions include measures to make Annual General Meetings more effective. Written questions may be submitted by shareholders before the meeting and a summary of points raised during the meeting should be circulated to all shareholders (para. 6.5). Institutional investors should be encouraged to make greater use of their voting rights and to seek contact with companies at a senior executive level. They should take particular interest in boards where there is a concentration of power in the hands of the chief executive and should seek to promote the influence of non-executive directors. In general they should be encouraged to bring about changes in underperforming companies rather than to dispose of their shares (paras. 6.7–6.8).

The emphasis on the role of institutions in improving corporate governance creates a problem of equal treatment of different categories of shareholder. The Committee recognizes that the information available to financial institutions is superior and suggests that significant statements about a company must be made available to all shareholders (para. 6.9). It also accepts that closer relations with managements can result in institutional investors gaining price sensitive information which makes them insiders (paras. 6.9–6.10). While encouraging discussions between institutions and management, the Report does not go so far as to recommend the formation of shareholders' committees and the participation of shareholders in the appointment of directors and auditors. The Report questions whether such bodies could be properly representative of shareholder interests and argues that shareholders should seek to influence boards directly rather than through committees (para. 6.2).

The Cadbury Committee has made useful proposals for improving the system of corporate governance in Britain. In some respects its recommendations seem unduly timid. The proposed voluntary Code of Conduct is lacking in effective sanctions. It will be relatively easy for companies to claim compliance without the provision of an adequate system for evaluating and monitoring the operation of the Code. The changes in legislation which are proposed are minor but the voluntary code should, it is proposed, be assessed after two years. Should it fail to bring to an end the more flagrant abuses of executive power, the case for more extensive changes in legislation will need to be reviewed.

REFERENCES

Artus, R. E. (1990), 'Tensions to Continue', in National Association of Pension Funds *Creative Tension?* (NAPF, London).

Ball, R. J. (1990), 'Financial Institutions and their Role as Shareholders', in National Association of Pension Funds, *Creative Tension?* (NAPF, London).

Bannock, G. (1990), *The Takeover Boom: An International and Historical Perspective*, Papers prepared for the Inquiry into Corporate Takeovers in the UK No 2 (David Hume Institute, Edinburgh).

Charkham, J. (1989*a*), *Corporate Governance and the Market for Control of Companies*, Bank of England Panel Paper No 25 (Bank of England, London).

—— 1989*b*), *Corporate Governance and the Market for Companies: Aspects of the Shareholders' Role*, Bank of England Discussion Paper No 44 (Bank of England, London).

Committee on Finance and Industry (1931), *Report* Cd 3897 (Macmillan Committee) (HMSO, London).

Committee on the Financial Aspects of Corporate Governance (1992), *Draft Report* (Cadbury Committee).

Committee to Review the Functioning of Financial Institutions (1980), *Report* Cmnd 7937 (Wilson Committee) (HMSO, London).

Cosh, A. D., and Hughes, A. (1987), 'The Anatomy of Corporate Control: Directors, Shareholders and Executive Remuneration in Giant US and UK Corporations', *Cambridge Journal of Economics*, 11: 285–313.

Davis, E. and Kay, J. (1990), 'Corporate Governance, Takeovers and the Role of the Non-Executive Director', *Business Strategy Review*, Autumn, 17–35.

De Bondt, W. and Thaler, R. (1985), 'Does the Stock Market Overreact?', *Journal of Finance*, 40: 793–805.

Edwards, J. S. S. and Fischer, K. (1990), 'Banks, Finance and Investment in West Germany since 1970', unpub. paper (Centre for Economic Policy Research).

Fama, E. F. (1970), 'Efficient Capital Markets: A Review of Theory and Empirical Work', *Journal of Finance*, 25: 383–423.

Florence, P. S. (1953), *The Logic of British and American Industry* (Routledge and Kegan Paul, London).

Franks, J. and Harris, R. (1989), 'Shareholder Wealth Effects of UK Takeovers:

Implications for Merger Policy', in J. Fairburn and J. Kay (eds.), *Mergers and Merger Policy* (Oxford University Press, Oxford).

—— and Mayer, C. (1990), 'Takeovers', *Economic Policy*, April, 189–231.

Gilson, R. and Kraakman, R. (1990), 'Reinventing the Outside Director: an Agenda for Institutional Investors', working paper No. 66 (Stanford University Law School, Stanford).

Grossman, S. and Hart, O. (1980), 'Takeover Bids, the Free Rider Problem and the Theory of the Corporation', *Bell Journal of Economics*, Spring, 42–64.

Hannah, L. (1983), *The Rise of the Corporate Economy*, second edition (Methuen, London).

Hay, D. A. and Morris, D. J. (1991), *Industrial Economics and Organization: Theory and Evidence*, second edition (Oxford University Press, Oxford).

Hirschman, A. (1970), *Exit, Voice and Loyalty* (Harvard University Press, Cambridge, Mass.).

Hughes, A. (1989), 'The Impact of Merger: A Survey of Empirical Evidence for the UK', in J. Fairburn and J. Kay (eds.), *Mergers and Merger Policy* (Oxford University Press, Oxford).

Jensen, M. C. (1988), 'Takeovers: Their Causes and Consequences', *Journal of Economic Perspectives*, Winter 2: 21–48.

Lipton, M. and Rosenbaum, S. (1991), 'Corporate Governance: An End to Hostile Takeovers and Short-Termism', *University of Chicago Law Review*, Winter.

Marsh, P. (1990), *Short-Termism on Trial* (Institutional Fund Managers' Association, London).

Mayer, C. and Alexander, I. (1990), 'Banks and Securities Markets: Corporate Financing in Germany and the UK', unpub. paper (City University Business School, London).

Miles, D. (1991), 'Testing for Short-Termism', unpub. paper. (Birkbeck College, London).

Milward, A. and Saul, S. B. (1977), *The Development of the Economies of Continental Europe 1850–1914* (Allen and Unwin, London).

Payne, P. L. (1974), *British Entrepreneurship in the Nineteenth Century* (Macmillan, London).

—— (1978), 'Industrial Entrepreneurship and Management in Great Britain', in *The Cambridge Economic History of Europe*, vii. P. Mathias and M. M. Postan (eds), *The Industrial Economies: Capital, Enterprise and Labour*, pt. 1 (Cambridge University Press, Cambridge).

Peacock, A. and Bannock, G. (1991), *Corporate Takeovers and the Public Interest* (David Hume Institute, Edinburgh).

Plender, J. (1990), 'Some Policy Options', in A. Cosh, A. Hughes, A. Singh, J. Carty, and J. Plender, *Takeovers and Short-termism in the UK*, Industrial Policy Paper No. 3 (Institute for Public Policy Research, London).

Prais, S. J. (1976), *The Evolution of Giant Firms in Britain* (Cambridge University Press, Cambridge).

Schliefer, A. and Summers, L. (1988), 'Breach of Trust in Hostile Takeovers', in A. Auerbach (ed.), *Corporate Takeovers: Causes and Consequences* (Chicago University Press, Chicago).

Shiller, R. (1981), 'Do Stock Prices Move too much to be Justified by Subsequent Changes in Dividends?', *American Economic Review*, 71: 421–36.

Summers, L. (1986), 'Does the Stock Market Rationally Reflect Fundamental Values?', *Journal of Finance*, 41: 591–601.

Sykes, A. (1990), *Corporate Takeovers: The Need for Fundamental Rethinking*, papers prepared for the Inquiry into Corporate Takeovers in the UK No. 9 (David Hume Institute, Edinburgh).

Sykes, A. (1991), 'The Lessons of Venture Capital Financing for Quoted Companies', Venture Capital Report.

APPENDIX

The Code of Best Practice

1. Board of Directors
(a) The board must meet regularly, retain full and effective control over the company and monitor the executive management.
(b) There should be a clearly accepted division of responsibilities at the head of a company, which will ensure a balance of power and authority, such that no one individual has unfettered powers of decision. Where the chairman is also the chief executive, it is essential that there should be a strong independent element on the board, with an appointed leader. (para. 4.6)
(c) The calibre and number of non-executive directors should be such that their views carry significant weight in the board's decisions. (para. 4.8).
(d) Boards should have a formal schedule of matters reserved to them for decision to ensure that the direction and control of the company is firmly in their hands (paras. 4.19–4.20)
2. Non-executive Directors
(a) Non-executive directors should bring an independent judgement to bear on issues of strategy, performance, resources, including key appointments, and standards of conduct. (para. 4.8)
(b) The majority should be independent and free of any business or financial connection with the company apart from their fees and shareholding. Their fees should reflect the time which they commit to the company. (paras. 4.9–4.10)
(c) They should be appointed for specified terms and reappointment should not be automatic. (para. 4.14)
(d) There should be an agreed procedure for non-executive directors to take independent professional advice if necessary, at the company's expense. (para. 4.12)
(e) Non-executive directors should be selected through a formal process and their nomination should be a matter for the board as a whole. (para. 4.13)

3. Executive Directors
(a) Directors' service contracts should not exceed three years without shareholders' approval. (para. 4.33)
(b) Directors' total emoluments and those of the chairman and highest paid UK director should be fully disclosed and split into their salary and performance-related elements. The basis on which performance is measured should be explained. (para. 4.32)
(c) Executive directors' pay should be subject to the recommendations of a remuneration committee made up wholly or mainly of non-executive directors. (para. 4.34)

4. Controls and Reporting
(a) Boards must establish effective audit committees. (para. 4.29)
(b) Directors should report on the effectiveness of their system of internal financial control. (para. 4.26)
(c) Boards should ensure that an objective and professional relationship is maintained with the auditors. (para. 5.7)
(d) It is the board's duty to present a balanced and understandable assessment of their company's position. (para. 4.41)
(e) The directors should explain their responsibility for preparing the accounts next to a statement by the auditors about their reporting responsibilities. (para. 4.22)
(f) The directors should state in their report that the business is a going concern, with supporting assumptions or qualifications as necessary. (para. 5.23)
(g) The chairmen of the audit and remuneration committees should be responsible for answering questions at the Annual General Meeting. (paras. 4.29, 4.34)

2

Corporate Strategy and Corporate Accountability

PROFESSOR JOHN KAY

2.1 INTRODUCTION

This paper is concerned with the relationship between corporate strategy and corporate accountability. I shall argue that in Britain, and in Anglo-Saxon countries generally, there are substantial areas of weakness arising from this relationship.

The corporate chief executive is increasingly cast as a fund manager, who chooses industries and businesses in the same way as an investment manager chooses sectors and stocks. He manages a portfolio of activities as the investor manages a portfolio of shares. Taken as a whole, the evidence that this activity adds value is slight, and that evidence suggests that wealth is created by nurturing and developing individual businesses rather than by putting them together in different or distinctive combinations. Competitive advantages arise, and rents accrue, at the level of the individual operating unit, not in the industry or to the corporate entity (see, for example, Rumelt (1991), but also Schmalensee (1985)). Yet the role of dealmaker suits many managers, to whom it offers opportunities for rapid growth, media attention, and the thrill of the chase—and it suits the financial services industry, to which it offers transactions fees, market activity, and arbitrage opportunities.

This corporate activity is not simply irrelevant to the creation of competitive advantage; it may in important respects prove actively destructive of it. Many competitive advantages are based on architecture (Kay 1993); on the creation of a network of relational contracts (Macneil 1974; 1978), or trust relationships (Fox 1974), whose terms are largely implicit and which are enforced not by legal process but by the expectation of the parties involved that they will go on doing business with each other. Such architecture may exist within the firm, or between the firm and its customers and suppliers, including those who supply it with capital. It allows the sharing of information (rather than its strategic deployment) and encourages the development of fast and flexible responses to a changing environment through a process in which decisions are taken by reference to maximization of mutual gain rather than for the benefit of individual parties.

The existence of relational contracts necessarily gives scope for opportunistic behaviour (Williamson 1985; 1986). One party may make an immediate gain at the cost, in general, of terminating the relationship or at least the ability of the parties to the relationship to continue to operate under established rules. In the last decade, in particular, such opportunities have repeatedly been taken. The outcome is not only the loss, in specific cases, of the gains from relational contracting but the creation of a climate in which this style of business relationship becomes more difficult for everyone. The social and commercial penalties for opportunistic behaviour have been reduced, and the assurance of stability in personnel and ownership structure, essential to the maintenance of confidence in such relationships, has largely disappeared. Relationships are increasingly replaced by more tightly specified contracts, and formal monitoring of performance. In such a world, information is managed strategically, and co-operative behaviour induced only when it clearly corresponds to an individual interest as well as a collective one.

While these changes are not without their advantages, it is striking that our most successful industrial competitor is a country whose business culture strongly emphasizes the stability of commercial relationships, both between firms and within them. It is a country which has an environment which systematically creates and emphasizes social and economic penalties for opportunistic behaviour, and in which business relationships are characterized by an absence of legal process virtually incomprehensible to Western society. It is also a society which benefits from the creation, and sharing, of organizational knowledge, speed and flexibility of response, and from a readiness to engage in co-operative behaviour—precisely the competitive benefits which an emphasis on the role of architecture would lead us to predict.

In section 2.2 of this chapter, I review some of the more common fallacies about the nature and sources of competitive advantage. I emphasize throughout that the source of competitive advantage is a distinctive capability that is both *sustainable* and *appropriable*. Such capabilities are not replicable by competitors, draw on unique characteristics of the organization, and can be exploited for the benefit of the corporation itself. (I distinguish this latter case—where distinctive capability is *appropriated* for the benefit of the firm—from those where the corporation acts as vehicle for the distinctive capabilities of those who work for, or supply, it.) Section 2.2 describes characteristics of firms which, although widely emphasized, fail to meet these tests of appropriability and sustainability—characteristics such as size, scope, market share, corporate leadership, and the choice of markets and market position. In section 2.3, I consider the nature of distinctive capabilities which *do* fulfil the requirements of sustainability and appropriability: innovation (in limited circumstances), reputation, and architecture. I go on to describe how competitive advantages are built around them.

Section 2.4 describes architecture in more detail, emphasizing the relationship between architecture and the governance structure of the corporation. In the concluding section 2.5, I comment on short- and long-termism and draw some policy implications.

2.2   HOW COMPANIES DO NOT DERIVE SUSTAINED COMPETITIVE ADVANTAGE

2.2.1   *Scale Economies and Critical Mass*

Phrases like 'critical mass' and 'global players' are in wide circulation to emphasize the need, and the likelihood, of further rationalization and concentration of firms both within Europe and in the international economy more generally. In much casual discussion of strategic issues in Europe, size appears to be viewed as the principal source of competitive advantage. Sometimes, indeed the impression is given that size is the *only* source of competitive advantage. This increasing focus on a small number of companies in most industries may be the vision which many strategists have of the future. The verdict of the market-place does, however, seem to be different.

While through the twentieth century the clear trend has been one of increasing concentration, that now seems to have been halted and reversed. The check seems to have occurred in the United States around 1960. In the UK, the merger boom of the 1960s substantially increased concentration, and the peak was reached at the end of that decade. Since then the average size of large firms and their share in total output have declined markedly, and the same tendencies are evident in individual markets. In Germany and France, some increase in concentration seems to have continued into the 1970s. (See Hughes 1991 for a recent survey of this evidence.)

There is a tendency to confuse the indicators of success with the causes of success. The king may wear a crown, but it does not follow that you will become king by wearing a crown. When we look at Boeing or Toyota or IBM we observe companies which are both large and successful. But the causation runs from their success to size, not from size to success, and it is quite mistaken to believe that by replicating their size one could replicate their organizational effectiveness.

If scale were a primary source of competitive advantage, then the greatest competitive advantage ever enjoyed by any firm was that held by General Motors in the 1950s. GM was the world's largest and most respected corporation, pre-eminent in an industry unquestionably characterized by substantial scale economies. Following the failure of Kaiser and Studebaker it was generally assumed that the automobile industry would concentrate around a smaller number of existing players. The notion that GM's dominance might be challenged by a new entrant to the industry then appeared inconceivable. Yet that is precisely what has occurred and it is now Toyota, rather than GM, which is the world's leading producer of motor cars. The key lesson is that size cannot be a sustained source of competitive advantage, because if size is its only source, then size is something which a competitor with a true competitive advantage, based on a distinctive capability, can ultimately replicate.

2.2.2 *Market Share as Competitive Advantage*

If size, as such, is not a competitive advantage, what of market share? One of the clearest findings of the PIMS database (Buzzell and Gale 1986) is that high market share and high profitability are closely associated. But as with the nexus between size and success, it is important not to confuse the manifestations of competitive advantage with the causes. Firms with competitive advantages are likely to have both high market share and high profitability, but it does not follow that a firm without a competitive advantage will increase its profitability by increasing its market share through price cutting, advertising and promotion, or market development. Nor, for that matter, does it follow that a firm which does have a competitive advantage will increase its profitability by increasing its market share.

At the very least, however, the correlation may suggest that building market share is likely to be a part of the creation of competitive advantage, and that a firm with low market share is unlikely to have a sustainable position. But there is less to this observation than it seems at first sight. BMW has little more than 1 per cent of the world car market, but if we redefine the market as the luxury car sector we get a much higher percentage. The underlying issue is that almost all successful firms enjoy a large market share relative to their perceived competition—it could hardly be otherwise.

The PIMS database, appropriately for its purposes, asks firms to define their 'served market' by reference to these perceived competitors. For an outside observer, any firm which has a competitive advantage will have some market, suitably defined, in which it is dominant. If 'build market share' 'means 'build market share even if that is not the most effective way of developing our competitive advantage', then the prescription is a misleading one. If it means only 'build market share if that is the most effective way of developing your competitive advantage', then it adds little to our understanding of competitive strategy.

2.2.3 *Attractive Markets and Market Positions*

Much strategy discussion focuses around the relative attractiveness of different markets. This approach forms the basis of the portfolio planning which was popular a decade ago (Hapselagh 1982), and still retains considerable influence on corporate behaviour. It is, at first sight, obvious that rapidly growing markets, such as those for financial services or electronics, are more attractive than declining markets, such as those for steel or tobacco. Yet it is the very obviousness of the proposition that is the problem. If these markets are objectively attractive, then they are attractive to everyone, and that will impinge on industry profitability as rapidly as entry can occur. We can identify an industry as attractive just as we can observe that Glaxo is a good share or the Polish zloty is a weak currency. It does not follow that a firm should enter an attractive market any more than investors should buy Glaxo or sell zlotys. The issue for the potential investor in every case is how much of that attractiveness, or lack of it, is already discounted by the market.

The term 'efficient market' is most frequently used of trading in securities, where there is extensive evidence of a high degree of market efficiency.[1] An efficient market is one in which there are no bargains, because all relevant information about the product is already reflected in its price. The advice, 'buy Glaxo shares because Glaxo is a well-managed company with outstanding products' is worthless advice, even though it is a type of advice that is often given, because these facts about Glaxo are well known and fully incorporated in the price of Glaxo shares.

In broader business terms, the implications of market efficiency are much the same. Opportunities that are available to everyone are not likely to be profitable for anyone. What other people can equally see and do will rarely be a sustained source of advantage. Having correctly perceived the attractiveness of markets like financial services or electronics, many firms have entered these markets, and many have lost money doing so. It should not occasion surprise that often the largest money-losers are firms whose competitive advantages lie in quite different fields of activity but which see the appeal of a growing industry. Observe Exxon's losses in the small computer market or BAT's in insurance. At the same time, firms like Hanson and BTR have built highly successful businesses by targeting acquisitions in industries which other firms saw as objectively unattractive.

If market selection is not a basis for competitive advantage, but a means of exploiting a distinctive capability which is specific to a particular firm, the same is true of market positioning. PIMS does show that high returns are associated with quality positions (Buzzell and Gale 1986). However, these are not returns to market position as such. They reward the underlying distinctive capability which allows that firm, but not others, to attain a high-quality position. For many firms, their competitive advantage is best

---

[1] The efficient market hypothesis for financial markets is described in any corporate finance text, e.g. Brealey and Myers (1981) and Fama (1970). Its implications for strategy are well set out in Oster (1990).

exploited in a high-quality position. It does not follow that the same position would produce the same returns for other firms, and our presumption must be that it would not. The success of Mercedes does not mean that it is possible, or sensible, to recommend the same market position to Hyundai. Each should select positions which reflects its—quite different—sources of competitive advantage.

The confusion between good positioning and competitive advantage is a particularly common management error in markets for fast moving consumer goods. Another British retailer, the Next Group, provides a chastening example (Cronshaw and Kay 1992). Next successfully identified an underdeveloped market for fashionable clothing of moderate quality for women aged 20–35, and sales and profits grew very rapidly. Mistakenly believing that its good fortune rested, not on its market position, but on competitive advantage in retailing systems, the company diversified into mail order, interior design, and financial services, with marked lack of success. At the same time, established retailers with strengths in retailing systems invaded its market niche, and brought the company to the verge of collapse.

Positioning is unlikely to provide sustained competitive advantage because positioning is rarely appropriable. Most market positions can be replicated, and if profitable they will be. Some market positions, as with that of Mercedes, are truly hard to emulate, but that demonstrates that the true competitive advantage lies in quality of engineering, and in consumer recognition of it, rather than in the market position as such. An exception to this general rule is found when a market niche is sufficiently small that it will support one profitable incumbent but not two. CNN is replicable but it is probably not profitable to replicate it.

2.2.4 *Competitive Advantage Through Merger*

Despite the central role which acquisition plays in most discussions of corporate strategy, evidence on the consequences of mergers points to one clear conclusion. Taken as a whole, merger activity adds very little value.

There are several ways of assessing post-merger performance. The simplest is to ask companies themselves whether they think mergers have been successful, an approach adopted by Hunt *et al.* (1987) who established that on this self-rated basis around half of mergers succeeded and around half failed. They went on to identify the relative size of acquiror and acquiree as the single largest influence on the probability of success. An alternative way of finding out companies' own opinions is to see what they subsequently do. Ravenscraft and Scherer (1987) analysing over 6,000 US mergers over a twenty-five-year period, found that just under half of all acquisitions were subsequently divested, a result confirmed in a smaller but more recent exercise by Porter (1987).

The most objective means of measuring added value from a merger is a comparison of pre- and post-merger profitability, and several British studies do this, normalizing by reference either to the experience of other firms in the same industry, or matched non-merging firms. The pattern is one of general relative decline. Ravenscraft and Scherer (1987) established a similar picture for the USA: substantial profit deterioration in those firms which were subsequently divested, more modest but still distinct deterioration in those which were retained. The most optimistic conclusion is that of Mueller *et al.* (1980) in the only major study also to cover mergers in other European countries. They observe that 'no consistent pattern of either improved or deteriorated profitability can therefore be claimed across the seven countries. Mergers would appear to result in a slight improvement here, a slight worsening there.'

Evidence from the stock market is rather more supportive (Franks and Harris 1989). Acquirors almost invariably pay a bid premium, so that merger announcements lead to an increase in the market value of the acquired firm. Sometimes the share price of the acquiror rises, sometimes it falls, but the principal studies both in the UK and USA have established that these broadly balance out, so that merger announcements are, on average, neutral in their effect on the acquiror's share price. This indicates that the market's assessment of the combined value of the merged firm is greater than its assessment of the firm's value as independent units, and this gain—which accrues principally to the shareholders of the acquired company—is a measure of the value added through merger.

There are, however, some problems with this interpretation of the data. Acquired firms tend to have performed worse than the stock-market in general in the period before (though not immediately before) acquisition, and acquiring firms rather better. When the stock-market performance of acquiring firms is measured over a longer period of time than that of the merger announcement, the average pattern is one of underperformance, implying that a portfolio of newly merged companies can be expected to do worse than the market. The stock-market's initial assessment (like, perhaps, that of the managers of the companies involved) is unduly optimistic.

The most likely explanation of these facts, and their reconciliation with accounting data, is that the timing of acquisitions tends to reflect valuation discrepancies. Mergers tend to be consummated when the acquiror's share price is relatively strong and the acquiree's is relatively weak. The apparent gains from merger reflect the correction of these discrepancies rather than the added value of the merger as such.

None of this evidence should be interpreted as indicating that no merger is ever successful. Clearly, many mergers match expectations and do add value to the businesses which they bring together. But there is no evidence to suggest that merger activity, taken as a whole, is an important means of adding value, and plenty of evidence to suggest that it is not.

2.3   How Companies do Derive Competitive Advantage

A firm is, in essence, a set of relationships.[2] It makes contracts to buy materials and to hire employees: it makes contracts with its bankers and its shareholders, who provide it with capital; it makes agreements to sell output to customers. Each firm's distinctive identity is built from the distinctive character of the totality of these relationships.

The first task of the management of any firm is to establish the *consistency* of its contracts, to ensure that the committed output can be achieved with the planned inputs. But there is a second, and equally fundamental, task. Each contract matches a physical flow—of goods, services, labour, materials—with a financial flow (Table 2.1). The firm also seeks to maximize the value of the set of contracts which makes up the firm. That means ensuring that each individual contract is at least as good as any other available in the market-place. It means hiring the best employees and minimizing the cost of capital.

Table 2.1   *The firm as contracts*

Physical flows	Financial flows
− Sell to customers	+ Sales proceeds
+ Obtain materials	− Pay suppliers
+ Hire employees	− Pay wages and salaries
+ Buy capital services	− Pay for capital services

But it is equally important to ensure that the set of contracts *taken as a whole* is the best available. This latter task—that of choosing the complete set of contracts by defining the nature of the firm's activities, and its positioning relative to its competitors and potential competitors—is the central task of business strategy. While the physical flows of outputs sum to zero— since output is matched by inputs of materials, labour, and capital—the financial flows do not. The balance is the economic rent, or added value, associated with the operations of the firm.

Such added value is the outcome of the quality and distinctiveness of the contract portfolio. The distinctiveness is at least as important as the goodness. In an efficient market there are few opportunities to make good contracts. It follows that making contracts on better terms than are generally

---

[2] This approach owes much to that of Alchain and Demsetz (1972).

available in the market is not a principal means of adding value, since it is an opportunity unlikely to be systematically available for long. Added value is, in the main, achieved by developing a set of contracts which others are unable to make. There are four broad ways in which this can be done.

One is to make a novel contract or arrangement of contracts. This might be for a new type of good or service—as with product or process innovations. The innovation might be in the *form* of the contract itself, as is often the case in financial services. The difficulty in establishing competitive advantage from this source is quickly apparent—most innovation can be quickly replicated—and sustained competitive advantage depends on the ability to protect the innovation, through legal restriction, copyright, or patent protection, or through strategy.

Added value may be created if customers or suppliers are systematically willing to make contracts with the firm on terms which they would not make available to other people. Usually this is a result of the supplier's *reputation*. International car hire firms offer the same models of car on the same formal contract terms at higher prices than do local firms (Star 1991). They attract customers, not because the quality and reliability of the service is necessarily any better, but because customers know that the reputation of the franchisor provides them with an assurance of that quality and reliability.

The distinctiveness of a set of contracts may rest in the group of contracts taken as a whole, in the *architecture* of the firm. While any part of it can be reproduced, the complexity of the set defies imitation. Typically, this requires that many of the contracts have implicit, or relational terms. If you can write a contract down, others can make the same contract. This architecture is a major part of what distinguishes Marks & Spencer, both in its internal architecture—its relationships with its employees—and its external architecture—its relationships with its suppliers. Architecture is the phenomenon that makes Liverpool a better team than the aggregate of its players, while Manchester United, with players of broadly the same calibre (as measured by transfer value or international representation) gets broadly the results that these levels of playing standard would imply (dell'Osso and Szymanski 1991).

And a final means of establishing a distinctive set of relationships is to make contracts which others are unable to make. This may be the result of exclusive access to a scarce factor (a television franchise or a national resource) or it may be the product of regulatory restriction, natural monopoly or strategic action. It is a criminal offence, for example, to operate a public telecommunications network without a licence. Until 1980 no licences were available and since then only two have been awarded.[3]

---

[3] To British Telecom and Mercury Communications.

2.4 ARCHITECTURE

2.4.1 *The Purposes of Architecture*

Architecture is a structure which achieves the growth of organizational knowledge, or the development of a co-operative ethic, within the firm itself. Both these things sound more common than they really are. All firms possess organizational knowledge, in the sense that an insurance company knows about insurance and an automobile manufacturer knows about automobiles. But what an insurance company knows about insurance is, as a rule, what its employees know about insurance, and is much the same as what other insurance companies know about insurance.

Organizational knowledge (Dyerson and Roper 1991) is distinctive to the firm, it is more than the sum of the expertise of those who work in the firm, and it is not available to other firms. If an insurance company builds up data and skills in the assessment of a particular category of risk, and if those data and these skills are truly those of the company and not those of a small group of employees, then it has created organizational knowledge. That organizational knowledge gives it a distinctive capability and is a competitive advantage in the market for that risk category. Most of an automobile company's base is derived from technical skills that are general to the industry, but the very large investment now involved in the development of individual models leads to the creation of organizational knowledge which is specific to that design.

As both these examples illustrate, organizational knowledge is often distinctive only at the price of being applicable to a narrowly defined market. Large competitive advantages come when the organizational knowledge is unique, appropriable to the firm, and relevant to a market which is large or a range of markets which is wide. This does not happen often. It was, perhaps, achieved by IBM, but was eroded even there as the knowledge base became diffused and the market more fragmented.

All firms would hope to establish a co-operative ethic. But the key issue here is what Williamson (1985) calls the difference between perfunctory and consummate co-operation—the difference between what is involved in mutually beneficial exchange, and true pooling of information in pursuit of a shared objective—the difference between a relationship with the local telephone company and a relationship with a marriage partner. While consummate co-operation is often achieved in small groups, it is rarely attainable across large organizations, where strategic bargaining between units is generally inevitable. Still less often is it accomplished in relationships between firms or with groups of firms. In markets which require flexibility of response or rapid flows of information, the creation of such a co-operative ethic can be a distinctive capability and a prime source of competitive advantage.

2.4.2   *The Nature of Architecture*

Both these purposes—the creation of organizational knowledge and the establishment of a co-operative ethic—depend on a supporting system of relational contracts. There are two distinct, but closely related, issues here. One is that of imitability. If the structure of relationships which achieves these things could be formalized and made routine it could also be imitated, and would at that point cease to be a source of competitive advantage.

Many books have been written which purport to describe IBM (e.g. Sobel 1981; Rodgers 1986; de Lamarter 1986; Mercer 1987), and Marks & Spencer (e.g. Rees 1973; Tse 1985; Goldenberg 1989; Sieff 1990). These books are available in any public library. They have been avidly read by would-be imitators of IBM and Marks & Spencer. Many employees have left Marks & Spencer and IBM and are available for other firms to hire, and competitors have done that too. Yet attempts to replicate the architecture of these organizations have not been at all comparably successful. Clearly, there is more to the architecture than these books contain; more to the architecture than any individual employee, or group of employees, knows. Neither reading the book nor recruiting the employee achieves the transfer of organizational knowledge, the implantation of the co-operative ethic, nor brings sufficient understanding of the structure of contracts and relationships which makes these things possible.

The second issue is the underlying nature of the relationships involved in the creation of organizational knowledge and a co-operative ethic. These are activities with 'Prisoner's Dilemma' properties and are best resolved in a context in which players see themselves as participants in a repeated game, with well-understood strategies for repeated play, as participants in a system of relational contracts.

We see this in the characteristics of organizations which have successfully established a strong architecture. There is an expectation of long-term relationships both within the firm and between its members, a commitment to a sharing of the rewards of collective achievement, and a high, but structured, degree of informality. This informality is sometimes mistaken for disorganization—in popular discussion of chaos, entrepreneurship, or 'ad-hoc-cracy', as conditions for innovation (see for example Peters 1988)—but truly chaotic organizations rarely perform well, and a system of relational contracts substitutes an extensive set of unwritten rules and expectations of behaviour for the formal obligations of the classical contract.

If we look at historical examples of immensely powerful organizational architecture—ancient Greece and Rome, medieval Italy, British India—we see all of them characterized by unwritten codes of behaviour, of great strength and considerable complexity. Indeed, many of the tragic heroes of literature are individuals who, for apparently good reasons, broke these codes and were destroyed by them. All these societies were founded on extensive systems of relational contracts.

The essence of architecture is that it is determined by a system of relational contracts. These contracts may be those that exist within the firm itself, between the firm and its employees, and in the implicit contracts which employees have with each other. They may rest between the firm and its suppliers, of goods and services, or of finance. They may be between the firm and its customers. Competitive advantage may be gained from relational contracts among a group of firms in a cluster or a network.

2.4.3 *Financial Architecture*

Relational contracts are often of particular importance in the finance of industry (Mayer 1992). Those who finance an activity will wish to monitor both the objective magnitude of the risks they take and the quality of the performance of those who manage them. However, those who have responsibility for the activity have clear incentives to distort that flow of information; to underestimate the risk, to overestimate the performance relative to these risks (Grossman and Hart 1983). It is therefore necessary to devise a contract structure that is robust to these problems. I consider three—the complete classical contract, the relational contract between the firm and its financiers, and internalization within the firm itself.

A common reaction to the information problems I face if I allow someone else to spend my money—and this is the situation everyone who funds a business encounters—is to impose a detailed contract of a classical kind. Often this does not work well. It can go wrong in one of two ways. If I am to be strictly bound to my promises, I will be reluctant to make promises at all. The legal obligations directors carry for statements they make in a company prospectus are generally very onerous, and as a consequence, prospectuses frequently contain only a bare minimum of factual information. If we make a detailed contract, I can only be held to the specifics of the contract, not to its objectives. Perhaps circumstances change, and we would do better to take a longer- or a shorter-term view. Classical contracts can be renegotiated, but the parties to them may well not exchange the information which would enable them to reach a mutually superior bargain.

Relational contracts are an alternative mechanism, and this is why financial institutions often talk about relationships, even if they are rarely successfully achieved. Close and enduring relationships between finance and industry are relatively uncommon in Britain and the United States, where financing is typically of an arm's length classical contracting kind. But Germany has traditionally enjoyed close relationships between its universal banks and industrial firms; these banks not only make loans but are responsible for significant equity stakes in the companies concerned. Japan has similar banking relationships and in addition networks of cross-holdings of shares between companies which have commercial relationships. Sweden has a particularly intricate structure of financial relations between its banks and industrial companies, centred around the Wallenberg group.

Financial centres are examples of geographically concentrated networks (Porter 1990). It is apparent that geographical proximity is important to networking, although the role it plays is not entirely obvious. At first sight it seems absurd that at a time when capital markets have become international, and world-wide communication of data, funds, and information has become instantaneous, the financial institutions of the world should be investing in building taller and taller high-rise blocks in tiny, and fabulously expensive, areas of lower Manhattan and east London.

The key issue is the need to establish trust and penalize opportunism in a network of relational contracts. This is facilitated if business relationships are supported by a corresponding network of social relationships. We are all more inclined to trust people we know; a view which is partly based on instinct and emotion, partly on our capacity to make our own judgements (we are also inclined to mistrust some people we know), and partly on a rational calculation that people are less likely to cheat us if by doing so they sacrifice a social reputation as well as a commercial one.

The extensive entertainment which is integral to Japanese business serves to reinforce relational contracts in this way as does the geographical concentration of the networks of small contractors which are characteristic of much of Italian industry. It may be no accident that the City of London's pre-eminence rested on the homogeneity of the background and values created by the English class and school systems. These factors may also explain why conscious attempts to eliminate the competitive advantages of networking through replication are rarely successful.

It follows that some social environments are more conducive to the development of competitive advantage through architecture than others. Since the essence of architecture is that organizations or groups of organizations have values—social and economic—distinct from those of their members, there is a direct conflict between individualism and the creation of architecture. This conflict is reinforced by the absence of powerful sanctions against opportunistic behaviour in an individualistic environment. Competitive strengths based on these architectures are therefore less evident in those environments where the prevailing ethos is strongly individualistic. Where they are apparent—as in the financial sector, in networking activities in less developed countries, and in the performance of companies with a very distinctive corporate ethos—the activities concerned are commonly viewed by outsiders with a degree of hostility and suspicion. Nepotism is a term of abuse, and contact networks are often corrupt.

2.5 CONCLUSIONS: SHORT-TERMISM AND LONG-TERMISM

The need for a more long-term view of corporate strategy is a theme which has been repeatedly emphasized over the last decade. Yet, as is now generally recognized, the arguments which are commonly formulated in the attack on short-termism are wrong. It is not true that the increasing tendency to judge investment managers by their performance over a three-month period, or a year, requires the managers of corporations to take a similarly short-term view. To think this is to fail to appreciate the central role which financial intermediation has, and achieves successfully: a divorce between the time horizons of borrowers and the time horizons of lenders.

Yet exposing this clear technical fallacy (as in Marsh 1990; 1992) has not made the short-termism/long-termism argument die, and it is apparent that many thoughtful people continue to believe that there must be something in it. My arguments here are designed to explain why there may, indeed, be something in it. The development of an environment in which organizational knowledge can be created and a co-operative ethic established requires an assurance of long-term relationships and a climate supportive of relational contracting and which is hostile to opportunistic behaviour.

The system of corporate governance we have in Britain has not established that, neither within firms themselves nor between firms and those who supply them with finance. Moreover the broad direction of change is away from, rather than towards, that outcome. Lifetime employment is perceived as something that can no longer be afforded. The tenure of senior executives has become markedly more insecure. Transactions banking has replaced relationship banking, and the most important financial innovation of the 1980s was the development of tighter controls associated with high levels of gearing as a means of securing managerial accountability. Such architecture as we have has been significantly undermined.

This is as much the fault of managers themselves as of the financial system. The shift to a deal-driven culture with its emphasis on the role of acquisition and divestiture in corporate strategy, the emphasis on the management of the corporate portfolio, and the readiness to behave opportunistically when occasion offers itself are not matters which the City has imposed on reluctant managers, but trends which executives have enthusiastically developed for themselves. We should understand that the principal issue of accountability in takeovers is not the responsibilities of institutional investors in the acquired company, or the need for more restraints from government agencies or company law. We need instead to develop the obligation, and opportunity, for shareholders in the acquiring company to stop what is generally a profitless activity, both for them and for the community.

REFERENCES

Alchian, A. and Demsetz, H. (1972), 'Production, Information Costs and Economic Organisation', *American Economic Review*, 62: 777–95.

Brealey, R. and Myers, S. (1981), *Principles of Corporate Finance* (McGraw-Hill).

Buzzell, R. D. and Gale, B. T. (1986), *The PIMS Principles* (The Free Press, New York).

Cronshaw, M. and Kay, J. A. (1992), *Whatever Next?* (Centre for Business Strategy Case Study, London Business School).

de Lamarter, R. T. (1986), *Big Blue: IBM's Use and Abuse of Power* (Dodd, Mead & Company, New York).

dell'Osso, F. and Szymanski, S. (1991), 'Who Are the Champions? An Analysis of Football and Architecture', *Business Strategy Review*, 2/2, Summer (Centre for Business Strategy, London Business School).

Dyerson, R. and Roper M. (1991), 'When experience becomes know-how: Technology management in financial services', *Business Strategy Review*, 2: 2, 53–73, Summer (Centre for Business Strategy, London Business School).

Fama, E. F. (1970), 'Efficient capital markets: A review of theory and empirical work', *Journal of Finance*, 25: 383–417.

Fox, A. (1974), *Beyond Contract: Work, Power and Trust Relations* (Faber and Faber, London).

Kay, J. A. (forthcoming), *Foundations of Corporate Success* (Oxford University Press, Oxford).

Franks, J. and Harris, R. (1989), 'Shareholder wealth effects of corporate takeovers: The UK experience 1955–1985', *Journal of Financial Economics*, 17: 5–26.

Goldenberg, N. (1989), *Thought for Food: A Study of the Development of the Food Division, Marks & Spencer: An Autobiography* (Food Trade Press, Orpington).

Grossman, S. and Hart, O. (1983), 'An analysis of the principal–agent problem', *Econometrica*, January, 51/1: 7–45.

Hapselagh, P. (1982), 'Portfolio planning: Uses and limits', *Harvard Business Review*, January/February, 58–72.

Hughes, A. (1991), 'The Impact of Merger: A Survey of Empirical Evidence for the UK', in J. A. Fairburn and J. Kay (eds.), *Mergers and Merger Policy* (Oxford University Press, Oxford).

Hunt, J. W., Lees, S., Grumbar, J. J. and Vivian, P. D. (1987), *Acquisitions: The Human Factor* (Egon Zehnder International, London).

Macneil, I. R. (1974), 'The Many Futures of Contract', *Southern California Law Review*, 47: 691–748.

—— (1978), 'Contracts: Adjustments of Long Term Economic Relations under Classical, Neoclassical and Relational Contract Law', *Northwestern University Law Review*, 72: 854.

Marsh, P. (1990), *Short Termism on Trial* (Institutional Fund Managers Association, London).

—— (1992), 'Market Assessment of Company Performance', Chapter 3 of this volume.

Mayer, C. (1992), 'Stock Markets, Financial Institutions and Corporate Performance', Chapter 9 of this volume.

Mercer, D. (1987), *IBM: How the World's Most Successful Corporation is Managed* (Kogan Page, London).

Mueller, D. C. *et al.* (1980), *The Determinants and Effects of Mergers* (Cambridge).

Oster, S. (1990), *Modern Competitive Analysis* (Oxford University Press, New York).

Peters, T. (1988), *Thriving on Chaos* (Macmillan, London).

Porter, M. E. (1987), 'From Competitive Advantage to Corporate Strategy', *Harvard Business Review*, May/June.

Porter, M. (1990), *The Competitive Advantage of Nations* (Macmillan, London).

Ravenscraft, D. J. and Scherer, F. M. (1987), *Mergers, Sell-Offs, & Economic Efficiency* (The Brookings Institution, Washington, DC).

Rees, G. (1973), *St. Michael: A History of Marks & Spencer* (Pan Books, London).

Rodgers, F. G. (1986), *The IBM Way* (Harper & Row, New York).

Rumelt, R. P. (1991), 'How Much does Industry Matter?', *Strategic Management Journal*, 12/3, March, 167–186.

Schmalensee, R. (1985), 'Do markets differ much?', *American Economic Review*, 75, June, 341–351.

Sieff, M. (1990), *Management the Marks & Spencer Way* (Fontana, London).

Sobel, R. (1981), *IBM: Colossus in Transition* (Times Books, London).

Star, J. (1991), *Car Hire* (Centre for Business Strategy Case Study, London Business School).

Tse, K. K. (1985), *Marks & Spencer: Anatomy of Britain's Most Efficiently Managed Company* (Pergamon Press, Oxford).

Williamson, O. E. (1985), *The Economic Institutions of Capitalism* (The Free Press, New York).

—— (1986), 'Transaction-Cost Economics: The Governance of Contractual Relations', *Economic Organisation* (Wheatsheaf Books, Brighton).

3

Market Assessment of Company Performance

PAUL MARSH

3.1 INTRODUCTION

This chapter deals with the important question of whether share prices reflect company performance and prospects.

Many people argue that they do not. The stock-market is often likened to a casino, where stock prices are simply betting odds, set as a by-product of a giant game. On this view, share price movements have little to do with the underlying economic performance of the companies concerned, but instead are determined by fads and fashions, and by which way the herd of investors stampedes or places its bets.

Against this general scepticism, several quite specific criticisms are levelled against the stock-market. First, the market is frequently alleged to be short-termist, placing too much weight on current profits and dividends, and too little on the longer-term. Second, it is often claimed that the market is too concerned with accounting measures of performance, such as earnings per share, rather than with the underlying economic profitability of businesses. This problem is made worse, it is said, by the questionable reliability of accounting information, and the 'flexibility', or even laxity, of auditors.

Finally, still others argue that there is a serious 'dual-pricing' problem. This is believed to arise because share prices are thought to be mostly determined by day-to-day supply and demand conditions in the market. As such, they will simply represent the values at which small minority stakes change hands in marginal transactions. This, it is alleged, results in relatively low market valuations, which, in turn, lay companies open to hostile takeover bids. Predators are attracted by the inherent prospects of arbitrage resulting from the duality of share prices—in marginal transactions versus in takeover bid situations. Implicit in this criticism is the belief that the level of takeover activity has been excessive, and that takeovers have been bad for industry and bad for the nation.

This chapter investigates each of these allegations in turn to see how well they stand up in the light of the now very large body of evidence on how share prices are determined. It concludes that most of these accusations against the stock-market have no basis in fact, and simply do not square with the available evidence.

This chapter is organized as follows. In section 3.2, we begin by asking what function the stock-market should perform, and what market prices ought to reflect. Section 3.3 then briefly reviews the evidence on stock-market efficiency, and concludes that market prices do, in fact, broadly reflect values. Sections 3.4, 3.5 and 3.6 then look in turn at short-termism, at analysts' apparent fixation on short-term results, and at the question of whether or not analysts are too concerned with accounting numbers and/or are fooled by accounting manipulations. Section 3.7 then examines the worries which have been expressed about dual pricing, while section 3.8 looks at the closely related issue of whether takeover activity reveals market inefficiencies.

In section 3.9, we put forward a number of possible reasons why the workings of the stock market are so poorly understood by many businessmen and policy makers, and why the various allegations examined—and then dismissed—in this chapter might have come into common currency. Finally, in section 3.10, we look at a number of ways in which the stock-market could be made more efficient in terms of its assessment of corporate performance. These relate to financial reporting and disclosure, the role of auditors, the quality of analysts, and improved communications between industry and the investment community. Section 3.11 then provides a brief summary and conclusion.

3.2   WHAT SHOULD STOCK MARKET PRICES REFLECT?

Before evaluating how well the stock market does its job, it is important to establish what job it should be doing. All stock-markets carry out at least two functions. First, the so-called primary market provides a mechanism whereby companies can sell shares to investors in order to finance capital expansion. The secondary market, on the other hand, provides a forum in which investors can buy and sell outstanding shares. The two functions are, of course, inextricably linked. Investors would be far less willing to provide cash to companies via the primary market if there was no secondary market in which they could subsequently sell their shares.

The functioning of both the primary and secondary stock-markets has long been of interest to financial economists. Economists define a 'well-functioning' market as one in which companies can raise new money at a fair price; and equally, where prices are fair for investors buying and selling 'second-hand' securities. This of course begs the question of what constitutes a fair price.

In theory, the share price of any company should reflect the present value of the company's stream of future cash flows.[1] At first sight, this suggests

[1] There are many approaches to share valuation besides the discounted, or 'free', cash flow method. These include the stream of dividends approach, the earnings approach, the growth

that all we need do to check whether a company's share price is 'fair' is to
estimate its future cash flows, compute its cost of capital, carry out a discounted cash flow calculation, and then compare the answer with the company's current market value.

The problem with this procedure—as anyone who has ever tried it has
discovered—is that it can provide you with any answer you want. First,
this is because subjective judgements are required to estimate the cost of
capital, since the latter will depend on the level of risk involved. Not only
might we all differ in our judgements of future risk, but there is also still
some debate about the precise relationship between risk and the cost of
capital.[2] Second, and even more problematic, we need to estimate the magnitude of expected future cash flows. Unfortunately, the latter are not a
matter of objective fact, but are simply estimates in the mind of the analyst.
Furthermore, apparently quite small differences in judgements about, for
example, future growth rates can lead to widely differing estimates of
value.

These problems have led financial economists to conclude that the only
meaningful measure of whether stock-market prices are fair is whether or
not they reflect all available information. Markets where prices are fair in
this sense are then termed efficient (Fama 1970), and research on equity
markets has therefore focused on tests of market efficiency.

3.3   DO SHARE PRICES REFLECT VALUES?

We cannot *prove* that markets are efficient, since, as we noted above, we
can never be sure that a particular company's share price fully reflects all
available information. All we can do is try to *disprove* market efficiency by
looking for counter-examples to an efficiently functioning market. Such
counter-examples might be investment systems which are consistently successful, or individuals who regularly achieve superior performance in the
market-place. This would suggest that at least some people have access to
information which is not already discounted in share prices.

Early researchers, therefore, set out to find investment systems which
outperformed the market averages. They failed. As time went on, the
emphasis shifted to looking at how rapidly share prices responded to the

opportunities approach, the asset valuation approach, together with various combinations of
these. Although these different methods vary in focus and outward appearance, it can easily be
shown that, properly defined, and with consistent assumptions (e.g. on payout ratios, future
new equity issues etc.), they are all equivalent (see Miller and Modigliani (1961) for the original proof of this, or any standard textbook on corporate finance).

[2] One of the best known and most commonly used approaches to estimating the relationship between risk and the cost of capital is the Capital Asset Pricing Model (CAPM).
However, the CAPM itself has many variants and extensions, and there are also alternative
models based on arbitrage pricing theory (for a readable summary, see Brealey and Myers
(1991), ch. 8).

announcement of new information. Again, careful research revealed no ways of achieving outperformance. Prices responded far too rapidly to the news. Finally, researchers began to look at the performance of professionally managed portfolios. Surely here they would find evidence of a group of professionals who could consistently beat the market. In fact, these studies have concluded that, after taking account of differences in risk, no group of institutions has been able to outperform the market consistently, and that even the differences between the performance of individual funds are no greater than one would expect from chance.[3]

All this suggests that there is no obvious category of information, or group of individuals with access to information, which is not already fully discounted in stock-market prices. On the other hand, no one is claiming that markets are totally efficient, and in any market, there are bound to be occasions when prices are unfair. Indeed, there is now a well-documented literature on certain empirical regularities and stock-market anomalies. It remains a matter of debate as to whether these reflect market inefficiencies, or simply some missing ingredient in our theories of expected return.[4] But even if the strongest possible interpretation is placed on this anomalous literature, any balanced assessment of the vast body of evidence on share

[3] See Fama (1970) for a review of the development and results of early research on market efficiency, and Fama (1991) for the 'sequel', which discusses and reviews the cumulative market efficiency literature to date. For the early, and rather depressing evidence that professionally managed funds were unable to achieve outperformance even on a before-expenses basis, see Jensen (1968), Bogle and Twardowski (1980). Several more recent studies on professionally managed funds (e.g. Ippolito 1989) suggest that mutual fund managers do, on average, have enough information to cover the costs they impose on investors. This finding is consistent with the notion that because it is costly to generate and process information, informed investors are compensated for the costs they incur to ensure, through their trading, that prices adjust to information. The market is thus less than fully efficient (some private information is not fully reflected in prices) but in a way that is consistent with rational behaviour by all investors. Unfortunately, however, the recent evidence that professional managers have enough skill to cover their costs is partly counterbalanced by other studies, which suggest that they do not (e.g. Brinson, Hood, and Beebower 1986).

[4] Out of the many hundreds of tests of market efficiency, there have been a few which appear to reject market efficiency (for summaries of these, see Jensen (1978); Dimson (1988); Fama (1991)). In nearly all cases, however, these studies are testing whether the market is efficient, conditional on the validity of a specific model of how returns should vary across shares (e.g. the CAPM). In many cases, therefore, an apparent rejection of market efficiency could equally well be interpreted as a rejection of the joint hypothesis, i.e. that the particular model assumed is itself not valid. Even if one places the strongest possible interpretation on the anomalies literature, the bulk of the studies have at most rejected market efficiency for select segments of the market (see Merton 1987). One exception here is the controversial literature which claims that the entire stock-market is subjects to 'fads' and speculative bubbles, and that this makes long-run returns predictable, and causes the market to be 'too volatile', all this being inconsistent with 'rational pricing' (e.g. see Shiller (1981); 1984; Shleifer and Summers (1990)). In an excellent review of this literature, Fama (1991) argues that the evidence on long-run return predictability is most likely to be the result of rational variations over time in expected returns, rather than irrational bubbles, although he concedes that distinguishing between the two is never clear-cut.

price behaviour still has to conclude that the notion of market efficiency is remarkably well-supported by the facts.

3.4   IS THE MARKET SHORT-TERMIST?

One popular criticism of the stock-market is that it places too much weight on current profits and dividends, and by implication, marks down the share prices of companies which invest for the longer term.

To investigate whether there is any truth in this, we first need to define what is meant by giving 'too much weight to the short term'. As we noted above, the share price of any company should reflect the present value of its stream of future cash flows. This means that cash flows (and hence profits) in the near term should necessarily be given greater weight, since future cash flows must be brought back to present values by taking full account of the cost of capital. Giving too much weight to the short term thus needs to be redefined as 'giving more weight to the near term than is justified by the cost of capital'.[5]

Unfortunately, as we have already noted, it is virtually impossible to utilize the discounted cash flow approach to prove that a particular company's share price is undervaluing the long term. The reasons for this relate to the essentially subjective nature of the future forecasts which would have to be used—as outlined in section 3.2 above. Instead, however, we can return to the body of evidence on market efficiency, since the claim that share prices are short-termist is itself an allegation that the stock-market is inefficient.

For example, if the stock-market places too much weight on current dividends, then presumably, low yielding stocks are undervalued, relative to their expected future cash flows. As long-term investors in a short-sighted world, we should therefore be able to make money by investing in these low yielders and holding them for the very long term, when 'true value must out' if the short-termist proposition is valid. Similarly, if the market places too little weight on future prospects, we could again make money by buying growth stocks (i.e. shares with high PE ratios, but where the PEs should presumably be even higher), and holding them for the very long

[5] There is, of course, a long-standing debate on whether or not Germany and Japan have enjoyed a competitive advantage over the UK and USA through having a lower cost of capital. It would appear that any differences which do exist have been greatly exaggerated (see Baldwin (1987); Marsh (1990)). But even if a particular country were handicapped by a higher cost of capital, then both corporate managers and the financial community would have to accept this as the appropriate hurdle and capitalization rate. They could not be accused of short-termism for failing to invest in projects where the promised returns were insufficient to cover this cost of capital, and indeed, investment in such ventures would simply diminish corporate wealth still further. Thus while differences in the cost of capital (if they exist) could help to explain international differences in the level of real investment, short-termism *per se* needs to be defined relative to the ruling cost of capital, where the latter is taken as given.

term. Or if the market marks down the prices of companies which invest for the longer term, we would simply need to identify companies which are about to announce major capital investments or expenditures on R&D, and then sell them short, or at least avoid them like the plague (until after the announcement, when presumably they might be good long-term buys).

These issues all now become testable propositions, amenable to scientific enquiry. But the results of such tests do not support the proposition that the market is short-termist. In reality, for example, the evidence on dividends, both in the USA and UK, is that historically the market has had a preference for capital gains rather than dividends, and that high yielding shares have been more lowly valued.[6] This apparent anomaly is more likely to be attributable to historic taxation considerations than to a tendency for the stock-market to be too long-termist. Similarly, in the case of PE ratios, the only controversy arising out of careful empirical research on both the British and American stock-markets is a concern that the shares of companies with good growth prospects may have been *overvalued* rather than the contrary.[7]

Finally, a number of large-sample US studies have documented how share prices react to announcements of decisions on capital expenditure, R&D, and investment in new products.[8] Far from causing alarm and dismay, all these studies indicate that such announcements are regarded as good news, and result, on average, in share price increases. Furthermore, the researchers in question have also partitioned their samples in different ways, and thereby been able to explain differential reactions to various types of announcement by different groups of companies. For example, one study (McConnell and Muscarella 1985) showed that announcements of new capital investment projects by US utility companies—which are essentially constrained to make only 'normal profits'—are greeted with an average share price rise of zero—precisely as expected. However, the same study concluded that for industrial firms,

announcements of increases in planned capital expenditure are associated with statistically significant increases in the market value of common stock, and announcements of decreases in planned capital expenditure are associated with statistically significant decreases in the market value of the common stock.

The evidence cited above has a direct and obvious bearing on the issue of whether the market is short-termist. However, there is also much indirect evidence, related, for example, to the way the market reacts to earnings announcements, dividend announcements, changes in accounting practices,

---

[6] See, for example, Blume (1980); Litzenberger and Ramaswamy (1982); Levis (1989).

[7] See, for example, Reinganum (1981); Basu (1983); and Levis (1989).

[8] See McConnell and Muscarella (1985); Woolridge (1988); Jarrell, Lehn, and Marr (1985); and Chaney *et al.* (1989).

fund raising operations, and mergers and acquisitions.[9] This all supports the general hypothesis that the stock-market is broadly efficient, and that it is concerned with, and on average discounts correctly, the long-term as well as the short-term implications of relevant news items and key events.

3.5 ARE ANALYSTS FIXATED ON SHORT-TERM RESULTS?

In spite of the evidence cited above, investment analysts often give the impression that they are excessively pre-occupied with short-term earnings and dividends, and with the current price earnings (PE) ratio. A recent survey (*3i* 1990), for example, found that over 80 per cent of UK finance directors believed that analysts used earnings per share (EPS) as the main basis for valuing shares, and 91 per cent believed that the City was too focused on short-term earnings. US surveys reveal identical beliefs (Business Week/Harris Poll 1987).

In fact, attention to the current year's results and to PE multiples need not imply that analysts are taking too short-term a view. In a well-functioning stock-market, a company's share price should, at any point in time, reflect all the information which is available about its future prospects. Share price changes should therefore occur only in response to new information. Dividend and earnings announcements are a very important source of such news. In addition, they can convey (and are generally accompanied by) significant information about the future. Analysts and fund managers would therefore be negligent to ignore them. Furthermore, while on occasions it is possible for companies to enhance their short-term profits at the cost of sacrificing long-term returns, more often than not, good short-term profitability—derived from good management, or a strong product market position—is likely to herald good long-term performance as well.

Companies also typically use earnings and dividend announcements as a signal of future performance prospects. For example, there is extensive evidence that finance directors on both sides of the Atlantic attempt to manage the firm's future dividend growth path.[10] Thus when setting the current year's dividend they take into account their own judgements about future profitability and cash flows, and set a dividend which is consistent with this, and with sustaining a steady growth rate of future dividends. Current dividend announcements are thus an important signal of management's own (inside) knowledge and judgements about the longer-term future of the companies they manage.

---

[9] Besides the two Fama review articles cited above (Fama 1970; 1991), further reviews of this evidence for markets on both sides of the Atlantic can be found in Brealey (1983); Foster (1986); Richards (1979); and Keane (1985).

[10] See, for example, Lintner (1956); Watts (1973); Edwards and Mayer (1984); and Marsh and Merton (1987).

Similarly, earnings announcements do not simply convey current results, but also provide information about future prospects. There are two interrelated reasons for this. First, one of the design features underlying accounting principles is that they should lead to a measure of sustainable earnings (Black 1980). Second, and superimposed on this, is the fact that accounting practices also allow a degree of flexibility, thereby giving managers quite considerable discretion over the earnings they report in any one year. Thus reported earnings can be adjusted downwards in years when 'true' earnings appear unsustainably high, and managers can then spread the surplus into future years; and, of course, they can do the opposite when the current year's 'true' earnings would paint too gloomy a picture of long-term prospects (Ronen and Sadan 1981). This smoothing process—with both its designed-in and discretionary elements—means that analysts and fund managers are justified in placing considerable importance on the current year's earnings announcement, because it will convey information not just about the current year, but also about the longer term and about management's own expectations.

While it is therefore quite appropriate for analysts and fund managers to be concerned with dividend and earnings announcements, any suggestion that this is their sole focus is simply not supported by the facts. For example, although share prices do respond to earnings and dividend announcements (and in the way they should), in practice, much of the market's reaction is anticipatory.[11] This suggests that more timely information sources than the dividend and earnings announcements are used in the share price valuation process (Foster 1986).

Nor is there any evidence to support the 'myopic hypothesis' that the stock-market has a short-run focus on the current year's reported earnings rather than a multi-year horizon. Certainly, the vast majority of UK and US security analysts claim to have a multi-year horizon for earnings forecasts (Arnold, Moizer, and Noreen 1983). Even more importantly, there is strong evidence that share prices themselves reflect a multi-year earnings forecast horizon (Brown, Foster, and Noreen 1985).

Analysts are also sometimes criticized for placing too much emphasis on the current PE ratio. But this would be a concern only if they were applying the same PE ratio to all shares, whatever their future prospects. This is evidently not the case: PE ratios vary widely. Furthermore, research studies have long confirmed that PE ratios depend—as theory indicates they should—on prospective long-term earnings growth, the retentions needed to

---

[11] See, for example, Ball and Brown (1968); Watts (1973); and Maingot (1984). Of course, the fact that analysts spend time *anticipating* earnings may give little comfort to their critics, since this is part of the popular complaint. However, it would be very hard to argue that they, or the market-place, were doing a good job if share prices *failed* to anticipate predictable information.

finance this growth, and the rate of return needed to compensate for the risks involved.[12] There is also considerable evidence that PE ratio differences can also be attributed to the accounting methods used,[13] providing further confirmation that analysts and fund managers are discriminating in their interpretation of what earnings figures really mean, and what they imply for valuations.

Thus while it is easy to see how analysts as a group might be deemed guilty of 'conduct likely to mislead' (see also sections 3.9.1 and 3.10.4 below), their actual behaviour, correctly interpreted, is far less short-sighted than is alleged. Furthermore, however analysts may behave or appear to behave, we saw in sections 3.3 and 3.4 above that there is simply no evidence that their actions have 'damaged' share prices by causing them to reflect a short-term bias.

3.6   ARE ANALYSTS FOOLED BY ACCOUNTING MANIPULATIONS?

Just as analysts are alleged to be too short-termist, so too are they accused of being overly concerned with accounting measures of performance, such as EPS, rather than with the underlying economic worth of a business, as measured by the discounted value of its expected future cash flows. This problem is believed to be exacerbated by the ease with which accounting numbers, particularly EPS, can be manipulated.

Once again, however, the key issue is not how analysts appear to behave, nor ultimately, even how they actually behave. Instead, the question is one of how *share prices* behave, and whether the stock-market correctly assesses accounting information.

There is, in fact, an extensive research literature on how the stock-market reacts to new accounting information, and to a company's choice of accounting methods. Indeed, over the last twenty years, this market-based accounting research (MBAR) has emerged, at least in the USA, as the dominant theme in accounting research. But even outside the USA, it has formed an important research stream, particularly in the UK, Australia, and Canada, and even to some extent in Japan and Continental Europe.[14]

The MBAR literature provides strong evidence that accounting data—in spite of all the caveats and reservations relating to its quality and reliability—conveys useful and relevant information to investors. As noted in section 3.5 above, however, much of the stock-market's reaction to accounting results is anticipatory, indicating that supplementary and more timely information is also widely used by investors. Furthermore, the rela-

---

[12] See Whitbeck and Kisor (1963); and Beaver and Morse (1978).

[13] See Beaver and Dukes (1973); and Foster (1986).

[14] For several excellent surveys of this literature, see Ball and Foster (1983); Chow (1983); Foster (1986); Griffin (1982); and Lev and Ohlson (1982).

tionship between reported accounting numbers and share returns is not a mechanistic one, i.e. the market does not take accounting numbers at face value, but uses a broad-based information set in interpreting their information content.

There is also very strong evidence that the market looks behind the accrual accounting numbers in order to determine the cash flow implications. Accounting changes which increase cash flows (usually because they affect tax), even if they reduce reported EPS, are generally regarded as good news. In contrast, changes which increase reported earnings without increasing cash flow are regarded as neutral, or, more likely, as bad news. In other words, the fact that these companies feel the need to indulge in cosmetics in order to boost their reported earnings is taken as an indicator that their underlying performance is less favourable than that of other companies who can afford to save up the accounting change for a 'rainy day'. This interpretation is certainly borne out by extensive further evidence which suggests that companies which are performing badly are more likely to indulge in accounting changes.

The MBAR research thus provides strong evidence that the market is concerned with the underlying cash flows of the business, rather than accounting numbers *per se*. In addition, the market also looks at the signal conveyed by the reported numbers, in terms of what it might tell them about current and future performance, and about management's future actions. Furthermore, once investors have been informed about the basis on which a set of accounts has been prepared, there is no evidence to suggest that they are misled by the use of alternative accounting measurement and disclosure techniques. At least in this sense, they seem well able to see through the veil of accounting practices.

There is no room for complacency about accounting numbers, however. The MBAR literature demonstrates that investors *can* be temporarily fooled by accounting numbers. In particular, an announced increase in EPS derived purely from accounting changes can be perceived as good news in the period between the earnings announcement and the publication of the annual report if the change of accounting method is not disclosed at the time of the announcement.

Research shows that these short-run distortions are corrected rapidly once the market learns about the true basis on which the figures have been prepared (e.g. see Kaplan and Roll (1972)). However, there may be many occasions when the annual report does *not* provide adequate disclosure of either the facts or the accounting methods, or when management has deliberately set out to be economical with the truth. The auditors may either be unaware of this, or else may condone it, deeming the accounting methods to fall within the letter (if not the spirit) of the rules. Markets cannot be expected to be efficient with respect to information they are not given, or where they are deliberately fed misleading data. This is an issue to which we return in section 3.10 below.

3.7 IS THERE A DUAL PRICING PROBLEM?

It is sometimes claimed that the stock-market suffers from a serious 'dual-pricing' problem. For example, Plender (1990) argues that:

> On a normal day-to-day basis, a company's stock-market capitalization reflects the price set by marginal trading in the shares between portfolio investors. But . . . the stock-market operates on two distinct sets of values. One for trade in small parcels of shares that reflect only a fraction of the total number of shares in issue; another for whole companies that are expected to change hands. The existence of this gap between the different bases of valuation provides arbitrage opportunities for predators and investors.

This statement could be seen as misleading in at least three ways. First, it could be taken to imply that day-to-day share prices are determined mostly by fluctuations in supply and demand between sellers and buyers, rather than fundamentals. Second, it suggests that share prices should and do reflect one valuation basis or the other, and that 'dual pricing' is wrong. And third, it claims that 'dual-pricing' provides arbitrage opportunities.

While share prices do obey the laws of supply and demand, it is important to understand the nature of the trading process. Many stock market trades are liquidity-motivated, and are driven by investors' savings, liquidity, or rebalancing needs (e.g. an individual may wish to buy a car or finance school fees; or a pension fund to make disbursements to pensioners, or invest contributions). Other trades, however, are information-motivated, i.e., the deal is prompted by a belief that a share's price does not reflect its value.

If the market consisted solely of liquidity-motivated and uninformed traders, then day-to-day share price movements might well simply reflect the balance of buyers and sellers, rather than economic fundamentals. But this is not the case. The market place also contains a large number of professional, information-motivated investors, all of whom are trying to identify shares whose prices fail to reflect values. If they believe that buying and selling pressures from uninformed traders have moved prices away from values, this provides a profitable trading opportunity. But in an efficient market, the resultant trading activity quickly moves prices back into line.

The nature of the demand curve for a company's shares thus differs from many people's preconceptions. The dual pricing view implicitly assumes that demand curves slope downwards, i.e. an increase in the supply of shares on offer will depress the price, while an increase in demand will generate a price rise. The alternative view, consistent with market efficiency, is that the demand for a particular company's shares is close to being perfectly elastic, so that an increase in supply will not in itself lead to a fall in price. This high demand elasticity stems from the existence of very close substitutes, since if shares are efficiently priced on the basis of their risk and expected return, one share will prove a close substitute for another. Thus, if a share price moves above its intrinsic value, *no* informed investors will wish to hold that share; while if it moves below, *all* will wish to buy it. On this view, share prices respond not to shifts in the marginal supply of shares on offer, but only to new information, i.e. prices do not rise or fall because of a shift *along* the demand curve, but because the entire demand curve itself moves up or down in response to the new information.

There is much evidence to support this view. Direct evidence that share demand curves are highly elastic is provided by studies of large share sales, both by investors (block sales) and by companies (new equity issues).[15] In addition, the very extensive literature on market efficiency referred to above provides much supporting evidence, namely that share prices move in response to new information about a company's fundamentals, and that share prices reflect values. The notion that day-to-day share prices are simply set by the price pressures emanating from marginal transactions thus not only offends against theory and common sense: it is also wholly unsupported by the evidence.[16]

Why then do share prices change when a bid is in prospect, and is this evidence of 'dual-pricing' and market inefficiency? To address this question, we first need to recognize that in a efficient market, a company's share price *should* reflect a mixture of a number of bases of valuation. First, it should reflect the going-concern value of the company under its existing management. Second, it may also reflect the value of the company as an independent concern, but with a changed management team. Third, it may reflect the disposal or closure value of all or part of the company's business, in cases where the company's assets are potentially worth more in alternative uses. Fourth, it may reflect the amount other companies might pay to win control, and this, in turn, may encompass the different potential synergy values to several alternative possible suitors.

Except in the very exceptional case of a company where a change of management, asset usage, or ownership was quite inconceivable, we would

---

[15] For studies of large block sales, see Scholes (1972); Dann, Mayers, and Raab (1977); and Holthausen, Leftwich, and Mayers (1987). For evidence relating to new equity issues by companies, see Marsh (1979); and Asquith and Mullins (1986).

[16] At the market micro-structure level, short-run trading activity *is*, of course, likely to impact on prices and spreads. This is because market makers cannot in general distinguish between informed buyers and sellers and uninformed traders (liquidity and 'noise' traders), and will therefore move their prices and spreads in response to the flow of transactions. Thus even uninformed deals can lead to transitory price variations which are not linked to any underlying information flow about the company. In an efficient market, such short-term pricing errors due to noise will, however, subsequently be reversed (see French and Roll 1986).

expect a company's stock market value to be some weighted average of its values under these different scenarios, where the weights accorded to each mirror the perceived likelihood of that scenario occurring. Dual pricing, if it existed, would thus be wrong, first because it was dual rather than multiple; and second, if it attached probabilities of either zero or one to each valuation basis, rather than some intermediate probability which reflected the likelihood of that scenario occurring.

There is much evidence to indicate that share prices do reflect a mixture of many different valuation bases. For many companies, therefore, their share prices contain some 'bid prospects' element. Frequently, no bid appears. But in other cases, we observe sharp price rises when bids are announced or foreshadowed. This happens because investors are revising the weightings they apply to each basis of valuation to reflect the fact that a (successful) bid is now a probability rather than a possibility. There are no arbitrage opportunities here, as proponents of 'dual-pricing' would argue. Indeed, there are no abnormal profit opportunities at all (riskless or otherwise) unless the market is inefficient at assessing the likelihood of bids, and/or their probable implications. We turn to the evidence on this in the next section.

3.8 DO TAKEOVERS REVEAL MARKET INEFFICIENCIES?

There is now a very large body of research on takeovers, covering experience on both sides of the Atlantic.[17] This documents how the share prices of both the acquiror and the victim react to stake changes, bid announcements, bid rejections, the introduction of anti-merger provisions, competitive bids, bid revisions, the successful consummation of acquisitions, and failed bids. It also provides evidence on how the acquirer's share price behaves in the post-merger period.

Two main conclusions emerge from this research. First, the market reacts rapidly and in an unbiased manner to the announcement of bid-related events, i.e., on average, it correctly assesses the impact and implications of the news, and adjusts its valuation bases and assumed probabilities in an unbiased way. Second, studies of post-merger abnormal share price performance show that, on average, the ultimate value of the benefits of the merger were correctly foreshadowed in the market's initial share price response to the news. This is precisely what we would expect in an efficient market, and at the same time, it demonstrates clearly that there are no arbitrage profits for investors in connection with takeover.

Many commentators, however, are less concerned about the efficiency of the stock-market with respect to takeovers, than they are about the work-

[17] See, for example, Jensen and Ruback (1983); Dodd (1983); Marsh (1986; 1990); Jensen (1986); and Franks and Harris (1989).

ings and efficiency of the market for corporate control. Indeed, from the comments of some industrialists, one might easily conclude that acquisitions were an unequivocally bad thing. For example, Laing (1990) writes: 'By the time it becomes evident that our totally free market in corporate control is seriously damaging to the nation, it will be too late.'

The concern here is not so much with whether the stock-market correctly assesses the implications of bids for future corporate performance, but with whether takeover activity itself has a deleterious impact on the economic efficiency of the corporate sector.

Once again, we can turn to the substantial body of evidence on takeovers to correct this misapprehension and to shed light on this question, at least from the shareholders' perspective. All of the empirical studies indicate that takeovers have resulted in large gains to the acquirees' shareholders. Indeed, nearly all studies suggest that it is the worst performing companies which tend to get taken over by their better-performing counterparts. Acquirors, for their part, appear to have reaped modest gains—or at least not lost—from their activities, even after taking account of the premium they have paid. On average, therefore, the combined entity has enjoyed a higher market capitalization than the sum of its two components when run separately. Acquisitions have thus historically allowed companies to reap economic and efficiency gains, and in this sense, acquisitions have, on average, been a virtue rather than a vice.

This finding needs some qualification. First, it relates to average behaviour. Thus although, on average, mergers have increased shareholders' wealth, many have failed. And while takeover victims have tended to be poorer performers, well-managed companies also sometimes get taken over against their managements' (but not their shareholders') will. Second, the available evidence relates mostly to shareholders' interests. Possibly, shareholders' gains have been counterbalanced by welfare reduction for consumers and other stakeholders. The evidence we do have on this, however, suggests that this has not been the case (see Healy, Palepu, and Ruback 1900).

Third, the published evidence does not take account of the hidden costs and benefits of takeover activity. For example, there are substantial costs—in terms of fees, management time, and employee motivation—associated with failed bids. Furthermore, managers who find that their company is threatened by a bid may behave in a short-termist manner, cutting back on long-term investment in order to bolster short-term profits as a defence against takeover. While such actions are likely to be counterproductive to their intended cause,[18] and to impose a real cost on shareholders, threatened managements undoubtedly sometimes behave in this way.

Balanced against these costs are the substantial benefits which can flow

[18] Such actions are likely to be counter-productive since they are based on a fundamental flaw, namely that the share price will respond favourably if the company cuts long-term

from the threat of takeovers and the value of keeping managements on
their toes. Indeed, in the UK and USA, contested takeovers are one of the
most effective disciplinary devices available, both as a deterrent, and as a
measure of last resort. This raises the obvious question of whether there
might be better, cheaper ways of ensuring effective corporate control than
leaning so heavily on acquisitions. Indeed, two of the most successful industrialized nations, Japan and Germany, have done very well without the disciplinary mechanism of contested bids. If improvements in relationships
between companies and their shareholders, and more effective corporate
governance could yield shareholders the same gains they have achieved
from takeover activity without the associated costs, this would clearly be
worth striving for.

3.9   WHY IS THE MARKET MISUNDERSTOOD?

We have shown above that many of the allegations made against the stock-
market—namely of market inefficiency, short-termism, a fixation on
accounting numbers, and dual pricing—are simply not supported by the
evidence. So why have these ideas come into common currency, and why
are the workings of the stock-market so poorly understood by many businessmen and policy makers? In this section, we offer five possible explanations.

3.9.1   *Markets Act Smarter than Most Players in Them*

Businessmen frequently judge how well the market assesses company performance by the quality of the investment analysts they meet. The top analysts in each sector generally have an excellent understanding of the
companies they follow. But as in all professions, the stars are relatively few,
and average and poor analysts dominate numerically (CBI 1987). Thus analysts as a group, via their dialogue with companies, and the questions they
ask, and fail to ask, often convey an unhelpful impression of short-termism,
and of ignorance about companies' businesses, markets, technologies, and
longer-term prospects.

Yet the poor quality analysts have little following or influence, and thus
do no harm (nor good for that matter) to the market's price-setting process.
Indeed, the evidence suggests that share prices, because they represent a dis-
tillation and consensus of the best judgements available, behave as though
they were influenced only by the top analysts. But while poor analysts may
not damage share prices, they can certainly damage the market's reputation.

investments in order to boost current earnings. But if these longer-term investments were
worth undertaking in the first place (i.e. if they had positive NPVs), then all the evidence suggests that the market will mark the share price down rather than up as soon as it becomes
aware of what is happening (see section 3.4).

For, sadly, businessmen are generally unaware of the research findings on market efficiency,[19] and thus do not always recognize that markets act smarter than most players in them.

3.9.2. Markets Are Sometimes Wiser even than Insiders

Managers often complain that their company's share price is too low (except in the depths of a recession, when they occasionally seem to believe the opposite). Because they are 'insiders', they believe their judgements to be superior to the market's, and this causes them to generally distrust market prices.

From time to time, managers will, of course, be genuine insiders, in possession of price-sensitive information that has not yet been disclosed to the market (e.g. see Jaffe (1974); Seyhun (1986); and Pope, Morris, and Peel (1990)). But possession of such information is likely to be an occasional rather than a regular occurrence, and markets cannot be deemed inefficient (except in the strong form sense) for failing to take account of undisclosed, inside information.

The more normal situation, however, is that managers are simply taking a different—and often more optimistic—view of already-published information. These differences may arise because markets are more detached and objective than the company's own managers, or else because managers are not skilled in valuation methods. Alternatively, they may arise because managers have done a poor job of communicating their future plans and prospects to the market (see section 3.10.3 below). But if the message *has* been communicated, and the share price remains low, then managers would do well to heed the unwelcome message, namely that there is a credibility gap, which may well have its origins in the quality of the management team itself.

3.9.3 Markets Look Ahead

A fundamental reason why managers find markets hard to understand is that markets look ahead. Frequently, however, managers' own lives are dominated by the here and now, giving rise to various standard complaints such as: 'The economy is in deep recession, but the market is hitting all-time highs. Its incomprehensible (and indecent)' or 'We worked all year to cut costs and boost sales, and despite the tough climate, we increased profits. Yet when we announced the results, the (ungrateful) market scarcely responded.'

---

[19] The evidence for this statement is based on (admittedly casual) observation of executives attending courses at the London Business School over the last twenty years. Despite the popular notion that British managers are financially oriented, in reality, those with 'financial' backgrounds have mostly been trained as accountants (see NEDO 1987) rather than as financial economists. In practice, British (and indeed European) managers generally have a fairly poor knowledge and understanding of financial markets, investment, and corporate finance.

Most managers, of course, understand, at least at the intellectual level, that markets look ahead, anticipating economic up- and down-turns, and corporate performance. Yet they often find this frustrating and disappointing at the emotional or gut-reaction level. Indeed, in many ways, they would like to have their cake and eat it. First, they would like the market to react favourably to the new contract won, the research breakthrough, or the recent excellent acquisition. To the extent that such events are news, the market will react obligingly, capitalizing the future implications of such news in today's share price in an unbiased way. If the market's assessment is correct, however, there should then be no subsequent price action unless there is further good news. But meanwhile, for the managers concerned, all the real hard work of implementation still lies ahead. They would therefore like to be fully rewarded, first in advance, and second, on delivery. Unfortunately for them, however, efficient markets do not double-count.[20]

The stock-market is thus damned because it does look ahead, and damned because people believe it does not. Its far-sightedness can confuse and frustrate managers. Yet those same managers are quick to accuse it of being short-termist, even though there is no evidence to support such claims.

3.9.4 *Markets are Volatile*

Industrialists often question how share prices can reflect values when they move around so much. Financial economists turn this on its head by pointing out that prices cannot reflect values *unless* they vibrate randomly, i.e. unless prices *do* change in response to new information, which, by definition, is as likely to be good news as bad (see Samuelson (1965)).

Share prices could still, of course, be too volatile. Indeed, we might caricature the businessman's complaint as: 'The factory is still there. The order books are unchanged. Yet the share price is 20 per cent lower (higher) than a month ago.' Such complaints are no proof, of course, that the market is too volatile. Perhaps the market is looking ahead and re-evaluating *future* growth prospects in the light of new information. Or alternatively, real interest rates, or risk/the risk premium may have changed, thus altering the market's capitalization rate. Indeed, in judging volatility levels, at least three factors need to be borne in mind. First, the company's business risk, which can be substantial, will be a major source of volatility. Second, share price volatility will be amplified by any financial gearing. And third, even

---

[20] Markets do not double-count, but they frequently single-count in instalments. For example, on the news of a profitable new venture which has not previously been anticipated, the share price should rise by the venture's net present value, assuming successful implementation, multiplied by the probability of success. Subsequently, if the likelihood of success increases or becomes a certainty, there should then be a further share price increase.

quite modest changes in expected future growth rates or in the capitaliza-tion rate, can lead to marked changes in value (see, for example, Brealey and Myers 1991: 299).

Notwithstanding these arguments that share price volatility is endemic, a few researchers (and many laymen) maintain that stock-market volatility in part results from speculative activity. The belief here is that changes in fashions and fads, and a 'herd instinct' cause investors to misprice shares in alternating waves of interest and disinterest, leading to 'speculative bub-bles', and to volatility levels which cannot be justified on the basis of fun-damentals. The best-known empirical work here is by Shiller (1981), who claimed that stock-market prices were far more volatile than could be justified by the much lower volatility of dividends. It now seems clear, how-ever, that such inferences are invalid, and that volatility tests of this kind are not informative about market efficiency, but instead simply demonstrate that expected returns vary through time. Furthermore, there is growing evi-dence that these changes in expected return are linked to business condi-tions.[21]

There is no evidence, therefore, that stock prices are too volatile. What does seem clear is that managers confuse volatility with capriciousness and irrationality, and that this causes them to distrust stock-market prices.

3.9.5 *Markets are Frequently Wrong*

In an efficient market, prices reflect all that is known, or anticipated, today. Since the world is risky and ever-changing, today's information rapidly becomes yesterday's, and stock prices adjust to an unfolding sequence of 'news'. If this 'news' is *truly* new information, prices cannot be expected to reflect it in advance. We can expect stock markets to be efficient, but we cannot expect them to be omniprescient.

With the benefit of hindsight, of course, almost all past share prices are proved 'wrong'. But even without hindsight, an individual who bets against market prices even in a perfectly efficient market can still expect to win roughly half the time. For if prices reflect all information, new information is as likely to be good news as bad.

All this serves to provide market critics with a wealth of anecdotes about how markets have 'got things wrong', for particular companies, countries,

---

[21] A central assumption of the early volatility tests (e.g. Shiller 1981) was that expected returns were constant, and that variation in stock prices was driven entirely by shocks to expected dividends. Subsequent researchers, notably Marsh and Merton (1986) have pointed out that Shiller's analysis essentially ignores what we know about the way managers decide on dividends, namely that they try to 'smooth' them out over time. Later criticisms have focused more on the assumption of constant expected returns. For reviews of the now extensive litera-ture on volatility tests, see Cochrane (1990) and also Merton (1987). For an excellent review of the associated literature on long-term predictability, see Fama (1991) (and also footnote 4 above).

markets, and/or at particular times. But while the more extreme anecdotes can be hard to dismiss, and provide genuine food for thought (e.g. the South Sea Bubble, the 1987 Crash, and the rise and fall of Polly Peck), the real test is to find individuals who are consistently wiser than the market with foresight, rather than hindsight. The evidence on market efficiency suggests that such individuals are extremely rare, and that while market prices may often be wrong, they are seldom systematically or predictably out of line.

3.10   HOW CAN THE MARKET BE MADE MORE EFFICIENT?

In the preceding sections, we have argued that, contrary to the popular view, the evidence supports the notion that stock-market prices reflect fundamentals; that the market is broadly efficient; and that the market evaluates new information relating to a company's performance and prospects in a rapid and unbiased manner.

These conclusions do not, however, provide cause for complacency. We argued in section 3.2 that a key role of the stock-market is to provide a fair valuation mechanism, i.e., one where prices reflect all information. Mostly, and for obvious reasons, tests of market efficiency examine whether prices reflect public information. Yet much relevant information is not in the public domain, while much public information is 'noisy' and of questionable quality. The market can hardly be expected to do a good job of evaluating information which it is not given, or of interpreting information which it is given, where the data has been deliberately packaged to mislead.

Undoubtedly, therefore, markets could—at some cost—be made even more efficient if they were provided with more and better-quality information. We therefore examine below three closely interrelated issues, namely financial reporting, the role of auditors, and communications between companies and the investment community, with a view to exploring how the quantity, quality, and flow of information to the market could be improved. Finally, we examine how the quality of analysis, particularly by fund managers and investment analysts, might be enhanced, since this, too, has a direct bearing on increasing the efficiency of the market.

3.10.1   *Financial Reporting*

There is currently a widespread consensus—at least in the UK, and arguably, internationally—that financial reporting is in need of reform.[22] In particular, it is felt that too much flexibility has led to many accounts

---

[22] Sir Ronald Dearing, Chairman of the new Financial Reporting Council, an assembly of senior figures from UK industry, the City and the accounting profession, stated that not one member of the Council was happy with the current state of affairs in accounting (*Financial Times*, 17 Oct. 1990). This view has been supported in the submissions to the new Accounting

becoming misleading, and even to abuse. In response to these concerns, the new UK Accounting Standards Board (ASB) is embarking upon a programme of reform, and has promised to 'turn the shape of accounts upside down'.

Our concern in this chapter is with the market's assessment of company performance. If accounts are to be made more useful from this perspective, then any programme of reform must take into account the needs of sophisticated investment analysts, the requirements of financial valuation theory, and the empirical evidence from MBAR. This implies that any suggested changes should be predicated on the fact that analysts and investors are ultimately concerned with cash flows rather than accounting numbers; the future rather than the past; the disclosure of relevant information, rather than with the way accountants package it; and the raw data required to estimate economic values, rather than with pre-calculated measures of balance sheet values. With these criteria in mind, we suggest below a number of ways in which accounts could be made more useful. Reassuringly, many of these coincide with the ASB's proposals for reform.

The first proposal, namely to replace the funds flow statement by a cash flow statement, has already been set in motion by the ASB. This move is now beginning to provide analysts with new information on cash flow and liquidity which could often not readily be inferred from the old-style accounts. To further support this change, companies should now also be required to disclose any constraints on the remittability of cash from their various overseas subsidiaries.

Second, a number of measures should be introduced to make past results more informative about the future. Arguably, two of the key roles of accounts are to help shareholders and analysts distinguish between (a) one-off effects and continuing phenomena, and (b) expenses which are operating costs and those which are investments. From a valuation perspective, these distinctions are crucial, since they represent (a) the difference between one-off cash flows and annuities, and (b) cost annuities and (presumably) positive NPV investments.

To address the first of these problems, companies should be required to disclose the proportion of profits which come from continuing businesses (those owned at the start of the year), as well as businesses acquired and sold during the year. In addition, conglomerates should be required to disclose profit information about their subsidiaries, allowing analysts to see each unit's contribution to group earnings. Finally, companies should be required to identify and disclose any other one-off costs and benefits. Note

Standards Board by the CBI, the 100 Group of finance directors, the National Association of Pension Funds, and the Institute of Chartered Accountants in England and Wales, all of whom have argued that financial reporting is in need of fundamental reform. These views have been echoed at the international level by the International Accounting Standards Committee whose declared objective is to end the 'global accounting muddle'.

that the key issue here is not whether such items are presented or permitted above or below the line (the issue which raises all the passions), nor even how they are labelled (e.g., exceptionals, extraordinaries, etc.), but whether they are clearly disclosed and explained in a way which allows analysts to distinguish between one-off effects and costs/benefits which are likely to recur.

A breakdown of profits by continuing/acquired/sold businesses is already being implemented by the ASB. But the second proposal, namely of requiring accounts to distinguish between expenses which are operating costs and those which are investments presents more problems. This, too, was included in the ASB's original agenda, but is at a less advanced stage of development, and will be more costly and controversial to implement. In principle, the objective here is to break expenses down into a number of subcategories representing investments for the future, e.g., R&D, training, and development, various categories of strategic marketing expenses, etc. This is a much tougher assignment because of the difficulties involved in defining these categories, distinguishing between 'investment' and 'operating' expenditures, and satisfying concerns about not revealing commercially-sensitive information to competitors.

Despite these obstacles, however, moves towards greater disclosure in this arena would be of enormous value to analysts. It would also provide companies with less scope for short-termist behaviour, since profit increases achieved simply by cutting investments would be starkly identified. Furthermore, most companies could disclose far more information than at present without any danger of revealing sensitive information to competitors. The ASB thus deserves—and will need—strong support for its efforts in this direction.

The ASB has promised at least two other major reforms; first, to require that balance sheet assets be shown at current values, and second, that accounting standards should be tightened up to ensure greater uniformity and to curb abuse. The first of these, namely the move from historic costs to current values, is presumably motivated by the belief that accounts should reflect economic reality. Unfortunately, this goal is largely unattainable. True values depend on future cash flows, and since accountants are neither in the business of forecasting, nor are they trained in valuation, any attempt to make accounts reflect economic values is doomed. Either it will lead to the meaningless application of mechanistic rules (e.g. the application of published, but inappropriate indexes to adjust historic costs to current values), or else it will require extensive, costly use of specialist valuers, who will generate unauditable, 'black-box' valuations.[23]

---

[23] This, of course, is precisely what happened under current cost accounting (CCA) (see Marsh 1991). CCA opened up major divisions both between companies and the accounting

The latter are of little value to analysts except in the limited context of assets for which there is a reasonable second-hand market (e.g., marketable securities, property, etc.) where modified historic cost accounting is already widely used. In almost all other cases, what analysts require is not valuations, but more disclosure, so they can form their own judgement of value. A well-documented case of this is the inclusion of brand names in balance sheets. Typically, companies which have chosen to do this have published just a single, overall 'value', and have disclosed virtually nothing about the valuation methods, the brands, or even which brands have been included. Analysts are unanimous in regarding such numbers as unhelpful. Instead, what they would like is more disclosure about the breakdown of profits and projected growth rates between brands (see Barwise *et al*. 1989).

The best way to promote the cause of economic reality is thus not to insist on current value balance sheets, but instead, to require much greater disclosure, both about the accounting methods companies use, and also about the companys' underlying business.[24] Disclosure of accounting methods is particularly important, given that analysts are concerned with the underlying cash flows, rather than with accounting numbers. They thus need to know what assumptions and transformations the accountant has made if they are to unlock the many black boxes which they currently find in accounts (e.g., leases, pensions, provisions, deferred tax, and long-term contracts). This is frequently not possible at present.[25] Reform is thus required to ensure that wherever there is a choice of accounting methods, the accounts should specify not only which method has been chosen, but also all the key assumptions and figures which have been used, so that analysts can in principle rework the figures for themselves.

Besides fuller disclosure of accounting methods, analysts would also find it helpful if companies were obliged to disclose more information about their underlying businesses. One of the most useful steps forward here would be to require public companies to adopt a new standardized report-

profession, and within the profession itself. Ultimately, CCA fell mostly into disuse, and arguably, the whole debate was a set-back for accounting reform.

[24] Following this line of reasoning, it is the accountant's job to assemble, audit, and report financial information, not to conduct valuations. It is then the job of analysts and investors to use this information, together with other relevant data, to assess the firm's future prospects and hence its value. If these two roles are confused, this can lead to the potentially dangerous circularity of companies and accountants letting stock-market ratings influence their decision as to what earnings figure they should report (see Treynor 1972) or what balance sheet values they should show (see Barwise *et al*. 1989).

[25] To take just one example, although there is an accounting standard on pension costs (SSAP24), Mercer Fraser (1990) estimate that only 10% of companies disclose all the information necessary to make reliable and sensible comparisons of different companies' pension costs. Key assumptions, such as the amortization period for pension surpluses are frequently not disclosed. This is yet another example where black box valuations (in this case, actuarial valuations of pension fund surpluses or deficiencies) are of little use to the analysts unless they are accompanied by full disclosure of the key assumptions and figures.

ing format along the lines of the 10-K report which US companies have to file under Securities and Exchange Commission rules. This would be a major advance in terms of facilitating comparisons between companies and giving investors more complete information.

This emphasis on enhanced disclosure and more standardized reporting formats would also make a major contribution to the other area for ASB reform, namely the tightening up of accounting standard to curb abuse.[26] Note that the aim here should be clarity, transparency, and the avoidance of abuse, rather than uniformity *per se*. 'Abuse' in this context is defined as the bending of accounting standards in such a way as to hide salient information. The appropriate response to this is clearly a systematic tightening up of disclosure requirements to ensure that the relevant facts and accounting policies are disclosed, and that such disclosure is properly policed by the auditors (see section 3.10.2). In addition to the reforms outlined above, this will also involve changes in the treatment of off-balance-sheet items, and consolidated accounts, as well as measures to ensure that accounts reflect the economic substance of business transactions, not just their legal form.

Note that the definition of abuse proposed above, namely a deliberate attempt to mislead via the non-disclosure of relevant information, might be viewed as somewhat narrow. Currently, a more hawkish view is in the ascendant, namely that any discretionary use of reporting options designed to alter a company's profit figure should be regarded as an abuse. The logical extension of this view would be that companies should be placed in an accounting strait-jacket with no discretion over how, or what figures, they report. This would not only be virtually impossible to implement, but it would anyway be an unfortunate development since it would remove management's ability to use accounting numbers to signal future prospects. This could make accounts less, rather than more, valuable.

Flexibility in accounting is not, therefore, an unequivocally bad thing, but simply a variable to keep in balance. For, while too much flexibility can lead to abuse, too little can lead to the impoverishment of accounting numbers (e.g. see Black (1980) and Myers (1988)). Where flexibility does exist, however, the key issue in terms of the reform of accounting standards is to ensure that it is accompanied by full disclosure, so that intelligent analysts can understand what is going on, and if they so desire, make their own adjustments to the published figures.

Unfortunately, this point is all too often lost in the debate about

---

[26] Arguably, the ASB's other objective of moving towards current value balance sheets would actually conflict with, rather than contribute towards, this desire to tighten up accounts. For if accounts are to reflect current values, the accounting rules used would need to be flexible, and judgement would have to be elevated over uniform rules. But this is at odds with the ASB's view that there is currently too much flexibility in UK accounts and that this has led to an undesirable free-for-all.

accounting standards, where the most impassioned arguments often seem to be about the least important issues, for example, identifying the correct treatment or categorization of a particular item, such as goodwill or extraordinary items, rather than simply ensuring that there is full disclosure and complete transparency.[27] Indeed, it would be a great pity if the ASB became side-tracked into these traditional debates about accounting 'packaging', and lost sight of the fact that the key issue is one of disclosure about what is contained in the package.

3.10.2 *The Role of the Auditor*

The widespread concern about UK reporting also extends to auditors. There is currently an 'expectations gap' between what most people think auditors should be doing, and what auditors believe their duties to be. This gap is at its widest in the context of the auditor's role in relation to company failure, and management incompetence or fraud. These may be relatively rare events, but when they do occur, they are often not foreshadowed in, nor picked up by, the audit report. A further criticism of auditors is their apparent willingness to endorse the bending of accounting rules.

Auditors seem to believe that they can close the expectations gap simply by issuing disclaimers, namely that it is the companies' directors rather than the auditors who are responsible for both the financial statements and for uncovering fraud, and that auditors are simply carrying out an external check on material supplied by corporate directors, and verifying this on a sample basis only. They also cite the 1990 House of Lords *Caparo* decision that the company's auditors do not owe a duty of care to potential investors or the company's individual shareholders.

To restore confidence in the value of the audit report, the expectations gap needs to be closed in a more substantive way. A general strengthening of accounting standards (see above) would play a key role here, since this would provide auditors with more ammunition to stand up to client companies who wish to bend the rules in a misleading way. But arguably, a change in the law may also be required to extend the audit firm's liability for any negligence on their part. This, in turn, would have the healthy by-product of encouraging auditors to qualify accounts more often if they are dissatisfied with the quality or the presentation of the figures. At the same

---

[27] To be fair, we are viewing this debate from the somewhat partial perspective of the investment analyst's needs. The composition of accounting numbers may be important from a number of other perspectives other than just disclosure, e.g., executive remuneration, borrowing limits, Stock Exchange consent requirements, etc. It is also possible that management decisions within firms may (incorrectly) be influenced by accounting numbers rather than economic reality. Indeed, managers may genuinely believe that even purely cosmetic reductions in EPS will reduce share prices, either because they are poorly trained in finance, or else because they have a low opinion of analysts, and mistakenly believe that this is how the market works.

time, shareholders should also be given access to the auditor's report to management which details any accounting and control deficiencies and the company's response to them. This would allow shareholders to judge the quality of the accounting, control, and fraud-prevention systems.[28]

To reinforce the notion that auditors should be independent agents acting in the interests of shareholders, it might also be helpful to insist that the audit firm—or at least the partner in charge of the audit—be changed every few years. Companies should also be required to disclose all their relationships with their auditors, including consultancy. Finally, in line with the recommendations and Code of Best Practice of the Cadbury Committee (1992) companies should set up audit committees composed mainly or wholly of independent non-executive directors, and responsible, *inter alia*, for considering the scope of the audit, the choice of the auditors and the audit fee. Such committees should be urged to place audit quality ahead of price at the top of their list when selecting auditors.

3.10.3 *Communications*

Although financial reporting is very important, it is by no means the only channel through which information flows to the market. Indeed, many commentators, and most review bodies, which have examined the workings of the financial markets have placed at least as much emphasis on the importance of direct communications between companies and the investment community. Indeed, one of the major conclusions of the CBI Task Force (1987) was that:

At the heart of the problem lies a communications and educational gap between management [and] owners of companies . . . The communications challenge . . . can be met by:

(a) companies making more effort to keep the market informed about their longer-term strategic intentions and in particular about spending on R&D, as well as training and other aspects of innovation . . .

(b) financial analysts being better trained in the skills necessary to provide a strategic assessment of a company's prospects.

While cynics may label such statements as homilies, it is clear that communication is very important. Indeed, for the individual fund manager or analyst, his or her prime source of potential competitive advantage lies in making better, more informed investment judgements or recommendations. A regular and open exchange of views with the companies which they invest in or follow should help to deepen their understanding not only of the businesses, but also of the management teams. Similarly from a com-

---

[28] Several of the proposals listed here were advocated by Mr James Leek, chief executive of the Caparo Group in a talk to the London Society of Chartered Accountants on Wednesday 17 Apr. 1991.

pany's perspective, this provides them with a channel to explain strategy, to correct misapprehensions, and to prevent underpricing of the company's shares. Such dialogue can also serve other important functions, such as providing companies with information on what institutional shareholders expect of them, and providing a channel for monitoring, control, and influence, as well as information exchange.

There are, of course, costs and impediments to communications. First, improved communications, disclosure, and investor relations can be costly and involve considerable senior management time. Second, information relating to future strategy is often commercially sensitive, yet companies cannot seek to maintain confidentiality by revealing the information to key shareholders on a selective basis, since if the information is price sensitive, this flies in the face of their obligation to treat shareholders equally, and, anyway, makes the recipients of such information insiders. And third, if greater communications facilitates better monitoring and control, this will not necessarily be welcomed by executive managers, whose objectives may not always be precisely aligned with those of shareholders (Berle and Means 1932; Jensen and Meckling 1976).

In spite of these impediments, there have, in recent years, been major changes in both the extent, and channels, of communication between companies and their major shareholders. A case could certainly be made that historically, many companies had somewhat neglected their shareholders (Ball 1990). More recently, however, there has been an increasing awareness of the importance of investor relations, as indicated by the growth in both the corporate PR and investor relations industries. At the same time, there has been a shift away from using stockbrokers as the principal intermediaries between companies and their investors in favour of multiple channels, more direct dialogue (Plastow 1990), and, indeed, more company visits.

While momentum and commercial self-interest should ensure that these trends continue, additional pressures and encouragements might also prove productive. The publication and dissemination of 'how to' guides and checklists which typically outline what needs to be communicated and what questions should be asked[29] may have some influence on both companies, and analysts and fund managers, as may better training and education (see below). A more powerful force in the short term, however, is likely to be the trend towards greater direct pressure from institutional shareholders, coupled with the implicit message that their future support for management is not automatic, particularly if prior communications have been poor. Companies, in turn, are increasingly recognizing that investor relations is a long-term investment, and not something which—together with shareholder

[29] See, for example, Innovation Advisory Board (1991); Confederation of British Industry (1987); Stewart and Glassman (1984).

'loyalty' and understanding—can simply be switched on when the bankers
or predators are at the door.

3.10.4   *The Quality of Analysis*

The level of market efficiency depends not just on the quantity, quality, and
flow of information, but also on the way such information is processed,i.e.,
on investment analysis and the quality of analysts.

Analysts are frequently criticized for their dangerously uneven quality;
for having 'only the haziest understandings of the markets, technology and
competitive pressures under which a company is operating; for their failure
to ask intelligent or penetrating questions, particularly about future strategy
and innovation; for their failure to detect warning signs in the accounts of
some recent corporate failures; and for failing to produce original
research.'[30]

Such criticisms have led to demands for improvements in the standards
of investment analysis on the grounds that this will enhance market
efficiency. But this may itself reflect faulty analysis. For while there are
undoubtedly many analysts for whom a number of the above criticisms are
valid, the top analysts in each sector generally have a good understanding
of the companies they follow (see CBI 1987). Even more importantly, share
prices behave as if they were influenced by only the most sophisticated
players in the market (see section 3.9.1). Furthermore, empirical evidence
on the skills of top analysts suggests that they do add value, and that they
also operate within the context of a highly competitive environment (see
Dimson and Marsh 1984).

It is plausible, therefore, that there are enough good analysts to keep
share prices in line with values. But this does not imply that efforts to
improve the standards of investment analysis are misguided. For even if
these fail to enhance market efficiency, they will almost certainly pay dividends in other ways—not least in terms of improving the profession's—and
the City's—image.

The main levers for improving investment analysis are clearly recruitment
policy, and training and education. In terms of recruitment policy, analysts
are sometimes criticized for being too young and inexperienced, and for
often not having a background in terms of education or work experience in
the sectors which they cover. Yet youth and varied backgrounds may not
be inappropriate, given some of the skills required of an analyst, such as
high intelligence, numeracy, a systematic and analytical frame of mind,
investigative skills, originality, and the ability to take an alternative and

---

[30] See CBI (1987); Innovation Advisory Board (1990); and also the comments made by Mr.
Pen Kent, associate director of the Bank of England at a *Financial Times* Conference on
Financial Reporting (*Financial Times* 11 Oct. 1991).

detached view. Over the years, brokers and fund managers have certainly experimented with recruiting alternative types of analyst, and any biases we currently observe presumably reflect their accumulated wisdom about what makes a good analyst.

On the question of the training and education of analysts, there is arguably a need here to extend beyond the existing syllabus laid down by the Society of Investment Analysts, to include more practical issues, such as hands-on, supervised case analyses, use of data sources, investigative and interviewing skills, and the art of asking good questions. Many analysts (and fund managers) would also benefit from a rather broader management education, embracing operations management, marketing, and business strategy, ideally leavened with some first-hand exposure to business and management issues. But the educational and experience gap here is not just one-sided. Many senior corporate managers who come into contact with analysts and fund managers are not well-versed in the world of investment, financial markets, or even corporate finance, and there is also a strong case for better management education in this arena to enhance the level of effective dialogue and debate.

3.11 SUMMARY AND CONCLUSIONS

In this chapter, we have outlined a number of popular beliefs about the stock-market, namely the allegations that share prices fail to reflect values or the fundamentals of company performance; that they are short-termist; that analysts are fixated on short-term performance and are fooled by accounting manipulations; and that there is a serious dual-pricing problem, which manifests itself particularly in the context of takeover bids.

We have examined each of these assertions in turn to see how well they stand up in the light of the now very large body of empirical evidence on how share prices are determined. We have concluded that most of these accusations against the stock-market have no basis in fact, and simply do not square with the available evidence.

The substantial body of evidence on market efficiency, for example, indicates that stock-market prices do, in fact, broadly reflect values. There is thus no evidence of any short-term bias in share prices, nor of any tendency for the market to penalize companies which invest for the longer term. Furthermore, the extensive evidence from MBAR research provides strong evidence that, however investment analysts may sometimes appear to behave, the market is concerned with the underlying cash flows of the business, rather than accounting numbers *per se*. Nor does the market appear to be misled by the use of alternative accounting measurement and disclosure techniques.

Similarly, an examination of the worries about dual-pricing reveals that these largely reflect a misunderstanding of the basis on which share prices are determined. Furthermore, the closely allied concerns about takeover activity seem largely misplaced, since there is no evidence of any systematic market inefficiencies around the time of takeovers. Nor is it even correct to assume that takeovers are somehow a bad thing. For, at least from the shareholders' perspective, the evidence on takeover activity suggests that it has, on balance, been a virtue rather than a vice.

These conclusions should not, however, provide cause for complacency. Given that one key role of the stock-market is to provide a fair valuation mechanism, we have argued that markets could be made even more efficient (albeit at some cost) via improvements in the quantity, quality, flow, and interpretation of information. We have therefore outlined a number of ways in which this might be achieved through improvements in financial reporting and disclosure, changes in the auditor's role, better communications between companies and the financial community, and improvements in the standards and quality of investment analysis.

REFERENCES

Arnold, J., Moizer, P., and Noreen, E. (1983), 'Investment Appraisal Methods of Financial Analysts: A Comparative Survey of U.S. and U.K. Practices', working paper (University of Manchester).

Asquith, P. and Mullins, D. W. (1986), 'Equity Issues and Offering Dilution', *Journal of Financial Economics*, 15: 61–89.

Baldwin, C. Y. (1987), 'Competing for Capital in a Global Environment', *Midland Corporate Finance Journal*, 5: 43–64.

Ball, Sir R. J. (1990), 'Financial Institutions and their Role as Shareholders', in National Association of Pension Funds, *Creative Tension?* (London).

Ball, R., and Brown, P. (1968), 'An Empirical Evaluation of Accounting Income Numbers', *Journal of Accounting Research*, 6: 159–78.

—— and Foster, G. (1983), 'Corporate Financial Reporting: A Methodological Review of Empirical Research', *Journal of Accounting Research*, 20: 161–234 (supplement).

Barwise, T. P., Higson, C., Likierman, A., and Marsh, P. R. (1989), *Accounting for Brands* (The Institute of Chartered Accountants in England and Wales, London).

Basu, S. (1983), 'The Relationship between Earnings' Yields, Market Value and the Returns for NYSE Stocks: Further Evidence', *Journal of Financial Economics*, 12: 129–56.

Beaver, W. H. and Dukes, R. E. (1973), 'Tax Allocation and Depreciation Methods: Some Empirical Results', *Accounting Review*, 11: 549–59.

—— and Morse, D. (1978), 'What Determines Price–Earnings Ratios?', *Financial Analysts Journal*, 34: 65–76.

Berle, A. A. and Means, G. C. (1932), *The Modern Corporation and Private Property* (Macmillan, London).

Black, F. (1980), 'The Magic in Earnings: Economic Earnings vs. Accounting Earnings', *Financial Analysts Journal*, 36: 19–24.

Blume, M. E. (1980), 'Stock Returns and Dividend Yields: Some More Evidence', *Review of Economics and Statistics*, 62: 567–77.

Bogle, J. C. and Twardowski, J. M. (1980), 'Institutional Investment Performance Compared: Banks, Investment Counsellors, Insurance Companies and Mutual Funds', *Financial Analysts Journal*, 36: 33–41.

Brealey, R. A. (1983), *An Introduction to Risk and Return from Common Stocks*, second edition (Cambridge, Mass., MIT Press).

—— and Myers, S. C. (1991), *Principles of Corporate Finance*, fourth edition (New York, McGraw-Hill).

Brinson, G. P., Hood, L. R., and Beebower, G. L. (1986), 'Determinants of Portfolio Performance', *Financial Analysts Journal*, July–Aug., 39–44.

Brown, P., Foster, G., and Noreen, E. (1985), 'Security Analyst Multi-Year Earnings Forecasts and the Capital Market' (American Accounting Association, Sarasota, Fla.).

Business Week/Harris Poll (1987), 'Survey of Corporate Attitudes', *Business Week*, Oct. 23, 28.

Cadbury Committee (1992), *Report of the Committee on the Financial Aspects of Corporate Governance* (Gee and Co., London).

Chaney, P. K., Devinney, T. M., and Winer, R. S. (1989), 'The Impact of New Product Introductions on the Market Value of Firms', Report 89–105 (Marketing Science Institute, Cambridge, Mass.).

Chow, C. W. (1983), 'Empirical Studies of the Economic Effects of Accounting Regulation on Security Prices: Findings, Problems and Prospects', *Journal of Accounting Literature*, 2: 73–110.

Cochrane, J. H. (1990), 'Volatility Tests and Efficient Markets: A Review Essay', manuscript (University of Chicago).

Confederation of British Industry (1987), *Investing for Britain's Future: Report of the City/Industry Task Force* (CBI, London).

Dann, L. Y., Mayers, D., and Rabb, R. J., Jnr. (1977), 'Trading Rules, Large Blocks and the Speed of Price Adjustment', *Journal of Financial Economics*, 4: 3–22.

Dimson, E. (ed.) (1988), *Stock Market Anomalies* (Cambridge University Press, Cambridge).

—— and Marsh, P.R. (1984), 'An Analysis of Brokers' and Analysts' Unpublished Forecasts of UK Stock Returns', *Journal of Finance*, 39: 1257–92.

Dodd, P. (1983), 'The Market for Corporate Control: A Review of the Evidence', *Midland Corporate Finance Journal*, 1: 6–20.

Edwards, J. and Mayer, C. (1984), 'An Investigation into the Dividend and New Equity Issue Practices of Firms: Evidence from Survey Information', IFS working paper 80.

Fama, E. F. (1970), 'Efficient Capital Markets: A Review of Theory and Empirical Work', *Journal of Finance*, 25: 383–417.

—— (1991), 'Efficient Capital Markets: II', *Journal of Finance*, 46: 1575–1617.

Foster, G. (1986), *Financial Statement Analysis*, second edition (Prentice Hall International, Englewood Cliffs, NJ).

Franks, J. R. and Harris, R. (1989), 'Shareholder Wealth Effects of Corporate Takeovers: The UK Experience 1955–85', *Journal of Financial Economics*, 23: 225–49.

French, K. R. and Roll, R. (1986), 'Stock Return Variances: The Arrival of Information and the Reaction of Traders', *Journal of Financial Economics*, 17: 5–26.

Griffin, P. (1982), *Usefulness to Investors and Creditors of Information Provided by Financial Reporting: A Review of Empirical Accounting Research* (FASB, Stamford, Conn.).

Healy, P. M., Palepu, K. G., and Ruback, R. S., 'Does Corporate Performance Improve After Mergers?', working paper 3149–90 (MIT Sloan School of Management).

Holthausen, R. W., Leftwich, R. W., and Mayers, D. (1987), 'The Effect of Large Block Transactions on Security Prices: A Cross-sectional Analysis', *Journal of Financial Economics*, 19: 237–67.

Innovation Advisory Board (1990), *Innovation: City Attitudes and Practices* (Department of Trade and Industry, London).

—— (1991), *Getting the Message Across: The Innovation Plans Handbook* (Department of Trade and Industry, London)

Ippolito, R.A. (1989), 'Efficiency with Costly Information: A Study of Mutual Fund Performance, 1965–84; *Quarterly Journal of Economics*, 104: 1–23.

Jaffe, J. F. (1974), 'Special Information and InsiderTrading', *Journal of Business*, 47: 410–28.

Jarrell, G. A., Lehn, K., and Marr, W. (1985), 'Institutional Ownership, Tender Offers, and Long-Term Investments' (Office of the Chief Economist, Securities and Exchange Commission, Washington, DC).

Jensen, M. C. (1968), 'The Performance of Mutual Funds in the Period 1945–64', *Journal of Finance*, 23: 389–416.

—— (1978), 'Some Anomalous Evidence Regarding Market Efficiency', *Journal of Financial Economics*, 6: 95–101 (and *passim*).

—— (1986), 'The Takeover Controversy: Analysis and Evidence', *Midland Corporate Finance Journal*, 4: 6–32.

—— and Meckling, W. H. (1976), 'Theory of the Firm: Managerial Behaviour, Agency Costs and Capital Structure', *Journal of Financial Economics*, 3: 305–60.

—— and Ruback, R. S. (1983), 'The Market for Corporate Control: The Scientific Evidence', *Journal of Financial Economics*, 11: 5–50 (and entire volume).

Kaplan, R. S. and Roll, R. (1972), 'Investor Evaluation of Accounting Information: Some Empirical Evidence', *Journal of Business*, 45: 227–57.

Keane, S. (1985), *Stock Exchange Efficiency: Theory, Evidence and Implications* (Philip Allan, Oxford).

Laing, Sir H. (1990), 'The Balance of Responsibilities', in National Association of Pension Funds, *Creative Tension?* (NAPF, London).

Lev, B. and Ohlson, J. A. (1982), 'Market-Based Research in Accounting', *Journal of Accounting Research*, 20: 249–331 (supplement).

Levis, M. (1989), 'Stock Market Anomalies: A Re-assessment Based on the UK Evidence', *Journal of Banking and Finance*, 13: 675–96.

Lintner, J. (1956), 'Distribution of Incomes of Corporations among Dividends, Retained Earnings, and Taxes', *American Economic Review*, 46: 97–113.

Litzenberger, R. H. and Ramaswamy, K. (1982), 'The Effects of Dividends on Common Stock Prices: Tax Effects or Information Effects', *Journal of Finance*, 37: 429–43.

Maingot, M. (1984), 'The Information Content of UK Annual Earnings Announcements: A Note', *Accounting and Finance*, 51–8.

Marsh, P. R. (1979), 'Equity Rights Issues and the Efficiency of the UK Stock Market', *Journal of Finance*, 34: 839–62.

—— (1986), 'Are Profits the Prize of the Prey of the Predator', *Financial Times Mergers and Acquisitions*, May 4–7.

—— (1990), *Short-Termism on Trial* (Institutional Fund Managers Association, London).

—— (1991), 'Cash Flows and Accounting Numbers', unpublished teaching note (London Business School).

Marsh, T. A. and Merton, R. C. (1986), 'Dividend Variability and Variance Bounds Tests for the Rationality of Stock Market Prices', *American Economic Review*, 76: 483–98.

—— —— (1987), 'Dividend Behaviour for the Aggregate Stock Market', *Journal of Business*, 60: 1–40.

McConnell, J. J. and Muscarella, C. J. (1985), 'Corporate Capital Expenditure Decisions and the Market Value of the Firm', *Journal of Financial Economics*, 14: 399–422.

Mercer Fraser (1990), Report on the Implementation of SSAP24 (Chichester).

Merton, R. C. (1987), 'On the Current State of the Stock Market Rationality Hypothesis', in Dornbush, R., Fischer, S. and Bossons, J. (eds.), *Macroeconomics and Finance: Essays in Honour of Franco Modigliani* (MIT Press, Cambridge, Mass.).

Miller, M. H. and Modigliani, F. (1961), 'Dividend Policy, Growth and the Valuation of Shares', *Journal of Business*, 34: 411–33.

Myers, S. C. (1988), 'Signalling Methods of Accrual Accounting', working paper (London Business School).

National Economic Development Office (1987), *The Making of Managers* (London).

Plastow, Sir D. (1990), 'Corporate Strategy and the Institutional Shareholder', in National Association of Pension Funds, *Creative Tension?* (NAPF, London).

Plender, J. (1990), 'Some Policy Options', in *Takeovers and Short-termism* (Institute for Public Policy Research, London).

Pope, P. F., Morris, R. C., and Peel, D. A. (1990), 'Insider Trading: Some Evidence on Market Efficiency and Directors' Share Dealings in Great Britain', *Journal of Business Finance and Accounting*, 17: 359–80.

Reinganum, M. (1981), 'Misspecification of Capital Asset Pricing: Empirical Anomalies Based on Earnings' Yields and Market Values', *Journal of Financial Economics*, 9: 19–46.

Richards, P. H. (1979), *UK and European Share Price Behaviour: The Evidence* (Kogan Page, London).

Ronen, J. and Sadan, S. (1981), *Smoothing Income Numbers* (Addison-Wesley, Reading, Mass.).

Samuelson, P. (1965), 'Proof that Properly Anticipated Prices Fluctuate Randomly', *Industrial Management Review*, 6: 41–9.

Scholes, M. (1972), 'The Market for Securities: Substitution versus Price Pressure and the Effects of Information on Share Prices', *Journal of Business*, 45: 179–211.

Seyhun, H. N. (1986), 'Insiders' Profits, Costs of Trading, and Market Efficiency', *Journal of Financial Economics*, 16: 189–212.

Shiller, R. J. (1981), 'Do Stock Prices Move Too Much to be Justified by Subsequent Changes in Dividends?', *American Economic Review*, 71: 421–36.

—— (1984), 'Stock Prices and Social Dynamics', *Brookings Papers on Economic Activity*, 457–98.

Shleifer, A. and Summers, L. H. (1990), 'The Noise Trader Approach to Finance', *Journal of Economic Perspectives*, 19–33.

Stewart, G. B. and Glassman, D. M. (1984), 'How to Communicate with an Efficient Market', *Midland Corporate Finance Journal*, 2: 73–9.

3i (1990), 'Corporate Attitudes to Stock Market Valuations: 3i Shareholder Value Survey', *plc UK*, 1 (entire issue) (3i, London).

Treynor, J. L. (1972), 'The Trouble With Earnings', *Financial Analysts Journal*, 28: 41–3.

Watts, R. (1973), 'The Information Content of Dividends', *Journal of Business*, 46: 191–211.

Whitbeck, V. S. and Kisor, M. (1963), 'A New Tool in Investment Decision-Making', *Financial Analysts Journal*, 19: 55–62.

Woolridge, J. R. (1988), 'Competitive Decline: Is a Myopic Stock Market to Blame', *Journal of Applied Corporate Finance*, 1: 26–36.

4

A Larger Role for Institutional Investors

J. P. CHARKHAM

4.1 INTRODUCTION

Now that there is broad international consensus that market-based systems are the most efficient way of organizing the production and distribution of goods and services, attention has begun to focus on which particular model is consistently most effective. It is consistency that counts; in the short run almost anything goes.

Countries employ the system which their history has bequeathed to them and which suits their social conventions. Formal structures tend to be adapted to accommodate national idiosyncrasies. Most systems provide for companies to have a board of directors, but what they do and how they do it vary greatly. The component parts of each system fit together but are generally unsuitable individually for transplantation into another system.

To talk of company structure is unhelpful if it conveys an image of rigidity: companies being composed of people are living organisms; and it is company dynamics that are crucial. We are never far away from 'agency costs', a behavioural phenomenon with economic consequences. Agency costs are a reflection of motivation. Motivation alone does not ensure competence; even the highly motivated sometimes fail.

4.2 THE BASIC PRINCIPLES

A study of the various models suggest that there are two fundamental principles.

1. That the management of the enterprise, whether it be collective or more individualistic in nature, must have reasonable freedom to push it forward towards longer-term objectives without undue interference by the bureaucracy and without undue fear of litigation or takeover.
2. That the management operates within an adequate framework of formal or informal accountability for its strategy and performance.

It appears that the first principle is observed in most countries *except* that in the USA and the UK the threat of takeover is often a negative factor, and in the USA litigation may sometimes be a problem despite the business judgment rule. The second principle is satisfied in Germany by a combination of informal accountability to the banks and formal accountability to a supervisory board. In Japan accountability is even more informal, to the banks, to colleagues in the keiretsu, to other companies connected by shareholdings or a business relationship, and to various elders such as the chairman (and previous chairmen) and certain advisers. In France accountability is more patchy and depends mainly on whether the board has major shareholders on it or not.

For historical and political reasons the banking systems of the UK and the USA have during the last fifty years or so not been part of the framework of accountability within which industrial and commercial management operates. Management accountability is left almost exclusively to boards and thus depends almost entirely on their composition and quality. At best accountability is excellent, at worst non-existent. This problem has long been recognized, hence the strenuous efforts that have been made to improve the quality of boards by increasing the number of able, independent, directors on them, and by the insistence on audit committees of the board in the USA. Although in the UK a proper board structure is a correct first step, it is not a complete answer for many reasons, for example

1. Some management does not want to be accountable; it wants to be comfortable. So it picks its outside directors (if it picks any) from people it calculates will not 'rock the boat' however distinguished they may sound.
2. Some management is not good enough, and it picks its outside directors in its own image.
3. Nominating committees, if properly composed, are helpful but not a total solution.
4. Some chairmen make poor use of potentially good boards because they do not want interference or because they are inept, perceiving themselves to be far less autocratic than they appear to others.
5. Some outside directors disappoint through lack of knowledge, experience, and courage.

It is notoriously difficult to see from the outside how well a board is working, at least in the short term. Eventually the figures tell their own story especially when they are compared with other firms in the same or related sectors. In practice it is often clear that a board is lopsided, overdominated or simply not good enough.

In the UK system the German and Japanese informal influences are not available and it would not be practicable to copy them—though doubtless a closer relationship with bankers might yield benefits to both parties.

As things stand, there is no alternative in the UK and the USA but to look towards the owners of the business to make sure that the board's stewardship is adequate and that it is keeping management up to the mark. It is not helpful to be deflected by the argument that a company has many stakeholders of whom shareholders are only one party. In fact, shareholders come at the end of the queue, because in the long run their prosperity depends on the prior satisfaction of customers, workforce, creditors, and banks. The supremacy of the shareholders is a myth except in a limited sense—they are the only party with a legal right to elect the board. In the UK model we are therefore driven inexorably to consider this right, unless we believe that takeovers are an adequate substitute for accountability. Takeovers have their uses, but they are a blunt instrument often providing the wrong solution at unnecessary cost.

4.3 INSTITUTIONAL INVESTORS

To say that the role of institutional investors is clearly crucial is not to deny the rights of other investors. Private shareholders too can raise their voices at AGMs, but few of them have the knowledge to do so. But private investors can rest easy in the knowledge that if the institutions take up the cudgels their interests will be served too; all they need to worry about is whether the institutions are in fact ready to bear a private cost for a public good (the free-rider problem).

There are various views of institutional investing. Here are two examples from opposite ends of the spectrum. The first is M&G's published policy statement.

A: M&G's investment philosophy is to concentrate on long-term value with an emphasis on income and recovery, and a general reluctance to invest in highly rated fashionable stocks. M&G funds have holdings of 5 per cent or more in the equity capital of about 220 companies. We believe that as substantial investors we should have a firm and lasting relationship with the managements of companies in which we have a large interest, and we make a point of getting to know the people who run those companies. We do not presume to tell the management how to run their business but, if a company's actions are likely to jeopardise the interests of shareholders, we find that constructive intervention can often be preferable to disposing of a holding. This means that we take a long-term view of performance and try not be deflected by short-term considerations.

Here is a contrasting view from a top fund manager

B: I do not believe that it is sensible to expect shareholders to step in and sort out management problems, except as the very last resort. We do not have the resources nor are our clients likely to be willing to pay for them. More important though, our overriding responsibility is to our clients who judge us on the investment results achieved each year.

Note that neither of these statements envisages interfering with everyday management decisions. In the first, the role of the shareholder is to be sufficiently informed to exert influences in the rare cases where an obvious lapse of general standards makes this essential in the interests of all the stakeholders, including the shareholders. It is not wholly an agency problem. The board may be doing its best but not be good enough.

These statements do not say that policy is limited by statutory or common law constraints. In the USA Professor Bernard Black's work for the Institutional Investor project of Columbia University of New York describes the US legal battlefield and concludes that even there the obstacles are not insuperable. In the UK the constraints are minimal. There are no cases of trustees being sued because they did or did not accept a takeover offer for a given share; or dealt too little; or took too long a view. The choice between these two views is unaffected by the law.

The policy statements given above both come from highly regarded institutions, but reflect differing characteristics. Characteristics of type A are: concentration of the portfolio on fewer stocks; larger stakes in individual companies; close communication with companies in which such investments are held; high loyalty factor to these companies; few dealings in those shares and less freedom to deal with whole stakes because of the effect on the market; and a general interest in corporate governance matters. Type B is the opposite in almost every way, its characteristics being wide diversification; small stakes in each company; superficial communication with companies, mainly about short-term influences on the price; loyalty factor; frequent dealing; and a virtually non-existent interest in corporate governance.

These views represent almost the two ends of the investment spectrum, on which all institutions can be placed. The most celebrated exponent of type A is Warren Buffet with his Berkshire Hathaway fund. Many of our major insurance companies and major pension funds that are managed in-house see themselves as closer to type A than type B.

Many fund managers, however, see their responsibilities as being satisfied by a type B approach. It might have been assumed that the choice between the two should be determined by the purposes a particular fund was created to satisfy, but it is not so. Many pension funds whose objectives are longer-term are under type B management, while some unit trusts which can be bought and sold every day in the market are managed on type A. The reasons are a complex mixture of assumptions about investment strategy, motivation, and personal skills.

4.3.1 *Personal Skills*

To take the second point first, many fund managers are not equipped for the type A programme, since they do not understand industry but do understand short-term markets. It is not of course that they would be incapable of developing the necessary skills, but simply that their job specifications do not require them to do so. It is no use blaming fund managers for not doing a job their firms do not want done.

4.3.2 *Motivation of Fund Managers*

This takes us to the second point—motivation. We all know that measurement motivates. Motivation is a two-edged sword but the sharper of its cutting edges is fear. Fund managers are driven by fear of losing business. The ways in which they will lose business are to present themselves poorly for the clients, or to manage the funds poorly. To stay in business they do not need to care about the ultimate beneficiaries or the national interest but must keep abreast of their competitors by holding a respectable place in a quarterly league table.

The motivations for fund managers are bound to institutionalize the herd instinct, so as to minimize the short-term risk of failure. There are fewer prizes for coming first than there are penalties for arriving last.

4.3.3 *Motivation of Trustees*

The trustees of a company pension fund should have one main aim, to ensure that the fund can meet its obligations when they fall due (on which they will receive actuarial advice). If, however, a manager of the company is also a trustee, he has another aim i.e. to maximize the value of the pension fund so as to minimize the firm's contribution (pension 'holidays'), or the amount it has to add if the fund needs topping-up. Furthermore, if he can legally do so, he would like to take surpluses from the fund back into the company to swell its profits. The pressures he exerts on his fund managers are related far less to the pension fund's beneficiaries than to the pension fund as a profit centre. All company managers want their own shareholders to belong to the type A school. If they put pressure on their own pension fund managers for short-term results they push them towards type B.

Trustees' motivations may well be mixed. Whether they are or not there is no excuse for failing to lay down the necessary ground rules for the fund managers they engage—and this takes skill.

4.3.4 *The Ground Rules*

The first issue is the diversification of the portfolio. The crucial question is how many different companies' shares should be brought. What is the evidence to suggest that there is benefit in ever wider diversification? Could not most of the benefit of diversification be captured by putting the bulk of the portfolio into 30–50 shares (unless the fund is so big that the resulting holdings would be disproportionate to the size of the companies held)?

With fewer shares bought, the fund could afford a better depth of analysis, and a closer relationship with companies becomes possible. Fewer decisions are needed and they would be more carefully weighed. It *is* more difficult to sell out a big holding than a small one, but the need ever to do so will be correspondingly less. Ought it not be a golden rule that managers should buy only as many different shares as they can study in depth and follow in detail? Even then, there is probably little point in wide proliferation.

A similar point should be made, but even more strongly, in regard to excessive trading. Trustees generally leave fund managers free to trade as little or as much as they like—and the fund managers like to be active. Various studies show that active and highly diversified management seldom beats the relevant index—even before expenses. (In the USA in any year only about one quarter do so.) Furthermore, as many UK companies find 80 per cent or more of their shares held by trustees, every transaction between them diminishes the value of the beneficiaries' holding viewed in aggregate (by the amount of the transaction costs). It is a minus sum game for them.

The differing motives of trustees, the diversification of portfolios, and excessive trading are issues worth further consideration. Just imagine for a moment a regime in which they did not apply. The trustees, being barred from raiding the pension fund or declaring a pension holiday, could afford to look towards long-term performance and that alone might persuade them to offer managers five-year contracts so they could concentrate on the longer term. These contracts might limit diversification so as to induce fund managers to think more deeply about the decisions they had to take. Limiting turnover would strengthen these tendencies mightily. And both requirements would keep costs down.

Fund managers might not welcome such a regime because of the disciplines it would impose and the new skills they would need to acquire. Companies would begin to look like combinations of people producing goods and services and not mere gaming chips. They ought to fear index-matched funds, as they are cheaper than active management and most of the time better for the beneficiaries. There is an argument that trustees owe it to the beneficiaries to insist on either the type A model for their fund managers or indexation.

Indexing does not provide an excuse for inactivity. If trustees persuade their fund managers to buy the index there is a tendency to walk away from it (subject to discussions from time to time on asset allocation or weighting). It is easy to understand why—in all but the largest funds the holdings in individual companies, if one buys the index, are very small. If every company in the index increases its profits by 10 per cent this year, individual share prices will reflect this and so will the index. Holders of indexed funds have a common cause to achieve this result and it would be entirely logical for them to take a common interest in corporate governance.

4.3.5   *Trustees*

Individuals who manage their own assets can please themselves and act irrationally if they choose. Everyone else, whether formally a trustee or not, has no such freedom. Trustees or quasi-trustees bear responsibility for the bulk of the nation's savings. They may delegate management to fund managers but they remain responsible for the terms on which delegation is given. The previous paragraphs have suggested some deficiencies which may be found in this system. There is a sound case for ensuring that trustees are better trained for their difficult task.

4.3.6 *Dividends and Cash Flow*

Company management always has tricky decisions to take in the retention/distribution equilibrium which is part of the present/future balance. Japanese management feels confident it can pursue a retention/future policy because that is what its shareholders will want, or at least tolerate: the same is true to a lesser degree in Germany. Our shareholders, who have turned to equities as a hedge against higher rates of inflation, have a much keener interest in distribution and would like high dividends, though they also want investment for the future. Alas this is impossible in *real terms* in markets where there is strong international competition. There is no obvious answer to the dilemma except better communication between company management and shareholders to develop an understanding of the companies' strategy. Shareholders will be more inclined to be patient if they have confidence in management *and confidence in their own ability to do something about the management if it consistently fails*. The important aspect of the Japanese and German systems is not just that the providers of capital and finance are better informed, but that they have influence over companies, and know it. There is no doubt that a type A approach is superior in this regard and must on that account be a help to industry in developing long-term plans.

4.4   THE TYPE A APPROACH RE-EXAMINED

4.4.1   *The Free-rider Problem*

The arguments for a type A approach have been well rehearsed over the years but one of the main reasons why trustees and fund managers have been slow to espouse it is the free-rider problem. They see no reason to incur a private cost for a public gain—and perceive, perhaps incorrectly, the cost of communication with companies as higher than that of constant trading. Small funds feel this keenly as they are quite modest about their potential influence. The bigger the fund, the weaker is the free-rider argument, and it is further diminished if costs can be shared.

There are already cases where institutions act jointly *ad hoc*, but as yet no more systematic approach to co-operation has been found attractive, even though this was envisaged as far back as the 1970s when the Institutional Shareholder Committee was established. An interesting proposal has been made in the USA that institutions might subscribe to a Warren Buffet type fund which would take big stakes on a long-hold basis in a few companies and keep a careful eye on them.

4.4.2 *Foreign Companies and Holdings*

Although this paper is confined to UK companies because it is concerned with our corporate governance arrangements, the greater internationalization of stock-markets cannot be overlooked. UK trustees will need to consider this aspect when they instruct fund managers to buy abroad. The interlocking arrangements between banks, shareholders and company management in Japan, Germany, and France, mean that there is little scope for exerting any influence—but there is some. AGMs are usually formalities in all three countries (and in many others, including the UK), but no management likes serious well-directed shareholder questions which achieve good press coverage.

There is, however, a special point with regard to the USA. UK shareholders cannot be forced to use their votes in US companies and most do not do so. US fiduciaries on the other hand (if they come under ERISA legislation) *must* cast their votes or see they are cast by their fund managers. We can expect to find them routinely doing so. UK shareholders had better look to their laurels if US pension funds start taking big stakes in UK companies, since AGMs here often go through on total votes of 10–14 per cent. The US authorities regard the right to vote as part of the pension plan assets and it cannot be neglected; the principle behind this rule seems sound.

4.4.3 *Insider Trading*

In the first type of arrangement, shareholders become much better informed about the company. Much of what they learn would not qualify as being inside information, but some of it may. If they get it, they must not trade on it: once it is generally known of course it is no longer 'inside'. But as they do not have a trading stance, this element of restraint is tolerable. The only people to suffer from knowing too much are those whose system requires them to react to every twitch of the market. Systems are constructed on different premisses and they do not mix.

4.4.4 *Responding to a Bid*

The type B approach implies a total absence of loyalty in the case of a bid; the only question being to get the best price. Sometimes a bid can be decided by a market shudder which carries the target company's price down with it, and below the bid level. On such a slender accident the fate of the ownership of companies has hung. Of course, the type B holder may feel that the target's restructuring may be so effective in the short term that it is a better bet even than the bid premium, and many contested bids do in fact fail (perhaps because too few shares are in type B hands!).

Type A holders may sometimes be tempted if the price looks advantageous even taking the long view of the company's prospects. In any case absolute protection against a bid is undesirable. As a footnote I might add that some people feel that if a bid comes from quarters which are themselves bid-proof, there may be a fair reason for government intervention.

A bid premium is inherent in our double function market and is crystallized every time the market becomes a market for companies, and not a market for shares.

4.4.5 *'We've never done it that way'*

The type B process is so deeply engrained that it will be hard to alter. For years many fund managers have regarded selling in the market as an answer to managerial shortcomings. As the organization of some big firms of fund managers is highly devolved, a 'Growth Fund' sale may become a 'Recovery Fund' purchase, all in the same firm.

Buffet's simple formula is to concentrate on fundamental value coupled with a judgement of when the market's pricing mechanism is mistaken. If one believes in a perfectly efficient capital market this cannot happen, but human beings who comprise markets are no more perfectly informed or fully rational in the economic sphere than in any other.

The tendency to concentrate on the current price and not on fundamentals shows itself particularly in a bull market. A rising price sanctifies all—poor board structure, erratic policies, and even behaviour of a dubious standard. Even type A holders are reluctant to intervene for fear of affecting the share price whatever their misgivings. Those who conduct dialogues with companies and may raise the points that trouble them, such as the weakness of the non-executive elements on a board, are often reluctant to press too hard, lest the paragon in command resigns and the markets react adversely. Smaller holders can sell in the market without moving the price, and even big holders can do so gradually, but only too often they hold on, waiting for something to turn up, such as a bid. What happens frequently is that the market weakens, and the faults are exposed. The price then goes through the floor and the paragon departs (heavily compensated), followed by a struggle for survival. This sequence could have been avoided had action been taken in time and the paragon been tamed. The acid test for the institutions is to discover whether a board has the capacity to say no to the chief executive if necessary. If it has not, danger is on the way whatever the share price may be today.

Even on the present basis of judgement, fund managers' perception of how to realize their self interest may be mistaken, but it would take courage, and might be a high short-term risk, for a type B fund manager to switch to a Warren Buffet strategy. It would, moreover, call for different skills and the perception of managers that they are unsuited to such a switch may be correct. They fear that being ultimately proved right is no consolation if in the meantime they have lost the business. They also fear that their skills are not attuned to being ultimately right but rather to not being immediately wrong. Without a firm lead from the trustees of the funds under management it is unrealistic to expect fund managers to change.

Some institutional trustees are showing positive intentions. The Association of British Insurers in a paper entitled 'The Responsibilities of Institutional Shareholders' in March 1991 states that:

1. Institutional investors should encourage regular systematic contact at senior executive level for the purposes of an exchange of views and information on strategy, performance, board membership and quality of management.
2. Institutional investors should take a positive interest in the composition of boards of directors, with particular reference to:
    (a) Concentrations of decision-making power not formally constrained by checks and balances appropriate to the particular company.
    (b) The appointment of a core of non-executives of appropriate calibre, experience and independence.
3. Institutional investors support the appointment of remuneration and audit committees.

This sounds admirable as far as it goes but the ABI does not speak for all institutions and the free-rider principle affects them as well as others. They too can be mesmerized by the share price in a bull market and the representations of individual insurance companies can be ignored. In the end, whether it is organized *ad hoc* or more systematically, some kind of joint action will be needed both to spread costs and reduce the free-rider problem, and to act quietly and effectively. Teddy Roosevelt's famous dictum might have been written specially for them—'Speak softly but carry a big stick'.

4.5 ACCOUNTABILITY

Let us end where we began—with accountability. Accountability for the use of power has been for centuries the main theme of the development of the UK political and judicial systems. The concentration of economic power in the hands of a few people at the top of companies is in its own way no less important. Not only the effectiveness of the system, but also its legitimacy, depends on there being adequate accountability on the way in which this power is exercised. This chapter has argued that under UK arrangements there is no alternative to this being in the hands of institutional shareholders; they, more than anyone, are the guardians of the savings of the people. Where they are principals as in the case of insurance companies, they act as both trustees and managers. Where these roles are separated as in the case of pension funds, the managers are accountable to the trustees and it is for the latter to establish the terms on which accountability is to be exercised. In no case should institutions see their task as being to manage, or even to control those who must call the managers to account—i.e. the board—but to monitor the board. The institutions are the guards of the guards, so to speak, and their task should be an occasional one, but it is none the less critical. If they do not exercise their power, eventually others will.

There is one final twist to accountability. To whom are the institutions themselves ultimately accountable? It may be their own shareholders, or their policyholders, or both. The fact that there is no simple answer does not invalidate the rest of the argument. It is another argument for another occasion. If, in a democracy, we waited for perfect rulers we would wait a long time. In the world of corporate governance it would be an advance if our institutions with all their imperfections were to play a fuller part.

The acid test of any proposition is to look at the negative aspects. What is to happen if the shareholders continue *not* to care? I suggest that: more companies will continue to underperform; more companies will fail, and more value will be lost. (I reject the argument that liquidations or insolvencies merely result in a beneficial redistribution of assets. They are, rather, immensely wasteful.) I also believe that more UK companies will disappear; more beneficiaries will suffer; and more fund managers will be dismissed as their costly practices are exposed.

4.6 A FUTURE PROGRAMME

The areas which need further investigation are as follows.

1. Methods of uncoupling pension funds from companies to stop management using the pension fund directly or indirectly as a profit centre.

2. The qualifications of trustees and quasi-trustees and their role, with particular emphasis on:
   (a) Incentives to fund managers to think long by granting long contracts.
   (b) The reduced diversification of portfolios.
   (c) Guidelines on the amount of trading a fund manager should conduct.
3. Some better arrangements for joint action by shareholders, including:
   (a) Joint action by *individual* shareholders (for which some enabling machinery is necessary).
   (b) Joint as well as individual action by institutions when a board is clearly not working satisfactorily.
   (c) The establishment by some institutions of a fund operating on Warren Buffet lines in which they would take shares.

5

Proposals for a Reformed System of Corporate Governance to Achieve Internationally Competitive Long-Term Performance

ALLEN SYKES

Boards should be structured . . . to strike the right balance between the entrepreneurial drive which is essential for competitive success and a proper degree of regulation and control. (Sir Adrian Cadbury, *The Times*, 5 March 1991)

[Commenting on pressures on institutional investors to behave more like responsible proprietors: a power vacuum is developing that will be filled by some other economic or political interest group if the institutional investors fail to wake up . . . [There is] the need to broaden the input into company boardrooms and to get the institutions off the hook of voting obligations which they cannot live up to but which they are terrified of losing to other interests. (Barry Riley, *Financial Times*, 29 February 1992)

If they [the investment institutions] do not exercise their power, eventually others will. (Charkham 1991)

real ownership of most of the equity in American corporations is impossible. The most obvious reason is that their primary fiduciary responsibility is to their investors and beneficiaries, which can lead to a conflict of interest with their acting as owners. (Lorsch 1991)

Somehow a class of investor should be created which is interested in corporate governance. (Jacobs 1991)

THE last few years have witnessed a marked upsurge of interest in the subject of corporate governance in both Britain and the USA. At least three related developments have contributed to this. First, there is widespread unease about the damaging long-term results from which is now considered to be an excessive level of takeover activity during 1985–9, often financed by imprudent amounts of debt. Second, the pay levels of senior executive directors in general, and chairman and chief executives in particular, has far too often risen to excessive levels when related to performance. Not infrequently it has been inversely related. Third, and most important of all, there has been a growing perception that British and US corporations, particularly in the manufacturing, high technology, and construction industries are increasingly uncompetitive with most of their main rivals in Western Europe (as typified by Germany) and in the Far East and South East Asia (as typified by Japan). For a particularly convincing analysis of these diverging economic and efficiency trends of at least twenty years standing see Eltis, Fraser, and Ricketts (1992), Ishihara and Prestowitz (1991) and Jacobs (1991) for the United States. Much of the analyses for each country would apply to the other.

A unifying, underlying feature of the three developments is that it is increasingly perceived that all of them are exacerbated by major weaknesses in the similar British and US systems of corporate governance. More and more, thoughtful observers are coming to realize that the systems of corporate governance which once served both nations so well have so changed their fundamental characteristics as to now constitute a major handicap to growth and efficiency. This is *not* to say that flawed corporate governance is the only important cause of a relative decline in corporate and national growth and efficiency. Indeed, Eltis, Fraser, and Ricketts (1992) have shown persuasively that there are a number of major causes for Britain's relative decline in comparison with Germany and Japan, notably the much lower inflation and much superior macro-economic stability which those two countries have long enjoyed; their significantly lower cost of capital (both equity and debt), the benefit of knowledgeable, long-term banking relationships; their better-educated and trained workers; their superior record on industrial relations; their dedication to quality and continuous innovation, with more sustained and effective research and development; and the like. It is clear, however, from the many important recent British and American contributions to the corporate governance debate that major improvements in our systems of corporate governance are needed. Indeed, with the exception of creating low inflation and greater macro-economic stability which are the province of governments, improvements in overcoming all the other main handicaps to improved economic performance either depend upon, or would greatly benefit from overcoming the main weaknesses in corporate governance. It is this perception which gives particular importance to the rethinking of corporate governance that is now taking place in Britain and America. It should not therefore be thought that improved corporate governance is a relatively minor matter which should be of interest only to a few specialists. Rather it is at the heart of corporate efficiency and significantly influences both nations' international economic and hence political influence.

5.1   THE CORPORATE GOVERNANCE MALAISE

The present unease between industrialists and their institutional shareholders—the City—has become widespread in both Britain and the United States over the last 2–3 years. There is concern that our system of corporate governance is in need of adaptation and reform, although there is no general agreement on what these changes should be (Jacobs 1992; Charkham 1991; Sykes 1990a; 1990b). Common to most of those involved in the debate is the view that boards of directors need to take more and better account of the views of their owners and particularly of the investment institutions who are the overwhelmingly important class of owners (owning nearly 70 per cent of shares, compared with individual owners who own 20 per cent). Many suggestions have been put forward for redefining the roles of directors in general and non-executive directors in particular.

The whole subject of corporate governance is seen by many as being bound up with the need for British industry to be able to achieve long-term performance comparable with its main international rivals. At present, industry is too frequently under pressure to achieve short-term results. Part of the concern about short-termism relates to what many see as an excessive level of hostile takeovers which was common to both Britain and America in the 1980s and particularly in the last five years of that decade. While takeover activity has much abated in the last three years, particularly because of the serious recession, most commentators expect it to come back at a high level when the recession lifts even if it does not reach the frenetic levels of 1985–9. Indeed, since the last quarter of 1991, takeover activity has picked up significantly.

It is against this background that I shall examine the need for reforming corporate governance to achieve long-term, internationally-competitive performance, and ways of achieving it. I cannot undertake this examination, still less make recommendations for change, without first examining briefly the present system of corporate governance. I consider our structure of corporate governance has so changed its originally successful basic characteristics that it seriously handicaps long-term corporate efficiency and hence constrains long-term economic growth. It satisfies none of its main participants, a clear sign that something fundamental is wrong. *There are generally no successful systems of corporate governance without committed and knowledgeable long-term shareholders, managements with the preconditions and incentives for long-term performance, and with such managements being properly accountable to their shareholders.* These were characteristics of British and US capitalism in our heydays, and of our more successful Western European and Pacific Rim rivals today. They are also the characteristics of most of the successful venture capital industries in both countries. We do not so much need to invent new approaches but to remember old approaches which have served well before, and which need reinterpreting in a practicable, modern context.

The corporate governance debate has become polarized and sterile with the City and industry blaming each other for short-termism. Academics generally support the City's view but financial journalists are increasingly doubtful. Before considering the desirable reforms for each system of corporate governance I wish to examine very briefly the two main forms of world capitalism. First, there is the British and US system which exists in most of the English speaking world. Second, there is the system that has developed in most of Western Europe, Japan, and the newly industrializing Pacific Rim countries. As this latter group is located at either end of the Eurasian continent I have called them for convenience 'the Continentals'.

5.2   THE TWO MAIN FORMS OF CAPITALISM

For further discussion of the two forms of capitalism see Sykes (1990) and *The Economist* (1990).

5.2.1   *The British (and US) System*

Under the British/US system most external long-term funds are raised from the stock-market and that market is also an open and highly active takeover market. It is the main, indeed some would argue the only, effective way of imposing accountability on management under our present system, since shareholders find it difficult to impose their views save in a crisis. It is a system which is widely acknowledged within the countries concerned (and by their main rivals) to favour the short term over the long. Most significantly our system of capitalism performs less well than most of the Continentals, and this has been true for twenty to thirty years (see Eltis, Fraser, and Ricketts 1992). While economic growth continues it is significantly less than that of the Continentals and this looks set to continue. In other words, there is a relative decline in long-term economic performance and this shows up in a generally shrinking manufacturing and high-technology base.

Amongst shareholders the investment institutions are dominant but largely passive. They lack the long-term commitment and knowledge to be active investors, and regularly and freely admit they lack the appropriate expertise and resources. But more importantly, in the main they choose not to be active investors.[1] The investment institutions want the freedom to buy and sell shares freely. They do not want to co-operate with other investors save in a serious crisis when there is no alternative. This is because they are in fierce competition with each other to attract and retain investment funds, a competition that requires short-term performance over 2–3 years at best

---

[1] This has led one notable US commentator (Lorsch 1991) to conclude that real ownership of most of the equity in US corporations is impossible. It may be impossible *directly*, but it must be made possible indirectly, or procured by other means since if investment institutions cannot somehow exercise the ownership function between them there will remain a fatal vacuum at the heart of corporate governance.

(although many would say much less) and it is this process which inevitably institutionalizes short-termism in our systems.

There are a minority of investors in Britain and the USA who do take the long-term view. They hold their shares for long periods, and even indefinitely (e.g. Warren Buffet's Berkshire Hathaway fund). In his examination of this matter, Charkham (1991) has called these investors type A. They have many of the attitudes of investors and banks in Continental systems of corporate governance. He contrasts them with the other and overwhelmingly dominant type B investors who are fundamentally interested only in their portfolio of shares, rather than their shareholding in any particular company. They are concerned to maximize the value of their portfolio as a whole and are active and frequent traders of stocks (see, in particular, *The Economist* (1990)). But, as we know from numerous studies in Britain and the United States, few funds can consistently beat the index by active trading, and their high dealing costs are largely wasted. This has led many investors to put significant proportions of their funds into portfolios which replicate an index. If one cannot beat an index this is a sensible action, but it is a complete abnegation of ownership. Suggestions have been made in both countries (see Jacobs 1991 and Charkham 1991) that investment institutions could diversify risk satisfactorily with say only 20–50 well-chosen stocks and the fund managers could then know their companies and their managements well, and could start to fulfil the role of owners, at least in part. These solutions have much to commend them. My own proposals (see section 5.5 below) are designed on not dissimilar lines.

Boards of directors are necessarily self-appointed because, save in very rare cases, the investment institutions deliberately take no part in their appointment. Hence, most boards are not generally accountable to their shareholders. Compared with Western Europe the pay of British executive directors is relatively low, their rewards are mainly short-term and they tend to lack long-term incentives. In the United States the pay of chief executive officers (CEOs) (often the only senior manager who is a director) is by contrast often high, even excessively high. In both countries I would argue that pay is often too high in relation to short-term performance (the main, indeed overwhelming type of incentive) and usually quite unrelated to long-term performance and hence quite inappropriate for achieving what is most relevant.

5.2.2 The Continental System

The Continental system works differently. Here the majority of external long-term finance tends to come from long-term debt with cheap loans from banks with supportive long-term relationships being of great importance. Companies tend to have committed and knowledgeable shareholders, often including banks which themselves have strong board representation. It is the general business culture in Continental countries to take the long-term view and therefore to support long-term investment and heavy research and development (R&D) expenditures. (In Britain, apart from pharmaceuticals, R&D expenditure as a proportion of sales is only around half that of Germany and Japan (Eltis, Fraser, and Ricketts 1992). This supportive long-term business culture is generally shared by owners, bankers, customers, suppliers, management, and workers.

Under the Continental system there are few hostile takeovers but managements are held accountable and changed or removed for underperformance without the cost and trauma of takeovers. Most importantly, the Continentals achieve significantly superior long-term performance (Eltis, Fraser, and Ricketts 1992; Ishihara and Prestowitz 1991; Jacobs 1991; and Drucker 1991). *The challenge facing Britain and the US is to reproduce the best Continental characteristics in a practicable context reflecting our national cultures.* The corporate governance malaise we suffer from is no-one's fault, rather it is a system fault. It has happened because our system has evolved into a *system* where the fundamental characteristics of committed owners and accountable managements with the preconditions for long-term performance have changed. The fundamental change is the substitution of passive investment institutions in place of active, knowledgeable shareholders (Sykes 1990a; *The Economist* 1990; and Drucker 1991). The systems may look superficially the same as in our heydays, but they no longer deliver internationally-competitive long-term results.

5.3 IDENTIFYING THE JUSTIFIED AND NECESSARY REQUIREMENTS OF OWNERS AND MANAGEMENTS

If we are to design a superior system of corporate governance we need to look at the justified and necessary requirements of both owners and managers.

5.3.1 *The Interests of Owners*

First, let us consider owners. All classes of owners are fundamentally interested in the highest achievable long-term returns. Individuals owning 20 per cent of shares in Britain and 30 per cent in America are advised not to invest in equities unless they have a time horizon of five to six years. Those investing in unit trusts (mutual funds) or investment trusts have a rather longer time horizon, perhaps 7–10 years. For pension funds and insurance companies the time horizons for their investors, clients and policy holders are typically 15 years or more. A weighted average of these time horizons would be in the region of 8–10 years, but as I have already pointed out, paradoxically, we have a system which imposes at most 2–3 year pressures on investment institutions, i.e. the period over which most fund managers have to perform to retain clients. Indeed, many are now required to perform over much shorter periods. This in turn puts a similar time pressure on boards of directors and explains why their performance incentives are nearly always short-term. *It is this process which institutionalizes short-termism.* Thus the true long-term needs of the ultimate owners of the investment institutions, or of the funds which the institutions invest, are not well served by our present system. The pressure for short-term performance which competing investment institutions put on fund managers is in direct contradiction to the fundamental interests of the ultimate beneficiaries. This should not be acceptable to any of the parties concerned.

The investment institutions value highly their present freedom constantly to change their investment portfolios, but this freedom is illusory for two reasons. First, in practice it is only the freedom to earn less than the Continentals regularly achieve over any recent decade (Eltis, Fraser, and Ricketts 1992 and Drucker 1991). Second, most institutions effectively own such a wide portfolio of shares that they have interests on both sides of most takeovers. They thus cannot gain takeover premiums unless it can be shown conclusively that there is an overall net benefit from takeovers in aggregate. There is no overwhelming evidence for such benefits in Britain and, of course, our overall corporate and economic performance falls significantly short of the best Continentals. (There is slightly better evidence of net takeover gains in the United States and corporate returns are higher than in Britain but well below Japan and its near neighbours.) If in fact institutions cannot sell out of shares on a significant scale, then they ought to care for the underlying performance of their investments in a much more active way. One way or another they must collectively provide or procure effective, knowledgeable, proactive ownership. They must find the means to hold managements generally accountable for long-term performance and thus have the power to change them when necessary. It is very difficult to see how investment institutions can do this without procuring the appointment of some non-executive directors to represent their interests, directly and independently, on the boards of the main companies (Eltis, Fraser, and Ricketts 1992). I discuss this later.

Finally, owners should have a major say in the remuneration of senior management, especially when there is frequent criticism of excessive pay which is unrelated to performance, and when such incentives as do exist are mainly short-term. As investment institutions seldom play any part in appointing non-executive directors who largely influence pay, this requirement can only be met by their greater and more direct participation in corporate governance.

5.3.2   *The Interests of Managers (Directors)*

Under the present system, it is important to appreciate just how powerful and dominant chairmen and CEOs can be. They effectively appoint all their executive director colleagues who typically owe their past, their present, and, usually, their future to them, more particularly when the roles of chairmen and CEO are combined in one person. They also appoint the non-executive directors: hence they are extremely powerful. It is unease over this concentration of power which underlies the widespread view that the offices of chairman and CEO should not be combined in the same person.

The non-executive directors, because they are usually appointed by the chairman (and perhaps his senior executive colleagues), typically have little connection with either individual or institutional shareholders, and hence have neither independent support nor independent information about the company. For the latter they depend on their executive colleagues. It is fashionable to argue that these non-executive directors should take upon themselves all the burdens of controlling and monitoring their executive colleagues. Further, they are expected to do this for only modest remuneration, in case they have too much to lose from resigning when the situation requires it. Given that they are usually chosen and appointed by the chairman and have no link with or support from institutional shareholders, too much is expected of them.

Against this unsatisfactory background we can now consider what are the justified and necessary requirements of managers (here defined as senior managers, i.e. mainly the executive directors in Britain). First, they want conditions for internationally-competitive, optimal long-term performance. To get it they must have knowledgeable and committed long-term owners and the means of aligning their interests with that of owners. In other words they need a suitable form of 'owner-capitalism'. It is desirable that they should have appropriate incentives to achieve long-term performance such as exists with management buyouts (MBOs) and other venture capital investments which represent a particularly successful activity in both Britain and the United States (in contrast to Continental countries). Here, managers are typically required to invest and risk 1–2 years' salary, but a successful performance over 5 years or so could bring them 10–12 times these sums, with even higher rewards for exceptional performance.

If managers are to have such prospects, however, proper accountability to shareholders is essential. Indeed there are no generally successful systems of corporate governance where managers are not accountable. Too many prominent managers, when complaining of hostile takeovers, would like to see such takeovers severely restricted or even banned. At present this is the main form of accountability to shareholders. It may be rough, expensive, and often arbitrary, but it cannot be abandoned or reduced until something better is put in its place.

5.4 THE BRITISH SYSTEM FAILS TO SATISFY OWNERS OR MANAGERS

To sum up the present position, our system of corporate governance fails to meet the long-term interests of both owners and managers. In many years investment institutions fail to equal even the performance of the stock indices. (See Barry Riley, *Financial Times*, 20 April 1990 for Britain, and Jacobs (1991) for America). In short, we have a system under which everybody loses. It is a system fault, however, and it is quite capable of being remedied, providing the fault is recognized, and there is the will to change it.

Many schemes are currently under consideration in Britain and America to overcome the system fault, but few are very satisfactory because they do not comprehensively address all the difficulties. I turn now to my own detailed proposal which I have tested out on a number of knowledgeable people on both sides of the Atlantic. I believe it addresses all the main issues and commend it for consideration.

5.5 A RADICAL AND COMPREHENSIVE PROPOSAL: A COMPACT BETWEEN OWNERS AND MANAGERS

5.5.1 *The Proposal in Outline*

My proposal is for a radical compact between owners and managers, or to define it more precisely, a compact between institutional owners and executive directors, starting with the top 100 companies. (Most of what follows applies essentially to British conditions. Later on I comment briefly on its adaptation to American conditions.) In outline I propose that the executive directors and institutional shareholders should negotiate 5–7 year performance-targets. The executive directors would be required to risk 1–2 years' salary. This would be forfeit for non-performance but could lead to very generous bonuses of, say, 10–12 times the salary for meeting performance, and to much higher rewards for exceptional performance. In return, executive directors would agree to accept 3–5 non-executive directors nominated by the investment institutions.

It would not be possible for all the major investment institutions to co-operate in selecting their own nominees for non-executive directors but I believe there should typically be 3–5 investment institutions taking a significant interest in each of the major companies and preferably holding say 15–20 per cent of the shares in a company between them (with a lesser shareholding in the very big companies). Each 'inner core' investment institution would appoint a non-executive director to the board of a company. (I shall call them 'shareholder directors'). Their task is to carry out the monitoring and target setting functions. To do this they will need the support of a secretariat in *each* of the investment institutions which appoint them. Executive directors would still be free to appoint other non-executive directors if they wished. Such directors would not have monitoring functions but would be appointed to help the executive directors to run the business better, and to negotiate and achieve their performance targets.

This major restructuring of boards of directors would greatly change and I believe improve, corporate governance. The chairman/CEO would no longer be an unduly dominant figure. Like every other executive director he would be chosen for his general competence to achieve long-term performance. If his contribution fell below standard it would be the strong, and indeed irresistible, wish of his executive colleagues (as well as the shareholder directors) for him to alter his performance, or as a final resort, step aside. When executive directors are risking sizeable sums, and have the hope of very substantial rewards, they will not countenance underperformance anywhere in the executive team. Thus, when executive directors choose to band together to negotiate a 5–7-year performance target, they will take the greatest care to have the best and strongest team they can find and the strongest self-discipline will prevail throughout their association.

5.5.2 *Partially Concentrating Investment Institutions to Take an Ownership Position in Major Companies*

I turn next to the procuring of 3–5 inner core investors for the major companies. In Britain there are around 60 major investment institutions which probably own rather more than half of the shares in the top 100 companies. They cannot each be expected to take a direct interest in each of the top 100 companies. If they are to perform the ownership function, they can do this only by splitting the responsibilities between themselves. If each investment institution were to appoint one shareholder director in 5–8 of the top 100 companies, this would suffice to provide 3–5 shareholder directors per company. I believe that it is important to have 5 shareholder directors for the task rather than 3. If so, each investment institution would have to take an interest in, on average, 8 of the top 100 companies. It is desirable that these inner core investors, should between them hold 15–20 per cent of the shares of the companies in which they are active, although for the very large companies this might be only around 8–10 per cent.

The inner core investors would be making a 5–7-year implied commitment to the companies in which they invested although they would have to be free to recommend any takeover bid which seemed likely to offer better value than continuing with the 5–7-year plan. If the ownership burden was split in the way I have suggested—and I realize I am talking about the general adoption of the system although I fully recognize it would have to start in quite a small way—each of the top 60 investment institutions would still be free to deal freely in 92 per cent of the companies. In other words, they would have almost the same investment freedom as exists at present. However, all of the top 100 companies would have effective owners because 5 active shareholders would be appointing shareholder directors to each company.

There is nothing new in the idea of sharing the burdens of ownership. It has been practised in the international mining industry for over a century where frequently four or five companies have an interest in a mine but one of them assumes the management responsibilities. This same system is found in the international oil industry, particularly on the large and risky exploration blocks, where there are many owners but one company has the responsibility for being the operator.

5.5.3 *Providing the Part Time Directors for the New Roles*

The shareholder directors would need to be businessmen of wide experience. This should be apparent when one considers the very large responsibilities they would be assuming. It would be their task to agree the 5–7-year performance targets and to assess the executive directors (senior management team), to ensure they were fully experienced and competent for the role. These tasks require judgement of a high order. In addition, they would have to agree the executive directors' remuneration and incentives. They would thus have to take on the responsibility for the board audit and executive directors' remuneration, i.e. all the main monitoring functions. To help them discharge these responsible tasks each director would need to be backed up by a suitably staffed secretariat in the investment institution which had appointed him. Thus each investment institution should have a secretariat specializing in all that could be publicly known about the 8 companies in which it was an inner core investor. Thus each of the 5 shareholder directors would have independent advice. This, plus the inside information they would glean from their directorship duties, should make them well informed and together fully capable of dealing on equal terms with the executive directors.

The shareholder directors would typically have to give 30–40 days a year to their duties which would be much greater than is asked of most non-executive directors under the present system. Accordingly they should be much better paid than non-executive directors in the top 100 companies who are now paid (say £15,000 to £20,000) for typically only a 10–15-day annual commitment. Neither the shareholder directors nor the members of the secretariats should be allowed to deal in the shares of the companies with which they are involved. Hence, there must be a 'Chinese Wall' between the shareholder directors and their secretariats taken together, and the fund managers of the investment institutions concerned. By this means there would be informed shareholder directors but no abuse of power or inside information. (It is also desirable and probably essential for an investment institution's secretariat to be housed in a separate location from the institution.)

The proposal would not work well if one or more of the 5 core investment institutions were completely to sell out of a company in which they nominated a shareholder director (save in a takeover). However, by isolating their shareholder director and the secretariat, they could add or subtract from their core shareholding if such action were deemed generally acceptable to the representative bodies of the institutional investors.

It might cost say £250,000 to £300,000 annually to run a secretariat within an investment institution to support 8 shareholder directorships in the 8 companies. The 2–3 investment analysts involved would be expected to be familiar with all publicly available knowledge on the companies concerned, including research papers. They would liaise with and support their institution's shareholder director appointees thus giving them both support and an informed independent view. The benefits, if the system were widely applied, would be considerable by leading to significantly higher long-term returns, and would greatly outweigh the cost. However, the benefits would arise for all shareholders, whether private or institutional. Accordingly, it would be appropriate for an annual charge to be made for say £30,000 to £40,000 to the company on whose board a shareholder director sat.

Finally, it should be noted that, the role of a shareholder director should be an attractive and challenging role to suitably experienced businessmen. There should be no shortage of candidates. Because of the time commitment involved it would probably appeal most to senior businessmen in the last ten years of their career. The need to appoint 500 shareholder directors would not mean finding 500 people because on average most candidates for the role might be expected to take on two or, occasionally three, such directorships. Hence, in practice, no more than 250 individuals would be needed. Further, a majority of the necessary suitable candidates are already non-executive directors of major companies. They already have the necessary competence, but under the proposal would have the independence, knowledge, and support to discharge their duties much more effectively.

Lastly, I consider the role of the other part-time directors, those to be appointed by the executive directors. There would be no requirement to appoint such directors: that would be up to the executive directors. They would choose any such part-timers for their knowledge, imagination and business acumen. In short, they would help to formulate the 5–7-year performance plan and then help accomplish it. Like the full-time executive directors they too would risk 1–2 years' fees and participate pro rata in the bonus incentive scheme. Their fees would reflect their worth to their executive colleagues in achieving the 5-year plan and carrying conviction with the shareholder directors. Such fees would often and deservedly be much higher than the typical non-executive director fees currently paid. In sum, these part-time directors would be quite distinct from the shareholder directors and would have no specific monitoring functions, although in common with all other directors they would retain general responsibility to act in the best interest of the company and its shareholders. I believe such directorships would be a much more challenging and rewarding role than present non-executive directorships, and again there should be no shortage of candidates. Many able businessmen who are not attracted to the role of non-executive directors at present would find part-time directorships on the proposed terms particularly attractive. They could be expected to add significantly to overall, long-term corporate performance.

5.5.4 *Adapting the Proposal to the United States*

The proposal as put forward for Britain requires adaptation for the somewhat different conditions in the United States. There, the same concentration of shareholdings in the top 100 (or 500) companies does not exist. Lorsch (1991) points out that one of the largest state pension funds owns less than 1 per cent of the shares in any one company in its large corporate investment (whereas in Britain this would more probably be 3–5 per cent). This in part underlies his previously quoted view that 'real ownership of most of the equity in America's corporations is impossible'. It is of course correct that direct ownership is impossible unless US investment institutions either reduce the number of their holdings or procure ownership by other means. As mentioned above (section 5.2.1) it would be feasible greatly to reduce the number of holdings with little effect on risk. If that route is not widely acceptable—and there could be high, perhaps prohibitively high transaction costs in condensing the very large number of investment portfolios concerned—then two other routes are possible. First, as Jacobs has suggested (1991) one could set up special investment management intermediaries looking after only 15 stocks and taking the same active interest in corporate governance as in my proposal. These special firms could be partly new firms set up by individuals with the right experience, and partly investment co-operatives set up by the investment institutions themselves. Competition would soon identify the most competent. Second, following a suggestion of Gilson and Kraakman (1990) the main investment institutions could co-operate to appoint independent directors to all major corporations and to put particular pressure on underperforming companies. There may well be other routes that would achieve the same effect (see in particular

University of Chicago Law Review 1991). But as Jacobs (1991) has aptly remarked, 'Somehow a class of investors should be created which is interested in corporate governance.'

It is interesting to note that all of these US proposals are based on similar principles to my own proposals and those implicit in many other contributors to the corporate governance debate. It suggests a welcome and reassuring convergence of proposed remedies.

5.5.5   The Effect on Fund Managers

The adoption of proposals on the lines I have outlined would eventually lead to changed terms of reference for many fund managers. As companies agreed 5-year performance targets with their shareholder directors, and as the threat of hostile takeovers would then be much reduced (see 5.6.4 below) it would no longer be appropriate to appoint fund managers as at present for very short terms only. Much longer terms would be appropriate and thus remove one of the chief causes of short-termism. Further, many fund managers could well come to specialize in highly selective portfolios of 20–50 companies about which they were very knowledgeable. Well run, such funds should offer better long-term returns and be welcomed by investment institutions. In Charkham's words (1991), there would be more 'type A' fund managers, a development much to be welcomed.

5.5.6   Interests of Owners Versus Other Stakeholders

I would like to make a final point. A number of contributors to the corporate governance debate believe the present system in Britain and the United States should be changed to include the other main stakeholders (customers, creditors, and employees). This, it is argued, would bring the two countries more into line with the systems of many of the more successful Continentals, particularly Japan. This is a tenable viewpoint. My own view is that by far the most serious weakness in British and American corporate governance is the absence of effective knowledgeable, owners who can take the long-term view and hold management to account. If this is done the interests of other significant stakeholders would be very much improved, and would be sufficient change to make in corporate governance for the forseeable future.

5.6   CONCLUSIONS

5.6.1   Widespread Appeal

I believe that the form of corporate governance I have outlined should appeal to executive and non-executive directors alike, and also to investment institutions. There should be no shortage of suitable candidates for either form of part-time directorship because the roles would be much more satisfactory, stimulating, challenging and rewarding than typically exist at present.

5.6.2 Need for Experiments

I believe there could be no improvement in the roles and effectiveness of directors, whether executive or non-executive, without major corporate governance changes, broadly along the lines I have set out. I believe the proposals now need expert study by investment institutions, directors, and their major representative institutions. There is a need for experiments to prove whether the system would work well and to find out what practical changes and improvements may be needed. Major improvements in corporate governance cannot be expected to come from study, conferences, and investigative bodies alone. They are the necessary first steps, but, as with all important changes, we need practical experiments. If the proposed system, or a modified version of it, is seen to work satisfactorily it should spread rapidly by example. If only 10–12 major investment institutions were to give it vigorous support its adoption should be assured.

5.6.3 The Most Likely Initial Company Candidates

The most eager initial candidates for the proposed compact system would be those companies who feel themselves particularly handicapped by the undoubted short-termism in British and US industry, mainly in manufacturing, construction, and high technology. It is no coincidence that the relative decline of these industries has been most marked in the last ten to twenty years. The other eager potential candidates would be firms fearing hostile takeover bids who would like to give themselves a chance to achieve long-term performance and whose senior management would be willing both to be held accountable and to risk significant sums in return for the prospect of serious reward. Finally, by giving management attractive, long-term incentives it obviates the need for most corporate buyouts.

5.6.4 Reducing Hostile Takeovers and Protectionist Mergers

It is important to note that the adoption of the proposals will reduce but not eliminate hostile takeovers. I would emphasize that I am not against a free market in corporate control but I am convinced that it would be much more effective when applied under a strong, efficient, and *knowledgeable* system of corporate governance, the basic ingredient of any efficient market. (A major weakness in the case for leaving it to the takeover markets is the lack of such knowledge among investors). The adoption of the proposal would also reduce and probably eliminate cosy protectionist mergers. As in the case of takeovers, a management would have to convince its shareholder directors that a merger was in the interests of its company and shareholders and not of management comfort or aggrandizement. In all these cases the executive directors (senior managers) would have to agree mergers, takeover bids, or defences with their own knowledgeable shareholder directors. If the latter were overruled, it would be likely that at the subsequent meeting of shareholders which would be called, the views of the shareholder directors would typically be backed, not only by the 5 institutions providing the directors, but by most other investment institutions. In these conditions the abuse of management power should become comparatively rare, and takeovers and mergers largely confined to those cases where genuine and substantial benefits would be likely.

5.6.5   No Direct Government Role

I see no need for direct government involvement, i.e. no need for legislation to force the new system to come to pass: but government encouragement would be welcome. The present British Government widely supports a free market in corporate control but it needs to recognize that our present system of corporate governance is clearly insufficient to deliver internationally-competitive, long-term performance. The same argument applies to the Federal and State Governments in the United States.

5.6.6   Enhancing Long-term International Competitiveness

I believe the proposals would provide Britain with the pre-conditions for greatly enhanced long-term performance. It would provide a system from which all the main participants would gain. The same would follow from suitably adapted proposals for the United States.

Long-term corporate efficiency is ultimately the main determinant of national economic efficiency and hence of international political influence. The relative economic decline of British and US industries (particularly in manufacturing and high technology) can be expected to continue unless we fundamentally improve our system of corporate governance. That improvement is readily achievable if we recreate the fundamental characteristics of the corporate governance of our heydays. Such features are the main characteristics present in MBOs and the venture capital industry as a whole, and the same as enjoyed by our Continental rivals. To repeat, there are no generally successful systems of corporate governance without committed and knowledgeable *long-term* shareholders, managements with the pre-conditions and incentives for long-term performance, and with such managements being properly accountable to their shareholders. If Britain and the USA want optimal long-term performance one of the most important preconditions is a major reform of corporate governance to build in long-termism. If in so important a matter this is not done by co-operation between senior corporate managements and investment institutions, then as Charkham and Riley remind us (see opening quotations) other economic or political entities may step in to fill the gap. The choice is ours.

REFERENCES

Charkham J. P. (1991), 'A Larger Role for Institutional Investors', NEDO Conference, 21–22 November.

Davies, E., and Kay, J. (1990), 'Corporate Governance, Takeovers and the Role of the Non-Executive Director', *Business Strategy Review*, Autumn.

Drucker, P. F. (1991), 'Reckoning with the Pension Fund Revolution', *Harvard Business Review*, March–April.

Economist, The (1990), 'Punters or Proprietors? A Survey of Capitalism', 5 May.

Eltis, W., Fraser, D., and Ricketts, R. (1992), 'The Lessons for Britain from the Superior Performance of Germany and Japan,' *National Westminster Quarterly Bank Review*, February.

Gilson, J., and Kraakman, R. (1990), 'Re-inventing the Outside Director: An Agenda for Institutional Investors', working paper no. 66, August (J. M. Olin Program in Law and Economics, Stanford Law School, Stanford, Calif.).

Ishihara, S., and Prestowitz, C. (1991), 'America and Japan: Forget Pearl Harbour', *The Economist*, 30 November.

Jacobs, M. (1991), *Short-Term America: The Causes and Cures of Business Myopia* (Harvard Business School Press, Cambridge, Mass.).

Lipton, M. and Rosenblum, S. A. (1992), 'A New System of Corporate Governance: The Quinquennial Election of Directors', *University of Chicago Law Review*, 58/1, Winter.

Lorsch, J. W. (1991), 'Real Ownership is Impossible', *Harvard Business Review*, November–December.

Sykes, A. (1990), *Corporate Takeovers: The Need for Fundamental Rethinking* (David Hume Institute, Edinburgh).

—— (1900b), 'Corporate Governance: Bigger Carrots and Sticks', *Financial Times*, 31 October.

—— (1991), 'The Lessons of Venture Capital Financing for Quoted Companies', *Venture Capital Report*, June.

6

The Changing Relationship Between the Banks and Business in the UK

DOUGLAS MCWILLIAMS and ANDREW SENTANCE

6.1 INTRODUCTION

A recession imposes strains on the relationships between banks and their business customers. Yet the extent of the strains that were revealed during 1991–2 in the UK have no parallel in recent memory.[1] Moreover, these concerns have emerged despite the fact that UK banks' profits have been weak and (before the flurry in April 1992 caused by bid speculation) banks' shares have substantially underperformed the main stock-market indices.[2] By contrast, in the 1979–81 recession there was less apparent dissatisfaction despite banks' profits reaching levels that encouraged the imposition of a special levy on their current account assets in the 1981 Budget.

Some of the discussion of these strains has drawn attention to the changed role of the banks in the 1980s in the light of financial deregulation. But there has been no attempt to relate these changes to those in the structure of UK business in the 1980s.

Our contention is that it is not so much the changed structure of the UK banking system, but rather the interaction between that and the changed structure of their business customers, which has had an important influence on recent developments.

This chapter looks first at the developments in UK banking since 1980 and then at changes in the structure of UK business over the same period. It then discusses the interaction between the changes in the financial system and those in the structure of business, and the consequences of this interaction for relationships between banks and their business customers.

6.2 DEVELOPMENTS IN BANKING AND BUSINESS IN THE 1980s

Though progress has been obscured by the current recession, the performance of the UK economy improved in the 1980s, in comparison both with

---

[1] A valuable summary of these strains and the banks' responses is given in 'The Availability of Bank Credit and Interest Rates', House of Commons Treasury and Civil Service Committee 6th Report 1990–1 Session July 1991.

[2] e.g. in the 5 years between 1 Jan. 1987 and 1 Jan. 1992 on a capital issues adjusted basis UK banks' shares have fallen by 36.6% against the UK stock-market. Source: IndEC data from London Economics (MES) Ltd.

Fig. 6.1. Growth in GDP per capita (% annual average increase). *Source*: OECD National Accounts

other countries and with its record of the recent past. Figure 1 shows that from 1980–90 the UK economy grew more rapidly than the average of both the European Community and the OECD countries. Comparisons of this type are sensitive to the time period chosen. However, the economic cycles which distort these comparisons affect all industrialized countries. Although the UK economy grew in the 1980s no faster than in the 1960s, the world economic background in the 1980s was much less favourable. It is this improvement in relative performance that is most impressive. Three key factors which contributed to this growth performance were:

1. Deregulation of financial services, which contributed to rapid growth in this sector and broadened access by other sectors to financial instruments.
2. An underlying improvement in profitability and productivity, particularly in UK manufacturing industry.
3. The establishment of many smaller companies, which contributed strongly to employment growth in the late 1980s.

These factors have also had a significant impact on the relationship between banks and business.

6.2.1 *Changes in the Banking Sector*

Critical to the changes in the banking sector in the 1980s was the deregulation of UK financial services. The key changes of relevance to the relationship between UK retail banks and their customers were:

1. The abolition of foreign exchange controls in 1979, which greatly widened the opportunities for foreign lending into the UK and for lending overseas from the UK.
2. The removal of the 'corset' in 1980, which had restricted the interest-bearing eligible liabilities of banks.
3. The abolition of hire purchase controls on consumer credit in 1981.

4. The ability of the building societies, from 1983, to raise funds through certificates of deposit and large time deposits, followed in 1986 by dereg- ulation of asset holdings as a result of the Building Societies' Act.
5. The breakdown of the building societies' interest rate cartel and the entry of the clearing banks into the UK mortgage market.
6. The breakdown of the informal rules preventing equity withdrawal by which borrowers could use their homes as security for borrowing for other purposes.

In addition, the widely publicized 'big bang' changes to the London stock- market in 1986 affected the structure of UK financial services activity, although their direct impact on the relationship between banks and their customers was much less than that of the changes listed above.

The developments listed above mainly affected the scope for personal borrowing. Of more relevance to business—particularly large businesses— has been the globalization and liberalization of international financial mar- kets. Companies are now faced with a wide range of new financial instruments (swaps, options, convertibles, futures, etc.), which are products of the innovation and globalization of the financial markets.

One consequence of the process of deregulation was an expansion of bank lending. Total bank lending to UK residents rose from £55 bn. at the end of 1979 to £414 bn. ten years later. Even after adjusting for the inclu- sion of Abbey National plc in the bank lending figures during 1989, this still represents an average real increase of over 13 per cent per annum over the decade. The ratio of bank lending to GDP rose from 32 per cent at the end of 1979 to 89 per cent of GDP (excluding Abbey National) at the end of 1989. Since 1989, bank lending has risen roughly in line with GDP.[3]

However, the most rapid expansion over this period was in lending to the personal sector rather than to business. As a result, lending to business as a proportion of total bank lending fell from 69.8 per cent in November 1980 to 52.6 per cent in May 1989 (see Table 6.1). The main shift in the composition of lending took place in the first half of the 1980s—the share of lending to the personal sector expanded from 14.3 per cent in November 1980 to 24.3 per cent in November 1985 while the share of lending accounted for by manufacturing industry fell from 27.6 per cent to 16.2 per cent over the same period.

There are a number of reasons why it would be wrong to interpret this trend as a withdrawal of bank support for industry and commerce.

First, the decline in the share of bank lending going directly to business was partly offset by increases in leasing and lending to security dealers. These increases partly reflect changes in the methods of obtaining finance, rather than a decline in total amount of finance available. Over the 1980s

---

[3] Various *Bank of England Quarterly Bulletins* and *The CSO Blue Book* (1991 Edition).

Table 6.1.   *UK bank lending to UK residents: % of total bank lending, amounts outstanding*

Sector	1980 November	1985 November	1989 May	1989* August	1991 November
Manufacturing	27.6	16.2	13.0	12.5	10.8
Agriculture Forestry & Fishing	5.0	3.5	1.9	1.8	1.5
Energy and Water	2.6	2.9	1.2	1.2	1.4
Construction	3.7	3.0	3.8	3.6	3.5
Services			28.7	27.1	27.4
	30.9	30.6			
Leasing			4.0	3.8	5.2
TOTAL	69.8	56.2	52.6	50.0	49.8
Securities etc.	—	—	5.0	4.8	7.5
	15.8	19.7			
Other Financial			18.0	16.1	14.7
Persons	14.3	24.1	24.3	28.9	28.0

* Inclusion of Abbey National plc added £27.4 bn. to bank lending to persons, increasing the total by 7.4%.
Source: Bank of England Quarterly Bulletin, various issues.

the proportion of investment in machinery and equipment that was financed by leasing rose from 5.9 per cent in 1980 to 16.3 per cent in 1989 before falling back slightly to 13.8 per cent in 1990.[4] Meanwhile increased borrowing by securities dealers and stockbrokers is likely to have facilitated companies' raising of capital through issuing securities.

Second, in relation to business activity, lending to business continued to rise during the 1980s (although it has fallen back during 1991). Table 6.2 shows that bank lending to business (including leasing) as a proportion of GDP rose from 23.2 per cent in 1980 to 49.2 per cent in 1990. Although bank lending to manufacturing industry rose by less than lending to other sectors Table 6.3 shows that lending rose in relation to value-added even in that sector, as well as in construction and distribution.

Moreover, the reports from companies themselves in the 1980s do not appear to indicate any difficulty in obtaining finance. Indeed, throughout the 1980s, the proportion of manufacturing companies citing, in their responses to the CBI Industrial Trends Survey, an inability to raise finance as a constraint on investment at no point exceeded 4 per cent. This compares with between 40–50 per cent of respondents citing the rate of return

[4] *The CSO Blue Book* (1991 Edition).

Table 6.2.   *Bank lending to business as % of GDP*

Year	Manufacturing	Construction	Services	Leasing	Total*
1980	8.7	1.2	8.8	1.1	23.2
1985	8.9	1.7	15.5	2.2	33.0
1986	8.9	1.7	15.2	2.4	32.7
1987	8.3	2.0	16.5	2.8	33.6
1988	10.1	2.7	19.7	2.8	39.3
1990	11.4	3.6	25.5	4.6	49.2
1991	10.4	3.3	24.7	4.9	47.7

* Total excludes persons and finance (except leasing)
Source: Bank of England Quarterly Bulletin.

Table 6.3.   *Bank lending by sector as % of value added*

Year	Manufacturing	Construction	Distribution
1980	33.1	19.3	29.0
1985	37.4	28.3	54.8
1986	37.4	28.0	53.5
1987	35.1	30.2	55.2
1988	43.4	37.6	57.2
1989	50.7	46.8	66.2
1990	50.7	48.0	63.6

Source: Bank of England Quarterly Bullet, The CSO Blue Book (1991).

as a constraint, and between 30–50 per cent citing uncertainty about demand over the same period.[5]

While banks were finding new ways of lending to their personal sector customers as a result of the deregulation of the UK financial services industry, global deregulation and financial innovation allowed large companies to tap the securities markets at less than the cost of borrowing from banks.

Table 6.4 shows how bank borrowings fell as a proportion of total liabilities outstanding for large companies (see the table for a definition of this term) from 64.3 per cent in Q4 1987 to 55.6 per cent in Q4 1990. Table 6.5 shows how for the whole industrial and commercial companies sector the net financing requirements were increasingly met during the 1980s and early 1990s from a range of sources—shares, debentures, preference shares, and overseas capital issues. From 1980–86 the sector's borrowing from the banks was roughly equal to its net financing requirement; from 1987–91

[5] *CBI Economic Situation Reports*, various issues.

Table 6.4 *Large firms'* liabilities* (£bn.)

Period	Total liabilities (1)	Bank borrowing (2)	Issues of commercial paper	Other	(2)/(1) %
87Q4	26.6	17.1	1.6	7.9	64.3
88Q4	37.7	24.4	3.3	10.0	64.7
89Q4	43.8	27.4	3.0	13.4	62.6
90Q4	46.8	26.0	4.1	16.7	55.6

* Companies with capital employed of more than £21.8 m. at end 1982 plus former public corporations which had become part of the company sector by the end of 1984

Source: Financial Statistics Nos. 339, 359, CSO.

Table 6.5. *Sources of finance for industrial and commercial companies* (£bn.)

Year	Net financing requirement	Bank borrowing preference	UK capital shares	Issue of debentures and preference shares	Overseas capital issues
1980	6.2	5.9	—	—	—
1981	3.4	3.3	—	—	—
1982	5.6	1.9	—	—	—
1983	0.0	1.6	1.9	0.6	0.0
1984	1.9	7.3	1.1	0.2	0.3
1985	8.4	7.5	3.4	1.6	1.2
1986	11.9	9.1	4.5	3.4	1.2
1987	26.4	12.2	13.4	3.6	2.2
1988	48.6	31.8	4.4	3.6	2.5
1989	51.6	33.1	1.9	5.6	7.7
1990	30.9	18.6	2.6	3.5	6.4
1991	20.7	−3.0	8.3	6.9	5.5

Source: Financial Statistics Nos 322, 339, 359; *Bank of England Quarterly Bulletin* 25: 2.

borrowing from banks made up only half of the net financing requirement. Indeed in 1991 UK industrial and commercial companies raised over £20 bn. from the capital markets and repaid £3 bn. of bank borrowing. The Bank of England commented that 'banks appear to have widened interest rate spreads in response to the increase in bad debt provisions resulting from the recession. This made capital issues a relatively more attractive source of funds for those companies able to borrow from the capital markets.'[6]

[6] *Bank of England Quarterly Bulletin*, 32/1 (February 1991), 39.

One of the consequences of these changes in the structure of bank lending has been the pressure on banks' profitability. As a consequence of the liberalization measures listed above, greater competition in the 1980s squeezed net interest margins, in particular on domestic lending. Margins (interest income as a proportion of interest earning assets) and spreads (the difference between the rate paid on interest bearing assets and on deposits) on domestic lending declined. Margins fell from 7 per cent in 1980 to 4 per cent in 1990. This was concentrated into two periods: between 1980 and 1983 as interest rates fell, margins declined although spreads increased; between 1987 and 1990 there were lower spreads due to greater competition for loans, in turn owing to lower margins on mortgage lending and on lending to large companies and due to changes in the deposit mix on the liabilities side (*BEQB* November 1991). In addition costs did not decline, as retail branch networks have been maintained and there was a greater reliance on labour intensive fee-generating activities.

A factor enhancing banks' interest in their personal sector customers in the 1980s has been the growing excess capacity of bank branches. The chief executive of Lloyds Bank, Mr Brian Pitman, has been widely quoted as saying that the UK in April 1992 had twice as many bank branches as necessary.[7]

This is the result of technology having reduced the need to use cash or to go to a bank branch to obtain cash. These excess branches have typically been situated in High Streets or near offices. UK banks have responded by attempting to keep these branches profitable through selling other financial products such as life assurance to personal sector customers.[8] Nevertheless, the most stable and successful sources of non-interest income have continued to be fees and commissions from more traditional banking services to corporate customers. There has in effect been cross-subsidization by the corporate sector of the personal sector which has enabled banks to market a broader range of fee-generating products to their customer base (*BEQB* November 1991).

Thus the twin themes of UK retail banking in the 1980s emerged: an increasing focus on personal sector customers, perceived to be the most dynamic element of the customer base and the market with the most potential to raise the profitability of the excess branches, while large business customers increasingly looked to the markets to satisfy their capital requirements. The priority attached by banks to business lending and their business customers over this period weakened.

---

[7] *The Economist*, 2 May 1992, 117.
[8] By 1991 all the main English banks had created or acquired an insurance subsidiary or joint venture.

6.2.2 Changes in the Business Sector

While the banking sector adjusted to the impact of deregulation and globalization, the UK non-financial business sector was also forced to adjust its behaviour sharply in the 1980s. The pressures imposed on many businesses as a result of the sharp financial squeeze in the recession in the early 1980s forced them to improve their financial management through achieving significant improvements in productivity and profitability. The improvement was most marked in the manufacturing sector. During the 1980s, UK manufacturing productivity increased at roughly the same rate as Japan and at double the rate of other EC competitors.[9] Profitability in the manufacturing sector also improved relative to other countries. For example, CBI estimates suggest that the adverse gap between UK and West German rates of return on capital was closed from 25 per cent in the 1975–80 period to just 5 per cent in 1988 before the recession of the late 1980s and early 1990s.[10]

These developments in manufacturing industry were part of a general trend. The rate of return on capital registered by non-oil UK industrial and commercial companies rose from 3 per cent in the cyclical trough of 1981 to 11 per cent at the peak of the cycle in 1988 before falling back to 7 per cent in the cyclical trough of 1991.[11]

Improvements in profitability were combined with cautious financial management in the early 1980s. Industrial and commercial companies were in financial balance or ran a financial surplus in every year from 1980–7. Although opportunities for acquisition and overseas investment caused these companies to run net financing requirements later in the decade, over the period 1980–90, the financial deficit averaged only 1.2 per cent of GDP.[12]

The improvement in profitability and productivity was associated with a new-found confidence on the part of British management, which has endured despite the recent recession. This confidence encouraged companies to adopt a less deferential attitude to their traditional financiers and to diversify their sources of finance. The effect has been to reinforce the breakdown of established relationships which was already in train as the result of financial innovation and increased competition.

In the mid- to late 1980s, the trend towards financial caution was reversed, with industrial and commercial companies running net financing

---

[9] See the Report of the CBI Manufacturing Advisory Group 'Competing with the World's Best' (CBI 1991).
[10] Ibid.   [11] See CBI Economics Situation Reports.
[12] Table 6.5 and *The CSO Blue Book* (1991).

requirements of 6.7 per cent of GDP on average from 1987 to 1991.[13] This partly reflected the major investments and acquisitions of this period and partly 'distress borrowing' as companies found their revenues unexpectedly depressed by the recession.

The other important trend in the UK business sector during the 1980s was the establishment of many new businesses.

In 1989, companies employing fewer than 200 people accounted for 31.6 per cent of manufacturing employment and 24.4 per cent of manufacturing value-added compared with respectively 25.9 and 22.0 per cent in 1981 (see Table 6.6). The number of businesses registered for VAT rose by 29.4 per cent during the 1980s, with the rate of increase accelerating after 1985 (see Table 6.7). Trends in self-employment tell the same story: total self-employment in the UK in 1990 was, at 3.3 million, 65.5 per cent higher than in 1980 (see Table 6.8)

Table 6.6. *Contribution of smaller firms* to manufacturing employment and output*

Year	% Employment	% Output
1971	20.9	17.9
1975	21.9	18.0
1981	25.9	22.0
1982	26.7	22.6
1983	27.8	22.8
1984	30.3	24.6
1985	30.4	25.3
1986	30.6	24.7
1987	31.1	24.1
1988	31.2	24.1
1989	31.6	24.4

* Enterprises with fewer than 200 employees
Sources: Reports on the Census of Production.

The growth in the number of smaller firms was undoubtedly encouraged by the Government's perceived ideology and various policies such as the small-firm loan guarantee scheme set up in 1981; the enterprise zones launched in 1981; the freeports launched in 1983; and the Business Expansion Scheme, also introduced in 1983.[14] However, the fact that similar trends were emerging in other English-speaking countries suggests that deeper cultural factors may have been at work, such as increasing desire for freedom and flexibility.

[13] Table 6.5 and *The CSO Blue Book* (1991).   [14] Johnson (1991).

Table 6.7. *VAT registrations*

	Total businesses registered (millions)		New registrations (weekly)
	All	<£5 million turnover	
End 1979	1.29	1.28	306
End 1987	1.51	1.49	864
End 1989	1.67	1.66	1,700

Source: Department of Employment

Table 6.8. *Number of self-employed*

1980	2.0 million
1988	3.2 million
1989	3.3 million

Source: Department of Employment

6.3 BANK–BUSINESS RELATIONSHIPS

The changes in the structure of banking and businesses, outlined above, have led to three developments: the increasing concentration by banks on their personal sector customers; larger companies using the capital markets at home and abroad to raise finance; and a fragmentation of the business sector with an increasing proportion of activity and employment accounted for by small firms. The banks responded to these changes by expanding the range of services available to small and growing companies. By September 1991 95 per cent of NatWest's commercial customers were small businesses (defined as with a turnover of less than £1 million per annum, of which 85 per cent had a turnover of less than £100,000 per annum). Barclays quoted in January 1992 that nearly 80 per cent of their business customers had an annual turnover of less than £100,000.[15] However, this shift in the composition of their business lending portfolio had important implications which do not appear to have been fully appreciated at the time.

1. New and small firms are inherently more risky than large established firms, as the unprecedented scale of business failures during the current recession has confirmed.

[15] House of Commons Treasury and Civil Service Committee Third Report, 1991–2 Session, 'Banking Codes of Practice and Related Matters', Minutes of Evidence provided by National Westminster Bank plc and Barclays Bank plc.

2. Smaller firms need much more advice and support than banks have been traditionally accustomed to providing as part of their normal lending to business.

One consequence of this is that with hindsight banks appear to have been effectively providing a form of (albeit often secured) venture capital while charging loan rates that—though substantially higher than for prime borrowers—have been much lower than is usual for that form of finance.[16]

Evidence of this is provided by the report of the Treasury and Civil Service Select Committee of 1991–92 on Banking Codes. First, the Select Committee found that none of the banks scored well on the issue of performance monitoring; in other words not enough attention was paid to assessing the risk of the particular small business and varying the interest rate accordingly. Instead the Committee found that such policies towards smaller businesses were increasingly set at regional or head office level, rather than making use of information which might have been available at the local level.[17] The banks appeared to rely on collateral as an alternative to assessing the risk of an investment.

Second, the Select Committee found there had been an erosion of relationship banking during the 1980s. The ability of the individual branch manager to authorize lending decisions had been eroded over the last ten years due to the growing complexity of business arrangements which had led to a specialization of functions between different branch managers.[18]

Third, the Committee noted that 'the bulk of small business credit finance is in the form of overdrafts, and there is very little use of long term loan or equity finance' although in a survey it appeared that 'over a fifth used their facility to pay for fixed assets, which may well have been more appropriately funded by fixed term loans'.[19] Despite efforts to encourage equity funding, there has been a reluctance by both small companies and banks. Small companies see raising equity as ceding control to the bank. On the banks' side, the illiquidity of equity in small businesses and the uncertainty of returns on that capital has made them sceptical of the feasibility of taking equity in small companies.[20]

Surveys of CBI members, and other research findings, confirm that there are specific funding difficulties in the areas of loan and equity financing of less than £250,000 but particularly in the £50,000–£100,000 range; the supply of finance where returns take longer than five years to appear; and

---

[16] A study by Morgan Stanley showed that the average venture capital return to investors in the US in the period 1945–91 had been as much as 13.2% above the return on government bonds, *The Economist*, 4 April 1992, 142.

[17] House of Commons Treasury and Civil Service Committee Third Report, 1991–2 Session, 'Banking Codes of Practice and Related Matters', 7–9.

[18] Ibid. 57–8.   [19] Ibid., p. xix.   [20] Ibid. 55.

the provision of finance for new products or processes in which the firm lacks a track record.

To summarize, the fragmentation of the commercial client base and the increased use of the capital markets by the larger customers moved the banks in an unplanned direction towards higher risk lending. Moreover, the risks associated with the lending were closely correlated with each other because of their joint dependence on the economic cycle.

The problems associated with this emerged in the recession of the early 1990s. The major UK banks have had to increase their provisions for bad debts among smaller businesses. For example, Barclays have had bad debts in the business sector 'well in excess of £1 million a day during 1991'.[21] The Treasury and Civil Service Select Committee argued that the recession of the early 1990s had been marked out as different from the previous two in the greater extent of losses at the smaller business end of the market. This was leading to a reassessment by the banks of how to cater for small businesses' needs. For instance it is now the practice to distinguish growing businesses that need more sophisticated treatment from those that will stay within the remit of the branches.[22]

At the same time, concern has been registered by smaller firms themselves that the banks are being insufficiently supportive in hard times. While some of the more extreme allegations proved unfounded, this issue became sufficiently important to warrant the intervention of the Chancellor of the Exchequer in the summer of 1991. It has also led to the publication, by the major banks, of codes of practice to cover their dealings with business customers.

6.4 CONCLUSION

The relationship between the banks and their smaller business customers will need to be carefully managed as the economy moves from recession to recovery. For example, the report of the CBI Manufacturing Advisory Group, 'Competing with the world's best' concluded that:

There needs to be a more balanced relationship between banks and smaller companies. Unlike larger companies, smaller firms do not have access to competitive international financial markets. They are dependent to a large extent on the major clearing banks, which normally provide loans secured by means of a fixed and/or floating charge over the assets of the company. Because of the dependence on property as the main source of security, the lender often has a fairly limited appreciation of the nature of the business they are investing in. Over the long-term, this is bad for both the borrower and the lender, which has been reflected in the high levels of bad debts and business failures in the current recession.

[21] Ibid., 'Minutes of Evidence provided by Barclays Bank plc', 34.   [22] Ibid. 57–8.

The relationship between UK banks and their business customers is a key element in the provision of finance for investment and economic growth. In general, this relationship is a harmonious one although developments in the early 1990s have placed strains on it. But there is a mutual dependence—a strong, profitable, and internationally competitive UK business sector will provide by far the most attractive customer base for UK banks. Similarly UK business will benefit from a financially sound banking sector which is able to take a long-term view of its commitments and support its customers through hard times.

This article has sought to demonstrate that the problems emerging in banking–business relationships in the early 1990s were not simply the result of the recession. They stemmed from structural change in both business and financial markets. These strains will not disappear with recovery and the ability of banks and their customers to manage their relationships successfully in the years ahead will have an important bearing on the UK's future prosperity.

7

Small Firms and Clearing Banks

MILES MIDDLETON, MARC COWLING, JOHN SAMUELS, and
ROGER SUGDEN

7.1 INTRODUCTION

Concern over the relationship between small firms and their clearing banks
dates back many years. In 1991 it resurfaced as an important and pressing
consideration, accompanied and prompted by considerable media attention.
There is little doubt that the issues raised by the relationship are potentially
very significant for the future development of the British economy and
accordingly warrant detailed and careful consideration. With this in mind,
in July 1991 the Association of British Chambers of Commerce commis-
sioned this independent report.

This is, of course, an area of particular interest to Chambers of
Commerce and Industry: in numerical terms, all Chambers depend on a
membership base widely representative of the small business sector; while
equally the banks have traditionally played—and continue to play—a major
part in the work of Chambers of Commerce by the provision of people,
expertise, and resources, through sponsorship and other forms of material
help. It is therefore vitally important to Chambers of Commerce and
Industry that these two sectors of their membership should have a better
understanding than is evidently the case at the present time.

Our analysis of the situation is split into two substantive parts. The first
is a critical review of some existing literature. The aim of this is to identify
and focus upon the major concerns. The second is a survey of small firms
which are members of the Chambers of Commerce. The survey was carried
out in the light of our literature review and is designed to provide detailed
and up-to-date empirical evidence. Our findings are summarized in section
7.2, with sections 7.3 and 7.4 reporting extensively on the literature review
and small firms survey, respectively. Section 7.5 draws some tentative conclusions. Further details on the survey can be found in the appendix.

In examining the results of the survey, it is important to emphasize that
it is a survey of small business views—the banks themselves were not
consulted—and it is therefore quite clearly a one-sided picture of the relationship.

We would like to thank David Bailey for research assistance and Paul Hackett for computer
support. This draft is based upon a report prepared for the Association of British Chambers of
Commerce.

7.2 SUMMARY

7.2.1 *Review of Existing Literature*

- There are allegedly three fundamental characteristics which stand out for consideration: banks' market power, banks' short-termism, and the 'distance' that banks and small firms maintain in their relationship.

- It has been claimed that competition between banks is more superficial than real; even though a recent government report exonerated the banks from behaving as a 'quasi-cartel', their alleged market power remains a concern.

- There is arguably a gap in the availability of longer-term capital for small firms; associated with this, British banks have been criticized for not taking equity stakes in small firms.

- It has been said that banks and small firms have failed to develop a close relationship, for instance banks making little effort to understand trading conditions, banks applying a uniform policy, and firms giving banks inadequate information.

- Arguably rooted in these alleged characteristics, three more specific issues have caused particular worry: interest rates, other bank charges, and security levels.

7.2.2 *Survey of Small Firms*

- A questionnaire was posted to 1,500 Chambers of Commerce members in the South, the West Midlands, and Scotland; 261 of the respondents were identified as small firms.

- Asked about their most significant concern with existing bank practices, the most important responses were bank charges (25 per cent of respondents), amount of security (22 per cent) and interest rates (20 per cent).

- The bank's final decision on loan applications was made at the bank's regional branch/headquarters in 49 per cent of cases, with less than 40 per cent of decisions being taken at a local branch, and 6 per cent at a special small business branch.

- On their last loan application, 69 per cent had requested either new or increased overdraft facilities.

- Medium or long-term loans had been approved for 26 per cent of respondents.

- Of the firms surveyed, 77.3 per cent were paying less than 3 per cent above base rate, with the most common interest charge being at least 2 per cent but less than 3 per cent above base; 49 firms were paying a higher percentage over base on their most recent loan compared to their second most recent loan.

- Over 56 per cent of respondents had been required to provide security of at least twice the amount of loan, and only 6 per cent a ratio of less than one.
- Asked why they chose the method of bank finance that they did, 16 per cent said it was the only source available, 31 per cent it was the cheapest, 28 per cent that it would avoid outside interference; a further 13 per cent mentioned the avoidance of outside interference as one of several reasons.
- Long-term funding had never been considered by 49 per cent of respondents; of those that had, 83 per cent said it is available.
- Equity had never been considered as a source of long-term funding by 75 per cent of firms, and 67 per cent said that they would object to an equity stake being held by their banks. Asked why they would object, 33 per cent feared bank interference, 28 per cent loss of control and 13 per cent did not trust banks.
- It was felt to be very important by 69 per cent of respondents that banks 'know you and your business'; 49 per cent rated their bank's performance as good/fairly good in knowing them and their business.

7.2.3 Conclusions

- There is clear evidence that interest rates, other bank charges, and security levels remain an important worry for small firms.
- It appears that the recent and popular horror stories over interest rates represent a minority and are not the norm, though they are not necessarily unimportant.
- Our findings on security levels are of greater concern than our findings on interest rates; banks' requirements with regard to security levels need to be questioned.
- The evidence we offer on market power is thin and says little one way or the other.
- There appears to be a problem of short-termism and although the study can say little about the supply of long-term capital, our results are consistent with the view that both banks and small firms should reconsider their time horizons.
- Our evidence is consistent with an excessive distance in the small firm–bank relationship due to the wishes of both small firms and banks.
- We are left suggesting that the relationship between small firms and banks is sterile, uncommunicative and unimaginative.

7.3 REVIEW OF EXISTING LITERATURE

Recent popular discussion of the relationship between small firms and clearing banks has focused on the costs of finance, specifically the interest rates and other charges that banks are said to impose. However, extensive research over a longer period reveals that a deeper set of concerns needs to be addressed. More particularly, we suggest that there are three fundamental characteristics which stand out for consideration. These are banks' *market power*, banks' *short-termism*, and what can be called the *distance* that both banks and small firms maintain in their relationship. In addition and related to these alleged characteristics, there are several more specific issues worthy of attention.

7.3.1 *Market Power*

Some of the current small firm and clearing bank research is focused on the claimed lack of competition amongst banks. This is significant because the presence of market power would influence both the quality of services that banks offer clients, and the prices that they charge for such services.

Particularly interesting is the work of Binks, Ennew, and Reed (1988; 1989; 1990). From their extensive survey of small businesses in Autumn 1987, they have concluded 'that there is competition between banks, but only at a superficial or "cosmetic" level (advertising and promotions), with a high level of consensus/consistency in the underlying product provision, evaluation criteria, price setting, collateral requirements, charges, etc.' (Binks, Ennew, and Reed 1988). They see this lack of competition as reflected in small firms' lack of movement between banks, for instance.

Potentially against the market power hypothesis, however, the banks were exonerated[1] by a Treasury and Bank of England inquiry that had been ordered in June 1991 by the Chancellor of the Exchequer, Norman Lamont. The aim was to examine bank charges because the public needed to be satisfied that 'the banks are not behaving as a sort of quasi-cartel'.[2] Similarly, the Director General of Fair Trading, Sir Gordon Borrie, has also claimed that there was no evidence of a cartel or collusion between banks in their dealings with small firms.[3] Nevertheless, even if this is accepted, it is worth noting that market power can be manifested in various ways. Indeed the analysis in Binks, Ennew and Reed (1988) is in terms of banks' inability to compete, rather than their active pursuit of profit via a cartel or collusion (although this point is addressed somewhat superficially). Hence the allega-

---

[1] *Financial Times* (18 July 1991).
[2] Norman Lamont quoted in *Financial Times* (3 June 1991).
[3] *Financial Times* (28 June 1991).

tion of market power is very much on the agenda of fundamental concerns for small firms.

7.3.2 *Short-termism*

It is often alleged that there is a 'gap' in the availability of longer-term capital for smaller firms. This would imply that finance provision is biased towards companies with high current and historical profit levels, and against dynamic small firms with long-term prospects.

The Wilson Committee (1979) noted that long-term lending by banks to small firms was virtually non-existent. Things have changed since then but there remains at least considerable concern over this issue in the 1990s, even though NEDC (1986) claimed that the position had changed in the first half of the 1980s and even though Aston Business School concluded from its detailed survey in 1991 that small firms face few difficulties in obtaining finance. For example, Hall and Lewis (1988) refer to a 1987 CBI survey which apparently revealed problems in funding new products and processes in which smaller firms lacked a track-record. The survey claimed a shortage of 'patient money (for investments) where returns take longer than five years to appear'. Moreover it has been argued that banks will reduce or remove funding, or call in the receiver, in the case of small firms with good medium- and long-term prospects but with short-term difficulties (Binks, Ennew, and Reed 1990).[4]

It is also worthwhile to note that, in contrast to their counterparts in continental Europe, British banks have not supported small firms with equity stakes, inherently a source of long-term funding (Bannock 1981; Minns 1988). Relevant to this is the 1985 statement by the then Chancellor of the Exchequer, Nigel Lawson: 'there can be little doubt that the growth of new businesses has been hampered by the existence of the so-called "equity gap". It has been notoriously difficult to raise very small sums of equity, say between £20,000 and £50,000'.[5]

7.3.3 *Distance*

In various respects, it has been argued that banks and small firms fail to develop a close relationship. Indeed an aspect of this is seen to be the absence of long-term funding and equity involvement.

Another aspect is the claim that banks make little effort to understand firms' trading conditions. As Storey (1990) reports, for instance, it has been argued that a bank can require so much security that it sees no need to understand a firm! However this could have important implications. For example Binks, Ennew, and Reed (1990) conclude that

---

[4] See *Financial Times* (13 Nov. 1990).   [5] Contained in NEDC (1986).

greater access to information would change the nature of the criteria which banks apply to the assessment of firms by altering their perception of risk. Because the banks tend to use a limited information set on their customers, and in particular, fail to give full consideration to their managerial skills, trading conditions and constraints, they leave themselves little alternative but to apply standard capital valuations.

Central to this allegation is the view that banks apply a uniform policy throughout Britain and are unable to respond to specific circumstances in particular localities. For instance Bannock (1981) compares the decentralized German banking system very favourably to the highly concentrated British structure (see also Minns 1988). He points to the link between small German banks 'deeply rooted in local communities' and their disproportionate share of lending to small firms. He perceives the British system as less sensitive to local needs due to the sheer size of banks, and the 'remoteness of a few policy makers at the centre from the thousands of branch managers and assistant managers in the field'.

Having said this, however, concern over distance is not simply a potential problem with banks. The relationship between banks and small firms is necessarily a two-way affair and it is not at all clear that it is only banks who have maintained their distance. For instance, Storey (1990) argues that firms could help banks' understanding by providing complete funding proposals. This does not always happen; he suggests that firms could usefully consult accountants or others providing business advice to ensure that their funding proposals are genuinely informative. Similarly, it could be argued that small firms should give greater thought to raising equity finance.

7.3.4   *More Specific Issues*

Arguably rooted in these three alleged characteristics of the relationship between small firms and clearing banks, three more specific issues have caused particular concern: interest rates, other banks charges, and security levels. We will consider each in turn.

7.3.4(a)   *Interest Rates*

The Wilson Committee (1979) claimed that, on average, the interest rate charged to small firms was 2 per cent higher than that levied on large firms. Whilst a premium on bank lending to small firms is arguably inevitable—bearing in mind the higher likelihood of failure amongst small firms, the fixed-cost of assessing loan applications, and the monopsony power of large customers—Hall and Lewis (1988) note that 'the implication of the Wilson Report was that (the premium) was simply too high to be justified on these grounds'. This concern is echoed in Hall (1989), referring to a study by Churchill and Lewis (1985) of the costs and revenues of a US bank;

although its loans to small firms were in total relatively more costly and more risky than its loans to large firms, they generated more deposits and overall were more profitable.

Concern has also been expressed about the absolute level of interest rates. For example, Binks, Ennew, and Reed (1988) surveyed over 3,000 firms in 1987. Approximately 20 per cent cited interest rates as their most significant concern with existing bank practices. More recently, the focus of criticism has been on the alleged failure of banks to pass on cuts in base rates.[6]

7.3.4(b) *Other Bank Charges*

The only greater concern than interest rates reported by respondents to the Binks, Ennew, and Reed survey was bank charges; this was the most significant worry for 31 per cent of firms. Binks, Ennew, and Reed (1990) focus on various issues: the cost of bank charges, their unpredictability, and banks' failure to justify or explain their specific application. Worries over charges are also seen, for instance, in a 1988 report by *What to Buy for Business*.[7] Surveyed small firms complained that they had run up overdrafts because of unforeseen charges, had not been invoiced for charges, and that they were charged when others' cheques bounced.

7.3.4(c) *Security Levels*

The Wilson Committee (1979) believed that small firms were unfairly treated in the level of security that they had to provide. For example, it felt that security ratios (company net assets to borrowing) were excessive, in the range of $2:1$ to $3:1$. Likewise, for instance of the 25 firms that Binks and Vale (1984) investigated in detail, 15 had ratios of over $2:1$ (Hall and Lewis 1988).

Another claim is that banks are very cautious in their methods of calculating security. They rely on standard asset valuations. Assets tend to be valued at their so-called carcas value, that is, their minimum realistic resale price. This understates their value to production (Binks, Ennew, and Reed 1989). Banks caution is also indicated by the fact that security is measured in terms of asset cover rather than in terms of future cash generation. For young, fast-growing companies, this is a constraint.

---

[6] See, for example, *Financial Times* (3 June 1991) and the *Evening Standard* (5 September 1991).

[7] See *Financial Times* (4 October 1988).

7.4 SURVEY OF SMALL FIRMS

7.4.1 *General Background*

To explore major concerns over the relationship between small firms and their clearing banks, a survey was conducted using a questionnaire posted to 1,500 firms.

The questionnaire draws on the one used by Binks, Ennew, and Reed in their aforementioned work, carried out for the Forum for Private Business, and to a lesser extent on a related questionnaire used on other occasions by the Forum. This overlap in questionnaires facilitates comparison of results at different points in time and in different economic conditions. Certain modifications and new questions were introduced in order to throw light on issues emerging from our literature survey.

The questionnaires were posted on 1 August 1991 to a stratified sample of Chambers of Commerce members from three geographical areas: the South, the West Midlands, and Scotland. It was felt that these three areas would provide an interesting cross-section. Further details about our sample selection are contained in the appendix.

The response rate was relatively high at 18 per cent, a total of 269 firms. Of these, 8 fell outside our small firm definition, set at a firm employing up to 200 people. This definition conforms to that used by the Bolton Committee (1971) for small firms in manufacturing, and to the guidelines laid down by the National Federation of Self-Employed and Small Business. Responses from firms with over 200 employees have been excluded from the subsequent analysis. Response rates across geographical regions showed some discrepancy. Both the South and the West Midlands accounted for 37 per cent of small firm respondents, a total of 97 firms each, whilst Scotland accounted for 26 per cent, i.e. 67 firms.

Our feeling is that we have sufficient information to provide a worth-while analysis. Nevertheless care is needed, especially on five counts. First, we have only questioned firms, not banks. Clearly a full understanding of the relationship between small firms and banks requires an appreciation of the banks positions and views. Second, respondents to questionnaires of this sort tend to be those more conscious of and interested in their environment. This implies a disproportionate number of respondents; for instance, firms happy with their bank's performance are likely to be under-represented. Third, the excessive attraction to dissatisfied firms is likely to be exacerbated by the media attention given to banks' activities immediately before and during the implementation of the questionnaire. Fourth, the survey was not posted to a representative cross-section of all types of small firms: it was confined to Chambers of Commerce members. Fifth, although the response rate is good and respondents are spread across

Britain, the questionnaire was sent out to a limited number of firms in a limited number of areas.

7.4.2 Discussion of Results

The questionnaire grouped questions into four sets, labelled: general information, financing conditions, competition, and bank services. We will examine the responses under these headings and in general following the order in which questions were asked. In doing so we will refer to our earlier literature review, and to the 1987 Binks, Ennew, and Reed survey, henceforth denoted BER.

7.4.2(a) General Information

Easily the most common form of business organization answering the questionnaire is the private limited company. They account for 70.7 per cent of respondents.[8] Most of the other firms are fairly evenly distributed between proprietorships and partnerships. The dominant sectors in the survey are (non-financial) services (31.8 per cent), and manufacturing (29.8 per cent). All other specified areas of activity record figures of under 10 per cent. Approximately 80 per cent of respondents said that they currently employed up to 50 people. Among this 80 per cent, there is a uniform distribution of firms with 0–5, 6–10, 11–20, and 21–50 employees. Only 7 per cent of firms currently employed over 100. As for sales turnover, a mere 3.9 per cent reported sales of under £50,000, the median firm had sales of between £500,000 and £750,000, and 35 per cent of respondents had sales of at least £1 million. The age of firms is considerably skewed in favour of more established businesses. Over 40 per cent had been in business for over 15 years. This may reflect the focus on Chambers of Commerce members, many of whom are likely to be well-established local businesses.

Asked about their most significant concern with existing bank practices, far and away the most important categories were bank charges (25.1 per cent of respondents), amount of security (22 per cent), and interest rates (20.1 per cent). These are the three more specific issues raised in section 7.3; they are clearly causing small firms considerable worry. At the other extreme, only 2 firms expressed their major concern as being loan duration. This suggests that banks' alleged short-termism is not worrying their small firm clients, although this may be explained by firms' lack of experience with long-term funding. Firms will focus on constraints that they see; lack of experience with a product would suggest ignorance of any constraints implied by the product's absence.

---

[8] Unless otherwise stated, figures refer to those firms replying to a specific question. For instance, of the 259 firms replying to the business form question, 70.7% were private limited companies.

7.4.2(b)   *Financing Conditions*

We focused on the last occasion that a firm tried to obtain a bank loan (defined as a fixed term loan, new overdraft facility, or increased overdraft facility). Of the firms surveyed, 42.7 per cent last requested a loan in 1991, 31.8 per cent in 1990, and 24.3 per cent before 1990. Very interestingly, 49.1 per cent reported that the bank's final decision on the request was made at its regional branch/headquarters, less than 40 per cent of decisions being taken at a local branch and a mere 6.3 per cent at a special small business branch. This is consistent with the charge that banks are too centralized for small firms' needs, raising the issue of excessive distance in the small firm–bank relationship. Moreover there is some suggestion of increased centralization; our results compare to the BER finding that 29.9 per cent of decisions were made at the regional branch/headquarters level and 60.6 per cent by local branches.

There appears to be a bias towards shorter-term finance, 69.1 per cent of respondents citing requests for either new or increased overdraft facilities. Whether this is a result of banks' short-termism is unclear from this evidence. It could be that small firms, banks, or both are exhibiting short-termist preferences. In addition, the bias towards overdrafts may be explained by the purpose of the loans; 65.9 per cent required working capital and only 27.4 per cent were financing fixed assets. This may reflect the presence of a short-run problem, a recession, requiring a short-run solution. Another possibility could be that, because of the high real interest rates at the time, investment in longer-term assets was being postponed.

Over 85 per cent of loan requests were approved by banks, although among these 16.6 per cent were approved only after further negotiation and 5.5 per cent were rejected by the firms themselves. Only 11.1 per cent of requests were turned down by banks. This indicates that some form of finance is readily available to small firms but that initial loan conditions may be unsatisfactory for a significant minority. Of the loan requests that were refused by banks, the most common reason given was that of bankers' unfavourable comment, cited by 10 firms out of 37.

Of approved loans, one third were for amount of over £100,000. There was a distinct skew towards loans over £20,000, nearly 70 per cent falling into this category. This could be associated with the aforementioned skewed distribution in respondents' sales turnover.

The preference for overdraft facilities explains why 58.3 per cent said that their loan payback period was not fixed. Of the 70 firms reporting on a fixed payback, 26 recorded a period of under five years. In short, only 26.1 per cent of firms had medium- and long-term loans.[9] This is consistent with short-termism.

---

[9] That is, loans with payback period fixed at 5 years or more.

7.4.2(b)(i) **Interest Rates** The response to the questions on interest rates are interesting and of relevance to the current debate. Of the respondents, 77.3 per cent were paying less than 3 per cent above base rate, with the most common interest charge being at least 2 per cent, but less than 3 per cent, above base (see Table 7.1). This seems to be in line with the recent report from Treasury and Bank of England officials to the Chancellor of the Exchequer, Norman Lamont. Moreover the comparison with BER suggests a distinct downward shift in nominal percentages above base since 1987. This evidence tends to endorse the banks' position in recent debates. It also suggests that many respondents identifying interest rates as their most significant concern with existing bank practices may really be objecting to government macro-economic policy, i.e. too high base rates, rather than bank overcharging.

Table 7.1 *Interest rates paid*

BER		This survey	
Percentage above base	Percentage of respondents	Percentage above base	Percentage of respondents
0–2	7	$0 \geqslant$ <2	29.5
2–3	38	$2 \geqslant$ <3	47.8
3–4	42	$3 \geqslant$ <4	11.9
4–5	11	$4 \geqslant$ <5	3.8

Having said this 72 respondents were paying a different percentage over base on their most recent loan compared to their second most recent loan, and of these 49 were paying more. This presumably causes concern to some firms, at least.

7.3.4(b)(ii) **Security requirements** More than one in five respondents cited security as their main concern. To explore this issue, we have looked at the type of security required by banks, and at security ratios. No security was required in 21 per cent of cases but some degree of personal security was required in 38.7 per cent of cases. This is presumably a source of worry (although not necessarily a criticism of banks). Perhaps more interesting, however, are the responses on security ratios. Over 56 per cent of respondents had been required to provide security of at least twice the amount of loan, only 6 per cent a ratio of less than one. This appears to be quite different to BER, where 20 per cent seem to have had a ratio of at least two and over 60 per cent a ratio less than one. It suggests that the issues raised by the Wilson Committee (1979) have still not been addressed. What in fact appears to be happening is that banks are taking a lower percentage above base but are cutting off relatively riskier investments by demanding higher security. From a bank's point of view, with a depressed economy and increasing business failure, the move to higher security is logical. However, such high and apparently increasing ratios are consistent with excessive and perhaps growing distance between small firms and banks; recall the argument that security requirements can be so high that a bank sees no need to understand a firm.[10] How can a bank justify a ratio of two or more on any new loan?

7.3.4(b)(iii) **Further Responses Concerning Distance** Various questions in the survey shed further light on the distance between small firms and banks. Of the respondents, 87.3 per cent said that their banks did not require managerial/operational changes in the business as a condition of the loan. Arguably, an economy where banks and firms are in close partnership would be one where funding precipitated useful change, although it would be wrong to read too much into this response. Likewise, 83.8 per cent reported that banks offered no alternative way of fulfilling loan requirements. This is consistent with a sterile relationship, lacking communication and reluctant to explore fresh possibilities.

From neither of these questions is it possible to apportion responsibility for excessive distance. Question-marks over the attitude of firms, however, are raised by the fact that 45.8 per cent took no funding advice outside banks. Only 19.6 per cent took advice beyond accountants.

Similarly, when asked why they chose the method of finance that they did, 15.7 per cent responded that it was the only source available, 30.5 per cent that it was the cheapest, but 27.6 per cent that it would avoid outside interference. Moreover a further 12.9 per cent mentioned the avoidance of outside interference as one of several reasons. Again, whilst these responses can be interpreted in various ways, they are consistent with the view that firms want to keep their distance from banks.

Section 7.3 also noted the argument that small firms should consider equity finance as a means of generating a closer relationship with banks. Yet 74.7 per cent reported that they have never considered equity as a source of long-term funding and, when asked if they would object to their banks holding equity stakes, 66.6 per cent said that they would. The main objection was that banks would interfere. This was mentioned by 33.3 per cent of respondents. Closely related to this, a further 28.9 per cent said that they wanted to keep control and 12.6 per cent that they did not trust their banks.

---

[10] Although the numbers involved are very small, it is also worth mentioning that, of the loan offers rejected by firms, the most commonly cited reason for rejection was security requirements. This affected 8 firms.

7.3.4(b)(iv) **Long-Term Finance** One major concern, much discussed in the literature, is banks' short-termism. With this in mind, it is interesting to note that 62.2 per cent of respondents report that their banks have a loan withdrawal clause in the lending contracts. This may be a simple safeguard but it may be symptomatic of a lack of long-run commitment.

However, as with the distance argument, it could be that any short-termism is at least in part the responsibility of firms. We have already raised the possibility of firms preferring short-run finance. Other responses are consistent with this view. It is quite startling that 49.4 per cent, some 124 firms, have not even considered long-term funding, an observation underlined by the aforementioned comments over equity. This evidence clearly suggests that there is a problem of short-termism but that it characterizes firms at least as much as banks. Indeed in banks' favour, of the small firms that have considered long-term funding, 83.1 per cent said that it is available (although not necessarily from banks).

7.3.4(b)(v) **Charges** The questionnaire did not explore bank charges—other than interest rates—in detail. Nevertheless, those firms accepting a loan were asked if the original conditions changed during the term of the loan, and the responses are fairly interesting. The majority (67.8 per cent) reported no change. Interest rates were the most common alteration, reported by 17.9 per cent. The only other change worth noting concerns fees. This affected 13.3 per cent, some 24 firms.

7.4.2(c) *Competition*

Several questions focused on bank competition. Firms were asked if they had noticed any change in competition for their business from banks over the last three years. Of the 225 respondents finding the question applicable, 48.4 per cent had seen no change, 9.3 per cent a fall in competition and 42.2 per cent a rise. Thus on balance, small firms seem to have seen an increase in competition. However our results are broadly in line with BER—more of our respondents have seen a change but this is split between greater and lower competition—and it should be remembered that BER concludes that bank competition was more superficial than real.

Of the respondents, 39.8 per cent have actively shopped for a different bank in the last three years, compared with approximately 22 per cent in BER. It is not clear what this rise means. One view is that firms perceive more to gain from shopping around because of greater bank competition. Another is that small firms are increasingly dissatisfied with their banks' performance and that this has pushed them to look for something better. The rise could explain why more of our respondents see a change in competition levels.

Of the firms that have not shopped around, the most common explanation is satisfaction with existing banks (57.5 per cent). At least as part of their explanation, 21.6 per cent felt that all banks are the same. All other explanations record under 10 per cent.

7.4.2(d) *Bank Services*

Small firms were asked about the importance they attach to eight different bank characteristics, and about their banks' performance on these characteristics. The results are summarized in Table 7.2 (by focusing on the polar responses for each characteristic). Great care is needed to avoid reading too much into such a descriptive presentation as this. Nevertheless, given the pressure that they have faced in recent months the banks will presumably be quite happy with these results. The proportion of respondents rating banks as good or fairly good for a characteristic is largely in line with the proportion rating the characteristic as very important. Similarly, the poor/fairly poor rating tends to be in line with the 'not important' proportion. The most notable exception to this is over the range of services, where the evidence is consistent with banks offering a wider range than clients desire.

Table 7.2 *Rating of bank characteristics*

Characteristic	Importance of characteristic (%)		Performance of characteristic (%)	
	Very important	Not important	Good/ fairly good	Poor/ fairly poor
Knows you and your business	69.0	5.7	49.4	23.3
Provides business advice	16.8	48.4	15.2	54.4
Offers finance	54.5	11.3	48.2	24.7
Continuity of staff	30.5	21.6	35.0	30.3
Industrial knowledge	15.3	49.4	11.8	58.0
Speed of decision/ service	46.9	7.4	47.1	19.0
Wide range of services	14.1	45.7	43.1	
Knowledge of local market	12.9	57.6	15.2	45.4

There is also a question-mark over banks' knowledge of 'you and your business'. This characteristic was rated as very important by 69 per cent of companies, yet only 49.4 per cent rates banks' performance as good/fairly good. More precisely, 61 firms saw banks as good in this characteristic and 64 as fairly good. Likewise, only 5.7 per cent felt the characteristic was unimportant yet 23.3 per cent saw performance as poor (22 firms) or fairly poor (37 firms). Compared to the BER findings on this characteristic, the importance ratings are very similar but banks' performance has apparently worsened; a precise comparison is impossible but, roughly, in BER 46.8 per cent rated banks relatively well and 16.2 per cent relatively badly. This is evidence in favour of excessive distance in the relationship between small firms and banks.

Bearing this in mind, it is interesting to delve slightly deeper into the two other knowledge characteristics that we examined. One of the most striking things is the low importance that firms attach to both industrial knowledge and knowledge of the local market; in both cases, approximately 50 per cent of firms feel that the characteristic is unimportant. Arguably, this again raises the point that any excessive distance in the bank–small firm relationship is a two-sided issue; both banks and small firms are responsible. Moreover, if distance is a problem, it is disturbing that things appear to be worsening. In BER, 25.2 per cent rated industrial knowledge as very important (compared to our 15.3 per cent) and 33.7 per cent as not important (compared to 49.4 per cent); similarly, 13.9 per cent rated banks relatively well in their performance regarding industrial knowledge and 37.3 per cent relatively badly (compared to 11.8 per cent and 58 per cent). Likewise, in BER 23.90 per cent rated knowledge of local market[11] as very important (compared to our 12.9 per cent) and 40.1 per cent as not important (compared to 57.6 per cent); 24.7 per cent rated banks relatively well in their performance as regards local knowledge and 18.6 per cent relatively badly (compared to 15.2 per cent and 45.4 per cent). Running against this apparent trend, however, our questionnaire also considered changes in characteristics over the last three years. Asked about local knowledge, 86.7 per cent said that there had been no change, the residue dividing fairly equally between change for the better and worse.

The question about changes also covered other areas. In all cases the majority reported no change. If anything, firms detected improvements in access to bank managers and in services offered. However, of the 27.7 per cent reporting changes in staff ability, over two-thirds felt that the situation had worsened. Queries over banks' staffing policy are also raised by the observation that 33.3 per cent saw changes in staff continuity, the vast majority of these seeing changes for the worse.

---

[11] BER actually refer to knowledge of 'local market/community'.

Finally, we asked two more general questions about banks' services. The responses raise more questions than they answer but we feel that they are none the less quite interesting. First, when asked whether bank services are flexible enough to meet the special needs of small firms, 66.8 per cent said no. Alongside other responses, this suggests that aspects of the relationship between small firms and banks need to be reviewed and revised. Second, are banks helpful to firms experiencing financial difficulties? This question focused on problems over the last three years. Of 154 respondents, 44.2 per cent said that their banks had been okay, 27.9 per cent not helpful and 27.9 per cent very helpful.

7.5 CONCLUSIONS

The evidence contained in our survey needs to be treated very cautiously, for reasons that have been indicated. It does not provide the final word on any particular issue. Furthermore, the interpretations that we have offered should be seen as the basis for discussion and for further analysis. Other interpretations of this sort of evidence could be presented and a more detailed study is desirable. Despite these reservations—or rather, keeping them uppermost in mind—various tentative conclusions can be drawn.

There is clear evidence that the three more specific issues that we identified as having caused particular concern in the existing literature—interest rates, other bank changes, and security levels—remain important to small firms. In fact they appear to be their major worries. Nevertheless our findings on interest rates are perhaps surprising. the percentage paid over base is on average at least 2 per cent but less than 3 per cent, and there is a suggestion that this average has declined since the late 1980s, although a considerable number of respondents are paying more above base now than in the past. It appears that the recent and popular horror stories over interest rates represent a minority and are not the norm, though they are not necessarily unimportant because of that. Much of the criticism levelled at banks is perhaps misplaced; the underlying issue could be the government policy of high real interest rates. Our findings on security levels are of greater concern in the bank–small firm debate and raise an important question. The average security ratio is at least two and appears to have risen; why?

Turning to the three fundamental characteristics which have been alleged to characterize the relationship between small firms and banks, various points arise. The evidence we offer on market power is thin and says little one way or the other. Far more interesting is the evidence on short-termism. Our survey undoubtedly suggests that there is a problem but that the problem is not simply inadequate supply of long-term capital. Indeed our study can say very little about supply. Rather, our results are consistent with the view that both banks and small firms should reconsider their time horizons. Recall, for instance, that half of the respondents had never even considered long-term funding. Equally interesting is the evidence on distance in the bank–small firm relationship. We can draw a similar conclusion to that concerning short-termism. The evidence is consistent with an excessive distance due to the wishes of both banks and small firms. In many ways this is our strongest point. On the one hand, for example, it is very interesting that banks appeared to make well under half of their loan decisions at local level. On the other hand, respondents put very little store by banks' local knowledge.

If we are to move towards longer-term relationship banking, then there must be a firmer basis for that relationship. No one was forced—even in the heady 1980s—to accept a loan, but a too common attitude was to treat the lender with some degree of contempt. If credit is accepted then it is not unreasonable to accede to requests for information by lenders. The provision of regular monthly accounts, of balance sheets, of budgets and cash flow forecasts should not be regarded as an intrusion which should be ignored. Any creditor is a stake holder in the business, and businesses should be prepared to make an effort in working towards a mutually (not one-sided) satisfying relationship.

This implies a total commitment by both parties to a long-term commercial relationship. Businesses as much as banks must make the effort to understand the needs and concerns of the other. Banks should not be surprised that businessmen are unhappy with apparently arbitrary charges and margins, but equally businessmen should not be surprised when their lender seeks to be reassured that the business is being efficiently managed. And, above all, both parties must honour their side of any bargain: no businessman can complain about excessive charges if at the same time he is breaching his agreed overdraft limit.

We are left with the suggestion that the relationship between small firms and banks is sterile, uncommunicative and unimaginative, and that both must take responsibility for the situation. There seems to be scope for an all-round reappraisal of positions.

These are hash words from independent observers of the business scene, and they are addressed to two significant groups within the Chambers of Commerce. To remove the barriers to a more productive working relationship is a task which we need to tackle in Chambers of Commerce and Industry and which is also equally relevant to the business community in general.

The first point, is that any progress can only be by persuasion: we cannot compel groups of our members to establish a closer relationship with each other if they are determined not to do so. What we can do, is to draw attention to the advantages which will accrue for both sides from a better understanding of, on the one side the range of financial options available, and on the other the day-to-day pressures and practical problems which beset a small business. In both these areas, I suggest, the role of training is paramount.

The second point raises wider implications. If our survey's conclusions on this matter are correct—and we have to accept that they are based only on the views of small businesses—is there scope for greater autonomy for the bank's regional office or even for the local bank manager when dealing with small business clients?

From the Chambers of Commerce which draws its strength from its regional local roots, I feel that, as we approach the Single Market, the European Community concept of 'subsidiarity' is not solely a matter for the public sector. This is particularly the case where 'UK plc'—including banks and small firms—is competing with vigorous regional economies elsewhere in the Community.

Codes of practice in this area are welcome for the degree—albeit small—of certainty around which relationships between banks and small firms can be built. Certainly, there is scope for better training of business-men, particularly in new business start-ups and in financial matters, and of bankers in commercial matters. Perhaps this is something that Training and Enterprise Councils (TECs) could address themselves to. There is indeed a role for business support organizations, such as Chambers of Commerce, to provide direct assistance to businesses in the very basics of preparation of their business plans and cash flow forecasts. We will cer-tainly wish to encourage a greater involvement of local bank managers and officers in their business communities through Chambers of Commerce or via valuable secondments. There *may* be a role for regulation of charging practices, or a better (or at least fairer) defined contractual relationship between banking parties.

These are all things to be considered, which could be implemented imme-diately. Moves towards more regional or local structures of banking require detailed consideration and would take longer to bring about.

One thing is clear, however. Although, like an unsuccessful marriage, there is fault on both sides of the relationship, and actions to be taken and attitudes to be changed by banks and businesses alike, the market force of the clearers puts the ball in their court. One firm—or even several—taking a positive initiative is not going to change practices and attitudes in the UK. Just one clearing bank taking an initiative certainly would.

APPENDIX: SAMPLE SELECTION

To select the sample, all Chambers of Commerce within the three chosen geographical areas were asked by the Association of British Chambers of Commerce to supply a full directory of members, listed in alphabetical order, and a set of printed labels with all member firms' addresses.

Chambers which failed to supply a directory were excluded from our survey. The geographical areas were defined by the Association.

From each of the three geographical areas 500 firms were selected. To do this for the South and the West Midlands, the total membership of each included Chamber within each area was counted. The sample drawn from each Chamber was allocated proportionately to that Chamber's contribution to total membership within its area. (For instance, the West Midlands sample drew on the members of three Chambers, including Birmingham. Their total membership was 5,367 firms, of which 3,721 came from Birmingham. Accordingly our sample drew

$$\left(\frac{3721}{5367}\right) 500$$

firms from the Birmingham Chamber.) Once these calculations had been completed, the total number of firms for each Chamber was added up on an alphabetical basis, and the sample stratified proportionately by the letter of the alphabet.

The Chambers used in our sample for the South and the West Midlands, and the number of firms questioned in each, are given in Tables 7.A1 and 7.A2.

Table 7.A1.   *West Midlands*

Chamber		Number of firms in the chamber	Number of firms in the sample
Birmingham		3,721	346
Dudley		405	38
Walsall		1,241	116
	Total	5,367	500

Table 7.A2.   *South*

Chamber	Number of firms in the chamber	Number of firms in the sample
Oxford	403	29
South East Hampshire	908	65
Federation of Sussex Industries	2,501	179
Swindon	782	50
Thames–Chiltern	2,478	177
Total	7,072	500

For Scotland, we received a complete directory listing all of the 8,373 Scottish Chambers of Commerce members. The sample was simply stratified on an alphabetical basis, as above.

REFERENCES

Aston Business School (1991), *A Report of a Survey of Small Firms,* in Department of Trade and Industry, Scottish Office, Welsh Office, *Constraints on the Growth of Small Firms* (HMSO, London).

Bannock, Graham (1981), 'The Clearing Banks and Small Firms', *Lloyds Bank Review.*

Binks, Martin, Ennew, Christine, Reed, Geoffrey (1988), *Banks and Small Businesses: An Interbank Comparison, Report to the Forum for Private Business* (Forum for Private Business, Knutsford).

— — — (1989), 'The Differentiation of Bank Services to Small Firms', *International Journal of Bank Marketing.*

— — — (1990), 'The Single European Act and the Relationship between Small Firms and their Banks in the UK', *Managerial Finance.*

— and Vale, P. (1984), 'Finance for the New Firm', NUSFU paper 2 (University of Nottingham).

Bolton Committee (1971), *Committee of Inquiry on Small Firms: Research Reports Nos 4, 5 and 16* (HMSO, London).

Churchill, N. C. and Lewis, V. L. (1983), 'The Five Stages of Small Business Growth', *Harvard Business Review.*

Hall, G. C. (1989), 'Lack of Finance as a Constraint on the Expansion of Innovatory Small Firms', in Barber, Metcalfe, and Porteous (eds), *Barriers to Growth in Small Firms* (Routledge, London).

Hall, Graham, and Lewis, Pam (1988), 'Development Agencies and the Supply of Finance to Small Firms', *Applied Economics.*

Minns, Richard (1988), 'Local Financial Markets', mimeo (Greater London Enterprise Board).

NEDO (1986), Committee on Finance for Industry, *External Capital for Small Firms: A Review of Recent Developments* (NEDO, London).

Storey, David J. (1990), 'Is there a Gap in the Financing of Small Firms?: A Review of Evidence from the UK', mimeo (University of Warwick).

Wilson Committee (1979), *Financing Industry and Trade,* Three Banks Review, London, HMSO.

8

The Role of the Banks

DAVID LOMAX

8.1 HISTORICAL PERSPECTIVE

This is a welcome opportunity to set out the role of the banks in supporting industry and commerce. This chapter starts with the banks' broad
strategic position in society at the present time. It will then deal with relationships with small and large companies, and will draw the appropriate
conclusions at the end.

Some ten or fifteen years ago the banks were tightly regulated, there was
little innovation, some markets were officially cartelized, and the risks perceived in the banking business were relatively slight. The banks tended to
rise and fall with the tide together, and over the business cycle there was
adequate profit for the banking industry as a whole. In the United States
this was characterized as 3–6–3 banking. The banks paid 3 per cent on
deposits, charged 6 per cent on loans, and the bankers went of to play golf
at 3 p.m. For its time this was not a bad system. But since then everything
has changed.

The banks are now forced to regard themselves as commercial organizations very much on a par with other companies in the industrial and commercial sectors. The banks' earnings are transparent, their share prices are
valued on the Stock Exchange in the same way as other companies, and
there is limited ownership protection, particularly in the context of the
forthcoming European harmonization of the legal framework surrounding
the banking industry. The profitability of banks is a matter of intense public interest and is the means of assessing the relative merits of the management of different banks.

Banking thus has to combine a substantial proportion of the pressures
faced generally by industry and commerce with the constraints stemming
from being the core of the financial system: banks must remain sound and
the Bank of England needs to guard against systemic risk. The need to
guard against such risk requires a great deal of regulation and regular
reporting to the authorities on the banks' business positions. Banks have to
be regulated, but they also have to be commercial. A modern banker needs
to be both traditionally minded to see the virtue of stability and risk avoidance, while at the same time commercially skilled like businessmen in other
fields.

8.2 CAPITAL ADEQUACY

In looking at the pressures and influences on banking it is difficult to over-estimate the importance of the capital ratios now imposed generally throughout the OECD area. These stem from the work of the Committee of Banking Supervisors meeting under the aegis of the Bank for International Settlements at Basle, once known as the Cooke Committee. The ratios which they set out have since been adopted by the European Community and by other authorities such as the Federal Reserve System.

The system requires banks to recalculate their assets into what are termed 'weighted risk assets'. The weighting is intended to be a broad reflection of the riskiness of those assets. Table 8.1 sets out the main cate-gories of weighted risk assets and the weighting which is applied. In deter-mining the appropriate capital ratios a bank has to multiply the amounts in different categories of assets by the appropriate weighting to recalculate a 'weighted risk asset' (WRA) balance sheet.

Table 8.2 indicates this calculation as performed for a notional UK com-mercial bank. It indicates in a stylized manner a conventional asset total of £92.1 bn., and this is reduced to a figure of £78.75 bn. for total weighted assets.

It would be much more complicated to present the figures for one of the existing banks, since the number of accounting elements and the risk weighting within different parts of the assets are much more numerous and more varied than in this example.

The aim of the WRA system is to link the capital weighting to the risk of the assets, and thus to relate capital to the risk of the portfolio of assets held by a bank. This process was not entirely without controversy.[1]

Can one find a strict link between the capital required and the structure of a bank's assets? The riskiness of a bank's assets depends not just on individual components but how they fit together in building a portfolio. In the event it proved impractical to link the weighted risk asset and the capi-tal required to any rigorous calculation of the riskiness of the entire portfo-lio of any particular bank. The only move in the direction of portfolio analysis was that the authorities have been empowered to apply higher cap-ital ratios to banks if they so wish. The Basle Accord ratio of 8 per cent is thus a minimum which regulators may increase if they think that a bank's portfolio would justify that action.

The capital which a bank has to keep is broken down into two compo-nents, Tier 1 and Tier 2. Table 8.3 sets out the definitions of capital. Tier 1 must be at least 4 per cent, unless the regulators specify a higher figure. Tier 2 includes a range of other forms of capital. It should be noted that

---

[1] D. F. Lomax, 'Risk Asset Ratios: A New Departure in Supervisory Policy', *National Westminster Bank Quarterly Review* (August 1987).

Table 8.1. *Main categories of weighted risk assets*

Risk weight (%)	
0	Cash and claims collateralized by cash deposits.
	Claims on, or guaranteed by, Zone A central governments (excluding securities).
	Claims on Zone B central governments (all those not qualifying as Zone A) denominated in local currency and funded in that currency (excluding securities).
10	Holdings of, or claims collateralized by, fixed-interest securities issued by (or guaranteed by) Zone A central governments with a residual maturity of one year or less, and floating-rate and index-linked securities of any maturity.
	As above for Zone B central governments but denominated in local currency and funded by liabilities in the same currency.
	Loans to discount houses, gilt-edged market makers and institutions with a money-market dealing relationship with the Bank of England.
20	Holdings of, and claims collateralized by, fixed-interest securities of Zone A central governments with a maturity over one year.
	As above for Zone B central governments but denominated in local currency and funded by liabilities in the same currency.
	Claims on, or guaranteed by, credit institutions incorporated in Zone A (or Zone B if for a residual maturity of one year or less).
	Claims on Zone A public sector entities (includes Local Authorities).
50	Mortgage loans to individuals.
	Loans to Housing Associations meeting certain criteria.
100	Claims on the non-bank private sector.
	Premises, plant, equipment, and other fixed assets.
	Real estate and trade investments.

Note: Zone A countries are those which are members of the OECD and those which have special lending arrangements with the IMF.

subordinated term debt may not exceed 50 per cent of Tier 1 capital. In principle, Tier 1 capital is equity or retentions and thus reflects the cost of equity capital. Tier 2 reflects instruments which in general are considerably cheaper than Tier 1 capital.

It is of course possible to criticize the capital adequacy system in terms of finance and portfolio theory, as a measure of the appropriate way of controlling the riskiness of banks' portfolios. But in the event this system, somewhat rough and ready as it might be regarded, has been adopted by banks and regulators around the world and they are committed firmly to it. It provides a level playing field for competition between banks. It prevents

Table 8.2   *Example of a stylized weighted risk asset calculation for a notional*
UK bank

	Conventional presentation of assets (£M)	Risk asset weighting (%)	Weighted risk assets (£M)
Coins, banks notes, and balances with the Bank of England and State banks abroad	1,000	0	—
Money at call and short notice with other banks	9,640	20	1,928
Certificates of Deposit	860	20	172
Investments in Government Securities : up to 1 year	1,200	10	120
: over 1 year	150	20	30
Mortgage Loans	4,500	50	2,250
Advances and other accounts	72,100	100	72,100
Investments in associated companies	500	Deducted from capital base	—
Premises and equipment	2,150	100	2,150
TOTAL	92,100		78,750

banks' balance sheets ballooning rapidly, with risks of inflationary surges. If it were to be abandoned it would be very hard to put anything else in its place, and we could again see anarchy in competition and unstable monetary developments.

The question of capital adequacy is also being addressed in the context of the European community in relation to the securities industry. Capital adequacy and investment services directives are under discussion. When these directives are in force, an analogous capital ratio control will apply also in that industry.

The banks are expected by the authorities to keep to ratios above the minimum. Higher ratios are seen by the investment community and rating agencies as a sign of strength, while at the same time providing flexibility for future business growth. The ratios maintained by the British banks vary. For National Westminster the total capital ratio at the end of 1991 was 9.6 per cent, with the Tier 1 ratio being 5.5 per cent.

The use of this rigid WRA system of capital control, together with knowledge of the cost of particular forms of capital, has led the WRA sys-

Table 8.3 *Main components of capital*

Tier 1
Allotted called-up fully-paid ordinary shares
Irredeemable non-cumulative issued preference shares
Disclosed reserves (excluding revaluation reserves)
Share premium
Current year's published retentions
Minority interests (in respect of Tier 1 capital items)

Tier 2
Undisclosed reserves and revaluations reserves
Current year's unpublished profits
General provisions (restricted to 1.5 per cent of weighted risk assets now but 1.25 per cent from 1.1.93).
Hybrid capital instruments
   perpetual cumulative preference shares
   perpetual subordinated debt
   convertibles
Minority interests (in respect of Tier 2 capital items)
Subordinated term debt (NB must not exceed 50 per cent of Tier 1)

Deductions
Investments in Associates and Unconsolidated Subsidiaries
Holdings of capital instruments of other banks and building societies
Connected lending of a capital nature

---

tem to have considerable influence over pricing policies of the banks. The cost of capital to a bank will depend on many factors. These include the yields demanded by shareholders, the dividend growth expected, inflation, the proportion of equity in capital, the real return on government debt, and the risk premium for corporate debt. Many factors will vary between banks, including for example the mixture of equity and other capital. For the purposes of discussing the impact of this on bank behaviour I will make the *assumption* for the rest of this chapter that these calculations, for our notional bank, lead to a pre-tax cost of capital of 20 per cent.

Table 8.4 sets out an example of how such a cost of capital translates into the margin required on an element of banking business. The example is of the cost of a £100 loan, which is 100 per cent weighted and so will require £9 of capital (clearing bank average) to back it. Taking into account the average cost of Tier 1 and Tier 2 capital, the margin required to cover the cost of that capital is 0.9 per cent over the 10 per cent cost of the deposits which support the asset. Thus before taking into account any

Table 8.4 *Relationship between capital ratios and pricing policy*

£100	Balance sheet assets (commercial loans)	Liabilities: capital (clearing bank average)	£9
		deposits	£91
100%	Weighting		
£100	Weighted Risk Assets		
	Capital required to support WRA of £100		
	Tier 1 plus Tier 2 (clearing bank average)		£9
	Annual pre-tax cost of capital (%)		20
	Cost of capital		£1.80
	Deposit interest rate: assumed (%)		10
	Cost of deposits: £91 × 10% =		£9.10
	Total cost		£10.90

Interest rate on loan needed to cover cost of capital and of deposit $\dfrac{10.9}{100} \times 100\% = 10.9\%$

Margin needed over deposit rate of interest: 0.9%

costs of administration or risk of loss, a bank would need to aim for a margin of 0.9 per cent in order to remunerate its capital appropriately.

With the modern development of computer models, the cost of the capital to back different forms of business may be calculated relatively easily. It is an obvious step from that for the capital cost to become incorporated into the pricing decision in relation to a particular business.

A balance sheet asset will need a certain margin to cover the cost of capital, a further margin to cover administrative costs and make a contribution to central costs, and a further margin to cover the risk of loss. As these calculations have been done it has become clear that some customers were by no means covering the cost of the capital required to do business with them. This applied most spectacularly to the large corporate sector which, in the boom years of the 1980s, was enjoying margins of 10–20 basis points (0.1 or 0.2 per cent) on certain forms of finance.

This situation developed for a variety of reasons. The banks perceived limited credit risk in this business. When they had not been under strict capital ratios, there was no capital cost in expanding their balance sheet in that way, indeed there was no absolute control over balance sheet levels. The period was one of rapid expansion in international finance by many banks, in particular by the Japanese banks, and their desire for a larger market share drove down margins. The banks who were already in the business did not always wish to lose their relations with corporate customers, so they stayed in the market but with much lower remuneration.

This situation persisted for several years but came under closer scrutiny as banks became more conscious of the capital constraint and of the need to deploy their assets in areas which should be expected over the medium term to provide an adequate remuneration.

Banks thus face the 1990s with the capital ratios setting a limit to the total amount of business they can do at any time, while at the same time pointing out clearly the cost of doing business in particular areas. The consequence has been inevitable. The banks have moved their business away from fine margin business to where a greater return on capital may be made. Banks will have reacted in different ways to this situation, but in general the move would have been away from business with the major corporate and institutional customers. This has had the effect of increasing margins to some extent in that business area. At the same time they have come to manage their balance sheets closely so as to ensure continuing control over their capital ratios.

8.3 CREDIT AVAILABILITY

This factor leads to fears of a credit shortage—can the banks supply the finance which British industry and commerce needs? The answer to this is that there is no credit shortage in the offing, for four reasons. The first is that the wholesale corporate sector has available to it the resources from the entire world-wide securities and banking markets. The world-wide financial system is extremely efficient in enabling top credit risks and large institutional and corporate organizations to obtain funds throughout the system.

Second, the banks have capital well above the minimum requirements at the present time. For instance the 1.6 per cent capital which National Westminster has over and above the internationally agreed minimum of 8 per cent would allow an expansion of weighted risk assets of no less than £20 bn.

Third, if the banks were forced to manage their balance sheets more closely, because parts of their business were expanding rapidly, then that management would almost certainly take place through controlling the exposure in the treasury area and with the largest corporations. It would not take place in relation to the companies banking with the branches up and down the country.

Fourth, banks are able to raise additional capital from the markets when the proceeds can be employed in assets that provide an adequate return. At the end of the day if there were a global demand for credit which was above the capacity of the banking system to provide, then the remuneration on such loans, the margins, would increase to such levels as to make that lending adequately profitable, so the banks would be able to raise capital in the markets and deploy that in their business. This is the 'long stop' reason why there could never be an ultimate world-wide credit shortage. The present system is a very long way short of this mechanism having to be brought into play.

8.4 RISK CONTROL

A key determinant of profit is the interest spread, the gap between interest received on interest bearing assets and the cost of funds. Under a regulated system, bank profits may be sensitive to interest rates, with the banks making large profits when interest rates are high, the so called endowment effect. This is now far less the case than it may have been in the past. Both deposit and lending rates are to a far greater extent market determined. The banks also deliberately take steps to manage their balance sheets so that they are much less interest rate sensitive. For example, National Westminster has sufficient fixed interest rate lending, such as business development loans, to protect itself against falls in interest rates, but at the same time that inevitably means that the bank does not benefit from rises. The markets for deposits are now much more competitive, with market rates being paid on a much bigger proportion of deposits, and on virtually the whole of the marginal increase in deposits.

The banking markets are now much more competitive. New entrants have entered the market-place, such as the building societies, the Trustee Savings Bank, and foreign banks. The public is now far more demanding and expects to receive market interest rates even on relatively small value deposits. A wide choice faces credit-worthy borrowers. The margin is thus determined heavily by competitive forces and the banks expect neither abnormal margins nor bonanzas from endowment effects to last.

The effect of the Basle capital ratios has been to make banks aware that the business they can do on their balance sheet is linked rigidly to the size of their capital. If banks wish to obtain further income, and a better return for their shareholders, then they need to do business which is profitable but not balance sheet related. This has led to a search for fee income.

The effect of this is that banks are becoming less homogeneous. Each bank finds a different way of trying to solve this conundrum, and as they do so, then the banks become more diverse. As banks were faced with the need to develop new sources of income, preferably fee-based rather than capital-based, so they were forced to take a decision as to which way to go. There were many possibilities. These included life assurance, estate agency, merchant banking, venture capital, investment management, stockbroking, treasury activity including foreign exchange business, and offering processing services such as in relation to credit cards. Banks tended to make different selections from among this choice and so tended to become more varied. This variegation of the banking system will be seen throughout Europe over the coming years, and indeed in most fully competitive banking systems where the banks are allowed to diversify into different industries. Another consequence of the Basle ratios is that the situation a bank finds itself in is cumulative. Success leads to success, and a lack of success to contraction. A good year leads to greater retained earnings, greater capital, and thus the possibility of further expansion in balance sheet terms. A bad year leads to fewer retained earnings, and a tighter restriction on the balance sheet business which may be done. The result of this is that banks feel greater pressure to earn income which is less dependent upon the balance sheet so as to expose themselves less to this cumulative twist.

One of the changes which has matched the move of banking from a regulated to a deregulated industry is an enormous change in the approach which the banks have taken to risk control. Twenty years ago this control was couched mainly in the language of the traditional banker, relying heavily upon credit assessment skills, and trying to achieve a 'well diversified lending book of high quality assets'. Such an approach was not to be derided. The description mentioned of the ideal lending book would produce a portfolio which would satisfy the most stringent financial analysis. At the same time the banks' treasuries would apply what by now would be regarded as fairly rudimentary controls over their business. Since then, the emergence of particular problems, difficulty in achieving significant margins, the development of new products, and pressures from the regulators have led to a substantial increase in the processes which banks go through to control risk, and in the sophistication of that process. Most banks have senior committees which examine all aspects of risk. Credit control is increasingly based on models and statistical processes. These include credit scoring both for persons and some companies, grading systems concerned with the quality of credits, and, in some cases, the application of processes which are not far short of those used by the credit rating agencies. The development of modern treasury products, such as swaps and options, has led to far greater sophistication in both the business itself and in the means required to control risk adequately. The risks in modern banking are considerable and the efforts deployed to minimize and control them are very substantial. But even so, at the end of the day it is not possible to encapsulate the logic of banking into one systemic process. Managing a bank as a whole, and managing individual parts of the business are bound to rely upon human judgement, and that will include using informal processes and rules of thumb. Banks are also large organizations which employ and are run by many people. Like any business, banks operate under considerable uncertainty about their environment. At present, and for the foreseeable future, it is unrealistic to think in terms of a single rational solution being found to the problem of how a bank should be run.

8.5   THE SMALL BUSINESS SECTOR

Within this framework the retail business sector plays an extremely important role in the business structure of the clearing banks. The country needs a small business sector.The small business sector needs banking facilities, and the banking sector needs customers which fit with the services it can supply and with its cost structure.

The National Westminster Bank defines the corporate sector which has branch relationships in three categories. The small business sector, including start-ups, covers businesses with a turnover of up to £1m. Medium-sized companies include those from there up to £130m. Large companies are those with a turnover of over £130m. All these kinds of companies are intensive users of the services provided by the branch network, including cash, other forms of payment, a range of deposit systems, international payment systems and relationships, and various forms of borrowing.

The small business sector is particularly important to the UK. We need entrepreneurs and new companies to provide us with the opportunities for the growth which the UK needs to catch up with our continental competitors. Our desired expansion could not come just from the large company sector. The large corporate sector is more than likely to be in a phase of cutting costs and staff, rather than of expanding its employment yet further. For reasons of employment generation and of creation of economic activity the small corporate sector is crucial, as indeed is the process of starting up new companies. Here we need to take into account a crucial feature of the banking industry, which sometimes comes as a surprise even to those in banking.

8.6   ASYMMETRY OF RISK

The risk reward structure facing commercial banks is extremely asymmetric. Banks are lending on a margin. If a company does well they get no extra benefit, apart from the repayment of their loan and/or the extension of further credit to that company; but if a company goes under, then a bank could lose all its loan.

The margins on loans vary from often significantly less than 1 per cent to the major wholesale sector in the 1980s, to an average of just over 3 per cent for the small business sector. Loans to the wholesale sector have in the past at times not even covered their capital costs, so the assumption has to be that there would be no credit risk whatever, for those loans to have any justification. Let us assume in the case of a small business loan that the margin is 3 per cent, and the capital and administrative costs some 1 per cent, leaving a margin of 1 per cent to cover the risk. This means that if a bank gets 99 per cent of its decisions right in any year it will have a profit, if 98 per cent it would just cover capital and administrative costs, and if only 97 per cent right then there would be a loss on that business.

This risk/reward structure needs to be set in conjunction with the known risk structure in business. Of start-ups, some 30 per cent cease trading, for a variety of reasons, within three years. The failure rate is highest among small businesses, then becomes less as one moves up the scale. Not many individuals would care to lend their own money widely throughout the small business sector, on an average margin of just over 3 per cent. Given the risk structure faced by banks, with its high degree of asymmetry, and the known riskiness of the small business sector, and in particular of start-ups, a great deal of care is required to make this relationship mutually beneficial on a continuing basis.

In 1991 this result did not occur. The pressure on that sector was such that the losses went well beyond the risk perceived by the banks, and they took severe losses. On the other hand, attempts by the banks to relate the margin more closely to the risk, in a modest way on average, led to charges by the small business sector that the amounts demanded were too high.

In 1991 the balance of provisions taken by the banks was heavily geared towards the small business sector. In National Westminster over 40 per cent of the loan losses were on amounts of less than £50,000, by value not by number.

The small business sector is very diversified. Over half of small business customers do not borrow. National Westminster has one million small business accounts. Among the borrowing small business customers, the average amount borrowed is £15,000. The vast majority of small businesses have retrenched and remained in business, despite the ferocity of the recessionary forces.

We thus have a business sector which is highly varied, has high risks in certain areas, and where these risks cannot easily be discerned in advance by outsiders.

The banks need to charge enough to cover the average risk. They have to be extremely careful in selecting which propositions to support, since a bad risk selection would be extremely expensive. Some argue that the banks undercharge for the risks they are taking. Is there a way around this problem through applying more sophisticated financial techniques or by developing different forms of business? If such a solution or solutions could be found then the banks would be very willing to adopt them. There are, however, many practical barriers in the way of doing things very differently. Should the banks charge considerably more for their loans to small companies then this would create a great deal of customer resistance. Moreover, although a banker knows that the portfolio of business he is taking on includes considerable risks, he must believe that each loan he makes is likely to be repaid. There comes a point, such as if a bank were allowing 8 or 9 per cent for the credit risk, where he would regard the proposition as fundamentally not bankable. Should the bankers do a great deal more work in assessing the risk? Undoubtedly, but management time is extremely expensive. If the average loan is £15,000, then the profit margin may be worked out easily, and that is to be compared with what management time would be required to make a thorough study of such a company. In any case, banks are doing all they can to improve the credit assessment of small companies, including substantially expanded training schemes for their staff. This is a very important part of the answer, but it can never be the complete answer.

Should banks try to obtain some up-side potential by putting equity into companies? As indicated later, many small companies are extremely reluctant to allow outside equity holders. Small businessmen are extremely independent. There is a thriving venture capital industry in the United Kingdom, in which the banks have significant involvement, and the experience has been consistently that such business is unprofitable at the small end. The combination of the relatively high risk of failure with the administrative costs of running any venture capital involvement makes this end of the business non-commercial.

Could more be done in various parts of the business sector, including small businesses, by adopting greater sophistication? Should one lend on assets rather than to companies? Could appropriate covenants be exercised such as through securities or through the lending process? There are limits to the extent to which lending situations can be controlled or made more sophisticated in this way. Banks, of course, try to keep fully informed about what is going on with their borrowing companies. Once a company has significantly breached the covenants or terms of lending it may be too late. Few assets, apart from some forms of property, have anything like the same value in a liquidation as in a going concern. There are many other ways of providing finance to companies of all sizes, apart from lending, such as through venture capital, factoring, leasing, or issuing securities. The banks are in many of these businesses on a significant scale. Lending banks use other mechanisms, particularly factoring and leasing, as means of helping the financial position of small and medium-sized businesses. But as far as the lending banker is concerned, a lending relationship is a lending relationship. If that cannot be made to work, particularly as regards the small business sector, then it is difficult to find anything else which may satisfactorily be put in its place.

Despite the bruises inflicted on all parties by the recession in 1991, the banks, including National Westminster, are determined to remain in the retail business markets, including the small business market and the start-up market. To do so, however, the banks need to generate a return sufficient to cover the costs and risks of being in such markets.

8.7 THE RELATIONSHIP WITH SMALL BUSINESSES

To maintain this relationship, with the high variety and diversity of the small business sector and the severe risks in some areas, will require careful selection of business. There are bound to be loans declined where the customer thinks the other way, and indeed there should be loan declines where the customer may disagree. The acid test is whether the vast bulk of companies get the money they need, and can afford, on terms which are supportive to their business.

In this regard, Chapter 7 and in particular the survey which Miles Middleton conducted among ABC members was very interesting and shed much light on this particular issue. One must regard such views as somewhat impressionistic, as well as revealing. A survey response of 18.1 per cent is not large. Those who feel most strongly will reply, and some of the views expressed were inconsistent with each other as is likely to happen.

For example, one charge is that the banks have a very short-term view, presumably implying a short-term commitment. Yet of the 49 per cent of respondents who had considered long-term funding, 83 per cent said that it was available. That implies a substantial willingness on the part of banks to offer long-term funding, and an understanding by the small business sector that such funding is available.

Also, 49 per cent of respondents rated their banks' performances as good/fairly good in knowing them and their business. This does not seem consistent with the view that there is an excessive distance in the small firms–bank relationship.

The responses by businesses show a clear desire to retain their distance from the banks, with 67 per cent saying they would object to an equity stake being held by their banks, and 33 per cent fearing bank interference, 28 per cent loss of control, and 13 per cent who 'did not trust banks'.

Of those who were asked why they took their particular form of finance, 28 per cent said that it would avoid outside interference, while a further 13 per cent mentioned the avoidance of outside interference as one of several reasons.

Such inconsistencies are inevitable when people have a chance of venting deeply held resentments and frustrations. People are not asked to put forward feasible alternatives to the present situation, nor to say what they are prepared to pay for. The banks recognize these resentments and frustrations. They are not complacent about their relationship with the small business community.

The nub of the relationship on a continuing basis between small firms and banks relates to risk perception and risk avoidance. Small firms are unwilling to give up equity to outsiders. The venture capital business is extremely difficult at the small firm level. Many companies will be highly geared, and they are naturally concerned at the cost of finance and at the information and security which the lender may need so as to minimize the risk.

On the other hand, the banks see a sector which has an enormous turnover of companies and a high level of risk. Selecting companies so as to achieve a good profile among that pool of borrowers is a difficult task, and there will undoubtedly be occasions where the perception as to risk between the company and the bank differs. Moreover, charges in all their forms need to be such as to cover the expected risks, among other costs in the business. Companies may think that the charges are on the high side. The experience of 1991 shows that the risks were extremely great, and in the event were not covered by the charges. Risk control and risk selection will continue to be key elements in maintaining the fruitfulness of this relationship.

8.8   RELATIONS WITH LARGE COMPANIES

Many issues between banks and the major corporations are different from those with small companies. A major corporation has a far greater range of choice as to its sources of finance and the financial services it will use. It will have flexible access to the capital and banking markets, it is likely to have multi-banking relationships, access to banks in many countries, and will be well placed to obtain the best quotes for the services it requires.

The major corporations are well informed about what is available in the market-place and about the best ways of handling their own affairs. The skills available in corporate treasuries have been increased beyond all recognition over the past decade or more, not least through the creation of the formidable and effective Association of Corporate Treasurers. In many companies the corporate treasury has to account for its contribution or profitability to the company. In some others the corporate treasury has even legally, and not just *de facto*, begun to operate like a bank.

Under these circumstances a bank conducting business with a major corporate is very much in the position of any other supplier of goods or services, having to compete fully on quality and price. No bank could begin to presume on the relationship without being shown the door.

Many top companies have extremely good credit ratings, in some cases better than the banks who wish to supply them with financial services. Under those circumstances it may be difficult for the banks to intermediate profitably between the company and the ultimate source of finance. The situation would tend to lead naturally to some disintermediation. The massive growth of the commercial paper market, particularly in the United States but also in parts of Europe, illustrates the much diminished role of banks in the direct funding of such companies. One or two massive global conglomerates would use the banking system only as a lender of last resort for credit purposes.

The basis of traditional relationship banking in the UK was an implicit bargain in which the bank agreed to provide support for the company in case of emergency and help it out over any problems it might encounter, while at the same time the company agreed to put a certain proportion of its banking business to that bank, without necessarily being totally ruthless as to pricing down to the last decimal point. There has been a swing back towards relationship banking during the recession, with virtually all corporates having swung back that way. They tend to restrict their banking panel to say 15–20 banks but in reality will use only 3 or 4 for major deals.

The structure of this relationship banking has broken down, to the extent it has, largely because the major corporates have come to put less value on the components of this bargain. Companies may think that they will not get into such difficulty as to require help from the banks. Or they may take the view that if they are in such trouble then the banks would have no choice but to help them out, so there is no point in paying for that benefit. The pressures to maximize profitability within the company sector have led to an unwillingness to pay over the odds. Indeed, companies have been unbundling their banking relationships by putting different services out to competitive tender, such as CP programmes, payments transactions, and syndicated loans. Local authorities normally put their transmission business out to tender, and move their accounts according to which bank offers the best terms.

The fact that the banks have a relationship with a company, as long as they have exposure to it, means that banks may at times come to play the role of restructuring agents, irrespective of the position of the shareholders. In the UK the traditional position of the shareholders, including the institutional shareholders, is that they feel they are not in the position to exercise management or ownership of a company, and their preferred option is to be able to sell and leave a difficult situation quickly, through liquid markets.

In recent years many British companies have faced difficulties, and restructurings have had to take place, in some cases with losses to the banks. But in every single case of which I am aware, the key negotiation and reorganization took place through the banks, with a small or even minimal role for the institutional shareholders. This is because the banks, with their continuing exposure to the company, had no choice but to try to sort the situation out. For a bank it is almost certainly always better to sell on a going concern basis, and get back say two-thirds or more of your money, than have a 'fire sale' and get back a good deal less than that. Despite their having more of an arm's length relationship in the UK than in some other countries, when push comes to shove the banks become very deeply involved in corporate reorganizations, because of the nature of their relationship, in virtually all cases a longer-term relationship than have the institutional investors.

The British situation seems to me markedly different from that in Germany. In Germany, through the system of share depositories, the banks are in a position to vote significant proportions of the shares of the companies. The banks will have members on the supervisory boards of companies, and in many cases bankers will be the chairmen and/or deputy chairmen. When strategic issues arise in companies, the banks may be influential in four ways, because of their position as lenders, as direct shareholders, as proxy voters for other shareholders, and on the supervisory boards. Nothing like that is seen in the UK. In the UK companies are independent of their banks and are determined to remain so. British companies would not voluntarily create the German situation, and there is nothing in the legislative or commercial pipeline likely to cause it to happen.

One of the fruitful areas of relationship between large companies and banks, which suits the commercial needs of both sides, is that between corporate treasurers and the treasury and capital market units of banks. The banks have facilities available to companies in a particular market. The banks devote their skills to designing products and offering liquid and efficient markets. Many of these markets become commodity markets in due course, with products being sold largely on price, but others involve special skills on which the banks can, at least for a time, hope for commensurate returns. These markets operate on the basis of there being virtually no credit risk, so pricing is on a fully competitive basis, with a very limited pricing element allowed for the credit risk involved.

Another area of successful relationships between banks and the major companies relates to projects and specialized financing structures. Lending large amounts of money to a major corporate is essentially a commodity business, and the big companies will demand prices which are likely to be rock bottom. The banks may try to counter this profitability issue by specializing in more complicated financial structures and by obtaining a return for those skills. This element of business is extremely management intensive, requiring very highly skilled people. It also involves deep knowledge of the companies concerned, with credit analysis skills on a par with those applied by the rating agencies. As an example of such project skills, a team in National Westminster originally analysed the Channel Tunnel and came to the conclusion that the tunnel on the lines being built could be financially viable. Obtaining a full return from this kind of project business is not easy, since it is based on the valuation of ideas and the control of risk. But this is one area where a close relationship between companies and banks may take place, a relationship which is profitable as well to the banks that have specialized skills in those fields.

Over the business cycle the banks are the residual source of funds to the corporate sector. The corporate sector's net position with the banks will vary sharply over the cycle. In 1989 companies borrowed net £33 bn. from the banks, whilst in the first three quarters of 1991 they repaid £3 bn. The capital markets are less important suppliers of finance net to the corporate sector, in the decade to 1990 supplying less than half the amount lent net by the banks.

The relationship between the corporate sector and banks will vary across the spectrum from close relationships to arm's length contracting, depending upon the position of the various parties and how they see their interests. UK commercial life, like that in North America, Western Europe and much of the rest of the world, is based on contract law. The banking business is highly asymmetric as regards risk, with a bank needing to get something near 99 per cent of its decisions right to make money. The downside risk is great, and the upside potential limited. Under those circumstances it would be an extremely brave, or perhaps foolhardy, banker who did other than rely upon the legal structure for protection of his interests. There are many sharks out there, in companies of all sizes.

In this regard, suggestion that informal relationships, as distinct from contractual law, should form the basis of the lending relationship would seem somewhat idealistic. There may well be informal elements in relationships, but the fundamental relationship must be based on contract law. The Japanese structure, with few lawyers and little recourse to the courts of law, is entirely different from that in the UK and in the West generally. Of course, bankers try to supplement their contractual relationships with companies with informal contacts at all levels and in many ways. These include membership of business fora up and down the country, bankers and companies being represented for example in the Association of Corporate Treasurers, close personal friendships being formed, and a host of social contacts from lunches and dinners to golf days. The fundamental relationship is of contracts between legally independent entities: no informal relationships can override that structure.

8.9 CONCLUSION

In conclusion, the banking industry is full of competition, technological change and innovation. It is difficult to argue that there are any serious gaps in the services provided. There are no obvious products, which would be commercially viable in terms of risk and profit, which are not available already in the market-place.

The UK economy needs a viable and vibrant small business sector. The small business sector needs financial services. The banking system needs a profitable relationship with the small business sector. Given this community of interests it is difficult to see any fundamental conflict which would prevent a long-lasting relationship being established in that field.

For the largest companies the banking relationship is essentially the supply of services, and they are as determined to obtain the best value in that field as in any other. The benefits from traditional relationship banking, as perceived in the UK, appear now to be valued rather less by the company sector, and this has inevitably pushed the situation more towards arm's length banking. The banks also face a major issue relating to the profitability of the link with the largest companies, where business is extremely price competitive. In this area the banks have moved heavily into a treasury relationship with large companies, and at the same time some have tried to build up highly skilled service teams, such as project-based teams, to be able to offer sufficient value added so as to obtain an adequate return.

The largest companies have access to the complete range of financial markets and to world-wide sources. There is no fundamental shortage of finance facing them. If shortages exist elsewhere, then they can always return to the banks who would be very willing to supply them, and pricing would move to the appropriate level.

In the UK the relationship between banks and companies takes place in the framework of corporate governance as we have it. This means an efficient market in corporate ownership and therefore the inevitable takeovers and mergers. There are good arguments in favour of looking closely at whether this is the best structure for the UK, but it is a structure which is unlikely to change through voluntary action, and legislation does not appear to be on the horizon. That structure of corporate governance will thus continue to be the backdrop to the banking relationships with companies.

9

Stock-markets, Financial Institutions, and Corporate Performance

COLIN MAYER

9.1 INTRODUCTION

Stock-markets are traditionally viewed as the centrepiece of capitalist systems. According to textbook descriptions, they perform four essential functions:

1. They establish share prices which assist in the monitoring of firms and the allocation of resources.
2. They provide risk capital for investment.
3. They encourage risk taking by spreading risks and rewarding profitable investment.
4. They allow managerial failure to be corrected through markets for corporate control.

The first function is an information aggregation property: the expectations of a large number of investors are summarized in prices that reflect aggregate demands and supplies of individual stocks.

The second function is financing: the transmission of savings from investors to firms. The third is a diversification and hedging function: a large number of small claims on corporate assets are created and traded on markets. These permit investors to diversify portfolios over a large number of firms and to match securities with off-setting risks.

The fourth function is corporate control. Equity claims have associated voting rights that allow investors to exert control over corporate activities. Control can be exercised through proxy battles, non-executive directors, and takeovers.

In analysing the performance of stock-markets, most attention has focused on the first and third functions. The first function raises questions about the efficiency of stock-markets in pricing securities. Despite decades of analysis, results on the efficiency of stock-markets remain inconclusive. There is some evidence of mispricings associated with excess volatility of

This chapter is based on a Centre for Economic Policy Research International Study of the Financing of Industry and an Economic and Social Research Council project on Capital Markets, Corporate Governance and the Market for Corporate Control (W102251003). I am grateful to members of these two projects, Ian Alexander, Elisabetta Bertero, Jenny Corbett, Jeremy Edwards, Tim Jenkinson, Julian Franks, and Myriam Soria for helpful comments and advice.

share prices and the tendency of share prices to revert to mean levels. However, the evidence is weak and difficult to distinguish from variations over time in the returns that shareholders require to induce them to invest. Even if inefficiencies in pricing could be firmly established, they are of uncertain policy relevance since they have nothing to say about whether better institutional arrangements can be designed.

The diversification and hedging functions of stock-markets are the subject of a large financial economics literature. In so far as stock-markets make investments more liquid, they encourage broader equity participation than would otherwise be the case.

This chapter will have little to say about either of these functions. Instead, it will concentrate on the financing and control activities of stock-markets. The paper will argue that there are a number of puzzles that surround the operation of stock-markets. The first puzzle is by now a familiar one: despite the central role that is traditionally accorded to stock-markets, they provide little finance for industry; little new finance is raised from equity markets in any major industrialized nation.

The second puzzle relates to the other form of equity finance, retentions. Dividend policy has been a source of puzzlement to economists for several decades. This chapter notes a variation in dividend policy across countries that cannot readily be explained in conventional terms.

The third puzzle is associated with a rapidly growing literature in economics: it is known as the 'equity premium puzzle'. This suggests that differences in returns between equity and debt are too high to be explained by standard descriptions of risk aversion. If this is true then it implies that the cost of equity capital is too high relative to that on debt.

The fourth puzzle relates to the corporate governance and control functions of stock-markets. Despite the fact that theory accords an important role to markets in corporate control in improving economic efficiency, most financial systems appear to function perfectly effectively without them. Why is managerial failure not rampant in countries in which there is no market in corporate control?

These puzzles do not sit easily alongside the conventional description of stock-markets as mechanisms for providing risk capital and correcting managerial failure. These functions can be performed in a variety of different ways and it is questionable whether stock-markets are best at doing them. Instead, this chapter argues that UK style stock-markets perform a different function: they provide a market in property rights which allows control to be readily transferred to those who attach the highest value to it.

This is very different from the situation that exists in most other countries. Elsewhere, ownership and control rights do not reside with outside shareholders. They are concentrated in a small group of insiders. Transfers in control require the agreement of a number of parties, including related firms, employees and banks. The advantage of this is that these other parties can protect their interests better than their counterparts in the UK and are thereby encouraged to participate in corporate investment.

The question that this raises is which system performs best. In answering this, the chapter begins by questioning the simple view that stock-markets impede long-term investment and risk taking: evidence is presented that UK stock-markets have contributed significantly to these. However, it goes on to argue that there are some functions for which the UK market is ill-suited. These are associated with collaborative investment by a number of stakeholders: product and market development and specialized production. The consensus systems of control of continental Europe and Japan probably have distinct advantages in these areas.

The policy question that this raises is whether there are impediments to the emergence of these ownership and control structures in the UK. Some argue that the UK has a liberal system of regulation that permits companies to organize themselves in whatever way they think appropriate. However, this chapter contends that this is misleading. In particular, the establishment of corporate groupings in the UK is impeded by the emphasis that corporate and financial regulations have placed on the operation of stock-markets and the protection of minorities. Furthermore, in view of institutional rigidities, the emergence of corporate groupings may require positive promotion rather than just neutral regulation.

9.2 WHERE ARE THE NEW EQUITY ISSUES?

Aggregate patterns of corporate financing in different countries have been described at length elsewhere, see Mayer (1988; 1990). These estimates are based on flow of funds data and report the extent to which corporate sectors in different countries fund their investments from alternative sources over a fifteen-year period from 1970–85. Figures are reported for both gross and net financing proportions, where the net figures record sources of finance net of accumulations of equivalent financial assets, e.g. loans raised from banks net of bank deposits.

A number of common patterns emerge from these analyses. First, by far and away the most important source of finance in all countries is retentions. In some countries nearly one hundred per cent of financing for investment on a net basis comes from retentions. Second, to the extent that firms raise external finance, this comes predominantly from banks: banks are the largest source of external finance for industry in all developed countries. Third, only in North America do bond markets contribute a substantial amount to the financing of corporate sectors as a whole. Elsewhere, bond markets contribute less than 10 per cent of total financing.

The main observation that is relevant to this discussion relates to new equity issues: stock-markets do not contribute much in aggregate to corporate sector financing in *any* of the countries reported. On a net basis, new equity finance is frequently negative, reflecting the fact that firms are either repurchasing their own equity or purchasing other companies' equity in larger amounts than they are issuing equity themselves.

In some countries the low level of new equity issues is not surprising given the small size of stock-markets. For example, in Germany there were just 450 quoted companies in 1986; in France there were 680 and in Japan 1,500. However, there were many more quoted firms in the UK and US. In the UK there were 2,500 in 1986 and in the US 6,000 on the NYSE and NASDAQ combined.

The larger size of stock-markets in the UK and US reflects a larger number of companies coming to the market for the first time (initial public offerings or unseasoned issues). Table 9.1 shows that during the 1980s unseasoned new issues in the UK were often ten times or more those in Germany. But despite the larger number of quoted firms and unseasoned new issues, the proportion of investment funded by new equity issues was actually lower in the UK and US than in other countries over the period 1970 to 1985.

Thus in contrast to the standard description, stock-markets are not a major source of external financing for industry and large stock-market

Table 9.1 *Unseasoned new issues by firms coming to the German and UK stock-markets for the first time.*

	Germany	UK
1980	2	21
1981	2	73
1982	2	61
1983	11	113
1984	21	128
1985	11	151
1986	26	159
1987	19	146
1988	13	138

Notes: German listings relate to all German Stock Exchanges.
UK listings include those on the Unlisted Securities Market as well as full Stock Exchange listings. Figures exclude introductions and transfers between the USM and the main market.

Source: Mayer and Alexander (1990).

economies do not raise more new equity finance for their industries than small. In any event, the observation that UK and US stock-markets are much larger than those elsewhere just raises another puzzle. Why is it that some corporate sectors with small stock-markets can apparently operate at least as efficiently as their large stock-market counterparts?

The fact that stock-markets do not make a significant contribution in aggregate to external financing does not mean that they do not make a contribution to any part of their corporate sectors. On the contrary, Mayer and Alexander (1990) report that medium-sized UK electronics firms (i.e. small quoted companies) raised substantial amounts of new equity finance over the period 1982–8. There is therefore a group of firms that, at least in the UK, accesses the stock-market on a regular basis.

9.3 WHY DOES DIVIDEND POLICY VARY SO MUCH?

Corporate dividend policy has been a source of considerable puzzlement to economists for some time. In principle, dividends should simply reflect the balance between residual earnings that are available for distribution and internal requirements for investment. In practice, dividends appear to be set according to conventions that include a strong reluctance to cut dividends below previous years' levels (Lintner 1956). In addition, there is only a limited relation between dividends and the tax liabilities to which their payment gives rise. This is particularly starkly illustrated in relation to the observation that some firms pay out dividends which create tax liabilities for their shareholders at the same time as they raise new equity from their shareholders.

Dividend policy shows marked variations across countries. Using a matched sample of firms of similar size in the UK and Germany, Mayer and Alexander (1990) noted that dividend payout levels (the proportion of earnings paid out as dividends) of the UK firms were around three times as high as those of German firms over the period 1982–8 (see Table 9.2).

The most obvious explanation for the differences is tax: the tax incentives to distribute dividends in the UK may be higher than those in Germany. In fact, exactly the converse applies: retentions are particularly heavily discouraged by the German tax system.

Neither of the other two obvious explanations do much better. First, unlike dividend yields (dividends over share prices) there is no obvious reason why dividend payout ratios should be affected by inflation. Furthermore, the difference in payout ratios survives a period of considerable variation in inflation rates in the UK. Second, the higher dividend payments of UK firms do not simply reflect lower investment requirements: the ratio of investment to profits of the samples of German and UK firms were very similar.

Table 9.2   *Dividend pay-out ratios in Germany and*
the UK 1982–1988 (%)

	Germany	UK
1982	15.0	26.5
1983	14.3	29.8
1984	10.9	24.5
1985	10.0	27.1
1986	11.3	31.3
1987	14.6	39.6
1988	17.6	34.5

Source: Mayer and Alexander (1990).

Franks and Mayer (1991) note a similar difference in relation to *changes* in dividends. In a sample of fourteen German corporate restructurings during the 1980s it was commonplace for firms to cut or omit dividends during the process of restructuring. Dividends were gradually re-established over a period of years after the restructuring. This ability to cut dividends stands in marked contrast to the downward inflexibility of dividends in the UK and US noted above.

The contrast between the UK and Germany in terms of dividend levels and changes bears a remarkably close resemblance to a comparison of large quoted and unquoted firms that was performed in the UK (Mayer and Alexander 1991). For one matched sample of 56 quoted and unquoted companies in the UK, the average dividend payout ratio of the quoted firms was 21.7 per cent over the period 1980–7 as against 9.9 per cent for the unquoted companies. The average number of dividend cuts over the period was five times as high amongst the sample of unquoted as quoted firms. Large UK unquoted companies behave very similarly to large quoted German firms: they pay out a lower proportion of their earnings as dividends and they are more willing to cut their dividends than quoted UK firms.

9.4   WHY ARE EQUITY PREMIUMS SO HIGH?

The equity premium puzzle is as follows. Table 9.3 shows equity and gilt returns over the period 1918–88. Arithmetic real returns on equities averaged 10.4 per cent over the entire period and 2.2 per cent on gilts, giving a risk premium of 8.2 per cent. Since the Second World War returns on equities have averaged 10.0 per cent and on gilts 0.1 per cent giving a risk premium of 9.9 per cent. Over these two periods geometric risk premia have

Table 9.3 *Arithmetic annual average real returns on equities and gilts over the period 1918–1988* (%)

	Equities	Gilts	Risk premium
1918–1928	21.7	8.8	12.9
1929–1938	9.3	7.9	1.4
1939–1948	1.7	−1.9	3.6
1949–1958	9.6	−3.1	12.7
1959–1968	12.5	−1.0	13.5
1969–1978	5.5	−2.0	7.5
1979–1988	12.5	6.7	5.8
Average			
1918-1988	10.4	2.2	8.2
1948-1988	10.0	0.1	9.9

Source: BZW.

been 6.1 per cent and 7.5 per cent respectively. Similar risk premia have been recorded for the US. The problem that these risk premia present is that it is difficult to reconcile them with models of risk-averse consumers.[1] On average over the period from 1889–1978, real per capita consumption grew at just under 2 per cent per annum and the variability (standard deviation) of real per capita consumption was around 3.5 per cent. Risk premia of around 6 per cent can only be explained by extremely high risk aversion on the part of consumers (relative risk aversion of around twenty-six).[2] Not only is this implausibly large (most estimates suggest relative risk aversion of between one and two) but it also implies a high discount rate of riskless returns of around 15 per cent in real terms. Thus the equity risk premium puzzle is one of reconciling high equity returns, low riskless returns, and plausible values for risk aversion within the confines of observed growth rates and variability in growth rates of consumption.

This is not the only equity premium puzzle. Another one that has been widely documented concerns discounts on new equity issues of companies coming to the market for the first time. Table 9.4 records discounts on unseasoned new issues in the UK. Discounts are measured as the percentage

[1] The equity premium puzzle was first discussed in Mehra and Prescott (1985). Since then it has generated a large literature including articles by Mankiw (1986), Reitz (1988), and Weil (1989).

[2] The risk premium should be equal to the product of relative risk aversion, the standard deviations of aggregate consumption, and the excess return on equities, and its correlation coefficient. The standard deviation of returns on the Standard and Poors 500 was 16.7% over the period 1890–1979 and its correlation with the growth of consumption was 0.4%.

Table 9.4   *Underpricing of initial public offering 1985–1988*

	1985	1986	1987	1988	1985-8
Underpricing (%)	6.6	8.1	24.4	6.7	12.2

Source: Jenkinson (1990).

increase in the price of a share between issue and the end of the first week of trading in relation to average stock-market movements over the period. They therefore record the returns that shareholders earned over the period of the issue (around ten days in the case of the UK) in relation to average market movements. The striking feature of the discounts is their size. Similar results have been reported in the US. They imply annual rates of return of well over 100 per cent.

An explanation for both observations can be provided by an assumption that some investors encounter particularly risky prospects. In the case of unseasoned new issues, the most widely cited explanation is described as the 'winners' curse' (Rock 1986). Private investors are competing with well-informed (presumably institutional) investors for shares that are usually offered at a fixed price. Those issues that are underpriced are oversubscribed and the uninformed private investors only receive a scaled-down proportion of their subscription. Those issues that are overpriced do not attract the well-informed investors and the uninformed private investors' are not rationed. The uninformed therefore receive more overpriced than underpriced shares. They require a large discount on average to encourage them to subscribe.

The equity premium puzzle can be explained if individuals are unable to diversify their portfolios and face private consumption risk that is greater than aggregate consumption variability.[3] If individual consumption is more risky than aggregate consumption, risk premia will be high and riskless rates will be low in relation to what perfect capital market theory would suggest. Thus both the equity premium puzzle and the discounts on unseasoned new issues point to imperfections in the operation of equity markets that limit diversification and raise the equity cost of capital relative to that on debt.

This observation of a high equity cost of capital may go some way to explaining the observation of a strong preference of firms to raise external finance in the form of bank finance as against new equity issues.

---

[3] Other explanations have included Reitz's (1988) examination of big crashes, Abel's (1988) study of heterogeneous beliefs, Constantinides' (1988) and Abel's (1990) models of habit formation, Mankiw and Zeldes' (1990) separation of stockholders from non-stockholders, and Cecchetti, Lam and Mark's (1991) inclusion of leverage.

9.5 HOW DO SOME COUNTRIES MANAGE WITHOUT A MARKET IN CORPORATE CONTROL?

The UK has an active market in corporate control. Over the last few years on average around one quarter of takeovers of quoted companies were hostile in nature (i.e. they were initially rejected by the incumbent management).[4] In contrast, there is little or no market in corporate control on much of the Continent and in Japan. In Germany, for example, there have been just four cases of hostile takeover bids since the Second World War. In France, a market in corporate control is beginning to emerge following changes in regulations concerning takeovers at the end of the 1980s.

Markets in corporate control are supposed to perform the function of transferring assets from poorly performing to successful firms. Firms are continuously up for auction to buyers who attach the highest value to purchasing control. In principle this should encourage corporate efficiency on a number of accounts. First, it provides a low-cost mechanism for removing control from poor management. Second, the mere threat of takeover may act as a spur to better management.

If markets in corporate control do have these desirable properties it is surprising to discover that markets in corporate control are uncommon. It has been suggested that markets in corporate control may be expensive (in particular in terms of managerial time and effort) and cause management to be short-term in their outlook. However, it is not clear that takeovers are more expensive than their alternatives (e.g. closer institutional involvement) and the link between takeovers and short-termism has never been made precise.

It may be that other countries have organized alternatives that are close substitutes for takeovers. For example, the German supervisory board may be an effective mechanism for controlling what would otherwise be agency problems. But here a problem arises in understanding why supervisory boards should not themselves be subject to similar agency problems to the management that they are controlling. To understand this it is necessary to examine differences in the structure of ownership and control structures across countries.

9.6 AN EXPLANATION

An important feature of the UK takeover process is that ultimate jurisdiction over whether a takeover succeeds rests with the shareholders: if they do not sell their shares then the bid fails. No other party can exert any

---

[4] Jenkinson and Mayer (1991) also report that this was true at the end of the 1960s and beginning of the 1970s.

influence over the outcome of a bid, save in circumstances where the Government is drawn in by competition or wider social issues. This is not true of any other country except the US and even there state legislation has introduced greater impediments to the takeover process than currently exist in the UK.

The reason for the difference between the UK and continental Europe can be found in the structure of ownership and control. Ownership of UK quoted companies is dispersed across a large number of investors, primarily institutions. While institutions in aggregate own about two-thirds of UK equity, the average holding of any one institution in a particular firm is small. In a sample of 56 quoted companies reported in Mayer and Alexander (1991), on average less than two holdings per company in excess of 5 per cent were recorded. Financial institutions account for more than half these reported holdings, but even in these cases the average size of these large holdings was less than 10 per cent. In contrast, Franks, Mayer, and Soria (1991) report that large holdings in excess of 25 per cent are commonplace in Germany. These are owned by other families, companies, and banks. Similar patterns are observed in other continental European countries.

The UK stock-market is therefore characterized by a large number of widely dispersed shareholdings. In contrast the continental model of shareholdings is one of large share stakes. Furthermore, cross-shareholdings (reciprocal ownership of shares by companies) and complex interlinkages of share ownership are commonplace. These cross-shareholdings and interlinkages create large corporate groupings. The groupings are strengthened by firms having representation on each other's boards. The presence of banks on the supervisory boards of firms is well known. Representation by large suppliers, purchasers and competitors is less well documented. Figure 9.1 contrasts the UK system of corporate ownership and control with that on the Continent and in Japan.

One of the main implications of the corporate groupings is that outside of the UK and USA, ownership and control of corporations is in large part retained within the corporate sector: the degree to which outside investors (small shareholders) can exert control over corporate activities is very limited. In contrast, in the UK, ownership and control resides outside the non-financial corporate sector, primarily in non-bank financial institutions, such as pension funds and life insurance firms.

The main method by which outsiders exert control in the UK and USA is through takeovers. The takeover mechanism is an efficient system by which a large number of dispersed investors who would otherwise have little incentive to be involved in the monitoring of corporations can exert control over corporate activities. Essentially, takeovers put firms up for continuous auction: those who attach the highest value can purchase control from

Outsider systems   **Insider systems**

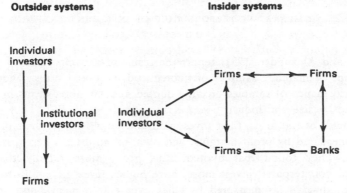

Fig. 9.1. Insider and outsider systems of ownership and control.

existing owners and managers. Takeovers allow owners to achieve maximum valuations without having to exert control directly themselves. Furthermore, the mere threat of takeover acts as an inducement to corporate efficiency.

While takeovers are the primary mechanism by which corporate control is exerted in an Anglo-American financial system, it is not the only one. Institutions exert control directly through the boards of firms and in the case of the USA through proxy battles. Overall, the level of outside investor intervention is high in the UK in relation to other European countries. This is indicated by high levels of chief executive and board room dismissals.

The common feature of all these forms of investor control is that they solely reflect the interests of shareholders. This is most clearly seen in the case of hostile takeovers, where competition for the ownership of firms results in changes in control being determined almost exclusively on the basis of highest bids (Jenkinson and Mayer 1991). This stands in marked contrast with the way in which corporate control is exerted in most other countries. The corporate groupings involve a large number of other stakeholders in corporate decision-taking, including suppliers, purchasers, banks, and employees. The structure of ownership and control creates a consensus in decision taking. This is not an outcome of some curious social convention or national characteristic. It is merely a reflection of the design of ownership and control structures.

The central questions raised by this distinction in ownership and control structures are, first, which system performs best and, second, to what extent can and should policy influence the structure of equity markets?

9.7 COMPARATIVE PERFORMANCE OF DIFFERENT PATTERNS OF
OWNERSHIP

Mayer and Alexander (1991) report the result of a comparison of the performance of matched samples of quoted and unquoted firms. They traced the performance of samples of large quoted and unquoted firms in the UK matched by size and industry over eight years from 1980–7. They examine the growth of the firms, their investment and employment, their profitability as measured by profit margins, and inflation-adjusted rates of return on capital. They found that quoted firms grow more rapidly than their matched counterparts, invest more, have higher levels of employment, are more productive (as measured by sales over employment), and are more profitable both in terms of profit margins and rates of return on capital employed. On all accounts therefore quoted firms outperformed their unquoted counterparts.

Perhaps most strikingly in relation to the short-termism debate, Mayer and Alexander found that quoted firms are more heavily concentrated in R&D intensive industries than unquoted firms of similar size. In other words, the distribution of large quoted firms is more heavily skewed towards high R&D industries than that of unquoted firms.

All of this suggests that stock-markets have contributed significantly to the performance of firms in the UK. Mayer and Alexander go on to provide an explanation for why this is the case despite apparent high costs of capital and low equity funding of investment. They note that quoted firms grew much more rapidly than their unquoted counterparts through acquisition. What the stock-market has allowed firms to do is to expand more rapidly through acquisition. This observation combined with the one that was previously made of a high level of firms coming to the stock-market for the first time suggests three ways in which stock-markets have contributed positively to UK corporate performance:

1. They allow growing firms to sell ownership and control to outside investors.
2. They allow existing owners of quoted firms to sell ownership and control to other investors.
3. They provide a mechanism, namely shares, by which ownership can be purchased by other firms..

In other words, the stock-market provides a mechanism by which property rights as well as equity claims to earnings streams can be traded. Such flexibility does not exist in other countries.

This right to transfer property rights is likely to be of particular benefit to certain activities such as entrepreneurship (firms coming to the stock-market for the first time), speculative investments (for example, oil exploration. and pharmaceuticals), and the formulation of corporate strategy where transfers of property should reflect divergences in expectations amongst investors.

This last function is consistent with the observation in Franks and Mayer (1991) that hostile takeovers in the UK are closely associated with changes in corporate policy as measured by chief executive dismissals, asset disposals, and corporate restructurings but only weakly related to pre-bid performance of the target firm. In other words, hostile takeovers appear to be motivated by expectations of improvements in performance rather than clear evidence of poor past performance. It is also consistent with the observation in Jenkinson and Mayer (1991) that hostile takeovers often appear motivated by the corporate strategy of the acquiring firm rather than managerial failure on the part of the target firm.

Markets in property rights suffer from two drawbacks. The first is that the separation of ownership and control, which is a feature of diverse ownership claims, makes equity financing expensive. Firms have to engage in costly signalling to their investors. This causes the level of dividends in the UK to be high and inflexible in relation to that in countries in which investors are more closely involved and in unquoted firms where separation of ownership and control does not arise. Second, the interests of other stakeholders (suppliers, purchasers, banks, and employees) in the firm are not represented. This discourages their participation in corporate investment.

UK-style corporate ownership is therefore likely to be least well suited to co-operative activities that involve several different stakeholders, e.g. product development, the development of new markets, and specialized products that require skilled labour forces. In addition, activities that require large amounts of external finance benefit from the close involvement of banks. The stage of corporate development at which this appears most crucial is when firms reach a medium scale of operation and seek stock-market participations in the UK, but receive long-term debt or equity finance from continental banks (Mayer and Alexander 1990). This difference is crucial to subsequent divergences in the control structure of UK and other countries' large corporations (Mayer 1991).

In summary, this chapter has argued that contrary to the traditional view described in the introduction, the primary function of UK-style stock-markets is neither the financing of firms nor the correction of managerial failure. Instead, it is the creation of markets in property rights for firms that allow transfers of ownership to occur in relation to investors' views about the likely future value of control and the appropriate strategies of firms. What this style of ownership does not accommodate is the interests of more than one group of stakeholders, in particular creditors. This implies that UK stock-markets may be well designed for certain activities but not those where collaborative investments between a number of interested parties and large external finance are required.

9.8   POLICY IMPLICATIONS

If this description of equity markets is correct then it raises a number of policy questions. The first is whether there is anything in either the UK or elsewhere that prevents companies from choosing appropriate ownership structures. If UK firms want to set up corporate groupings, is there anything to stop them?

Second, if choice is restricted by the nature of financial systems, is it possible for different arrangements to coexist? Could one imagine encouraging continental-style groupings in the UK or are these likely to be undermined by, or to put in jeopardy, existing stock-market activities? Finally, what policies are required either to reform existing systems or promote the emergence of alternatives to existing systems?

This is clearly too large an agenda to try to address here. Instead, I will restrict attention to the first question because there is a widely held view that the UK has a liberal system of corporate regulation that allows companies to choose whatever arrangement they believe appropriate. This is seriously misleading for two reasons.

First, the UK financial system has not evolved in such a way as to facilitate the formation of corporate groupings. Unlike Germany, the primary requirement of the financial system in the UK in the middle of the nineteenth century was not for large-scale financing of industry. Instead, it was for small-scale entrepreneurs to be able to realize returns from their investments. A stock-market served this function better than an integrated banking system. However, such developments are difficult to reverse. While technological change has created the need for larger-scale integrated processes involving investments by several related parties, transferring control from outside shareholders to insider groups requires fundamental changes. For example, the pervasive influence of German banks on the German financial system including the stock-market is unlikely to emerge in the UK.

Second, once the stock-market evolved as a centre-piece of the UK financial system, regulation was increasingly devoted towards improving its operation. Examples of such policy were the takeover code, insider trading laws and Stock Exchange conventions regarding dual class shares. These have had as their purpose the desire to increase participation on the stock-market by protecting minorities. Protection of minorities may have had a price: the extent to which firms can accumulate large share stakes without launching full bids, the willingness of institutions, including banks, to become party to privileged information, and the ability of firms to use dual classes of shares as takeover defence mechanisms have all been affected by these regulations. In sum, while there are few explicit impediments to firms choosing their form of corporate governance and control, the promotion of stock-markets and minority interests may have had a serious cost in discouraging the close involvement of insider groups in corporate activities.

REFERENCES

Abel, A. (1988), 'Asset prices under heterogeneous beliefs: Implications for the equity premium puzzle', mimeo (Department of Finance, Wharton School, University of Pennsylvania).

— (1990), 'Asset prices under habit formation and catching up with the Joneses', *American Economic Review*, 80: 38–42.

Cecchetti, S., Lam, P., and Mark, N. (1991), 'The equity premium and the risk free rate: Matching the moments', National Bureau of Economic Research discussion paper no. 3752.

Constantinides, G. (1988), 'Habit formation: A resolution of the equity premium puzzle', *Journal of Political Economy*, 98: 519–43.

Franks, J. and Mayer, C. (1991), 'Takeovers and the correction of managerial failure', mimeo.

— — and Soria, M. (1991), 'Corporate restructuring in Germany', mimeo.

Jenkinson, T. (1990), 'Initial public offerings in the UK, USA and Japan', Centre for Economic Policy Research discussion paper, no. 427.

— and Mayer, C. (1991), *Takeover defence strategies* (Oxford Economic Research Associates, Oxford).

Lintner, J. (1956), 'Distribution of incomes of corporations among dividends, retained earnings and taxes', *American Economic Review*, 97–113.

Mankiw, N. (1986), 'The equity premium and the concentration of aggregate shocks', *Journal of Financial Economics*, 17: 211–9.

— and Zeldes, S. (1991), 'The consumption of stockholders and non-stockholders', *Journal of Financial Economics*.

Mayer, C. (1988), 'New issues in corporate finance', *European Economic Review*.

— (1990), 'Financial systems, corporate finance and economic development', in Hubbard, G. (ed.), *Information, Capital Markets and Investment* (National Bureau of Economic Research, Chicago).

— (1991), 'Financing innovation', mimeo.

— and Alexander, I. (1990). 'Banks and markets: Corporate financing in Germany and the UK', *Journal of Japanese and International Economies*.

— — (1991), 'Stock markets and corporate performance: A comparison of quoted and unquoted companies', Centre for Economic Policy Research discussion paper.

Mehra, R. and Prescott, E. (1985), 'The equity premium: A puzzle', *Journal of Monetary Economics*, 15: 145–61.

Reitz, T. (1988), 'The equity premium: A solution', *Journal of Monetary Economics*, 22: 117–33.

Rock, K. (1986), 'Why new issues are underpriced', *Journal of Financial Economics*, 15: 187–212.

Weil, P. (1989), 'The equity premium puzzle and the riskfree rate puzzle', *Journal of Monetary Economics*, 24: 401–22.

10

The Role of the Venture Capital Industry in the UK

ADRIAN BEECROFT

THIS chapter assesses the contribution that venture capital makes to industry in various respects. There are two main areas of interest that relate to this. One is the provision of risk capital to small companies: what the problems are and how the venture capital sector copes with those in a different way from the clearing banks. The other relates to the question of governance: the way in which successful venture capital companies combine the provision of equity finance with hands-on involvement, not in the day-to-day running of the company, but in strategic guidance and help in dealing with management problems as the company grows and different functions develop. There are parallels between the role played here and the ideals presented in the papers by Dimsdale, Charkham and Sykes (Chapters 1, 4, and 5) as to what the non-executive director of a UK public company should be doing, and also parallels with the role played by a German bank with an equity stake and more relational contacts with its clients.

Criticisms of the industry in the context of broader UK financing problems are also addressed: in particular the relatively small proportion of funds that go towards high-technology ventures in the UK in comparison with the US and, related to that, the tendency for the largest proportion of venture capital to be directed towards lower-risk expansion or buy-out investments rather than towards start-ups or early stage investment.

The chapter is organized in the following way. Section 10.1 outlines the structure of the venture capital industry and its sources of funding, and looks at the different stances towards risk and return that can be adopted by the different types of company. Section 10.2 analyses the types of investment that have been undertaken and how they tie in with the types of company. The combination of funding with involvement in assisting in the growth of a small company is examined.

Section 10.3 looks at the contribution made by the industry in the wider context of the financing of small companies in the UK; in other words we compare some of the methods and attitudes of venture capital companies with those used by the banking sector in funding small businesses. We also look at some of the difficulties facing the venture capital industry in the UK in comparison with that in the USA and how those difficulties relate to the gaps in funding high-technology companies that still remain.

10.1 AN OUTLINE

10.1.1 *Structure and Size of the UK Venture Capital Industry*

The venture capital industry is composed mainly of the 120 companies in the British Venture Capital Association (BVCA). These have invested cumulatively between 1985–91 over £7 bn., investing around £1.5 bn. per year in 1988, 1989, and 1990. This fell to just over £1 bn. in 1991 (see Table 10.1).

Table 10.1 *Size of the UK venture capital industry (including buyouts)*

	1985	1986	1987	1988	1989	1990	1991
Amount invested (£m)	433	584	1,029	1,394	1,647	1,394	1,153
of which in UK	370	527	934	1,298	1,420	1,106	988
Number of companies financed	1,185	1,292	1,298	1,527	1,569	1,559	1,386
Cumulative amount invested since 1985 (£m)	433	1,017	1,780	3,174	4,821	6,215	7,368

Source: British Venture Capital Association

Table 10.2 illustrates the relatively rapid growth in the UK industry in terms of investment flows, although the pool of venture capital funds remains much larger in the USA than in the UK. The pool of US venture capital raised amounted to about $33.4 bn. in 1989, excluding buy-outs; the UK pool was around $7 bn. in 1989 and $9 bn. in 1990, excluding buy-outs.

The UK invested only 15 per cent of the amount of US investment in 1985. This grew to almost 50 per cent in 1990. The UK venture capital sector is the largest in Europe, investing between about 30–40 per cent of the total in Europe between 1987–90.

Table 10.2 *Amounts invested or disbursed by venture capital companies in the USA, UK and in the rest of Europe (excluding buy-outs and buy-ins) ($m)*

	1985	1986	1987	1988	1989	1990
USA	2,675	3,226	3,941	3,653	3,262	1,900
UK	422	471	690	1,006	906	936
Europe excluding UK	na	na	1,360	1,504	1,696	2,384

Source: NVCA, BVCA, EVCA

10.1.2 Type of Company or Vehicle for Venture Capital Funding

There are four types of vehicle which provide venture funding. These are the independent funds, the captive funds, 3i which must be considered in a category on its own, and Government sponsored funds such as the Business Expansion Schemes (BES).

Independent venture capital companies are either private or publicly listed. Independent means that the company is owned by its managers and other investors, but not by a bank or other financial institution. Independent funds accounted for 45 per cent by value of all venture capital investment made in the UK in 1990. Of these, 70 per cent were made by privately owned independents, 30 per cent by publicly listed independents (see Table 10.3).

Table 10.3 *Venture capital investments in UK by type of investment vehicle (total invested includes buy-outs) (% of total)*

	1985	1986	1987	1988	1989	1990	1991
Independent private	32	31	28	38	33	31	na
Independent publicly listed	9	18	15	11	10	12	11
Total independent	41	49	43	49	43	44	na
Captive bank	26	24	16	15	17	23	13
Captive pension fund	12	9	6	4	4	3	7
Captive other	10	11	4	1	5	8	5
Total captive	48	44	26	20	26	34	25
3i	na	na	26	28	29	20	na
BES	10	6	4	2	1	1	na
Government	2	1	1	1	1	1	1
TOTAL (£m.)	370	527	934	1,298	1,420	1,106	988

Source: BVCA

Independents raise fixed-term funds (usually ten-year funds) from international sources. The majority of funds come from pension funds and insurance companies, with the balance raised from banks, trading companies and individuals. The management company is paid an annual management fee—usually 2.5 per cent of the fund—and the directors or partners of the company receive 20 per cent of the net capital gains achieved by the fund. This 20 per cent reward structure, known as carried interest, is meant to act as a performance incentive, payable only once the institutional investors have recovered their initial investment. Investors receive no fixed annual yield but get the proceeds as and when investments are sold off. The management of the fund invests each fund in twenty or more companies in order to diversify away some of the risk of investment in unquoted companies.

Investments tend to be high risk and required returns are correspondingly high. This is compounded by the relatively illiquid nature of an investment in a private venture capital fund. However, a number of organizations now buy secondary positions in UK venture capital funds, which reduces the illiquidity for the investor in those funds. The average return required by an independent venture capital fund from UK venture capital investments is around 25 per cent; this covers the 15–20 per cent return that pension funds look for on their investment in venture funds plus the management fee and carried interest.

Independent funds are usually ten-year funds. During the first three or four years of the funds, two-thirds of the money is spent in initial invest-ments. The rest is held back for follow-on investments, the need for which arises either from rapid growth or from failure to meet goals within the ini-tial funding. Over the final six or seven years of the life of the fund, the venture capitalist nurtures and then exits from the investments. This means that the venture capitalist looks to exit from an investment on average after around six years. New funds need to be raised every three or four years to maintain the capacity to invest.

The need to invest and exit within the ten-year life-span of the fund limits the period within which a return needs to be made and therefore the types of investment that can be undertaken, a problem which will be discussed below. Exits have traditionally come from flotations and trade sales, around 50 per cent from each source. More recently it has become harder to float compa-nies; this may be a potential problem but it may simply reflect the recession and may improve when general economic conditions are better. (This has been the case in 1993). It is significantly easier to float companies at an ear-lier stage in the US than in the UK. This makes US investments much more liquid than in the UK, giving the venture capital fund an earlier exit route. This exit route offers the prospect of considerable returns being made to the venture capital company through selling publicly. The existence of a public market in the shares of the company, replacing private capital with public capital, breaks the constraint for the investment project itself to achieve returns within a relatively short period. There are, however, constraints imposed on young companies through being subject to the disciplines of the stock-market and share price volatility.

The second category of providers of venture capital is the captive funds. This term is used to describe funds that are directly controlled by pension funds, insurance companies, banks or other corporate bodies. This sector of the market has grown significantly over the past three years as a provider of funds. The BVCA figures show that captive funds were responsible for 20 per cent of the amount invested by the venture capital industry in 1988 rising to 34 per cent of the total in 1990 but falling back sharply to around 25 per cent in 1991. Within the captive funds category, bank subsidiaries showed the largest increase in investment in the late 1980s (see Table 10.3). However, the sharp fall in investment by such captive funds in 1991 was almost entirely by this bank sector.

The decision by a pension fund whether to invest in unquoted companies through independent venture capital funds or to set up a direct investment organization of its own (a captive fund) rests on a number of factors. One of these is size. Few pension funds will invest more than 1 per cent of their assets in unquoted companies, though some go up to 5 per cent. Therefore a pension fund needs to be substantial to justify setting up its own captive fund, since a minimum of £10m. per annum investment is required. It is a higher-risk strategy for a pension fund to invest directly in unquoted companies than to invest in independent venture capital funds. This has implications for the type of investment that they tend to make in the venture capital area (see below). There are further difficulties in recruiting venture capital managers within the constraints of the organization of pension funds or banks. Pension funds that have a captive fund in their home market will often use independents in overseas markets. In the UK, PosTel, CIN and the Prudential are among the organizations that make direct investments, but also invest in independent funds.

Pension funds and banks invest in unquoted companies partly because they believe that they can yield good returns and also on the part of some pension funds, in particular those for the local authorities, due to a feeling of social responsibility to invest in small companies. Banks have the advantage of branch networks by which to spot investment opportunities, although for reasons discussed in Chapters 6–8, they are often not adept at exploiting the information flows.

3i constitutes a category of venture capital vehicle on its own. It accounted for 20 per cent of all venture capital investment in the UK in 1990. The company was set up by the clearing banks after the war to help fill the equity funding gap identified by the Macmillan report (see Dimsdale, Chapter 1). It has done much to make the concept of unquoted investment acceptable to UK institutions and has acted as a training ground for many venture capitalists now working elsewhere in the industry.

3i is planning to float in order to allow at least some of the clearing banks to realize their stake. This raises a number of questions. Will it affect *3i*'s investment patterns? Will it mean that *3i* is less prepared to take risk and less prepared for early stage investment as concern for current profitability will increase? This is particularly of concern as *3i* have been the principal providers for small firms requiring equity under £200,000. Will pension funds shift their portfolios towards *3i* and get their exposure to unquoted companies through *3i* rather than investing in independent venture capital funds? Will *3i* raise new money or will there be no new issues in which case one might expect *3i*'s share price to rise in the event of increased demand from pension funds? It is felt that US pension funds, which form a substantial (around 40 per cent) part of pension fund investment in venture capital funds in the UK, will not invest through *3i* as they tend to be less worried about liquidity and understand the high-risk end of the market better.

The fourth category of venture capital vehicle is government-sponsored investment and Business Expansion Scheme funds. Activity in this sector is declining, with their contribution to the amount invested by the industry falling from £30m. in 1988 to £25m. in 1990—just over 2 per cent of the total.

10.2 TYPES OF INVESTMENT AND TYPES OF COMPANY

10.2.1 *The Governance of Small Companies*

There are broadly four types of investment, divided by stage of financing. These are early-stage or start-up investments, expansion capital, rescue capital, and management buy-outs or buy-ins. The early stage investment is very high risk with high failure rates, and high returns are required. Expansion capital has a lower rate of return than a successful early stage investment but is much less risky and there is the possibility of some running yield. Rescue capital is riskier than expansion capital, and possibly as high risk as early stage, and requires considerable management expertise to turn a failing company round. Buy-outs are relatively low risk, if the gearing is kept under control and if the business is not too cyclical.

Table 10.4 compares the proportions of investment by stage of financing in the USA and the UK. As US data does not include buy-outs and buy-ins, the UK buy-outs have been treated separately and the other stages are taken as proportions of the pool of venture capital excluding buy-outs.

The proportion of early stage and start-up financing fluctuated between 20–40 per cent of financing in the late 1980s, falling away to only 13 per cent in 1991. It held a much more constant share in the USA where it remained around 30 per cent of investment in the second half of the 1980s.

The share of financing directed to expansion capital has been over 60 per cent of the total, excluding buy-outs, in the UK for most of the recent period. This is higher than in the USA where between 40–50 per cent of funds are development capital. This might partly reflect some confusion in

Table 10.? Stage of financing (% of total excluding buy-outs)

	1985 USA	1985 UK	1986 USA	1986 UK	1987 USA	1987 UK	1988 USA	1988 UK	1989 USA	1989 UK	1990 UK	1991 UK
Start-up	15	19	19	27	13	18	13	12	13	16	15	8
Other early stage	15	10	16	13	15	11	15	11	15	23	10	5
Total early stage	30	29	35	40	28	29	28	23	28	39	25	13
Expansion	53	61	44	50	45	65	41	71	47	58	66	75
Other	17	10	21	10	27	6	31	6	25	3	10	12
Total excluding buy-outs ($m.)	2,675	422	3,226	471	3,941	689	3,653	1,006	3,262	906	936	785
Buy-outs % of total including by-outs	—	37	—	45	—	55	—	57	—	61	53	55
Total including buy-outs ($m.)	—	351	—	857	—	1,530	—	2,310	—	2,326	1,976	1,747

Source: BVCA and NVCA

the definitions here, as US data for the LBO and acquisition category might include some measure of buy-outs which are excluded from the UK data. This would bias downward the US proportions in the early and expansion stages, and bias upwards the US proportion in the LBO stage which is much higher than in the UK.

From the lower part of Table 10.4 one can see that increasing funds have been going to buy-outs of various sorts in the UK. The proportion of total funds including buy-outs rose from around 37 per cent in 1985 to over 60 per cent in 1989, falling off somewhat more recently. Financing buy-outs was particularly popular in the boom of the late 1980s and the concentration of buy-outs in cyclical service industries which have been prone to the recession has tempered this trend. The rising proportion of funds going to buy-outs in the late 1980s does suggest that this might have been at the expense of higher-technological earlier-stage financing.

This worry is substantiated if one looks at the type of industry to which funds were directed (see Table 10.5). It is assumed here that buy-outs have not been in technology sectors. A comparison was made between the USA and UK of proportions of funds (excluding buy-outs) going into technology sectors comprising the computer sector, electronics, medical, and biotechnology sectors, and communications. This shows the UK proportion to have been between a half and one-third of the US proportion of funds going into these sectors. The USA invested 80 per cent in 1985 falling to around 60 per cent in 1988 and rising back to 75 per cent in 1990 in high-technology industries. The UK proportion fell from 43 per cent in 1985 to around 20 per cent in 1988 rising back to 30 per cent more recently. Again this illustrates the propensity of the venture capital industry in both countries to move out of these sectors during the boom and back into them once boom conditions have subsided. This is worrying as those technology sectors themselves are relatively non-cyclical and should receive a fairly constant share of resources and not constitute a residual to fluctuations in low-technology sectors.

It is also germane to ask why the USA should devote a much greater proportion of its venture capital funds to technology-related enterprises. US venture capitalists have a much greater understanding of technology than in the UK. One might expect rewards to venture capitalists to be higher because of this.

In addition there are two other major differences which contribute to higher returns to such investments. Price–earnings ratios for technology-related companies are higher in the USA than in the UK. Newly floated companies also tend to attain their higher price–earnings ratios more quickly after flotation in the USA than in the UK. The presence of such a market in public equity in the USA particularly for these small young high-technology companies, which does not exist in the UK, itself enhances the

Table 10.5 Venture capital investment in the USA and UK by industry proportion of total investment excluding buy-outs by sector

Industry sectors	1985		1986		1987		1988		1989		1990		1991
	USA	UK	USA	UK	USA	UK	USA	UK	USA	UK	USA	UK	UK
Technology-related													
Computer	35	19	28	11	23	11	21	10	22	13	31	13	14
Electronics	26	12	24	8	18	9	18	3	19	5	17	5	8
Medical and biotechnology	15	4	15	9	18	11	20	4	22	8	23	9	5
Communications	4	8	5	8	5	4	3	3	4	5	4	3	1
Total %	80	43	72	36	64	35	62	21	66	32	75	30	28
Non-technology related													
Consumer	7	—	9	—	17	—	12	—	11	—	9	—	—
Industrial products and automation	6	—	5	—	6	—	6	—	7	—	4	—	—
Energy	1	—	2	—	2	—	0.4	—	0.5	—	1	—	—
Other	6	—	12	—	11	—	20	—	14	—	11	—	—
Total %	20	57	28	64	36	64	38	79	33	68	25	70	72
Total $ million excluding buy-outs	2,675	422	3,226	471	3,941	689	3,653	1,006	3,262	906	1,900	936	785

Note: It is assumed that buy-outs are not in the technological sectors. There is no break down of non-technological investment in the UK.

Source: BVCA and NVCA.

potential returns to venture capitalists holding original equity stakes in such companies. The trading in shares in small, high-technology companies is dependent less on the companies being ready to bring products to the market, but on their potential to do so. There is a considerable willingness of the US individual investor to back such companies in particular sectors such as biotechnology or electronics, although their enthusiasm comes in waves. The value of these shares once traded is frequently much higher than when the equity was originally created and hence original equity holders such as venture capitalists stand to reap substantial returns to their investment in this way. It also gives small companies a much deeper market for sourcing this type of investment.

The preference for technology-related activities also stems from the much larger market for technology-related products in the USA than for low-technology products. The whole of the USA is the market for a technology company whereas the market for companies producing many low-technology products and services is restricted geographically.

The different types of venture capital company favour different types of investment activity. Independent funds are more likely to invest in early-stage, high-risk and potentially high-return deals than are captive funds. This is partly because of the ways that the different vehicles are funded. The independents have ten-year money and no obligation to pay a running yield to their investors. Implicitly even independents' willingness to finance the riskier end of the spectrum has declined since 1988.

Captive funds, especially bank subsidiaries, and 3i either raise funds on the short-term money markets or from their parent companies. They need current income to pay their funding costs. They invest in later stage companies through a mixture of debt and equity and demand a running yield from their investments in the form of interest payments and/or dividends. Nearly all of 3i's investments take the form of debt with a small part invested as equity. This is similar to the role undertaken by German banks which take small equity stakes in many companies to which they lend. The UK clearing banks have chosen to hand this role to 3i rather than taking direct equity stakes themselves. This leads to a more restricted type of involvement by the banks in contrast to venture capital companies, which is a crucial aspect of the way venture capital companies contribute to the growth of small companies.

The independent fund is more likely to be run by people with an industrial background who can make a contribution to the companies in which they invest whereas captive funds tend to have more financial than industrial expertise. Many venture capital managers have considerable management experience and management education. When an investment is made, it is normal for the venture capital company to appoint at least one non-executive director to the board of the investee company. The venture capitalist can then advise and guide the entrepreneur on a variety of issues, fulfilling the role of a traditional non-executive director. The venture capitalist may take up an executive role within a company to fill a particular gap; this tends to happen more in rescue ventures and as a temporary measure. Venture capitalists have experience of sources of funding and of the generic problems of a growing business. These problems tend to be in two areas—personnel and control systems.

Occasionally the entrepreneur has recruited a complete management team, but it is more commonly the case that the team is incomplete. The venture capitalists can use their network of contacts to help build a team. As the company grows, management requirements change and it is frequent that the original entrepreneur is not the appropriate person to run a much larger concern. The other function which changes drastically is the financial one: a company with a turnover of up to £0.5m. probably needs a book-keeper/accountant whereas at the £2m. mark a financial manager is needed and at £5m. turnover a full financial director. These different jobs seldom suit the same individual. Loyalties within small teams develop to such an extent that company requirements are often not recognized by those inside the team. The venture capitalist fulfils this non-executive role of recognizing these changes and is also able to draw on a pool of managerial talent from a network of contacts. There are parallels between this role and that provided by a German banker, with an equity stake and reputation to protect, with a seat on the supervisory board and a network of contacts of managerial talent and competencies with which to suggest replacements if the need arises. This happens in particular in the case of rescues, when there has been obvious failure.

The ability to fulfil this function varies, depending in part on the degree of familiarity with the particular industry concerned. Some funds cover one or two industries in which they have specific expertise, whilst others cover a wider range of industries at a more general level. There are relatively few specialized funds in proportion to general funds. Out of 96 funds registered in the 1988 BVCA Handbook, over three-quarters of them were general. Only a small number of the specialist companies, maybe eight in all, concentrate on early-stage high-technology business. One problem of general funds is the inability to distinguish good from bad projects in relatively specialized areas of technology. The problem of identifying and managing early-stage and high-technology investments is difficult. It requires a level of expertise and experience which were not available to the venture capital industry when it began to expand in the early 1980s. As a result, some funds made significant losses from early-stage and high-technology businesses and have withdrawn from the area. This situation may lead to higher rejection rates than are warranted by the potential of the projects. It may also help to explain the relatively high proportion of funding of consumer-related investments or general industrial products and the relatively low level of technology funding in comparison with the USA. It seems likely that the experience of the early 1980s combined with more limited technological expertise in the UK means that funding of technology ventures is also lower in absolute terms than it should be in relation to the potential.

Another disadvantage that the venture capital industry cannot overcome alone is the relatively small pool of managerial talent on which to draw to commercialize the technical opportunities that do exist. There are not enough competent managers in Britain prepared to give up corporate jobs with fringe benefits and pensions to face the risks and uncertain rewards of starting or joining a small company. This is partly because, unlike the American counterpart, the average UK manager does not have the financial resources to support himself while a new business gets established. The venture capitalist can only help with this problem to an extent. Another disincentive to starting one's own business is higher rates of capital gains tax and less relief on it than in the USA and most of Europe.

In this context of difficulty in finding and establishing adequate teams of management and difficulties in finding commercial technological propositions, one can see why venture capital resources have been drawn into the management buy-out or buy-in sphere. The need for the venture capitalist to play a hands-on role in the development of the business is much less than in early-stage businesses. Many management buy-outs are of profitable companies with well-rounded management teams. The value that venture capitalists assist in creating derives either from the increased incentives due to the change in structure of ownership and control subsequent to the buy-out, or due to lack of funding of the business whilst it was contained within the larger company. The form of ownership and control structure is changed often from dispersed and passive public shareholders to a more concentrated, informed, and actively involved management and investing body. Better incentives derive partly directly from the management who now largely own and have more control over the company. The buy-out is also an example of a movement towards 'insider' control, protection from outside market pressures, which are discussed in Chapters 9, 12, and 15 in this volume by Mayer, Prevezer and Ricketts, and Corbett in particular.

For instance one motivation in buy-outs has been for management to increase their control over the business. Management achieve this partly through taking an equity stake in the business. The leveraging that has resulted from the management buy-out (MBO) process arises due to the management competing with a trade buyer and having to replace equity with debt. In this process the risk becomes more concentrated upon the smaller number of owners and the company is placed under higher risk of bankruptcy due to the much higher gearing. Such a process is only suitable for those businesses that are not intrinsically high-risk and can generate sufficient cash-flow to service sizable quantities of debt. The danger has lain in the cyclical nature of such businesses, often in the service sectors which are particularly prone to recession. Debt–equity ratios in MBOs at the time of the buy-out have, however, been brought down from around 6 in the first half of 1989 to just over 1 in the first half of 1991. The structure of the MBO market has changed as the banks have become more circumspect about lending to this sector. There have therefore been lower valuations of buy-outs and management have been accepting smaller equity stakes. The very high average debt–equity ratio in the late 1980s came from a limited number of very large transactions.

10.3   VENTURE CAPITAL IN THE WIDER CONTEXT OF FINANCING SMALL COMPANIES IN THE UK

This section addresses the issues of whether there is still an equity gap which is not filled by either the banking or venture capital sectors, and what lessons the banking sector could learn from the venture capital sector.

Venture capital financing offers a form and style of financing which is not provided elsewhere in the spectrum of financial services, in its combination of a certain length of commitment with greater involvement and a degree of influence over the companies in which equity stakes are taken. It is more flexible and imaginative in the financing packages that are put together than the banking sector has been (see Middleton and Hughes in Chapters 7 and 11). Its commitment includes help to companies in restructuring during the process of growth, helping to find suitable management, and assisting in rescue packages. Taking equity stakes in companies is crucial in providing the incentive to the venture capital company to take such an interest. The clearing banks' financing of companies might find that taking even small equity stakes, as is done in Germany and Japan, would increase the incentive to become involved in much the same way; there would be less reliance placed on collateral and a rigid schedule of relatively low interest charges, and more placed on equity-style returns through flexible dividends or the capital gain on the equity.

Certainly the banking and venture capital sectors are complementary in their financing of the small company sector. Nevertheless there is still a question as to whether gaps in funding certain sorts of small company remain. It still may be the case that relatively high-risk, early-stage companies specializing in technological investment find it harder to raise finance and assemble management teams than their counterparts in the USA for instance. This is not to say that all of the responsibility lies at the door of the venture capital sector to fill those gaps; there are certain strategic elements missing in the necessary conditions to make those enterprises viable—namely sufficient management skills within the small companies and enough flexibility in exit routes to make the returns required by the venture capital companies not prohibitively high. However, inadequate numbers of specialist skills in technology within the venture capital companies is a problem that the venture capital sector could tackle. For instance there could be more liaison between general venture capital funds and specialists either in large companies or universities and research centres.

Another type of company which may be slipping through the net in terms of inability to receive funding is the very small company requiring investment of under £200,000. Many venture capital funds do not find it worthwhile to commit their resources to such small ventures as there are economies of scale lost in the process. The alternative bank finance lacks the attention to assisting managerial competence that venture capital companies provide. There may be some scope for government assistance in providing training of management or additional management fees to those firms prepared to invest in and work with very small companies. A further opportunity may be for the clearing banks to take on the role that they previously subcontracted to 3i by taking equity stakes as well as making loans to such small companies. Equity returns could justify the higher management cost. It would, however, require the banks to rethink their role in relation to small companies. This is addressed in the chapters by Lomax, Middleton *et al.*, Hughes, and Dimsdale (1, 7, 8, and 11).

11

The 'Problems' of Finance for Smaller Businesses

ALAN HUGHES

11.1 INTRODUCTION

This chapter considers arguments and evidence for and against the view that smaller businesses in the UK have been constrained by equity or loan gaps in the past decade. The paper begins with an analysis of the comparative financial structure of large and small UK companies in the late 1980s, and of trends in their relative profitability since the late 1970s. Comparisons are made on both these scores with the relative experience of smaller firms reported in official inquiries for earlier decades (HMSO 1971; 1979). This is followed by a review of theoretical arguments which might account for the differences in financial structure which are observed. These arguments seek to explain the differences as optimal outcomes reflecting the relative ownership and risk structure of smaller firms, or as non-optimal outcomes reflecting various kinds of market failures arising in particular from inadequate or biased information flows. This discussion is followed by a review of developments in the supply of venture capital in the UK in the 1980s, and of recent survey and case study evidence on firms' perceptions of the financial constraints they face.

On the basis of these reviews the chapter argues that there is no compelling evidence of an overall failure in the supply of funds for smaller firms but that there may be problems in the *terms* on which finance is available. Emphasis is also placed upon difficulties faced by newer innovative firms. In so far as smaller firms experience problems, and in so far as these arise from the difficulties of banks in coping with the informational and risk problems of the small business sector, it is argued that the latter may help themselves by developing mutual guarantee schemes. In effect consortia of small firms should be encouraged to underwrite their own loan

This chapter arises out of the research programme into the Determinants of the Birth, Growth, and Survival of Small Businesses at the Small Business Research Centre, Cambridge. The programme is supported by the ESRC, The European Commission, Barclays Bank, the Department of Employment, and the Rural Development Commission. This support is gratefully acknowledged.

An earlier version of the chapter was presented at the NEDO Policy Seminar on the City and Industry: Capital Markets and Company Success in London on 21 November 1991. The author is grateful to 3i Plc and the British Venture Capital Association for the provision of data relating to their investment activities and John Knight of the CSO for advice on the Company Accounts database underlying *Business Monitor MA3 Company Finance*. Jane Humphries, Tony Lawson, David de Meza, Iain Smedley, and Peter Nolan provided helpful comments on an earlier draft. The usual disclaimers apply.

applications to banks. Existing European Community schemes are briefly described. The conclusion sums up the key findings of the paper.

11.2 THE COMPARATIVE FINANCIAL STRUCTURE AND PROFITABILITY OF LARGE AND SMALL COMPANIES

Table 11.1 presents a summary analysis of the balance sheet structure, gearing, and profitability of large and small UK non-financial companies in the UK in the period 1987–9. 'Large' companies are those ranked in the top 2,000 in terms of capital employed in the UK non-financial corporate sector. 'Small' companies are in a 1 in 300 sample of the remainder of the sector stratified by size of capital employed. Averages for these two groups may obviously conceal wide variations within them, and may also reflect the effects of aggregation across industries, characterized to different degrees by the presence of large and small firms. As a rough check on the latter effect a breakdown of the sample is provided into manufacturing and non-manufacturing industries. The data are the best available official statistics for the purpose in hand and may be compared with similar analyses specially carried out in the Bolton and Wilson Reports dealing, *inter alia*, with small business finance (HMSO 1971; 1979). It is worth emphasizing, however, that in the course of the 1980s increasing numbers of small companies took advantage of the dispensation to submit modified accounts in their returns to Companies House. This has led to an increase in the estimation involved in producing the data which is reported here. It is ironic that at a time when information on small company performance is of growing interest it is becoming increasingly difficult to obtain it in a useful form.

The data are presented as averages over the three financial years 1987–9. Each balance sheet item in Table 1 is shown as a percentage of total assets/liabilities whilst rates of return are shown upon total assets, net assets, and equity. A number of conclusions may be drawn from Table 11.1.

11.2.1 *Asset Structure*

1. Small companies have a relatively low ratio of fixed to total assets. In the non-manufacturing industries, for instance, small companies hold 30.9 per cent of their total assets in the form of fixed assets. For large companies the figure is 59.2 per cent.
2. Small companies have a relatively high proportion of trade debt in their asset structure. Thus in manufacturing, trade and other debtors comprise 37.9 per cent of total assets. For large manufacturing companies the figure is 23.6 per cent.
3. Small non-manufacturing companies have a high proportion of their assets in the form of stocks and work in progress (25 per cent) relative

Table 11.1. *The balance sheet structure, gearing, and profitability of large and small UK companies in the manufacturing and non-manufacturing industries (excluding oil) in the period 1987–89*

	Manufacturing companies		Non-manufacturing companies	
	Small	Large	Small	Large
	(Average % 1987–9)			
Fixed assets				
Net tangible assets	30.2	34.2	26.4	52.4
Intangibles	0.4	3.3	0.9	3.4
Investments	0.9	7.0	3.5	3.4
Total net fixed assets	31.5	44.4	30.9	59.2
Current assets				
Stock and work in progress	19.6	19.8	25.0	14.0
Trade and other debtors	37.9	23.6	36.0	19.3
Investments	1.0	2.8	0.6	1.7
Cash and short-term deposits	9.9	9.3	7.9	5.8
Total current assets	68.5	55.6	69.1	40.8
Total current and fixed assets	100.0	100.0	100.0	100.0
Current liabilities				
Bank overdrafts and loans	11.3	6.1	11.0	4.4
Directors' short-term loans	0.5	0.0	2.7	0.0
Other short-term loans	0.3	1.1	1.1	1.3
Trade and other creditors	35.3	23.6	41.9	21.9
Dividends and interest due	0.3	1.7	1.3	1.5
Current taxation	7.1	4.8	4.4	3.9
Total current liabilities	55.0	37.3	62.4	33.1
Net current assets	13.5	18.3	6.8	8.3
Total net assets	45.0	62.7	37.6	67.5
Long-term liabilities				
Shareholders' interest*	36.1	42.0	26.8	47.4
Minority interests and provisions	2.3	6.5	1.1	2.8
Loans†	3.2	11.5	6.3	15.4
Other creditors and accruals	3.4	2.7	3.5	1.9
Total capital and reserves	45.0	62.7	37.6	67.5
Total capital and liabilities	100.0	100.0	100.0	100.0

(cont.)

Table 11.1.   (*cont.*)

	Manufacturing companies		Non-manufacturing companies	
	Small	Large	Small	Large
Long-term loans as % all loans	20.5	61.7	29.4	72.9
All loans as % shareholders' interest	42.4	44.3	78.7	44.5
Interest expense as % of earnings				
before tax	15.4	12.4	21.4	14.7
Pre-tax return on net assets	15.9	19.6	19.1	14.4
Pre-tax return on total assets	12.4	14.3	13.0	17.6
Pre-tax return on equity	10.4	19.1	18.8	13.3

Notes: *Ordinary, plus preference plus capital and revenue reserves.
†Directors' loans, bank loans, convertible, and debenture loans, all of which have a duration
of over one year.
Source: Business Monitor MA3 Company Finance: Various Issues

to large non-manufacturing companies (14 per cent). In manufacturing,
however, there is little to choose between large and small in this respect.

11.2.2   *Current Liabilities*

1. Trade and other creditors are a higher proportion of liabilities for small
   than for large companies. In manufacturing, trade and other creditors
   were 35.3 per cent of total liabilities compared to 23.6 per cent for large
   companies.
2. Current liabilities are a higher proportion of total liabilities for small
   than for large companies, especially in non-manufacturing, where the
   respective percentages were 33.1 per cent and 62.4 per cent.

11.2.3   *Long-Term Liabilities*

1. Small companies are less reliant on shareholders' interests to finance their
   assets. In manufacturing for instance these accounted for 36.1 per cent of
   total small-firm liabilities compared to 42 per cent for large companies.
2. Small companies are more reliant on short-term banks loans and overdrafts than large companies (4.4 per cent and 11 per cent of total assets
   respectively in the non-manufacturing sector for instance).
3. In non-manufacturing, gearing (as measured by the stock ratio of total
   loans to shareholders interest, or by the flow measure of interest expense
   as a percentage of earnings before interest and taxes) is higher for small
   companies than for larger companies.

4. In manufacturing, small companies are slightly more highly geared on the flow measure but slightly less highly geared than larger companies on the stock measure.
5. In both manufacturing and non-manufacturing, small firms are much more reliant on short-term loans. Thus in manufacturing, long-term loans are only 20.5 per cent of all loans for small firms, but 61.7 per cent of all loans for large firms.

The basic findings for the asset and liability structures of small companies are broadly similar to those of previous investigations for the 1960s and 1970s (HMSO 1971). The high reliance on short-term finance provided by banks, and the relatively low proportions of assets financed by shareholders interests are clearly long-run persistent features of small business finance. The same is true of the relative importance of trade debt, and trade credit and the relative unimportance of fixed assets in their balance sheet structure.

11.2.4 *Profitability*

1. The profitability of small manufacturing companies is below that of large manufacturing companies on each of the three measures shown. Thus for example the rate of return on total assets (ROTA) was 12.4 per cent for small, and 14.3 per cent for large, companies.
2. The profitability of small non-manufacturing companies was above that for larger companies when measured as the return on net assets (RONA) or equities (ROE), but below that for larger companies on a ROTA basis. They earned a ROTA of 13 per cent compared to the 17.6 per cent ROTA of larger companies.
3. Profitability estimates based on ROTA are relatively low for small firms because of their much higher reliance on short-term liabilities in the form of trade credit. Netting out short-term liabilities to calculate returns on net assets inevitably raises estimated small company profitability compared to large companies.

These results are rather different from those reported in earlier periods.

The Bolton Report (HMSO 1971) provided estimates of ROTA, RONA and ROE for small and large businesses in 1986. These are shown in the first panel of Table 11.2, whilst the second panel shows estimates of RONA for 1973–5 prepared for the Wilson Committee (HMSO 1979). It is apparent from row c that small-firm profitability is between 8 per cent and 30 per cent higher than larger-company profitability, depending on the measure and time period. This superiority was also recorded in a number of other studies surveyed by the Bolton research team for the period 1958–68 (Tamari 1972, table 21, p. 29).

Table 11.2. *The relative profitability performance of large and small firms in the UK in 1968 and 1973–5*

	1968			RONA*		
	RONA*	ROTA*	ROE*	1973	1974	1975
a Small[†]	17.8	11.2	18.7	21.0	18.2	16.1
b Large[‡]	13.5	9.5	16.5	18.3	16.3	14.9
c as % of b	131.9	117.9	113.3	114.8	111.7	108.1

* RONA = Pre-Tax Return on Net Assets
  ROTA = Pre-Tax Return on Total Assets
  ROE = Pre-Tax Return on Equity
[†] Small firms in 1968 are those businesses employing less than 200 individuals in manufacturing and selected services who responded to the Bolton Committee's Financial Questionnaire. Small Firms in 1973–5 are a sample of 300 incorporated businesses with total capital employed of less than £4m. in 1975.
[‡] Large firms in 1968 and 1973–5 are companies included in the Board of Trade analysis of large non-financial companies. By the mid 1970s 98% of these companies had net assets of more than £1m. and 75% more than £4m.
Source: HMSO (1971), table 4.IV, p. 45; HMSO (1979), table 4.6, p. 60.

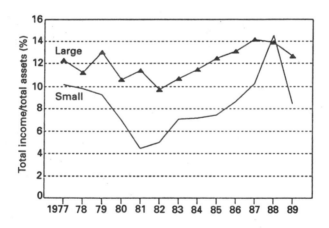

Fig. 11.1. Return on total assets, UK companies 1977–89. *Source*: HMSO (1977–89)

Figures 11.1–11.3 show that this favourable small-firm profitability gap for all non-financial companies was not permanent. Figure 11.1 shows that the ROTA for smaller firms was below that for large firms throughout the years 1977–89. The recession years of the early 1980s coincided with a decline and reversal of the relative performance of small firms in terms of

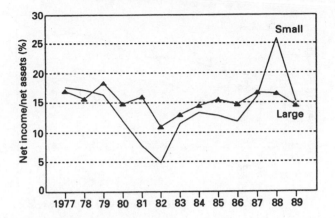

Fig. 11.2.   Return on net assets, UK companies 1977–89. *Source*: HMSO (1977–89)

RONA and ROE as shown in Figs. 11.2 and 11.3. Recovery in the economy
in the 1980s, however, led to movement back towards parity on these measures.

These average rates of return may of course contain very wide variations
across industries, and across companies. Figs. 11.4–11.9, which distinguish
between non-manufacturing and manufacturing trends in the 1980s, suggest
that small-firm profit inferiority is most marked in the latter. This inferiority shows up on all three measures in Figs. 11.4–11.6. In non-manufacturing
Figs. 11.7–11.9 show that small-firm profitability was much closer to that of
large firms, dipping below it in the period after 1983, but rising significantly
above it in 1988, and then falling back sharply in 1989. It is the peak of

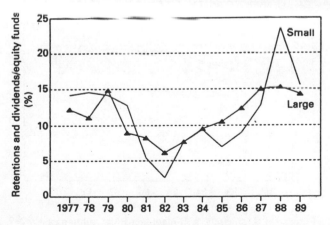

Fig. 11.3.   Return on equity, UK companies 1977–89. *Source*: HMSO (1977–89)

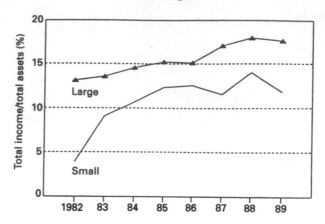

Fig. 11.4. Return on total assets, UK manufacturing companies 1982–9. *Source*:
HMSO (1977–89)

1988 which accounts for the favourable profit performance of small non-manufacturing firms shown in Table 11.1.

The relative movement of small- and large-firm profitability in these broad sectors may still reflect industry compositional effects within them. On the face of it, however, it appears that the small company sector in manufacturing was on average less profitable than the large firm sector from the late 1970s to the late 1980s. The performance of small firms in non-manufacturing was on average more on a par with large companies but was much more volatile. On this basis small firms should not have expected to be relatively attractive investment propositions and a worsening of the

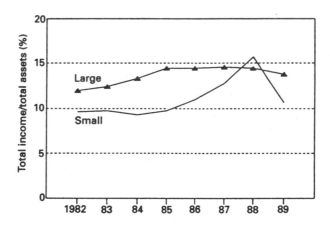

Fig. 11.5. Return on total assets, non-manufacturing companies 1982–9. *Source*:
HMSO (1977–89)

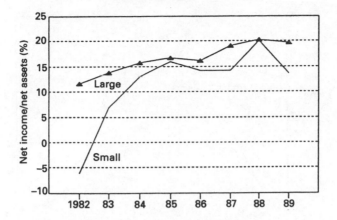

Fig. 11.6. Return on net assets, UK manufacturing companies 1982–9. *Source*:
HMSO (1977–89)

supply of both equity and long-term loan finance might have been expected,
compared with earlier periods.

11.3 ACCOUNTING FOR DIFFERENCES IN FINANCIAL STRUCTURE

The persistance over the long run of significant differences in financial
structure between larger and small firms in the UK is of course consistent
with a chronic market failure constraining small firms to a sub-optimal
position, or with a structure reflecting an optimal choice, or some combination of both.

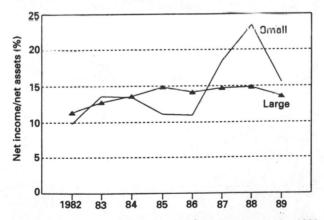

Fig. 11.7. Return on net assets, UK non-manufacturing companies 1982–9. *Source*:
HMSO (1977–89)

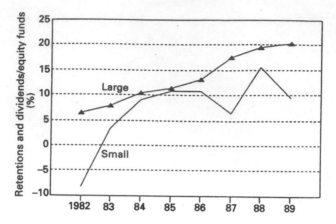

Fig. 11.8.   Return on equity, UK manufacturing companies 1982–9. *Source*: HMSO
(1977–89)

It may be argued, for instance, that the survival of small-scale proprietorships, partnerships, and closely held companies as part of the overall system
of business organization reflects an optimal trade-off. The avoidance of
agency costs, because residual claims are either explicitly or implicitly limited to owner/decision makers, is offset against the costs of foregone investment opportunities and inefficiency in residual risk bearing. The latter is
due to risk aversion reinforced by the over-reliance on human and financial
capital of owner-managers (Fama and Jensen 1985). In effect smaller companies avoid external finance and stay small by choice. It has also been
argued that the low fixed asset proportion in small firms may reflect a

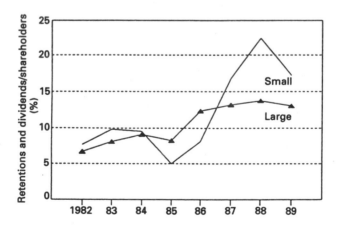

Fig. 11.9.   Return on equity, UK non-manufacturing companies 1982–9. *Source*:
HMSO (1977–89)

choice of flexible production methods, whilst the structure of long- and short-term liabilities may reflect a desire to maintain maximum freedom from external interference (Hay and Morris 1984). Thus small-firm owner managers may seek to avoid injections of capital from external equity sources, or from lending institutions where commitment of funds involves potentially enhanced reporting activity or restrictive covenants. More generally it has been argued that where wealth-constrained owners place an intrinsic value on ownership, and financiers care only about pecuniary returns, then standard debt financing may be the best way to implement control arrangements contingent upon various types of failure arising from the resulting conflict of interest (Aghion and Bolton 1992).

In the UK context it has been argued that these factors may be reinforced by a particular desire of suppliers of funds, especially loan funds, to keep an arm's length relationship with their clients. Overdraft finance and short-term loans allow banks the freedom to roll over the funding when things are going well, but to extricate themselves relatively quickly when things go badly. This may be especially attractive in relation to the small firm sector which is relatively volatile and risky. It also reduces the need to develop industry or firm specific knowledge on which to base longer-run or more interventionist strategies.

There is no shortage of evidence as to either the desire of some small business owners to place a high priority on independence, or of the lack of an industrial banking tradition among the leading clearers in the UK, not least as perceived by their small business clients. Thus, on the latter point, recent UK survey evidence points to the banks' lack of understanding of a firm's industry and market as being the most significant shortcoming which their small business clients identify (Binks *et al.* 1988; 1990). Equally it has been argued that the banks' primary responsibilities to their risk-averse depositors in the retail field predisposes them to operate an absolute upper limit on risk tolerance, beyond which they will not ration by price, but simply not lend at all (Hutchinson and McKillop 1992). Finally the difficulty facing businesses in transferring between banks in conditions of financial stress means that the balance of power is firmly with the banks rather than their small-business clients. The recent debate on the reactions of banks and their small business clients to recession and interest rate policy in the UK is an apt illustration. The twin reliance on trade credit and short-term loan finance is also doubly damaging in a recession. For just when small-firm cash flow is reduced by delayed payment by customers (especially large ones) and an inability to squeeze trade debtors (especially large ones), so are small firms most reliant on the short-term credit facilities provided by their banks. There are, of course, some solutions to these problems: the growth of factoring as a source of finance for small firms is one example of this, the development of codes of practice by banks, and of trade settlement codes by large firms and the Government, are others.

In the absence of a solution to the short-term credit problem, some firms may be willing to pay the price of 'lost independence' in order to avoid it. Is there then a market failure in provision for those who are actively seeking equity or loan finance, despite the potential losses of voting control or imposition of reporting controls or restrictive covenants which may be involved?

The arguments in principle are familiar enough. In so far as equity finance is concerned gaps may arise in the provision for small firms because of adverse selection problems, and appraisal and monitoring costs. Good quality entrepreneurs, it can be argued, prefer debt to equity. Where the suppliers of finance cannot judge quality, debt allows 'good quality' borrowers to earn a rent on their superior quality whereas they would be forced to share their payoffs with outside equity holders. Equity suppliers may therefore end up with relatively low-quality businesses, earn low returns, and be less willing than they otherwise might, to fund potentially profitable businesses whose owners are prepared to share the benefits of their success in high-risk ventures. Once equity funds are provided, insiders may seek to shirk their responsibility to generate funds for the equity holders, and monitoring costs will be incurred. In addition, where equity is supplied and risk is shared there is an incentive to invest resources in information gathering and appraisal. If there are indivisibilities in the costs of carrying out either of these roles then equity providers will be biased towards providing funds more cheaply to big rather than to small clients. Equity investors in small firms also run the risk of thin markets in the shares they hold. They are likely to trade at a discount thus raising the cost of equity capital to small firms. Finally the requirements for obtaining a listing on a Stock Exchange to obtain equity may be both onerous in terms of giving up control (e.g. minimum issues of shares to outsiders may be required) and impose expenses which are high per pound raised compared to large firms (e.g. because of indivisibilities in the production costs of prospectuses). The Stock Exchanges also impose conditions such as minimum lengths of past performance records, which will limit access for new firms. For all these reasons equity gaps may face small firms in their search for long-term funding, even if they are willing to cede the ownership rights which the pursuit of equity involves.

If for the moment we accept that equity gaps may arise, then the weight of long-term financing will be borne by loans. Here too, however, arguments in principle suggest that new and small firms may be at a disadvantage. The argument depends upon the effects of asymmetric information. Borrowers know more about the expected riskiness of their project than lenders, especially if they are small or new. There is likely to be less public information about their past performance on which lenders may base their decisions. If lenders try to use interest rate increases to allow for their perceptions of riskiness they are likely to drive out those who believe on their own private information that they are less risky than the bank does, and to attract those who believe they are more risky. The result for the bank will be a higher risk profile for its loans than it bargained for. Given two borrowers with the same expected mean return but different spreads around the mean, it is the borrower who believes he has the wider spread who is more likely to take up the loan. In that sense the good loans drive out the bad. The response to this may be to avoid interest rate increases as a discriminatory tool and substitute credit rationing by refusal to supply loans driving out some socially desirable investment. (Stiglitz and Weiss 1981). This argument is sensitive to the assumption that projects differ by mean preserving spreads. Consider two borrowers each of whom will earn the same return if their project succeeds but holding different views about the likelihood of success (and hence about their expected mean return) and a lender happy to share their view about the return if the projects succeed but uncertain about which borrower is more likely to succeed. The problem facing the lender is to charge an interest rate which yields the lender's required return, given the lender's views of the likelihood of each of the borrowers failing. Faced with an interest rate premium to reflect the lender's perception of the risk of failure of the borrowers taken together it is now the borrower who believes he has a lower risk of failure who will be most attracted. Those whose private information leads them to believe that they have a higher chance of failure and whose expected mean return is therefore lower will at the margin withdraw (DeMeza and Webb 1987). In practice there is likely to be uncertainty about both expected means and expected riskiness. This leads to some degree of pragmatism in arguing, for instance, for loan guarantee schemes to overcome the credit rationing results of our first example.

An alternative to using interest rates to solve the risk problem is to seek collateral. This helps elicit information about the borrower's risk perception. It also reduces the bank's downside risk in the event of a lender obtaining a loan and then pursuing higher risk/higher return projects than the one for which it was granted (the moral hazard problem). The collateral route has disadvantages. It erodes the limited liability of the owner. It also raises the problem of a debt gap for those otherwise viable projects whose originators are not already blessed with assets to back their judgement. Moreover the more conservative the valuation of the collateral the higher the disincentives for these firms. Recent evidence for the UK suggests that there is relatively little attempt to appraise individual project risk and use the interest rate to price for risk differentials. The more usual route is the pursuit of collateral and secured loans and the use of conservative 'carcase' valuations of collateral (HMSO 1990; Binks *et al.* 1988; 1990). The smaller-size classes contain a higher proportion of younger start-up firms who may face the asset constraint problem in a severe form. It is widely agreed that these companies may be forced as a result to be more reliant on retentions and personal funds than more mature businesses who at least have a 'carcase' to value (Churchill and Lewis 1983; Walker 1989; Evans and Jovanovic 1989).

It is important to note that there may be solutions to the credit rationing problem other than the interest rate mechanism or the pursuit of collateral, both of which operate at the level of relationships between individual borrowers and lenders. A way forward here is to devise institutional arrangements amongst *groups* of borrowing firms which allow their private information about debt worthiness across the group, and about the use to which loans are put, to affect borrowing behaviour, reduce monitoring costs, and ease borrowing problems for them all. If small firms coalesce into groups to form loan guarantee consortia of their own, then individual members of the group can approach lenders with their loan proposal underwritten by the group. Two benefits arise. First, the borrowers are likely to coalesce into groups which share similar risk attributes and to develop membership rules which minimize the likelihood of group members defaulting. In doing this they have the advantage of more detailed knowledge of their markets and industries than typical lenders. Second, since there is group liability for failure there is an incentive for peer group monitoring of behaviour (Stiglitz 1990). I will return to this issue. Before that it is necessary to consider briefly the evidence on whether the equity or debt gaps which may exist in principle do exist in practice in the UK.

11.4 EQUITY GAPS, DEBT GAPS, AND THE SUPPLY OF FINANCE TO SMALL FIRMS IN THE 1980s

In 1979 the Wilson Committee to Review the Functioning of Financial Institutions concluded in its report on the financing of small firms that they were at a disadvantage in terms of the cost of loan finance and the security often required to obtain it. The Committee felt that this reflected the inherent riskiness of small firms. However, they took the view that excessive caution by banks, especially in relation to new businesses, meant that small firms might face credit rationing and a debt gap as a result. They therefore recommended the introduction of a loan guarantee scheme. The Wilson Committee also recognized that external equity was difficult to find for small firms and was often available only on unfavourable terms. They noted that venture capital was especially hard to obtain.

The present equity gap is now seen as having two consequences—a shortage of initial capital for new start-ups, and a deficiency in the provision of development capital to finance the expansion of established enterprises. The latter is particularly serious for fast growing businesses coming up against gearing constraints. But similar problems also affect slower growing firms who may nevertheless want injection of outside equity or occasional marketability for their shares from time to time. (HMSO 1979: 9).

Despite these remarks they did not believe that the costs of raising capital as such were unfairly high. Instead they focused their recommendations on ways of improving the flow of the small amounts of capital which the large-scale-oriented markets failed to supply. Thus they sought to improve the marketability of small-firm equity (by promoting an over-the-counter market (OTC) in their stocks) and to resurrect 'Aunt Agatha', the family member who could be relied upon as a source of informal capital for entrepreneurial nephews. The demise of Aunt Agatha (brought to a premature end by the burden of taxation) symbolized the absence of small amounts of 'informal' risk capital which might otherwise be available to small-scale entrepreneurs. As a possible solution they suggested reforms to permit the development of Small Firm Investment Companies (SFICs). These would specialize in portfolios of unlimited companies and be given tax advantages to make them relatively attractive vehicles for savings.

Developments in the 1980s have gone some way to meet these objectives. First the Wilson recommendation for a Loan Guarantee Scheme was put into effect in 1981. Second, there was a switch in the balance of taxation away from direct income and capital taxes towards indirect taxation. This may have stirred Aunt Agatha in her grave, or at least perked up her descendants. Third, on the equity front the Business Expansion Scheme was introduced and set to run for ten years from 1983. This offered income tax relief at their highest marginal rate for individuals putting new equity investments in unlisted companies so long as they were held for a minimum of five years. Since one of the ways individuals could invest in BES was via specialist investment funds with portfolios of unlisted companies, this was reminiscent of the Wilson SFIC proposals. Fourth, the 1980s witnessed a large expansion in the venture capital industry, and the development of OTC markets, first via the formation of the Unlisted Securities Market in 1980 and then via the Third Market in 1987. Finally the Government, via the Enterprise Allowance Scheme, sought to encourage small business formation and *inter alia* provided financial support for small firms in innovation via the Special Merit Award for Research and Technology (SMART) Scheme, and on the regional front provided Regional Enterprise Grants for firms with fewer than 25 employees. There was also a broad programme of national and locally based initiatives to foster the provision of information and financial advice.

Many of the issues raised by the last major official inquiry into small firm's financing problems seem therefore to have been addressed. The most recent large-scale national survey of the SME sector by the Small Business Research Centre of the University of Cambridge reported that only a handful of firms who were seeking additional finance in the period 1987–90 were unable to get any (SBRC 1992: 37). Another recent major telephone interview survey conducted by the University of Aston concluded that:

small firms in Great Britain currently face few difficulties in raising finance for their innovation and investment proposals in the private sector . . . programmes of financial assistance are unlikely to have high additionality, unless the programme is rigorously limited to a 'lender of last resort' role . . . the institutional framework for investment finance for small firms is broadly adequate and not in need of further supplementation by public sector initiatives (HMSO 1991: 17).

Moreover there has been a substantial expansion in the numbers of small businesses operating in the United Kingdom in the 1980s. Whereas the Bolton inquiry was concerned with a small-firm sector in apparent long-term decline, and the Wilson Committee reported on a sector which had apparently stabilized its share, since then the sector has expanded (Daly 1990; Dunne and Hughes 1990; Hughes 1991). Some doubts none the less may be raised.

First, the Cambridge Survey revealed that manufacturing firms reported a higher level of all forms of constraint on meeting their business objectives than did service firms, and both groups rated access to finance the most significant of eleven possible factors constraining them (SBRC 1992: 27). The same survey also asked firms to score various factors in terms of their impact on limiting the introduction of new technology. As Table 11.3 shows, cost, and access to finance easily outscored the rest.

Studies focusing on barriers to growth in small firms using case studies,

Table 11.3. *Factors limiting the firm's introduction of new technology*

Factors	Mean value
Cost of purchase and installation	5.9
Cost of operation/support services	3.8
Lack of finance	5.2
Difficulty in recruiting skilled staff	2.1
Inability to recruit suitably skilled management	1.2
Problems in training staff	1.6
Resistance of staff/management to changes in work practices	1.1
Unsuitability of premises	1.4
Total responses (no.)	1,585

Note: Means are of ranked scores on a scale of 0–9: 0 no importance; 9 highly important.
Source: Small Business Research Centre (1992)

rather than survey methods, also raise specific doubts about the funding of fast growth and innovative firms. Thus a recent report by the Advisory Council on Science and Technology concluded that some smaller companies circumvented financial barriers to growth by giving up independence through takeover by a larger company, whilst the venture capital market and BES funds were not being focused on particularly high-risk or innovative activity, especially in manufacturing (ACOST 1990). They identified a particular difficulty for firms of between 50–500 employees in seeking small sums to maintain a sequence of innovations, and recommended *inter alia* initiatives to redirect the BES scheme and introduce SMART type competitions to boost support for innovation. In one sense this conclusion is not so much at odds with the Aston survey conclusions reported earlier which focused on very small companies, 58 per cent of which employed less than ten individuals and all of which employed less than fifty (HMSO 1991). Even amongst these, however, proposals for innovation were expected to face financial constraints. The authors reported that 30 per cent of those firms attempting to simultaneously introduce investment, and product and process innovation expected to experience difficulties (HMSO 1991: 13). In the light of these findings it is worth looking briefly at the BES scheme and the venture capital industry as a whole, to gauge trends in the 1980s in the sectoral and size distribution of funding from those sources.

It seems clear that venture capital funding is skewed towards larger investments. Over 90 per cent of British Venture Capital Association (BVCA) funds in 1990 were managed by businesses with a minimum investment level of over £50,000. Over 80 per cent of these funds were in businesses with a minimum level of £250,000 (BVCA 1991). A similar picture emerges when we look at the data for *3i*, the biggest venture capital investor in smaller firms. Table 11.4 shows that in 1990–1 50 per cent of *3i* funds were in investments over £1m., and only 1 per cent were in investments of less than £50,000. So small sums are in relatively short supply.

Figures 11.10 and 11.11 show that there has also been a decline in the percentage of venture capital funds committed to what might be considered high-tech sectors and companies. Thus the shares of the amount invested and of the numbers of companies financed in the computer-related, electronic, medical/genetics, and communication sectors all fell between 1984–6 and 1987–90. Investment in these sectors together averaged 38.1 per cent of total investment in the first period but only 23.8 per cent in the second. Venture capital funding has also switched emphasis away from start-ups and expansion towards management buy-outs and buy-ins as Fig. 11.12 illustrates. Between 1983 and 1986 around 23 per cent of funds were invested in start-ups and other early stage financing. This fell to an average of around 12 per cent between 1987 and 1990. The share of funds for expansion fell by 10 percentage points between the same two periods, while

Table 11.4. 3i *Investment by financing size range 1988–91*

Size range	Total amount invested (%)		
	1988–9	1989–90	1990–91
Up to £50,000	0.6	0.5	1.1
£50,000–£150,000	5.1	5.4	6.4
£150,000–£250,000	5.1	7.9	9.2
£250,000–£500,000	13.6	18.4	20.7
£500,000–£1m.	15.0	10.8	12.3
£1m–£2m	12.8	9.7	12.3
£2m and over	47.9	47.1	37.8
Total	100.0	100.0	100.0

Source: Data supplied by *3i* PLC

the share of buy-outs/buy-ins rose from 33.5 per cent to 57.9 per cent. Whilst there may be efficiency gains from the reorganization of existing assets between different managements it is apparent that the contribution of venture capital to small-business expansion has been less than might be thought from an examination of the raw totals of venture capital funding as a whole.

The Business Expansion Scheme data reveals similar problems. Although well over half of the number of investments made were in amounts of less than £50,000, and this proportion rose after 1983, the total amount of funds provided was much more heavily skewed to the upper end of the size distribution. By 1987–8, two-thirds of the BES funds were in investments of

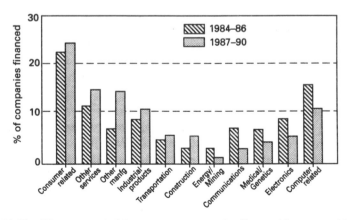

Fig. 11.10. Venture capital investment, companies financed by sector 1984–90.
Source: BVCA (1990)

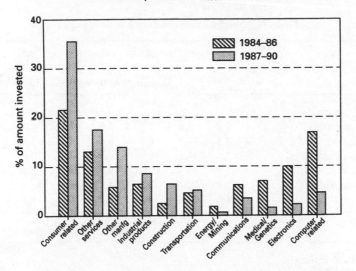

Fig. 11.11. Venture capital investment, amount invested by sector 1984–90. *Source*: BVCA (1990)

over £1m. with only 5 per cent in amounts of less than £50,000 (Inland Revenue 1990). Table 11.5 shows that manufacturing was increasingly neglected in terms of BES funds in the course of the 1980s. Between 1983–4 and 1987–8 the proportion of BES Funds in manufacturing fell from 33 per cent to 14 per cent. This compares with manufacturing's 27 per cent share

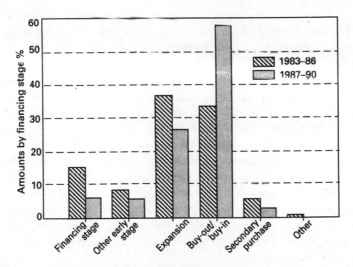

Fig. 11.12. Venture capital investment, proportion by financing stage 1983–90. *Source*: BVCA (1990)

Table 11.5. *BES scheme data industrial analysis*

	1983–4	1984–5	1985–6	1986–7	1987–8	1988–9	1989–90
Industry	Distribution by numbers (%)						
Agriculture, fishing & horticulture	3.2	1.6	2.1	2.8	5.0	4.5	4.1
Construction	4.5	6.1	3.7	4.5	4.6	3.3	1.3
Manufacturing	42.0	38.5	37.9	36.3	35.2	30.6	30.0
Wholesale & retail	18.7	14.9	18.0	19.7	18.7	18.8	19.8
Service industries	29.9	38.4	33.9	36.7	36.0	40.9	42.4
Others	1.7	0.5	4.4	0.3	0.5	1.8	2.4
	Distribution by amounts (%)						
Agriculture, fishing & horticulture	19.1	0.7	2.6	1.2	7.5	3.8	3.9
Construction	6.7	4.7	6.4	7.1	8.5	1.9	0.0
Manufacturing	33.3	23.7	22.3	21.9	13.9	28.8	23.5
Wholesale & retail	13.3	9.5	19.8	20.7	18.9	13.5	13.7
Service industries	23.8	60.8	44.0	49.1	51.2	50.0	56.9
Others	1.0	0.0	5.1	0.0	0.0	0.0	2.0

Note: The data for 1988/9 excludes sums invested in private rented housing schemes.
Source: Inland Revenue Statistics 1990, 1991.

of the numbers registered for VAT and which fall within the scope of the BES Scheme. The BES data for 1988–9 and 1989–90 exclude investments in private rented housing (PRH). The extension of the scheme to these projects in those years effectively meant the end of substantial funding for other sectors. Thus of £142m. invested in 2,442 companies in 1988–9, 80 per cent by number and 87 per cent by value went into PRH schemes. Between 1987–8 and 1988–9 funding for all other sectors dropped from £240m. to £50m., and the number of companies supported from 815 to 508. Within that total the number of manufacturing companies funded dropped from 287 to 154 and the amount invested from £24m. to £14m. (Inland Revenue 1990). Whereas BES investments (excluding PRH) were around 0.4 per cent of gross domestic fixed capital formation (excluding private sector dwellings) in the period 1983–8, this fell to 0.08 per cent in 1988–9. The winding up of the scheme announced in the 1992 Budget was hardly a great loss for manufacturing.

Set against the demise of the BES scheme was the introduction in February 1991 of Support for Products Under Research (SPUR) with the aim of providing £30m. over three years in the form of grants for single company innovative projects for those businesses employing less than 500 people. Specially targeted at the 50–500 group highlighted in the ACOST study SPUR offers firms up to £150,000. This is seen as complementary to the SMART scheme which supports smaller projects. It is too soon to evaluate its impact.

Taken as a whole the developments in venture capital funding and the BES scheme seem not to have been especially well focused on either the smaller end of the funding spectrum, nor on the most innovation intensive manufacturing sectors. This suggests, as the ACOST study concluded, that a finance gap may still exist in these areas. It is, however, difficult to argue that there were financial constraints on business formation as a whole in the 1980s or that there is a more pervasive market failure for small firms in the availability of funds at least in quantitative terms. In so far as they rely more than they would wish on short-term bank funding or their own internal resources, the 1980s may have posed particular problems for smaller firms. There was a decline in their relative profitability, and the decade began and ended in recessions which imposed severe strains on bank–small firm relationships. Nevertheless by the 1980s the Macmillan finance gap of £200,000 identified in 1931 had clearly been massively eroded. After all it would in today's prices be a gap of around £5.5m. Compared to that we appear to have come a long way. Smaller firms none the less continue to express the view that they are constrained by lack of finance, and by the attitudes of banks who they claim have still not developed with them the kind of closer long-term relationship to which they aspire (Binks *et al.* 1988; 1990). It is, however, possible to argue that the answer to at least some of the problems inherent in bank–small firms relations can best be tackled by the firms themselves. This is in particular true of those which arise from imperfect information and which we discussed in principle earlier in this chapter, and which the banks themselves may not be able to address efficiently. One possible way in which informational improvements might be brought about is discussed in the next section.

11.5 MUTUAL GUARANTEE SCHEMES

In contrast to arguments which berate the financial system in the UK for letting down small firms I would argue that the latter could do something to help themselves. What is required, however, is a recognition of the mutual interest of groups of small firms in pooling their private information about project riskiness and entrepreneurial quality, and developing mutual schemes to guarantee individual loan applications to banks by members of the group, after group screening based on the pooled information. Such group action may, if the group is large and well organized enough, also often improve negotiating power with banks over charges and the terms and conditions of loans.

Table 11.6 shows that Mutual Guarantee Schemes (MGS) are widespread in mainland Europe. They vary widely in industrial coverage, and in the extent to which they are based on local, regional or national organizations. The table shows that the sums guaranteed are, on average, quite small and the schemes in all countries rely on an elected or representative board to approve guarantees on behalf of the group. In Germany the regional Länder-based *Kreditgarantiegemeinschaften* are organized as mutual societies on a sector-by-sector basis and are correspondingly few in number compared to their more locally based French and Italian counterparts. Employers' associations, financial institutions, and local authorities play a central role in the German schemes, with maximum values of guaranteed loans and their permitted maturity varying by industrial sector. Both lenders and trade associations assess creditworthiness. Federal and State Government support takes the form of assistance with liquidity in the face of defaults, and the banks bear some of the default costs (Hull 1983; Bannock and Albach 1991).

Although the table reveals differences in detail between countries, the MGSs operated have some distinctive characteristics in common. Individual loan applicants are offered group guarantees after internal assessment by the group. Firms typically pay a fee to cover group administrative costs and the guarantee. They can then present their application to banks or other lending institutions backed by this guarantee. The lenders are thus faced with projects which have been screened on the basis of the general risk experience and in-depth knowledge of the borrowers as a group. Whilst the group benefits from the pooling of their risks across all their guaranteed projects the effect is to reduce the problems of adverse selection, credit rationing, and the pursuit of collateral which arise when the banks are faced with risky individual loan applicants. Thus mutual guarantee schemes help alleviate the problems which follow from asymmetric information. In addition the existence of a group scheme can lead to the effective dissemination of best-practice information and advice on industry and project risks across the members themselves. There may then be improvements in the quality and amount of information on which loan applications are formulated across the group as a whole (CEC 1991). Finally, the fact that the group pools risks means that members may be under greater moral pressures not to default or use their loans for riskier purposes than those specified in their project application. An example from Italy may help to illustrate this effect of these schemes (for more general examples and applications to rural credit schemes see World Bank (1990)).

In Italy, as Table 11.6 showed, local loan guarantee consortia are well established. In Modena in Northern Italy, for instance, one consortium

Table 11.6. *Mutual guarantee schemes in the European Community*

Member states	Number of MGSs	Average amount of finance guaranteed ECU (000's)	Geographical coverage of MGSs	Industry
Belgium	18	19	Organized locally often parallel with Local Credit Associations	All industry
Denmark	12	na	Mostly regional, otherwise national	Selected industries
France	286	11	Usually local or regional Approx 1/6 of all MGSs operate nationally	Selected industries
Germany	28	87	Organized regionally (Bundesland)	All lines of industry divided into four groups: – manufacturing – craftsmen – traders – restaurants/hotels
Italy	642	na	Provincial (local) mostly regional in their operations	Selected industries: – craftsmen – industrial – commercial – agricultural – craftsmen – traders
Luxembourg	2	16	National	All industries for regional MGSs: two for nationally operating SMEs: – road transport – construction industry
Spain	23	35	Regional, mostly one MGS per region with exception of four regions (of 17) and two national MGSs.	

Source: CEC (1991)

founded in 1974 had over 3,500 artisan members by the late 1980s. It has two functions. First, to guarantee members loans with ordinary credit institutions, and then in the event of default, to pay the institutions back, and seek recovery itself from the defaulter. Second, the consortium negotiates interest rates for its members with the banks at favoured rates reflecting the guarantee. The Modena consortium had by 1989 guaranteed 10 billion lire in loans and had only 70 million lire in unrecovered debts (Brusco and Righi 1989). This is attributed to the fact that loans are guaranteed by colleagues who have an incentive to monitor colleagues and help prevent default and because 'The person who receives a loan from the cooperative will stay up at night thinking of ways of repaying his loan. Whereas the person who receives a bank loan will stay awake at night thinking up ways of not paying back his loan' (Brusco and Righi 1989).

There are of course important trade-offs in these schemes. For instance the smaller the group acting together the less its ability to bear risk compared with a big lender such as a bank. This may be offset by the increased ability to screen effectively and monitor potential defaulters. Moreover, the incentive to free-ride is large in a big group and the costs of member default more widely spread (Stiglitz 1990). In all schemes of this kind there are also important private set up costs for firms initiating them. Since the benefits are public goods for all firms who subsequently join there is likely to be an undersupply of such schemes unless the State underwrites or subsidizes their creation. It is here that the State has a central role to play in facilitating institutional changes at national and particularly local level.

In the UK, of course, a critical issue has to be faced in proposing a move in this direction. That issue is the lack of collaborative or collective action by both large and small businesses in the conduct of their affairs. Nevertheless there are elements of an institutional structure around which schemes such as those outlined above could be built. The Chambers of Commerce, Local Enterprise Agencies and the Training and Enterprise Councils could perform facilitating and pump-priming roles. In the 1980s the notion of Enterprise has come to be associated almost entirely with individual action. There is, however, a great deal to be gained by exploring the benefits of collective enterprise by small firms.

11.6 CONCLUSIONS

At the end of the 1980s the financial structure of small UK companies continued to display certain well-known properties relative to that of larger ones. They were relatively more reliant on short-term loans and overdrafts and less reliant on equity finance. Trade credit also played a more important role on the liabilities side of their balance sheet, and trade debits a more important role on the assets side. In contrast, the data on small company profitability suggested a significant change in their relative position compared to previous decades. By the 1980s smaller companies had become less rather than more profitable than larger ones. Here in particular some caution is due because of the limited quality of the data produced by the reporting exemptions introduced for small business in the 1980s.

The theoretical literature suggests that the financial structure which characterizes small firms in the UK may reflect the wishes of entrepreneurs as much as constraints placed upon them by suppliers of finance. The survey and case study evidence reviewed does, however, suggest that a variety of market failures have produced problems in terms of both credit rationing and excess demands for collateral in certain areas, especially for newly established and innovative firms. The usual response to these problems is to argue for the augmentation or introduction of Government-backed loan guarantee schemes, or systems of grants and subsidies. Instead of entering directly into the debate over the merits or demerits of such schemes, this chapter has argued instead that some of the problems of risk evaluation and unequal or poor information about borrower qualities could be tackled by the borrowers themselves. Mutual guarantee schemes and other forms of collaborative self-help by small businesses are worthy of detailed policy consideration.

REFERENCES

ACOST (1990), *The Enterprise Challenge: Overcoming Barriers to Growth in Small Firms*, Advisory Council on Science and Technology (HMSO, London).

Aghion, P. and Bolton, P. (1992), 'An Incomplete Contracts Approach to Financial Contracting', *Review of Economic Studies*, 59: 473–94.

Bannock, G. and Albach, H. (1991), *Small Business Policy in Europe: Britain, Germany and the European Community* (Anglo-German Foundation for the Study of Industrial Society, London).

Binks, M. R., Ennew, C. T. and Reed, G. V. (1988), *The Survey by the Forum of Private Business on Banks and Small Firms* (Forum of Private Business, London).

—— —— (1990), *Small Business and their Banks* (Forum of Private Business, London).

Brusco, S. and Righi, E. (1989), 'Local Government, Industrial Policy and Social Consensus: The case of Modena (Italy)', *Economy and Society*, 18: 4, November, 405–24.

BVCA (1991), *Report on Investment Activity 1990* (British Venture Capital Association, London).

CEC (1991), *The Role of Mutual Guarantee Schemes in the Financing of SMEs in the European Community* (Commission of the European Community, Brussels).

Churchill, N. C. and Lewis, V. L. (1983), 'The Five Stages of Small Business Growth', *Harvard Business Review*, 83/3: 30–50.

Daly, M. (1990), 'The 1980's—A Decade of Growth in Enterprise', *Employment Gazette*, November, 533–65.

DeMeza, D. and Webb, D. (1987), 'Too Much Investment: A Problem of Asymmetric Information', *Quarterly Journal of Economics*, 102: 281–92.

Dunne, J. P. and Hughes, A. (1990), 'Small Businesses, An Analysis of Recent Trends in their Relative Importance in the UK with Some European Comparisons', *Small Business Research Centre Working Paper No. 1* (Department of Applied Economics, Cambridge).

Evans, D. S. and Jovanovic, B. (1989), 'An Estimated Model of Entrepreneurial Choices under Liquidity Constraints', *Journal of Political Economy*, 97: 4, 808–27.

Fama, E. F. and Jensen, M. C. (1985), 'Organisational Forms and Investment Decisions', *Journal of Financial Economics*, 14: 1, 101–19.

Hay, D. A. and Morris, D. J. (1984), *Unquoted Companies: Their Contribution to the United Kingdom Economy* (Macmillan, London).

HMSO (1971), *Report of the Committee of Inquiry on Small Firms* (Bolton Report), Cmnd 4811 (HMSO, London).

HMSO (1977–89), *Business Monitor MA3 Company Finance*, various issues (HMSO, London).

HMSO (1979), *Interim Report on the Financing of Small Firms* (Wilson Report), Cmnd 7503 (HMSO, London).

HMSO (1990), *An Evaluation of the Loan Guarantee Scheme NERA*, Department of Employment, Research Paper No. 74 (HMSO, London).

HMSO (1991), *Constraints on the Growth of Small Firms* (HMSO, London).

Hughes, A. (1991), 'UK Small Businesses in the 1980s: Continuity and Change', *Regional Studies*, October, 471–8.

Hull, C. (1983), 'Federal Republic of Germany', in D. J. Storey (ed.), *The Small Firm* (Croom Helm, London).

Hutchinson, R. W. and McKillop, D. E. (1992), 'Banks and Small to Medium Sized Businesses in the United Kingdom: Some General Issues', *National Westminster Bank Quarterly Review*, February, 84–95.

Inland Revenue (1990), *Inland Revenue Statistics* (HMSO, London).

Inland Revenue (1991), *Inland Revenue Statistics* (HMSO, London).

Martin, R. L. (1989), 'The Growth and Geographical Anatomy of Venture Capitalism in the United Kingdom', *Regional Studies*, 23: 5, 389–403.

SBRC (1992), *The State of British Enterprise: Growth Innovation and Competitive Advantage in Small and Medium-Sized Firms* (Small Business Research Centre, Department of Applied Economics, Cambridge).

Stiglitz, J. E. (1990), 'Peer Monitoring and Credit Markets', *World Bank Economic Review*, 4: 3, September, 351–66.

— and Weiss, A. (1981), 'Credit Rationing in Markets with Imperfect Information', *American Economic Review*, 71: 393–410.

Tamari, M. (1972), *A Postal Questionnaire Survey of Small Firms: An Analysis of Financial Data*, Committee of Inquiry on Small Firms Research Report No. 16 (HMSO, London).

Walker, D. A. (1989), 'Financing the Small Firm', *Small Business Economics*, 1: 285–96.

World Bank (1990), 'A Symposium on Imperfect Information and Rural Credit Markets', *World Bank Economic Review*, 4: 3, September, 235–366.

PART II

Germany and Japan

12

Corporate Governance: The UK Compared with Germany and Japan

MARTHA PREVEZER and MARTIN RICKETTS

12.1 INTRODUCTION

This chapter examines differences in the structure of corporate governance between the UK, Germany, and Japan. It looks at these structures from the point of view of the contractural relationships between the various parties involved. Thus shareholding is treated as conferring, in differing degrees, rights of ownership and control in the three countries. Likewise membership of a company board confers varying rights of control, and is associated in different ways with ownership interests in the company. Contractual relationships can be viewed as a spectrum varying from highly specific, short-term, 'classical' arrangements to vaguer, more long-term, 'obligational' or 'implicit' forms. The different mix between these types of contract that can be observed in the various countries has important consequences for business behaviour.

The chapter starts with a discussion of the problems which are encountered in transacting generally, and the special significance of these problems for the relationships between the firm and the providers of finance. It then uses this framework to examine differences between countries in the nature of shareholding, the structure of company boards, the mechanisms for monitoring and motivating managers, and the capital structure of firms. It draws on the findings of Part I of this volume about corporate governance, stock-market operations and the nature of banking–industry relations in the UK, and looks forwards to the rest of Part II in which the same issues are examined for Germany and Japan.

Transacting is hazardous. All economic approaches to the analysis of institutions start from this basic proposition. It was hazardous when Adam Smith penned his celebrated indictment of the 'negligence and profusion' associated with joint stock companies in the eighteenth century; it is hazardous in the UK still, and, notwithstanding some popular accounts of the universal goodwill which is said to permeate the fabric of her corporate life, it is hazardous in Japan.

In this chapter, some of the modern theory of contractual relations is used as a background against which to investigate the differing systems of corporate governance in the United Kingdom, Germany, and Japan. Sections 12.1 and 12.2 introduce the main concepts and ideas that have been developed to describe and explain the great variety of transactional relationships that exist in practice. The main sources of transactional hazards are outlined and some of the possible responses to them are discussed. In section 12.3, these ideas are related to differences in the property rights held by shareholders and other stakeholders in the corporate governance systems of the three countries. Section 12.4 uses the same conceptual framework to discuss the consequent differences in board structures and in the mechanisms used to motivate and monitor managers. Section 12.5 presents some empirical evidence on capital structures and relates it to the framework of transactional relations found in each country.

Coase (1937) devised the formulation of the firm as the hub of a radiating set of durable and loosely specified contracts with all the co-operating inputs. The importance of understanding the circumstances in which these arrangements reduce transactions costs and improve on entirely arm's length market relations has come to be recognized increasingly. One of the most hazardous contractual links is that between the firm and its financier.

1. Because the provider of finance is likely to have less information about future prospects than the user, the adverse selection problem arises. Information may be hidden from the provider of finance who will find it difficult to distinguish between good risks and bad. Borrowers may try to take advantage of the lender's ignorance by presenting a proposal which misrepresents the risks involved, while the lender, aware of this possibility, may be disinclined to finance projects which the borrower knows to provide excellent prospects (Arrow 1985).

2. Because it will often be difficult and costly to monitor the uses of finance, the problem of moral hazard arises (Jensen and Meckling 1976). Users of finance may take actions of which the providers would not approve were they in a position to know about them. For instance bondholders may fear that ill-considered risks may be taken, and this will affect the conditions under which they will be prepared to hold bonds. Shareholders may fear that some of their resources will be used in ways that benefit managers or other groups rather than in efforts to improve shareholder returns.

3. Because the finance of investment projects can involve long time periods, great uncertainty will usually accompany a decision. A wide range of possible outcomes associated with any project makes the task of discriminating between bad luck and bad management extremely difficult.

As well as these hazards in the relationship between financier and firm, there are difficulties encountered in the transactions between the firm and suppliers of other necessary inputs. Investment in one firm will often require other firms to supply specialized inputs and to adjust their plant or equipment accordingly. The firms supplying those inputs and making particular adjustments will need to have confidence both that the buying firm's financial arrangements are secure and also that their own contracts with the buying firm are well understood and trustworthy. This is especially the case if supplying firms have to produce items which are highly specific to a given investment project (i.e. whose value on the open market is small relative to their value to the project for which they were designed) or which require the use of specific assets in their production processes. In other words an investment project in one firm may well require a series of commitments down the supply chain to undertake other complementary and specific investments.

Firms committing themselves to supply specific inputs of this nature will be vulnerable to the possibility that the buying firm will attempt to renegotiate prices downwards after they have invested in the equipment or other assets required for production to take place. The absence of alternative uses for these assets reduces the bargaining power of the supplying firm. The possibility that the buying firm can act opportunistically and take advantage of the dependency of the supplier to appropriate the returns on specific assets is called the threat of 'hold-up'. Suppliers need to have confidence in both the buying firm's integrity and in its financial backing to be prepared to go ahead with investments subject to these hazards.

A similar problem arises when the people employed within the firm accumulate skills and know-how which are specific to the needs of that firm. If this know-how cannot be transferred to other uses or other firms but is indeed specific to that environment, a danger exists that shareholders might attempt to renegotiate contracts and divert the income generated by the know-how away from the labour force towards themselves.

These hazards of contracting are common to all countries, but efforts to overcome them can result in quite different institutional structures. These may in turn derive from different legal and cultural backgrounds, different industrial structures, and differing evolutionary time paths of economic development. We observe a variety of mechanisms in different countries to cope with the problems outlined above. They all imply the selection of a set of compromises to the trade-offs that have to be made; there is no unique solution to these transacting hazards.

For example, close monitoring of managers in an enterprise will help to overcome the moral hazard problem of managers' actions not being transparent to shareholders. But this system requires concentrated shareholdings to provide monitoring incentives along the lines of the classical capitalist system mentioned by Sykes in Chapter 5. It implies some integration between the functions of providing capital and managing an enterprise. It thereby sacrifices some of the advantages associated with dispersed shareholdings such as the wide spreading of risk and the use of specialized managerial expertise.

Another trade-off exists in dealing with the problem of hold-up (the danger that those people who invest in specific assets will find the returns appropriated by others). If the accumulation of highly specific know-how by team members is important, the potential for hold-up could be eliminated if the ownership rights to that expertise were held by team members and could not be transferred to outsiders. This, however, would restrict the amount of risk spreading that was possible, and would require a high proportion of debt finance (unless team members were rich enough to supply sufficient equity finance themselves). It would also create the management difficulties associated with labour-managed firms, and engender a reluctance to expand the number of team members, thus constraining the expansion of the firm.

An alternative strategy to reassure vulnerable holders of specific assets that the entitlement to the income generated by them is secure whilst allowing outside financial participation, would be to limit the possibility of takeover. This, however, removes a powerful source of management incentives. An alternative source of these incentives could be a highly developed managerial labour market in which past successes and failures were accounted for. This requires not only very good information but a highly mobile managerial class which contracts on the labour market at frequent intervals. It is therefore incompatible with the gradual accumulation of firm-specific knowledge over long periods, so prized by some modern students of the sources of competitive advantage. The use of sophisticated incentive packages linked to company performance, including stock options or other devices, offers another alternative form of management incentives. But this could be seen as linking managers' rewards too intimately with the shareholders' interests and ignoring their responsibilities to other stakeholders.

12.2   DIFFERENCES IN CONTRACTUAL RELATIONS

The complex trade-offs mentioned above are reflected in the differing institutional structures of the UK, Germany, and Japan. Recent studies of contractual relations have contrasted the broadly Anglo-Saxon approach with that of Japan. Although in every country a range of contractual forms can be observed, the USA and the UK seem to rely more heavily on transacting at arm's length using contracts with detailed written provisions which are then renegotiated periodically. Where conditions are so complex and uncertain that written contracts become unwieldy and imply a high probability of costly litigation, the response is to integrate vertically and undertake the activity within the firm so as to avoid the hazards of the market-place. Japan, in contrast, relies more heavily on implicit or relational contracting. Agreements will not incorporate extremely detailed descriptions of each party's obligations. Instead, a long-term relationship embodying high levels of trust between the parties is seen as the ideal which is enshrined in a basic agreement couched in extremely vague terms. A great deal of management time is invested in establishing reliable flows of information and resolving disputes without recourse to law. This system permits industries to be less vertically integrated without succumbing to transactional hazards.

In essence, the Japanese system encourages compliance by establishing accurate flows of information and threatening loss of reputation in the event of opportunistic behaviour. Cheating is less likely where it is understood that the present game is just one in a series stretching into the future, and where there are social as well as financial costs associated with breach of faith. The Anglo-US system encourages compliance by threatening specific penalties in the event of failure to accomplish particular terms of a contract. There may also be an implied threat not to deal again, but the lower expectation of repeat dealing combined with the lesser degree of dependency on a particular relationship makes this threat less significant even if more frequently implemented. The results of these broad differences can be seen in the structural characteristics of the car industry and the electronics industry. As Seiichi Masuyama points out in Chapter 16, the USA has relied to a greater extent than Japan on vertical integration in the car industry. Kester (1991) reports that General Motors purchases about 30 per cent by value of its parts from outside, compared with over 70 per cent for Japanese automobile assemblers. In spite of this it still relies on more than 2,000 different primary parts suppliers compared with 162 in the case of Nissan. A study by Sako (1990) of the British and Japanese electronic assembly and printed circuit board industries revealed similar differences in contractual relations between buyers and suppliers in the UK and Japan.

It should not be assumed that relational contracting is always to be preferred to arm's length arrangements. If contractual terms are fairly straightforward, and if the business environment is fairly stable so that contractual adjustments are needed infrequently, it would be irrational to sink management time into establishing costly relationships with suppliers. Similarly, some of the problems discussed above associated with the building up of specific assets (expertise or know-how within teams, or physical capital designed for specific investment projects) may be countered by contractual methods.

The main problem is to assign clear property rights to the returns from specific assets. In other words, contracts may be able to designate unambiguously who has the right to the returns on investment in specific assets, be they physical assets such as equipment or human assets such as know-how. Generally it may be easier to devise contracts to reward appropriately investment in physical assets than investment in human assets.

For instance, one firm may wish to buy a component from another. If the production of this component requires the use of highly specific equipment, the supplier will fear the possibility of hold-up. However, if the buying firm finances the specific capital equipment and leases it to the supplier, the latter should be reassured that the contractual terms will not be subject to adverse variation in the future. Any attempts by the buyer to reduce prices will, in principle, result in the supplier refusing further deliveries and transferring the non-specific assets of the firm to alternative employment. Of course, in practice this 'quasi-vertical integration' will require a degree of trust on both sides. From the supplier's point of view it is unlikely that even non-specific assets can be redeployed costlessly and immediately to alternative equally profitable activities. From the buyer's point of view, poor performance by the supplier or attempts to renegotiate prices upwards can be countered, in principle, by transferring the specific assets to an alternative supplier. Again, in practice it is unlikely that this could be achieved without incurring significant transactions costs.

Further, assigning property rights to specific know-how and human capital is even more difficult than establishing rights in physical capital. It is precisely in these areas that purely contractual solutions to problems posed by asset specificity break down. Unfortunately, as John Kay has argued, under modern conditions these assets can be seen as a major source of competitive advantage. It is from the specific human capital of the firm that its architecture is fashioned. It is therefore unfortunate for the UK that its dexterity with contractual solutions may be of limited benefit in an area which functions better with alternative more obligational relations.

In the rest of this chapter we look at corporate governance from this contractualist perspective, in the process referring to the contributions of Part II of this volume and linking some of the issues with the discussion of Part I. If the firm can be seen as a set of contracts, these contracts concern the disposition of property rights. Differing rights assignments produce different types of firm, and different incentives for the various contracting parties.

The property rights assigned to shareholders, for example, may vary considerably. Shares may convey the right to receive dividends alone, or they may in addition confer the right to take part in the selection of the management board. There may be restrictions (either formal or conventional) on the exchangeability of shares, as in Japan and Germany, or they may be freely traded on highly developed and impersonal stock-markets, as in the United Kingdom and the United States. The right to trade using information not available on equal terms to other shareholders may be circumscribed, as in the insider dealing restrictions of the United States and elsewhere. Rights may inhere in a named individual or may be exercised by the bearer of the shares or by an authorized proxy as in Germany. Where shares are held by financial institutions and the rights exercised by trustees (a very important arrangement in the United Kingdom), the decisions of the trustees may be constrained by rules governing their responsibilities to members of the fund over which they have jurisdiction. Limits may be set on the freedom of one firm to trade in the shares of another as, for example, with restrictions in many countries on the ability of financial institutions to hold shares of non-financial companies.

All these matters influence the background against which contracting takes place and the forms of corporate governance that evolve. The UK system has tended to produce an environment in which shares are held by institutions which trade them regularly on an active stock-market (as described in Chapters 1 and 3–5, by Nicholas Dimsdale, Jonathan Charkham, Allen Sykes, and Paul Marsh). In contrast, Japanese and German shareholding is relatively stable. The Japanese case is discussed in Chapters 15 and 16, by Jenny Corbett and Seiichi Masuyama. This fundamental difference affects the willingness of suppliers of human and other resources to invest in firm-specific assets. As already discussed above, implicit or relational contracting may be necessary where hold-up potential is great. In other words, a long-term commitment embodying high levels of mutual trust is necessary to give the transacting parties confidence to invest in specific assets and to reduce the fear of opportunism. Frequent change in the identity of shareholders will make it difficult for stakeholders (such as employees with highly specific know-how) to be confident that their vulnerability will not be exploited.

Takeovers provide another example of the possibility that implicit contracts are broken. They may threaten specific assets, such as teams of expertise built up in a particular organization, and so the willingness to accumulate these assets will be inhibited and efficiency reduced. Increases in returns to shareholders may not be derived from efficiency gains but from redirected rents (returns to specific assets). Takeovers then become a vehicle not for entrepreneurial flair, but for rent seeking. In section 12.3 the contrasting rights of shareholders are investigated in more detail.

A sedated market for corporate control has its disadvantages, however. The obvious danger is that the sedative effect will filter through to managerial effort. It is therefore not surprising that systems which rely less on a market for corporate control, and where the share price is less influential as an incentive than it is in the UK, have different mechanisms for monitoring and motivating managers. The structure and composition of UK company boards is discussed in Chapters 1, 4, and 5 by Dimsdale, Charkham, and Sykes; while in Chapters 13 and 14 Edwards and Fischer and Schneider-Lenné examine the German two-tier board system. These matters are reviewed further in section 12.4.

Differences across countries in property rights assignments and contractual relations are also reflected in sources of financing and in capital structures. Financial ratios are affected by the tax system, accounting conventions, and the riskiness of the firm's operations. However, transactional considerations will also be important. If providers of finance have better information channels they may be prepared to advance funds more cheaply and for longer periods, thereby permitting higher debt–equity ratios. If firms have obligational relationships with others in a supply chain, as happens frequently in Japan, this may result in larger outstanding claims on one another in the form of trade credits extended and received and this will again increase some measures of the ratio of debt to equity. The funding of employees' separation payments in Japan and pension entitlements in Germany also influences debt–equity ratios depending upon whether such implicit or explicit claims on the firm are regarded as debt or equity. The point here is that financial ratios have to be interpreted within the context of the contractual relations linking firms with their buyers and suppliers, their employees, and their bankers and shareholders. More information on capital structures is contained in section 12.5.

12.3   PROPERTY RIGHTS OF SHAREHOLDERS

12.3.1   *The UK System*

In a UK public company, managers are accountable to shareholders. A share entitles its owner to a vote at meetings for the appointment of directors, to receive any residual earnings from the firm's operations, and to exchange these rights without consulting managers or other shareholders. As a residual claimant, the shareholder is seen as the principal bearer of risk, although each individual can reduce his or her exposure by holding a diversified portfolio of claims.

Franks and Mayer (1990) have analysed differences in the rights attached to shareholding between countries. They argue that a key difference concerns the extent to which claims to the residual are associated with rights to select and control managers. In the UK system these rights are integrated. Further, the principle of equality of shareholder status is supported by regulatory bodies. Small shareholders, for example, have proportional voting rights and the same access to information as those who hold larger stakes in a company. This has been an important consideration in the regulations governing takeovers established by the Stock Exchange. It has led to the prevention of the undisclosed build-up of large stakes in a company, and to a system which discourages the acquisition of information which might make the recipient an insider. The very terminology is revealing. Shareholders in the UK system are expected, and to a degree encouraged, to be 'outsiders'. They are not part of the team.

Institutional shareholders dominate the trade in shares in the UK. The managers of these funds must consider the interests of the pensioners or others for whom they act as trustees. This does not, in principle, rule out choosing a stable portfolio of shares, or investing in detailed information about the activities of a group of companies. However, the desire to spread risks will tend to result in a diversified portfolio and a low return to intervening in any particular company, especially as insider status may thereupon restrict the ability to trade. In general, the result has been the development of a highly impersonal market in shares based on publicly available information. Marsh, in Chapter 3, presents the evidence concerning market efficiency. The fact that share prices quickly respond to all publicly available information, and that studies have been unable to uncover unexploited gains to arbitrage, does not in itself show that greater shareholder intervention would not have been profitable for those undertaking it. However, as the system has developed, management incentives have taken the form of the takeover threat prompted by an underperforming share price rather than any more direct method of monitoring by shareholders.

12.3.2   *The Japanese System*

If shareholders in the UK are predominantly outsiders, those in Japan are largely insiders, having some kind of commercial contact with the company. Thus, although the structure of shareholding—three-quarters institutions, one-quarter individuals—looks very similar to that in the UK, the nature of the institutional shareholding is very different.

The differences are of two sorts: the nature of the institutions and the nature of the obligations. The institutions are not independent pension funds and insurance companies with their own interests and obligations as described above. They are instead institutions such as banks who may have provided loan finance; supplying companies who may have a long-running association; or other companies linked by cross-shareholdings, who all may be part of a loosely structured keiretsu group. Corbett, in Chapter 15, explains in some detail the nature of the keiretsu and the type of contact typical of firms within the group. There tends to be considerable sharing of information and trading as well as financial contact within the group. However, the six largest keiretsu accounted for only 4 per cent of employees in Japan and 16 per cent of sales in 1989. Firms within groups and those outside may therefore be structured differently.

The second important feature of Japanese shareholding is that tradability of rights is more constrained than in the UK. It is estimated that nearly two-thirds of equity is held in the form of stable shareholding—*antei kabunushi*—which is distinct from interlocking shareholding—*kabushiki mochiai*—although the two may overlap. In Chapters 15 and 16, Corbett and Masuyama explain the nature of the stable shareholding agreements and their origins and rationale. Stability arises from an implicit agreement to waive the exercise of control rights (i.e. to hold shares as a passive friendly insider) and not to sell the shares to third parties, or at least to consult the firm whose shares are held if it is necessary to dispose of them. These obligations are implicit and do not entail shares never being sold. However, in practice it means that the most actively traded shares are those held by the household sector, the opposite of the situation in the UK. Stable shareholding practices are designed to raise the transaction costs of transferring ownership and to ensure greater continuity of control. As a result, hostile takeovers in Japan are almost unknown.

12.3.3   *The German System*

German shareholding practices do not involve the type of implicit shareholding agreements that exist in Japan. There are no equivalent barriers to the transfer of ownership. On the other hand, Franks and Mayer (1990) argue that there are barriers to the transfer of control. In Germany, for instance, public companies are able to issue non-voting shares to an amount equal to that of all voting shares. Capital can thereby be raised (up to a point) by means of equity without affecting the control of the enterprise. It is also common in Germany for banks, which may hold a relatively small equity stake themselves, to exercise voting rights on behalf of other shareholders who deposit shares with them (see Edwards in Chapter 13). Further, the rights of German employees are embodied in the co-determination law. They are represented on supervisory boards (discussed below) and also on workers' councils relating to terms of employment and dismissal. Such employee rights constitute an attenuation of German shareholders' rights in comparison with those in the UK where employee involvement in corporate decision making is at the discretion of the management.

12.4   BOARD STRUCTURE AND THE MONITORING OF MANAGERS

The different property rights and conventions surrounding shareholdings inevitably influence the means by which the management of a company is monitored. Under the UK system, the impact of direct monitoring is not great because the return to investment in monitoring from the point of view of a single holder of a small fraction of the total stock of equity shares is likely to be negligible. Shareholders can appoint auditors and external directors, of course, to act as their agents. But if the selection of these is effectively under management control, or if the probability of detecting poor performance on the part of auditors is sufficiently small, it is doubtful whether their impact on management behaviour will be substantial. In Chapters 1, 4, and 5, Dimsdale, Charkham, and Sykes discuss the structure of UK boards from this perspective and suggest possible ways of increasing the independence of non-executive directors and making company auditors more independent of executive management.

To give monitors an incentive to be effective requires that they have something substantial to lose from being ineffective. Direct monitoring is therefore only likely to be undertaken by a substantial stakeholder and then only if monitoring costs are not prohibitive. It is in this context that the separation of control rights from residual claims becomes relevant. Clearly, nothing is to be gained by a complete separation, since those with the control rights would then have no incentive to exercise them. However, to concentrate rights of control in the hands of a substantial stakeholder has the merit of lowering monitoring and control costs to this stakeholder. Those surrendering their control rights gain from a more efficiently run company and more valuable residual rights than otherwise might have existed had the control rights remained dispersed.

It is this strategy that, in essence, the German and Japanese systems can be seen as following, and it is the banks which seem to play an important part in its operation. The influence that the 'main bank' in Japan and the 'Hausbank' in Germany wields over a company is discussed in a number of chapters. Banks are allowed to hold equity stakes in companies, although these are limited to 5 per cent of equity in any one company in Japan, and in Germany amounted to 12 per cent of equity in 1988. In both countries, the role of shareholder is as important to the banks as the role of lender. This is so even in Japan where there is a higher proportion of investment financed by lending (see section 12.5). In Germany, banks' voting rights derive largely from the proxy votes they exercise on behalf of shareholders. In Chapter 13 Edwards gives details of the form and extent of these rights. In both countries banks have seats on company boards, although not necessarily dominant positions on those boards. Corbett in Chapter 15, suggests that the Japanese banks' positions on Japanese boards is more likely to stem from their role as shareholders than as lenders, with more directors appointed the higher is a bank's share of the equity.

Equity stakes, a proportion of the lending, and seats on the board give the German and Japanese banks a different association with companies than is typical in the UK. Information-flows between banks and companies may as a result be more developed. Corbett points out that Japanese banks send employees for stints as managers in client firms. Schneider-Lenné, in Chapter 14, refers to the long-term nature of relationship banking, the importance of company visits, the accumulation of information about many companies in a locality or region, and the interest in preventing temporary distress from spilling over unnecessarily to other business clients.

None of this means that banks control industry in Germany and Japan, nor that a single bank has exclusive contact with each company. It does imply, however, that the banks may be fulfilling some of the direct monitoring and information gathering functions which would be expected of owners. They do not do this from an altruistic attachment to shareholders' interests, but because their stakeholding in the firm is large enough to make monitoring worthwhile, and their control rights are extensive enough to make them influential. In the context of Japan, Aoki (1989: 148) supports this view that individual stockholders delegate the monitoring function to the 'main bank' of a company. 'The deviation from share price maximisation by the company at the sacrifice of individual stockholders and the phenomenon of overborrowing in the interests of the bank may in part be thought of as the "agency fee" paid by the individual stockholders to the bank for that service.'

Monitoring by banks may have a noticeable effect and benefit stockholders, but the overall structure of company boards in Germany and Japan gives voice to more than shareholder interests. Corbett points to the fact that Japanese boards are composed mainly of managers promoted internally. These managers do not see themselves as responsible to shareholders alone, but to a broad coalition of shareholders and other stakeholders. Managerial skills in Japan put great emphasis on the reconciliation of conflicting interests and the amicable resolution of disputes.

Indeed the Japanese firm can be looked upon as a 'coalition of the body of quasi-permanent employees and the body of stockholders' (Aoki 1989: 154). The distribution of the rents generated by this coalition is mediated by the management group in a complex bargain which is likely to involve higher growth rates and a greater concern with market share objectives than would be chosen by the stockholders alone. Masuyama, in Chapter 16, cites the lower rate of return on equity in Japan compared with the USA as evidence of this greater concern with market share.

Similarly, in the German two-tier board system described by Schneider-Lenné and Edwards, in Chapters 13 and 14, membership of the supervisory board is divided equally between employee and shareholder representatives. Although it formally appoints the management board, it does not exercise tight control over the management, meeting relatively infrequently and discussing social as well as matters of business. It is not possible for members of the board of managing directors to be on the supervisory board at the same time; and interlocking directorships are not possible either. On the other hand there are considerable links both between supervisory boards of different companies and between boards of managing directors and supervisory boards of other companies.

Although more direct monitoring and inside information gathering is associated with both German and Japanese systems than is the case in the UK, it would be wrong to conclude that shareholder interests are thereby more strongly represented. The activities of German and Japanese banks must be seen in the context of a board structure that encourages the representation of other stakeholder interests and which, in practice, leaves the management of each company with a wide area of discretion. The impersonal arm's length arrangements of the UK, because they are combined with an active market in corporate control, give powerful incentives to managers to worry about the share price. So concerned do they become that, it is claimed, they neglect the long-run interests of the company in pursuit of short-term shareholder returns, and will even rob other vulnerable stakeholders of their rightful property in takeover raids. The evidence for these propositions is not decisive (as can be see from, for example, Marsh in Chapter 3 and others) but the protection given to stakeholders other than holders of equity in the German and Japanese systems is a principal distinguishing characteristic. How far direct monitoring substitutes effectively for the incentives generated by the takeover threat, and, conversely, how far it is possible to protect other stakeholders within the UK's system through employee shareholdings or suitably structured anti-takeover measures, are as yet unresolved issues.

The indirect influence of shareholder interests in the UK system can be seen in a number of its characteristics—more contested takeover activity, higher dividend pay-out ratios, and a higher rate of return on equity, than are typical in Germany and Japan. Franks and Mayer (1990) attribute the UK's higher level of contested takeover activity than Germany's in part to the barriers to changes in control implicit in the arrangements discussed above. Despite the formal right to trade in shares, Germany's institutional structure (and even more so the Japanese structure) prevents outside raiders from acquiring control if those with existing controlling stakes do not wish it.

Dividend pay-out ratios are much lower in both Japan and Germany than in the UK. Comparable OECD data are available only for the UK, USA, and Japan (Table 12.1). From these it appears that the UK ratio of dividends to gross income has been consistently higher—at between 35 and 50 per cent—than that in the USA (around 25 per cent) or in Japan (around 15 per cent). Mayer and Alexander's (1990) comparative work between Germany and the UK based on a Datastream sample set shows UK dividend ratios to have been above twice those in Germany during the 1980s.

Complex linkages may connect dividend payment policy to structures of corporate governance. Differences in tax policy, accounting conventions, or the perceived availability of profitable investment opportunities within the corporate sector, might all be expected to play a part. The return of equity may either be in the form of dividends or capital gains. The equalization of overall returns to equity in international markets may lead to higher dividends in more slowly growing economies. In addition, however, the dispersed control rights associated with shareholdings in the UK are relevant. It has been suggested that fear of takeover motivates managers to distribute

Table 12.1.   *Ratio of dividends to gross income of non-financial corporations*

Year	UK (%)	USA (%)	Japan (%)
1974	—	24	17
1975	—	20	18
1976	—	20	17
1977	36	19	16
1978	37	20	15
1979	41	20	13
1980	45	23	14
1981	45	22	14
1982	49	25	15
1983	48	23	13
1984	45	21	12
1985	46	20	10
1986	34	22	12
1987	39	22	10
1988	42	21	10
1989	41	28	—

Source: OECD Financial Statistics

a higher fraction of earnings in the UK, although this would imply considerable informational inefficiency in the capital market if the sacrifice of profitable opportunities were thereby implied. An alternative view is that dividends are related to problems of monitoring. Managers pay dividends and are then forced into the capital market for resources. This subjects them to closer monitoring from the providers of new capital who will have an interest in appraising future plans carefully (Easterbrook 1984). Dividends may also be seen (De Alessi and Fishe 1987) as a way of reducing information and monitoring costs to shareholders. Regular dividend payments represent 'a commitment of minimum performance on the part of management'. The relative empirical importance of these possible influences has yet to be firmly established, but the higher dividend pay-out ratio in the UK than in Germany or Japan is at least consistent with the need for a different means of monitoring the management and conveying information to shareholders.

12.5   DIFFERENCES IN CAPITAL STRUCTURES

Contractual issues will also influence the observed sources of finance used by companies and the capital structure revealed in their balance sheets. The chapters by Mayer, Edwards and Corbett (9, 13, and 15) show comparable measures of the net sources of financing by companies in the UK, Germany, and Japan, and the following figures illustrate some of their key findings.

Outside finance, from the stock-market or banks, may not be appropriate for financing knowledge-based projects such as research and development, or projects which cannot be assessed in the absence of detailed firm-specific information. Kay (Chapter 2) points out that many company managers are themselves acting as fund managers. They aim to control risks within the company by diversifying the investment portfolio. They also screen for entrepreneurial talent using information generated within the firm. Developing a reputation for sound judgement of investment opportunities within the firm and retaining earnings for these purposes is an alternative to reliance on a sceptical and less well-informed outside market.

The degree to which companies in different countries finance new investment from retained earnings, that is, their self-financing ratio, is shown in Fig. 12.1. This indicates that all countries finance a large proportion of new investment from retentions. High retentions may be regarded as a response to information asymmetries that are particularly troublesome for longer-term high-risk projects.

However, Japan's proportion of financing by retentions is below the levels that prevail in the UK, Germany or the US, as can be seen in Fig. 12.1 and also Table 12.2.

Table 12.2 and Fig. 12.2 also show the higher proportion of debt financing in Japan than in the other three countries, at over 50 per cent of

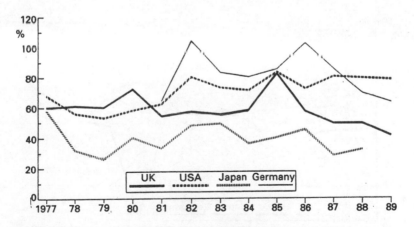

Germany: Issues of shares included in non-financial sources
Note: break in German series in 1986
Fig. 12.1.   Self-financing ratio. *Source*: OECD

Table 12.2. *Sources of finance as a proportion of total sources*

	UK		Germany		USA		Japan	
	1977–80	1981–9	1977–80	1981–9	1977–80	1981–9	1977–80	1981–9
Debt	23.4	30.4	33.2	18.4	35.1	33.7	56.3	54.2
Of which short-term debt	22.9	21.3	—	—	22.0	10.8	42.2	32.4
Of which long-term debt	0.5	9.2	—	—	13.1	22.9	14.1	21.7
Share issues	9.1	13.2	66.8	81.6	3.6	−5.3	5.1	6.4
Internal sources	67.5	56.4			61.3	71.6	38.6	39.5

Source: OECD Financial Statistics

sources of finance for investment. Higher debt financing and lower self-financing in Japanese companies may be seen as a function of greater information flows and obligations associated with the keiretsu. It may even be misleading to label such financing as external since the relationship that supports it may be closer to that of an insider. In Chapter 15 Corbett points to evidence that the keiretsu group provides insurance services, reducing profit variability at the cost of lower profit levels. As mentioned in

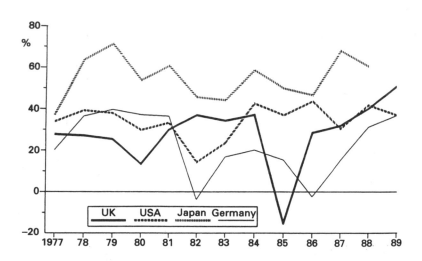

Fig. 12.2. Debt as a proportion of total sources. *Source*: OECD

earlier sections, Japanese company debt (heavily comprising short-term trade credits) may be linked to these keiretsu relationships. Further, the relationship with the main bank (discussed in section 12.4) reduces the agency costs of outside finance and may improve the assessments of risks. If this is so, higher levels of debt finance for new investment would be consistent with these contractual relationships.

The other distinction that emerges especially between Japan on the one hand, and the UK and Germany on the other, is the much greater stability in financing proportions in Japan. A relatively constant share of financing has been done with retained earnings and with debt. The main shift since the late 1970s is in long-term debt replacing short-term debt (see Table 12.2). This concurs with Corbett's impression (Chapter 15) that relationships between banks and industry in Japan have not altered dramatically over the 1980s, countering the claim that there has been a convergence in lending patterns between Japan and those in the West. This stability contrasts with the volatility of debt financing of the UK and Germany as Fig. 12.2 illustrates, with dips into aggregate debt repayment in the mid-1980s in both countries. External financing in the UK, Germany, and the USA seems to have been treated more as a residual, with switching between the different types of external finance according to conditions in the markets and of lending.

Balance sheet structure also reflects the contractual features prevalent in different countries. On the liabilities side, Fig. 12.3 shows that the UK and the USA have higher equity proportions than do companies in Japan and Germany. This crucially depends, however, on the classification of pension provisions in the German case and trade credits in the case of Japan. Table 12.3 shows that if German pension provisions are regarded as equity, debt–equity ratios are very similar in the UK and Germany. Provisions for pensions in German companies are retained by each company as liabilities on their balance sheet. They involve repayment obligations at a specified date in the future and in that sense are akin to debt. On the other hand Schneider-Lenné points out in Chapter 14 that these funds are seen by companies as a form of 'social capital', a form of equity contributed by those working for the company with implicit obligations attached to that equity.

Short-term trade credits and short-term borrowing are very important on both the liabilities and assets side of Japanese balance sheets. Figure 12.3 and Fig. 12.4 compare the structure of liabilities and assets respectively. Trade credits are classified as short-term liabilities in Fig. 12.3 and are marked separately where appropriate in Fig. 12.4. The network of inter-company financing is more important in Japan than elsewhere, reflecting closer supply chain links and a more widespread stakeholder influence compared with the UK.

Table 12.3. *Debt–equity ratio of non-financial enterprises*

Year	Japan	USA	UK	Germany	
				Provisions classified as debt	Provisions classified as equity
1974		0.56			
1975	5.60	0.52		2.56	1.84
1976	5.72	0.50		2.62	1.85
1977	5.49	0.51	1.06	2.60	1.82
1978	5.49	0.50	1.08	2.68	1.84
1979	5.49	0.49	1.06	2.77	1.88
1980	5.16	0.48	1.06	3.02	1.92
1981	5.04	0.47	1.10	3.09	1.96
1982	5.02	0.47	1.13	3.06	1.89
1983	4.84	0.50	1.10	3.05	1.83
1984	4.77	0.56	1.09	3.00	1.76
1985	4.40	0.61	1.04	2.99	1.72
1986	4.22	0.67	1.04	2.90	1.63
1987	4.36	0.71	1.03	4.19	1.51
1988	4.19	0.76	1.03	4.25	1.52
1989		0.82	1.14	4.33	1.53

Source: OECD Finance Statement

Note: Gross liabilities less equity as a proportion of equity.

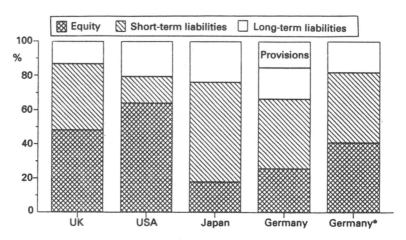

* Provisions are included as equity: Japan time period covered is 1977–88

Fig. 12.3. Liabilities of non-financial companies as a proportion of total liabilities 1977–89. *Source*: OECD

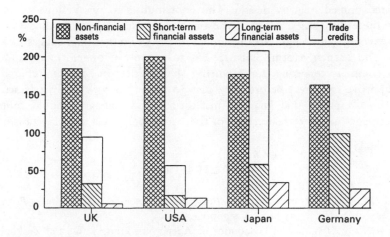

Fig. 12.4. Assets of non-financial companies as a proportion of value added.
Source: OECD

12.6 CONCLUSIONS

In this chapter, corporate governance in the UK, Japan, and Germany has been discussed from a contractualist point of view. Observed arrangements, it has been argued, are consistent with attempts to overcome the inevitable hazards which accompany transacting in every country. There is, unfortunately, no simple and obvious solution which can be adopted everywhere. Arrangements inevitably reflect historical circumstances to some degree, and there is room for disagreement about the scope for reform.

Contrasting the systems of various countries is instructive. But it cannot be inferred that policy makers are free to construct whichever of these symptoms appears upon calm reflection to have the best qualities. Not only are the trade-offs implied by different systems extremely difficult to quantify, but it may not be possible to create them piecemeal. Each system has a logic of its own, and bits of each may not fit together. Protecting stakeholders in the UK system by suppressing takeovers, for example, without putting into place the system of obligational relationships associated with other systems, might purchase some small efficiency gains at the price of discarding a major source of management incentives. Further, the power of conventions is substantial. Property rights are defined not merely by statute or legally enforceable rules, they also embrace conventions which may be enforceable only by the threat of loss of reputation. Such conventions and the associated confidence that the people with whom one is transacting will behave in reliable and predictable ways can only evolve. They cannot be created immediately by design. The contributors to this volume all recognize these difficulties. Most of the proposals discussed are modifications of the existing arms-length arrangements of the UK rather than suggestions for root and branch reform. This applies to proposals for improving auditing and company reporting, for requiring shareholders in acquiring companies to approve takeovers before they can go ahead, as well as Sykes's suggestion in Chapter 5 that financial institutions and managers should come to agreements which recreate some of the conditions of classical capitalism.

REFERENCES

Aoki, M. (1989), *Information, Incentives, and Bargaining in the Japanese Economy* (Cambridge University Press, Cambridge).

Arrow, K. J. (1985), 'The Economics of Agency' in Pratt, J. W. and Zeckhauser, R. J. (eds.), *Principals and Agents: The Structure of Business*, 37-51 (Harvard Business School Press).

Coase, R. H. (1937), 'The Nature of the Firm', *Economica*, vol. 4.

De Alessi, L. and Fishe, P. H. (1987), 'Why do Corporations Distribute Assets?: An Analysis of Dividends and Capital Structure', *Journal of Institutional and Theoretical Economics*, March, 34–61.

Easterbrook, F. H. (1984), 'Two Agency Cost Explanations of Dividends', *American Economic Review*, 74: 650–59.

Franks, J. and Mayer, C. (1990), 'Corporate Ownership and Corporate Control: A Study of France, Germany and the UK', *Economic Policy*, April, 191–231.

Jensen, C. M. and Meckling, W. H. (1976), 'Theory of the Firm: Managerial Behaviour, Agency Costs and Ownership Structure', *Journal of Financial Economics*, 3: 305–60.

Kester, C. W. (1991), 'Governance, Contracting and Investment Time Horizons' unpub. paper (Harvard Business School).

Mayer, C. and Alexander, I. (1990), 'Banks and Securities Markets: Corporate Financing in Germany and the UK', *Journal of Japanese and International Economies*.

Sako, Mari (1990), *Buyer-Supplier Relationships and Economic Performance: Evidence from Britain and Japan*, Ph.D. thesis, University of London.

13

An Overview of the German Financial System

J. S. S. EDWARDS and K. FISCHER

13.1 INTRODUCTION

The German system of providing finance for investment is commonly described as being a bank-based one, in contrast to the more market-based system of the UK, and is also commonly seen as having contributed importantly to German economic success. For example, Hallett (1990: 83) states that: 'Firms rely extensively on loan, as against equity, finance, and the banks exercise an important monitoring role through their representatives on the Supervisory Board . . . the role of the banks tends to counter "short termism", and provides a mechanism for reorganising management in good time, when a company starts running into trouble.' The aim of this chapter is to give an overview of the German system of finance for investment by means of a careful assessment of the role of banks in it.

There are three main sections in the chapter. Section 13.2 analyses the sources of investment finance for German non-financial enterprises over the period 1960–89 and compares them to UK non-financial enterprises' sources of funds. Section 13.3 considers whether German banks in their role as lenders to firms behave in a way which is significantly different from UK banks. Section 13.4 discusses the argument that German banks act on shareholders' behalf, via their control of equity voting rights and positions on supervisory boards, to monitor the management of large German firms. There is a brief conclusion to the chapter in section 13.5.

Before starting the main analysis of the chapter, it is necessary to describe the operation of the supervisory board system in Germany. This system applies essentially to larger incorporated companies. There are two major types of incorporated company in Germany: the Aktiengesellschaft (AG)—literally, stock corporation—and the Gesellschaft mit beschränkter Haftung (GmbH)—literally, limited liability company. In 1972 the share of total turnover in Germany accounted for by AGs was 19.1 per cent while

The research on which this chapter is based is part of the Centre for Economic Policy Research Project *An International Study of the Financing of Industry*. The German part of the study has been funded by the Anglo-German Foundation for the Study of Industrial Society to which we are most grateful. We are also grateful to the other members of the project—Ian Alexander, Elisabetta Bertero, Jenny Corbett, Tim Jenkinson, Colin Mayer, and Masako Nagamitsu—for comments and suggestions. We have also benefited from comments by Paul Borrett, Paul Seabright, and participants in seminars at Cambridge University, the Industrial Economics Study Group, and the London Business School.

that due to GmbHs was 17.1 per cent; by 1986 the shares of total turnover were, respectively, 21.1 per cent and 25.5 per cent.

All AGs must appoint a supervisory board (Aufsichtsrat) as well as a management board (Vorstand). The supervisory board comprises both shareholders' and employees' representatives. Since 1976 the legal position concerning these two types of representatives has been that one-third of the supervisory board members of an AG with 2,000 or fewer employees must be elected by the employees, while an AG with more than 2,000 employees must have one-half of its supervisory board members elected by the employees. In the latter case the chairman of the supervisory board, who is elected by the shareholders' representatives, can cast a second vote to break ties in supervisory board decisions. The shareholders' representatives on the supervisory board are elected (usually for the legal maximum of a five-year term) at the shareholders' general meeting. Shareholders' representatives can be dismissed before their term of office expires by a 75 per cent majority at the shareholders' general meeting. Employees' representatives are elected by the workforce.

The main function of the supervisory board is specified by the Aktiengesetz (Stock Corporation Act) as the control of management. This includes the right to appoint and dismiss members of the management board which directly manages an AG, and to fix their salaries. A member of the management board is appointed for a term of up to five years, with the possibility of reappointment, and cannot sit on the supervisory board. The management board is obliged to inform the supervisory board about future business policies, the performance of the company, and the conduct of business. The supervisory board can furthermore obtain any other information about the company from the management board which it feels is necessary. The supervisory board is not directly involved in management decisions, which are the responsibility of the management board, but it may, depending on the particular AG's articles of incorporation, be required to approve certain major decisions of the management board.

In contrast to AGs, a GmbH does not ordinarily issue shares and is only required to have a supervisory board as well as a board of managers if the number of its employees regularly exceeds 500. A smaller GmbH may provide for a supervisory board in its articles of incorporation if it so wishes. The same rules as for AGs apply for employee representation on supervisory boards which are mandatory for GmbHs.

13.2 THE FINANCE OF INVESTMENT BY NON-FINANCIAL ENTERPRISES IN GERMANY

Bank loans, it is often argued, constitute a particularly important source of investment finance in Germany (see, for example, Carrington and Edwards

(1979); *The Economist* (1990)). This claim is commonly based on capital gearing ratios derived from firm accounting data. The Bank of England (1984), for example, gives the following figures for the structure of liabilities of non-financial businesses in Germany and the UK at the end of 1981 (the figures are percentages of total liabilities):

Germany		United Kingdom	
Equity capital	19	Equity capital	49
Debt	81	Debt	51
of which short-term liabilities	48	of which bank loans	14
long-term liabilities	19	bond	8
provisions[1]	14	trade and other credit	25

[1] The provisions figure includes households' direct claims on enterprises in the form of pension provisions. As discussed below the appropriate categorization of this item between debt and equity is unclear, and in Table 13.1 it is classified as part of internally generated funds i.e. equity.

According to these figures non-financial enterprises' debt-equity ratio is much higher in Germany than in the UK, and, given that most firm debt in Germany takes the form of bank loans, bank lending to non-financial enterprises in Germany is also much higher than in the UK. However, international comparisons of the financing of investment based on balance sheet data are open to a number of serious objections. For example, in the absence of revaluations to take account of inflation the book value of equity capital can be substantially under-recorded. In the UK land and buildings are periodically revalued, but in Germany all assets are valued at historic cost, thus making any comparison of UK and German capital gearing ratios hazardous. Another problem is that the book values of assets and reserves are sensitive to depreciation schedules, and accounting conventions on depreciation vary appreciably across countries, partly in response to differences in corporate tax regimes. To illustrate the influence of different accounting systems on international comparisons of capital gearing ratios, Perlitz *et al.* (1985) showed, for instance, that the difference in the share of equity in total capital between Germany and the UK for a sample of very large corporations in 1979 and 1980 vanished if a series of adjustments to put both accounting systems on a roughly equal basis were made.

Because of these difficulties with balance sheet data, this paper follows the methodology set out by Mayer (1988; 1990) and uses sources and uses of funds data as a basis for international comparisons. In any period, enterprises' sources of funds must be equal to their uses of funds, and from this flow of funds statement it is possible in principle to establish how enterprises' investment in physical assets has been financed. Because the flow of funds statement describes current cash transactions it is naturally suited to answering the question of how investment has actually been financed. The uses of finance by enterprises in a particular time period include both the acquisition of fixed capital assets and stocks, and also the acquisition of financial assets. Some of the sources of enterprises' funds therefore go towards the accumulation of financial rather than physical assets. To identify the finance associated with physical investment it is therefore necessary to subtract enterprises' acquisitions of financial assets from equivalent increases in liabilities. This approach measures the finance of physical investment in terms of the net finance from various sources. However, a possible objection to analysing the finance of investment by a sector such as non-financial enterprises in terms of net sources of finance for physical investment is that, in a situation where some enterprises are borrowing from banks while others are depositing equivalent amounts of funds with banks, the net contribution of bank borrowing to financing physical investment by the sector will appear to be zero, which can be argued to understate the importance of bank loans as a source of finance. Even if banks are simply lending to some enterprises the funds deposited with them by others, the banks may be making an important contribution to the finance of the sector as a whole if, as is plausible, they have a comparative advantage over non-financial enterprises in the loan evaluation and monitoring process. For this reason figures are also presented showing the sources of funds of enterprises in terms of their share of investment in physical and financial assets, which are referred to as gross sources of finance.

The sources and uses of finance for the German producing enterprises sector are given in the capital finance account of the Deutsche Bundesbank, the transactions shown in which are valued at current purchase and sales prices.[1] The producing enterprises sector includes private and all public enterprises (regardless of their legal form): self-employed persons and partnership are also included in cases where their transactions relate to production and capital formation. By comparison with other countries, the definition of the producing enterprises sector in Germany is extremely wide, particularly in its inclusion of unincorporated businesses, so that care must be exercised when making international comparisons. This data source has the problem common to all national accounts flow of funds figures that some of the data are obtained as residuals from other components of the national accounts, which reduces their reliability and, because the allocation of such residuals is not standardized across different countries' national accounts, is another reason for caution when making international comparisons.

---

[1] Full details of the capital finance account of the Deutsche Bundesbank can be found in *Methodological Notes on the Capital Finance Account of the Deutsche Bundesbank 1960 to 1987: Translation*, Deutsche Bundesbank Special Series No. 4, 5th edition, June 1988.

Table 13.1 shows weighted average figures for net and gross sources of finance of investment for the producing enterprises sector over the period 1960–89. The weighted average figure for a particular source of finance is computed as follows:

$$\sum_{t=1960}^{t=1989} i_t^j \times \frac{P_t}{P_{1960}} \Bigg/ \sum_{t=1960}^{t=1989} I_t \times \frac{P_t}{P_{1960}}$$

where i_t^j denotes the amount of finance of type j in year t (measured in current prices of year t), $I_t = \sum_{j=1}^{n} i_t^j$ (there are n different types of finance) and P_t denotes the capital goods price index in year t. Hence the weighted average for a particular source of finance shows the contribution of that source of finance (measured in constant prices) over 1960–89 to either total physical investment (measured in constant prices) or total physical plus financial investment (measured in constant prices) over 1960–89. To put it another way, this weighted average is an average given by weighting the contribution of a particular source of finance to physical or physical plus financial investment in a particular year by the constant price value of physical or physical plus financial investment in that year. The broad conclusions which are drawn below are not sensitive to this particular choice of weighted average.

Comparing the net and gross figures in Table 13.1 it can be seen that internally generated funds are a significantly smaller percentage of

Table 13.1. *Net and gross sources of finance for investment, German producing enterprises sector 1960–1989*

	Net (%)	Gross (%)
Internally generated funds	79.3	62.9
of which provisions for pensions	3.9	3.1
Capital transfers from government	7.2	5.7
Bank borrowing	11.7	18.3
of which:		
long-term	13.3	6.4
short-term	−1.6	11.9
Funds from insurance enterprises	0.2	1.2
Bonds	−0.2	1.0
Shares	1.3	2.5
Other	0.5	8.3
of which foreign trade credit	−1.7	1.7
TOTAL	100.0	100.0

Source: Own calculations based on capital finance account of the Deutsche Bundesbank.

producing enterprises' investment in physical and financial assets than they are of physical investment alone, while short-term bank borrowing (short-term being defined as having an original maturity of less than one year) and other sources of finance are correspondingly significantly larger as a percentage of investment in physical and financial assets than of physical investment only. The category other in Table 13.1 mainly refers to financial transactions with foreigners. Thus the producing enterprises sector tends to accumulate foreign financial assets which when netted off the foreign financial liabilities it also accumulates makes this a relatively small net source of finance. Similarly, the producing enterprises sector tends to deposit more short-term funds with banks than it borrows short-term from banks, but netting short-term deposits from short-term borrowing obscures the fact that short-term bank borrowing is potentially quite an important source of finance for some producing enterprises, even though it is more than offset by short-term deposits with banks by other producing enterprises.

Bearing these qualifications to the use of the net sources of finance data in mind, we now focus on the finance of investment in physical assets (i.e. gross fixed capital formation and stockbuilding) by the producing enterprises sector over the period 1960–89. Internally-generated funds (the sum of retained profits, depreciation, and pension provisions) are by far the largest net source of finance for physical investment. One component of this source of finance which requires special attention is that which reflects households' claims under enterprise pension commitments. A feature of the German system of pension provision is that an important part of pension arrangements is provided by employers, partly via contributions to insurance enterprises and pension funds, and partly via direct claims of employees on firms as a result of pension contributions being invested in the enterprise. This latter category is what is shown as provisions for pensions in Table 13.1, and it can be seen that it is a non-trivial net source of finance for producing enterprises, amounting in size to one-third of the net bank borrowing figure over the period 1960–89. These contributions are classified as internally generated funds because they are indeed generated within enterprises, but as they carry with them a liability in the form of commitments to pay pensions to employees in the future they are clearly not equivalent to other forms of internal finance, and hence are shown separately in Table 13.1.

Long-term bank borrowing is the next most important net source of finance over the period 1960–89. Overall bank borrowing is a somewhat smaller net source of finance, reflecting the negative figure for short-term bank borrowing as a net source of funds for the producing enterprises sector. Capital transfers from the government appears as the next most important net source of finance for the producing enterprises sector, but this is slightly misleading, for although this item contains government subsidies it also contains, because of the structure of the German national accounts, the internally generated funds of government owned enterprises such as the Federal Railway and the Federal Post Office.

The remaining net sources of finance—bonds, shares, funds from insurance enterprises,[2] and other—are insignificant for the producing enterprises sector over the period 1960–89. One caveat which must be noted is that the figure for shares refers only to external equity raised by AGs, and so understates overall external equity finance. External equity raised by GmbHs is not identified separately and instead appears in the category of internally generated funds, as this figure contains retained profits, the computation of which includes residuals because of lack of data.

It is possible that the average financing figures for 1960–89 shown in Table 13.1 conceal changes in the relative importance of different sources of finance over the thirty-year period, and so Table 13.2 gives weighted average net sources of finance for the producing enterprises sector in each of the three decades which make up this period. It can be seen from Table 13.2 that there is little significant change in the relative importance of different net sources of finance over the period 1960–89. Internally generated funds accounted for a larger share of the producing enterprises sector's finance of physical investment in 1980–9 than in the previous two decades, and correspondingly the category other accounted for a smaller share in 1980–9 than in the two earlier decades. There is a gradual decline in the significance of overall bank borrowing as a net source of finance over the period, which is primarily due to short-term bank borrowing, there being no obvious trend in the share of long-term bank borrowing.

The overall picture which emerges from Tables 13.1 and 13.2 is that internally generated funds are by far the most important net source of finance for investment by the German producing enterprises sector over the period 1960–89. Although bank borrowing is the largest external source of funds in Germany, it is very much less significant quantitatively than internally generated funds. Whether bank loans are nevertheless a particularly important source of investment finance in Germany requires a comparison with the UK, to which we now turn.

Table 13.3 shows weighted averages over the period 1970–89, computed as in Tables 13.1 and 13.2, for net and gross sources of finance for investment for Germany, using the same data source as in Tables 13.1 and 13.2, and the UK, using national accounts flow of funds data. As always with international comparisons, there are reasons for taking care when making them. The figures shown in Table 13.3 are based on a definition of the non-financial enterprise sector for the UK which excludes unincorporated enterprises, in contrast to the definition of the German producing enterprises

---

[2] This latter category also includes funds from building and loan associations.

Table 13.2.   *Net sources of finance for investment, German producing enterprises sector, 1960–1969, 1970–1979, 1980–1989 (%)*

	1960–69	1970–79	1980–89
Internally generated funds	76.1	75.6	85.0
of which: provisions for pensions	2.0	4.3	4.9
Capital transfers from government	4.0	7.9	9.0
Bank borrowing	13.4	12.0	10.2
of which:			
long-term	11.5	15.6	12.6
short-term	1.9	−3.7	−2.4
Funds from insurance enterprises	0.9	0.5	−0.4
Bonds	0.7	−0.4	−0.7
Shares	2.4	0.6	1.1
Other	2.6	3.9	−4.1
of which: foreign trade credit	−1.1	−1.5	−2.2
TOTAL	100.0	100.0	100.0

Source: Own calculations based on capital finance account of the Deutsche Bundesbank

Table 13.3.   *Net and gross sources of finance for investment by non-financial enterprises in Germany and the UK 1970–1989 (%)*

	Net		Gross	
	Germany	UK	Germany	UK
Internally generated funds	80.6	98.0	62.4	62.1
Capital transfers	8.5	2.1	6.6	2.3
Bank finance	11.0	19.8	18.0	23.5
Bonds	−0.6	2.0	0.9	1.4
Shares	0.9	−8.0	2.3	7.4
Trade credit	−1.9	−1.6	1.8	1.9
Other	1.5	−4.1	8.0	2.4
Statistical adjustment	—	−8.2	—	—

Source: Germany, own calculations based on capital finance account of the Deutsche Bundesbank; UK, Mayer and Alexander (1991)

sector; and whereas the UK figures have a single large statistical adjustment to allow for problems with the quality of national accounts-based flow of funds data, Germany allocates balancing items to several different financing categories. Nevertheless the fact that the figures for the two countries are derived using a common methodology permits some meaningful comparisons to be made.

The striking conclusion that emerges from Table 13.3 is that German firms relied less on bank loans as a source of finance than did UK ones over the period 1970–89. Even if the separate statistical adjustment category for the UK means that the UK bank finance figures are somewhat overstated, it cannot be argued that bank loans were a significantly more important source of finance for investment in Germany than in the UK over this period. On the basis of these aggregate financing figures, there is no justification for the common characterization of Germany as having a bank-based system of finance for investment. However, there are other aspects of the role of banks which must be considered before rejecting this characterization entirely, namely the form in which banks provide loan finance, and the part they play in corporate control. These aspects are the subjects of the next two sections of the chapter.

13.3 GERMAN BANK LENDING TO FIRMS

There are several ways in which the form of bank lending to firms in Germany is argued to differ from that in the UK, to the benefit of German economic performance. German bank representation on company supervisory boards is argued to reduce the extent of information asymmetry between borrowers and lenders, so that bank loans are available on more favourable terms than in the UK. A characteristic feature of the relationship between banks and firms in Germany is claimed to be the existence of house banks, whereby individual companies use one large bank which provides most of their financial requirements and acts as lead bank wherever syndicated credits and other facilities are provided. Long-term relationships of this form between a bank and a firm mean that the bank understands the business and personnel of the firm to which it is lending well. Consequently the bank is seen as being better able to assess the risk of its loans, and can commit itself to supporting the firm with long-term loans. In particular the reduction in competition implied by the existence of house bank relationships is claimed to permit banks to be more supportive of firms in financial distress than would be the case in the UK, because the risk involved in providing rescue finance will be adequately compensated in the future and not be eroded by competition from other banks. German banks are also seen as being better able to provide loan finance to firms than is the case in the UK because they have ample staffs of technical advisers, capable of assessing industrial prospects and risks.

In this section evidence will be presented which casts doubts on these claims. Some of this evidence comes from interviews conducted by the author with German banks and firms in 1988.[3] One conclusion that

[3] Interviews were carried out with 16 banks and 13 firms, covering a range of different banks and firms in terms of size.

emerged very clearly from the interviews with banks was that they do not possess departments which have the technical expertise to assess whether particular projects for which finance is being sought are likely to be successful. It is interesting to note that the absence of this technical expertise on the part of German banks was remarked upon twenty-five years ago by Macrae (1966), who stated that: 'those famous technical and technological departments of the banks turn out to be rather myths; even in the biggest banks, they seem generally to be merely bankers with some knowledge of present trends in particular industries, rather than great innovating boffins in their own right'.

A second conclusion which emerged from the interviews was that bank representation on the supervisory boards of companies to which loans were made is generally insignificant as a source of information for the bank. This can be explained partly by the fact that in many cases supervisory boards have rather limited information about the operation of the company (see section 13.4 below for more details), and partly by the fact that bank representatives on such boards are often subject to Chinese walls which prevent them passing on information obtained on the supervisory board to their own bank. This conclusion is supported by a comparison of the sources of finance for investment for a sample of manufacturing AGs with the sources of finance for the producing enterprises sector as a whole. The AG is the only legal form of enterprise in Germany which must have a supervisory board, so that if bank representation on supervisory boards reduces information asymmetries and permits bank lending to take place on more favourable terms it would be expected that AGs use relatively more bank finance than does the producing enterprises sector as a whole. Weighted averages for net and gross sources of finance, computed in the same way as those given in section 13.2 above, were calculated for the period 1971–85, for the producing enterprises sector, and from aggregate company accounting data for a sample drawn from the population of all AGs in manufacturing over this period. The size of this sample is constant over two-year periods, but declines from 846 in 1970 to 576 in 1985. Given that the total number of AGs throughout this period was roughly 2,200 in any one year, this sample can be taken as representative of the behaviour of all AGs. The comparison shows that internally-generated funds were significantly more important for the sample of manufacturing AGs than for the producing enterprises sector (102.8 per cent as a net source of finance and 72.3 per cent as a gross source, compared to 77.5 per cent net and 60.1 per cent gross), while bank loans were significantly less important for the sample of manufacturing AGs than for the producing enterprises sector. Overall bank borrowing was a negative net source of finance for AGs in manufacturing (−2.7 per cent compared to 11.6 per cent for producing enterprises), and long-term bank loans accounted for 1.7 per cent of the net sources of finance for the sample of AGs, compared to 14.4 per cent for producing enterprises. The corresponding figures for bank borrowing as a gross source of finance were: overall—AGs 1.1 per cent, producing enterprises 19.3 per cent; long-term—AGs 1.2 per cent, producing enterprises 6.8 per cent. It follows from this comparison that enterprises without supervisory boards made more use of bank loans than did enterprises with supervisory boards over the period 1971–85. This conclusion does not support the view that bank representation on supervisory boards reduces problems of asymmetric information between borrowers and lenders, so improving the terms of bank loans and allowing more borrowing from banks to occur.

German banks do not therefore appear to have departments with specialist technical expertise which enable them to assess the riskiness of lending especially well, nor does their position on supervisory boards appear to give them additional information enabling them to make loans on better terms. Are German bank–firm relationships typically house bank ones of the form described at the beginning of this section, with the concomitant advantages? Table 13.4, taken from Braun (1981), casts some doubt on the view that the house bank relationship is the characteristic one in Germany. Even the smallest firms in the sample were unlikely to do all their business with one bank, and the larger the size of firms the larger was the number of bank connections. Indeed two-thirds of the largest firms in the sample shown in Table 13.4 had more than 10 bank connections. The number of bank connections does not, of course, reveal anything about their intensity, so that it is still possible that many of these connections are rather minor. The evidence from our interviews with banks and firms, however, supports the view that the house bank relationship is not typical in Germany. Although there was some evidence of house bank relationships of the form described above among medium-sized firms, even in this group such a relationship did not exist for most firms. Among large firms house bank relationships definitely do not exist. There is strong competition between German banks for large corporate customers, and the typical firm–bank relationship involves a firm having several main banks who share in all its financial

Table 13.4. *Number of bank connections by firm size in Germany*

Firm turnover	Number of bank connections (%)			
	1	2–5	5–10	>10
Less than 25 million DM	—	75	25	—
Between 25 and 100 million DM	7.7	38.5	38.5	15.3
Between 100 and 500 million DM	—	40.4	36.2	23.4
Greater than 500 million DM	—	11.3	21.8	66.9

Note: Total sample size 300 firms

business. The bank which is the house bank is usually the bank which has had the longest-standing connection with the firm, but its role is to act as the lead bank among a syndicate of several banks, rather than to be the exclusive supplier of financial services to a firm.

Table 13.5.   *Maturity of German bank lending (excluding housing loans) to domestic enterprises and self-employed persons* (%)

	Short-term	Medium-term	Long-term
1970	42.5	12.2	45.3
1980	39.5	9.3	51.2
1989	34.8	8.1	57.1

Note: Short-term refers to loans with an original maturity of less than one year, medium-term to loans with an original maturity of between one and four years, and long-term to loans with an original maturity of more than four years.

Source: *Monthly Report of the Deutsche Bundesbank*, various issues.

It is difficult therefore to argue that in Germany the existence of house bank relationships enables banks to commit themselves to firms by making long-term loans in a way that is not possible in the UK. However, much bank lending to firms in Germany is long-term, as Table 13.5 shows. The maturity of bank lending in industry in the UK is not published, but Vittas and Brown (1982) estimated that at the end of 1980 two-thirds of bank lending to industry was short-term. Bank lending in Germany may therefore enable firms to invest in projects which would not be undertaken in the UK because a firm that is committed to a particular investment project that has not yet yielded returns is in a weak bargaining position when further loans have to be negotiated after the original short-term loan is repaid, and so the firm may not embark on the project in the first place. However, it is not clear that long-term bank lending in Germany really does involve a completely binding long-term commitment of finance to firms by banks. German banks' general business conditions include the right of a bank to withdraw loans at any time if it thinks the borrower's position has worsened enough to cause concern. In practice it is difficult for the banks to use this right except when the borrower is clearly in serious financial difficulties, but in such circumstances German banks do use their right to withdraw loans, as can be seen in the discussion later in this section of bank behaviour when firms are suffering financial distress. The extent to which the higher proportion of bank lending in Germany that is long-term enables German firms to undertake more long-term investment than is the case in the UK, therefore depends on the extent to which UK banks refuse to renew short-term loans when firms are in circumstances which would not enable German banks to use their right to withdraw long-term loans. Unfortunately we have no evidence on this point.

German banks are often claimed to be more supportive of firms in financial distress than is the case in the UK, and to take a more active role in organizing rescues (see, for example, Dyson (1986: 132) and Prais (1981: 43)). As we have seen, it is difficult to argue that such behaviour, if it exists, is the result of long-term commitment of a bank to a firm in the form of a house bank relationship, or of the banks possessing great technical expertise. Nevertheless examples such as the role of the banks in rescuing AEG are often invoked to illustrate a difference in bank attitudes towards rescues between Germany and the UK. Leaving aside the point that the AEG rescue would not have taken place without substantial Federal Government financial support, so that it is wrong to see it as an example of German banks on their own rescuing a firm in financial distress, the question must arise of whether the AEG example is typical of German bank behaviour towards rescues. We now turn to this issue.

A survey by Drukarcyk *et al.* (1985) asked 282 banks what courses of action they would undertake after becoming aware of a severe financial crisis at a firm to which they had made loans. Three courses of action stood out as being typical: the cancellation of loans and attempts to obtain repayments, a measure that would be undertaken by 75.5 per cent of the responding banks (and an illustration of banks' use of their right to withdraw loans); giving advice to and attempting to influence management, undertaken by 64.2 per cent of the banks; and obtaining additional collateral, a measure used by 50 per cent of the banks. Although advising and attempting to influence management is consistent with the bank helping in a rescue, it is also consistent with other reactions to firms in financial distress, and the other two responses show that the typical response of German banks to a financial crisis at a firm to which they had lent is to try and protect their loans. This does not necessarily imply supporting a rescue attempt.

Table 13.6, which is taken from Gessner *et al.* (1978) and is based on the results of a written questionnaire completed by 122 banks referring to a total of 906 problem loans, shows that 23 per cent of such loans were rescued by the banks. This figure may underestimate the proportion of loans that were rescued because of the 20 per cent of the problem loans for which no procedure was specified. There is a high variance between banks in the proportion of problem loans rescued: 10 of the 122 banks which responded succeeded in rescuing all their problem loans, while 60 banks did not carry out a single rescue. One reason for the difference between banks in the numbers of rescues attempted is that, according to both Gessner *et al.* (1978) and our interviews, only the big three banks and a few other large banks have specialist departments which deal with problem loans. It

Table 13.6. *Procedures followed by German banks with respect to problem loans*
1975 (%)

Bankruptcy filed for but procedure not opened	14
Bankruptcy filed for and procedure opened	25
Settlement in court	6
Rescues	23
Silent liquidation*	12
Unspecified	20
TOTAL	100

*A silent liquidation occurs when a firm goes out of business but all creditors are paid off.
Source: Gessner *et al.* (1978: 241)

seems reasonable to conclude that those banks with specialist departments for dealing with problem loans are more active in attempting rescues and likely to have a higher success rate than the majority of banks which are not in such a position.

However, it does not follow that if a bank has a specialist department for problems it will invariably attempt to rescue a firm in financial distress. The specialist department has expertise only in the financial and legal aspects of problem loans: the interviews made it very clear that, in contrast to Japan (Corbett 1987), German banks do not usually get directly involved in the reorganization at the level of operational management, and do not possess any specialists at turning unprofitable firms around. The reason for this, besides a strong convention that industrial and bank management are distinct, is that a direct involvement of the bank in the rescue would inevitably raise liability questions for the bank if the rescue were to fail. The banks interviewed were unanimous in seeing a 'sound rescue concept' as a precondition for any reorganization being attempted. The central elements of such a concept were seen as relating to the quality of management and the market position of the firm. Although the rescue concept is sometimes developed by the bank itself, it is most often done so by management consultants, and in any case a management consultancy firm has to take responsibility for the validity of a rescue concept, because recent court cases have held banks liable for delaying insolvency with the consequence of inflicting damage on other creditors. As a rescue attempt which fails would potentially fall into the category of an insolvency which had been delayed to the detriment of other creditors, rescues now require a 'neutral third party' to certify that the behaviour of the bank is 'correct'.

According to Gessner *et al.* (1978) German banks have on average 80 per cent of their loans to firms which become insolvent covered by collateral. This relatively well-secured position of banks might be thought to have a favourable effect on their attitudes to rescue attempts, since in this position they seldom have a reason to enforce an insolvency. However, there was some evidence from the interviews that a high level of collateral actually reduces banks' incentives to mount rescue attempts, since the gains to the bank from a successful rescue are low when bank loans are well secured. This latter view is supported by the finding of Gessner *et al.* (1978) that the average loss in bankruptcy of those banks which had tried to organize a rescue was higher than that of those banks which had not attempted a rescue, which suggests that banks are more inclined to participate in rescues the more they stand to lose because a smaller proportion of their loans are secured by collateral.

We are not aware of evidence on UK bank behaviour towards firms in financial distress comparable to that quoted above, and in the absence of such UK evidence it is not possible to say whether German banks are more supportive of firms in financial crisis than are UK banks. However, the evidence we have presented shows that it is wrong to regard the typical response of German banks to firms in financial distress as being to attempt a rescue, and hence examples such as AEG should not be taken as representative of German bank behaviour towards problem firms.

13.4   GERMAN BANKS AS CONTROLLING AGENTS

The control of equity voting rights in large companies by German banks, and the banks' associated representation on the supervisory boards of such companies, has been argued to permit them to constrain the managements of large German companies to act more closely in accordance with shareholders' wishes and hence reduce the agency costs involved in the owner–manager relationship for large firms. To analyse the banks' role as controlling agents it is necessary to examine the extent of their control of equity voting rights, and also how far their position on supervisory boards enables them to influence management.

German banks' direct holdings of equity in German AGs are not large enough to enable them to exercise widespread control over the outcome of votes at shareholders' meetings. The best data source on share ownership in Germany is the Depotstatistik (security deposit statistics) collected by the Deutsche Bundesbank, which give the distribution of ownership in 1984 and 1988 of outstanding German shares (except insurance enterprise shares) based on nominal values. According to these figures banks held 7.6 per cent of German shares in 1984 and 8.1 per cent in 1988. The Depotstatistik give figures of 2.7 per cent for shares owned by investment funds in 1984 and 3.5 per cent in 1988: since the securities managed by investment funds have to be placed in the custody of a 'depot-bank', and investment funds are usually owned by their depot-banks, these figures for investment fund shareholdings should be added to the figures for banks to give estimates of the total direct bank equity holding, 10.3 per cent in 1984 and 11.6 per cent in 1988. These estimates of bank shareholdings need to be interpreted carefully when attempting to assess how much control they give banks. Bank shareholdings are concentrated in the hands of the big three banks. According to the *Monthly Report of the Deutsche Bundesbank*, May 1987 these banks' holdings of domestic shares account for about half of all German banks' domestic shareholdings. This means that the relatively small overall German bank direct equity holding is consistent with a small number of banks having significant shareholdings. Furthermore, bank shareholdings in particular companies tend to be a significant fraction of the total equity of these companies—the Gessler Commission found in the 1970s that over 90 per cent of the nominal value of bank shareholdings comprised 25 per cent or more of the nominal equity of the company. Nevertheless it remains the case that German banks are not in a position to exert control over more than a small minority of all German companies through their own shareholdings.

The major source of banks' voting power at shareholders' meetings comes not from their own holdings of equity, but from the proxy votes they exercise on behalf of those shareholders who place their shares with a bank for custody and administration. Because German shares are unregistered bearer ones, the banks' securities deposit service is widely used for shares. According to the Gessler Commission, 47.5 per cent of the nominal value of deposits of domestic shares with all banks were with the big three banks in 1977. Banks which hold shares for depositors can exercise the voting rights attached to these shares under the direction of the depositors. This means that a bank at which a shareholder has deposited shares in a company will indicate to the shareholder how it intends to vote on the various issues on the agenda at the shareholders' meeting of that company, and ask the shareholder for directions as to how the bank should exercise the proxy votes on behalf of the shareholder. If no directions are given by the shareholder the bank can exercise the proxy vote according to its stated intention to vote. The bank may only deviate from casting the proxy votes according to its original statement of intent if it can safely assume that under the circumstances the shareholder would have agreed to the deviation. In such a case the bank must inform the shareholder of its deviation and give reasons for it. Since many small shareholders do not give instructions on voting to their banks, the banks gain considerable influence from representing these votes, especially in widely held corporations.

A report of the German Monopoly Commission in 1976/77, based on a detailed study of banks' equity holdings, proxy votes, and supervisory board seats in the largest AGs in 1974, gives a great deal of information about banks' control of equity voting rights. These largest 100 AGs accounted for 55 per cent of the nominal equity and 75 per cent of the turnover of all AGs in 1974. The following data on votes represented by banks are derived from attendance lists of the shareholders meeting of the top 100 AGs in 1974: percentages of the total vote are computed on the basis of the share capital actually represented at the shareholder meetings.

In 44 of the 100 cases, the combined vote of banks, comprising both the banks' direct equity holdings and the proxy votes they exercised, was less than 5 per cent of the total share capital represented at the shareholders' meeting. These 44 cases were largely AGs where some other kind of large shareholder existed. Table 13.7 shows the combined bank vote for the remaining 56 cases in which this combined vote exceeded 5 per cent. Banks' control of equity voting rights is greatest among the top 10 AGs by nominal capital, and this strength is largely due to proxy votes. This is perhaps as would have been expected since the very largest AGs are usually also the most widely-held ones. The proportion of AGs for which the combined bank vote exceeds 5 per cent is smaller, though still significant, for the remaining 90 of the top 100 AGs, and the average combined vote in these AGs is also smaller though still significant. Proxy votes are always, on average, a more important source of bank control of equity voting rights than direct holdings, although there is a tendency for the difference between these two sources of bank voting power to narrow among AGs in the bottom half of the top 100.

The average figures in Table 13.7 do not fully reveal the significance of banks' control of equity voting rights in certain AGs. The combined bank vote exceeds 50 per cent in 30 of the 56 AGs, and in a further 11 cases the combined vote is above 25 per cent and hence sufficient to block certain important decisions, as these require a 75 per cent majority at the shareholders' meeting in order to be undertaken. Of the 30 cases where the com-

Table 13.7. *Bank control of equity voting rights for 56 of the top 100 AGs in 1974*

		1–10	11–25	26–50	51–100
(1)	Rank class of AGs by nominal capital				
(2)	Number of AGs with combined bank vote > 5%	8	6	14	28
(3)	Nominal capital of AGs in (2) as % of nominal capital of rank class	88.2	42.5	51.3	54.4
(4)	Average %age of bank vote in AGs in (2) due to banks' direct holdings of equity	3.56	6.10	14.65	13.52
(5)	Average %age of bank vote in AGs in (2) due to proxy votes	63.47	48.19	25.03	29.01
(6)	Average combined bank vote in AGs in (2)	67.02	54.29	39.68	42.53

Note: Averages are weighted averages with weights given by nominal capital of AGs

Source: Monopolkommision, II Hauptgutachten 1976–7

bined bank vote exceeds 50 per cent, there are 10 in which the banks can secure a majority from their direct equity holdings, 5 in which the banks' majority represents a mixture of direct holdings and proxy votes where the direct holding is above 25 per cent, and 15 in which the banks' majority is largely due to proxy votes.

It is clear from these figures that banks as a whole are in a position to exert considerable influence at the shareholders' general meetings of a substantial number of the top 100 AGs. Given the concentration of banks' direct shareholdings and the shares deposited with banks, it is not surprising that the total bank vote shown above is concentrated in the hands of the three big banks. Of the 41 cases where banks have a combined vote exceeding 25 per cent, 26 are due solely to Deutsche Bank, Dresdner Bank and Commerzbank. These three banks clearly control very substantial amounts of equity voting rights in the top 100 AGs, and this appears to be particularly important for AGs which do not have an important shareholder or shareholders and are therefore quite widely held. The German system whereby the proxy vote system gives banks—in particular the big three—a great deal of control of equity voting rights can thus be viewed as a mechanism to overcome the public-good problem of ensuring that the management of a widely-held corporation functions well. This problem arises because an individual small shareholder in a widely-held corporation has no incentive to devote resources to the monitoring and evaluation of management for there is a cost to obtaining the relevant information and essentially no benefit, since any small shareholder has a negligible effect on the outcome of voting over management teams at shareholders' meetings. The proxy vote system in Germany gives banks the ability to have a decisive influence on the outcome of voting at the shareholders' meeting of widely-held German AGs, and hence can be argued to give the banks incentives to acquire sufficient information to monitor and judge managements effectively—a role in which they may have a comparative advantage anyway due to their experience and expertise in assessing loan applications.

The monitoring and evaluation of the managements of large corporations is the function of the supervisory board in Germany, so that if banks are to monitor managements on behalf of shareholders it must be via representation on supervisory boards, the shareholders' representatives on which are elected at the shareholders' general meeting. The report of the German Monopoly Commission which was the source for the above discussion of bank voting power also examined bank representation on the supervisory boards of the largest 100 AGs in 1974. Bank representatives occupied 179 seats on the supervisory boards of the top 100 AGs: this compares with a total of 961 bank representatives on the supervisory boards of all AGs in 1974, and 1,344 bank representatives on the supervisory boards of all corporations (AGs and GmbHs). Banks were represented on 75 of the top 100

AG supervisory boards. Given that in 44 of the top 100 AGs banks' combined vote was less than 5 per cent of the total share capital represented at the shareholders' meeting, it follows that in at least 19 of the largest 100 AGs banks were represented on the supervisory board despite having an insignificant degree of control of equity voting rights. Bank representation on supervisory boards is not therefore always a result of bank control of voting rights and cannot therefore always be interpreted as reflecting a bank role of monitoring management on behalf of shareholders. The 179 seats on the supervisory boards of the top 100 AGs occupied by banks comprised 15 per cent of the total number of such seats. In 1974 employee representatives occupied one-third of the supervisory board seats of all AGs, so that bank representatives accounted for 22.5 per cent of all shareholder seats on the supervisory boards of the top 100 AGs in 1974.

Table 13.8 gives a breakdown of the 179 bank representatives on the supervisory boards of the top 100 AGs by banks and type of seat. The chairman of the supervisory board is the most important member of it, and is usually informed and consulted by management at least once a month. The dominance of the three big banks in terms of combined bank equity voting rights is reflected in their share of bank supervisory board representatives, but among the three Deutsche Bank is dominant, especially in terms of chairmen and deputy chairmen of the supervisory boards. The predominant position of Deutsche Bank in terms of chairmen and deputy chairmen arises in spite of the fact that in only one case could it command the majority of the vote at the shareholders' meeting by itself. There were, however, 9 other cases in which its combined vote exceeded 25 per cent, and 13 more where its combined vote ranged between 10 per cent and 25 per cent. The 55 seats held by Deutsche Bank gave rise to representation on 48 supervisory boards. The three big banks as a group were represented on

Table 13.8. *Bank representation on supervisory boards of top 100 AGs in 1974 by bank and type of seat*

	Chairman	Deputy chairman	Simple membership	Total
Three big banks of which:	21	19	62	102
Deutsche Bank	18	11	26	55
Dresdner Bank	2	6	18	26
Commerzbank	1	2	18	21
All other banks	10	16	51	77
TOTAL	31	35	113	179

Source: Monopolkommission, II Hauptgutachten 1976/77.

56 supervisory boards, outnumbering all the other commercial banks (37), the savings banks (14) and the credit co-operatives (2). In all of the 41 cases where banks had a combined vote exceeding 25 per cent they had at least one supervisory board seat. If banks had a direct equity holding of 25 per cent or more in an AG the chairman or deputy chairman of that AG's supervisory board was always a bank representative.

More recent reports of the Monopoly Commission give some less detailed information about bank representation on the supervisory boards of the top 100 AGs. In 1984 the representation of the big three banks on the supervisory boards of particular AGs among the top 100 in that year was as follows: Deutsche Bank 39, Dresdner Bank 22 and Commerzbank 15. Bank representatives as a whole accounted for 8.4 per cent of total supervisory board seats of the top 100 AGs in 1984, or 16.8 per cent of all shareholder representatives. It is clear that the number of bank representatives on supervisory boards of the top 100 has fallen since 1974, as has the number of AGs among the top 100 on which the big three have representatives. It is nevertheless still true that banks are extensively represented on the supervisory boards of the top 100 AGs, and that the big three banks, particularly Deutsche Bank, are particularly well represented.

The study of Gerum, Steinmann, and Fees (1988) gives some additional insights into the significance of bank representatives on supervisory boards of AGs. Gerum, Steinmann, and Fees investigated the supervisory boards of all the 281 AGs which had more than 2,000 employees in 1979 (i.e. all AGs for which half the supervisory board members were employee representatives). Table 13.9 shows the average composition of supervisory boards by different types of shareholder representatives. Representatives of domestic non-banks are the single largest group, holding more than twice as many seats on average than bank representatives. Banks' representatives account for 16.4 per cent of shareholder seats, a figure comparable to the 1984 figure reported by the Monopoly Commission for the top 100 AGs.

The average number of seats held by different types of shareholder representatives gives only a very general impression of the composition of supervisory boards, and Gerum, Steinmann, and Fees therefore used cluster analysis in order to identify typical patterns of supervisory board composition. This analysis revealed four different patterns:

1. Of the AGs, 33 per cent belonged to the 'majority ownership type', in which the representatives of an institution holding more than half of the equity occupied significantly more than half of all shareholder seats. Most of these AGs were either subsidiaries of other companies or public enterprises.

2. A further 14 per cent belonged to the 'minority ownership type', where representatives of minority owners usually occupied more than half of the shareholder seats. The ownership structure in these AGs was typi-

Table 13.9. *Shareholder representatives on supervisory boards of AGs with more than 2,000 employees 1979*

Type of shareholder representative	Percentage of total seats
Domestic non-banks	39.7
of which:	
holding more than 50% of equity	13.1
holding up to 50% of equity	8.1
holding no equity	18.5
Domestic banks	16.4
of which:	
holding more than 50% of equity	0.7
holding up to 50% of equity	4.4
holding no equity	11.3
Foreign firms	5.9
Government	13.2
of which:	
holding some equity	11.7
holding no equity	1.5
Private shareholders	5.7
Small shareholder associations	1.5
Former top executives	4.2
Consultants	13.5
TOTAL	100.0

Source: Gerum, Steinmann, and Fees (1988), table D-3, p. 48.

cally such that minority owners could exert decisive influence because there was no majority shareholder.

3. Another 34 per cent of the AGs belonged to the 'non-participation type', in which representatives of banks and non-banks without equity holdings usually occupied more than half of the shareholder seats. Two-thirds of the AGs in this group were widely held and classified as management controlled.

4. For the remaining 19 per cent of the AGs no clear-cut pattern emerged. The majority of these AGs belonged to the lowest size category of 2,000–10,000 employees, and in such companies private shareholders and consultants each held about one-third of the shareholder seats on average. Two-thirds of the AGs in this subgroup were classified as owner-managed firms.

Gerum, Steinmann, and Fees (1988) also found that the chairman of the supervisory board usually belonged to the same type of shareholder representative as did the controlling majority of shareholder seats on the supervisory board. Table 13.10 shows the distribution of supervisory board chairmen by type of shareholder representative for the 281 AGs in the sample, which is similar to the corresponding distribution of all shareholder representatives given in Table 13.9.

Table 13.10.   *Type of shareholder representative acting as chairman of supervisory board of AGs with more than 2,000 employees 1979*

Type of shareholder representative	Percentage of total chairmen
Domestic non-banks	37.4
Domestic banks	19.2
Foreign firms	7.5
Government	9.7
Private shareholders	8.2
Former top executives	7.1
Consultants	11.0
TOTAL	100.0

Source: Gerum, Steinmann, and Fees (1988: 54).

The overall picture that emerges from these analyses is that bank representation on supervisory boards of large AGs, both in terms of overall membership and chairmen of supervisory boards, is significant. However, representatives of banks are not, on average, the most important single group on such boards, and there is some sign that the number of bank representatives was smaller in the 1980s than it was in the 1970s. Gerum, Steinmann, and Fees' analysis suggests that bank representatives may well have been most important on supervisory boards of widely held AGs, where the proxy votes they exercised on behalf of small shareholders may have enabled them to achieve a dominant position among the shareholders' representatives on the supervisory board despite having no direct equity holdings in the AG. It should, however, be noted that the proportion of shareholder seats held by representatives of domestic non-banks with no equity holding in Gerum, Steinmann, and Fees' sample is larger than that held by representatives of domestic bank with no equity holding, so that the argument that proxy vote gives banks the power to put bank representatives on supervisory boards of AGs in which banks have no direct equity holding should not be pushed too far. It must also be remembered that the shareholder representatives comprise only half the supervisory board for the AGs in the above-mentioned sample, so that bank representatives account for only 9.2 per cent of the total membership of such boards.

German banks, and especially the big three, clearly do have considerable representation on the supervisory boards of AGs, particularly, it appears for widely held AGs. However, some bank representation is not the result of bank control of equity voting rights, which does not fit with the view that banks are monitoring managements on behalf of shareholders, and bank representatives, though significant, are not numerically dominant on supervisory boards. Against this latter point it can be argued that, because the proxy vote system gives banks a decisive position in voting at share-holders' meetings for widely-held AGs, the shareholders' representatives on supervisory boards, who are elected at such meetings, must be acceptable to banks, in the sense of reflecting the banks' interests, even if they are not bankers themselves.

A critical component of the argument that German banks ensure that managements of large companies act in shareholders' interests is the claim that the supervisory board controls the management of large corporations. As has been noted, the supervisory board appoints and dismisses members of the management board, and fixes their salaries, so in that sense controls the management board. But is the supervisory board in a position in which it can monitor and evaluate the performance of the management board accurately? The management board must inform the supervisory board about the general performance and prospects of the AG, and certain major decisions of the management board may, depending on the articles of incor-poration of the particular AG, have to be approved by the supervisory board. Gerum, Steinmann, and Fees analysed the articles of incorporation of the 281 AGs with more than 2,000 employees in 1979 to establish the extent to which specific management board decisions had to be approved by the supervisory board. They found that 37 per cent of these AGs had no management board decisions for which supervisory board consent was required by the articles of incorporation. Only 4 per cent had a list of such decisions which was comprehensive and in particular included decisions in the area of strategic planning. Particular investment or finance decisions which quite often required supervisory board approval were as follows: the sale of purchase of equity holdings in other firms (in 54 per cent of the 281 AGs); real estate matters (51 per cent); the setting up or closure of new production sites or sales offices (38 per cent); bond issues (36 per cent); and the taking up of loans (31 per cent).

The degree of formal control exercised by supervisory boards over man-agement boards in terms of decisions which require the former's consent, is therefore limited, although supervisory boards have the power to exert con-trol by withholding approval of specific management board decisions in a number of instances. However, it is claimed that supervisory board mem-bers often find it difficult to decide on particular issues in isolation with any confidence because they are not integrated into the strategic planning process of the AG. This point was made by Bleicher and Paul (1986), and was reinforced by Gerum, Steinmann, and Fees (1988), who found that the articles of incorporation of only 20 per cent of the 281 AGs they studied required supervisory board consent for the AG's general product or market strategy, while only 10 per cent required such consent for general business plans or investment finance plans. In a position of limited information it is difficult to assess whether a particular management board decision is good or bad, and hence the extent to which such decisions are in fact subject to close monitoring by the supervisory board must be open to some doubt. Gerum, Steinmann, and Fees found that for 86 per cent of the AGs in their study the supervisory board met only twice a year—the legal minimum number of meetings. This observation also casts doubt on the view that the supervisory board is in a position to monitor the management board closely.

Bleicher and Paul (1986) argued that the control of management decisions in large companies was less strong in Germany than in the USA. They found that there were many more board meetings in the USA than in Germany—ten to twelve meetings a year in the USA compared to two to four meetings of the supervisory board a year in Germany. They also found a larger input from non-executive directors in the USA relative to supervisory board members in Germany, due to the greater significance in the USA of subcommittees of the board in general and audit committees in particular.

A final reason for caution in viewing the supervisory board as a body which monitors the management of large companies in order to ensure that it acts in shareholders' interests is the fact that since 1976 employee representatives have constituted half the membership of supervisory boards of companies with more than 2,000 employees. Although the shareholder representatives are still in the more powerful position on the supervisory board, because of the second vote of the chairman in situations of stalemates, the extensive employee representation on the supervisory board has been argued to have led to a shift of focus of supervisory board discussion from business matters to general social and political questions. In turn this has given rise to a development in which managers try to circumvent the supervisory board as a whole by establishing more informal links with the chairmen of the supervisory board and the workers' council.

Despite this evidence which suggests that the supervisory board is not in a position to monitor the performance of the management board closely, it is still possible to argue that the German institutional arrangement of banks, proxy votes, and supervisory boards permits a closer degree of monitoring that managements of large, widely-held, corporations act in shareholder interests than do other institutions. But, given that the big three banks which are dominant in terms of control of equity voting rights are themselves AGs, the question arises of what the incentives are for these three banks to act as agents for shareholders to ensure effective monitoring and assessment of managements. As we have seen, although the big three banks do have significant direct equity holdings in some large AGs, in others their control of equity voting rights stems almost entirely from proxy votes. Thus for at least some large AGs the big three banks have no direct financial interest in ensuring that managements act in line with shareholders' wishes. Even for the AGs in which the big three banks have non-negligible direct equity holdings, the question arises of why the management of the big three should solely be concerned with maximizing the returns from these holdings. If agency problems give some scope for the managements of large German AGs to pursue their own interests at the expense of shareholders, then the managements of Deutsche Bank, Dresdner Bank, and Commerzbank may not have incentives to impose an external discipline on the managements of other AGs in order to maximize the profits from direct equity holdings by the big three banks. It certainly cannot be argued that the managements of these banks are subject to any control at their own shareholders' meetings, because the proxy vote system gives them effective control of themselves. A recent estimate (Pfeiffer 1986), of the proxy votes held by each of the big three at its own shareholder meeting was as follows: Deutsche Bank 47.2 per cent; Dresdner Bank 59.3 per cent; Commerzbank 30.3 per cent.

13.5 CONCLUSION

In terms of the aggregate financing of the non-financial enterprise sector, the German economy is no more bank-based than is the UK economy, as the comparison over the period 1970–89 in section 13.2 showed. However, it is possible that German banks benefit the German economy, not by providing an especially large volume of bank loans to firms, but in other aspects of their behaviour. Sections 13.3 and 13.4 of the paper examined two such aspects of German bank behaviour in detail. The terms of bank loan finance in Germany are often claimed to be favourable for firms because German banks are better informed than UK banks. It is suggested that this may be either because of the banks' technical expertise or because of their positions on supervisory boards. Section 13.3 suggested that there was no evidence of German banks deriving any information about the firms to which they lent from either of these two sources. It also showed that it is incorrect to regard the typical response of German banks to situations of financial distress on the part of firms to which they have lent as being to attempt a rescue. Section 13.4 of the chapter considered the possible role of German banks as monitors of management of large widely-held corporations on behalf of shareholders. Although a small number of German banks do have extensive control of equity voting rights due to the proxy vote system, bank representatives on supervisory boards comprise only a relatively small proportion of shareholder representatives on these boards, and the extent of control that the supervisory board has over the management board seems to be limited. Sections 13.3 and 13.4 do not provide a detailed comparative analysis of German and UK bank lending behaviour and mechanisms for controlling the management of large corporations. Consequently they cannot definitely establish that, in comparison with the UK economy, the German economy does not benefit from German banks' lending behaviour and control of equity voting rights. However, the evidence presented in these two sections does suggest that the commonly held views about the role of banks in the German economy are not self-evidently correct.

REFERENCES

Bank of England (1984), 'Business Finance in the United Kingdom and Germany', *Bank of England Quarterly Bulletin*, 24: 368–75.

Bleicher, K. and Paul, H. (1986), 'Das Amerikanische Board-modell im Vergleich zur deutschen Vorstands/Aufsichtsratsverfassung', *Die Betriebswirtschaft*, 3: 263–88.

Braun, P. A. (1981), 'Das Firmenkundengeschäft der Banken im Wandel', unpub. Ph.D. thesis (University of Augsburg).

Carrington, J. C. and Edwards, G. T. (1979), *Financing Industrial Investment* (Macmillan, London).

Corbett, J. (1987), 'The Finance of Industry: Evidence from Japan', *Oxford Review of Economic Policy*, 3: 4, 30–55.

Drukarcyk, J. *et al.* (1985), *Mobiliarsicherheiten, Arten, Verbreitung, Wirksamkeit*, Bundesministerium der Justiz.

Dyson, K. (1986), 'The State, Banks and Industry: The West German Case', in A. Cox (ed.), *State, Finance and Industry: A Comparative Analysis of Post-War Trends in Six Advanced Industrial Economies* (Wheatsheaf, Brighton).

Economist, The (1990), 'Punters or Proprietors? A Survey of Capitalism', May 5–11, 24.

Gerum, E., Steinmann, H., and Fees, W. (1988), *Der mitbestimmte Aufsichtsrat: Eine Empirische Untersuchung* (Stuttgart).

Gessner, V. *et al.* (1978), *Die Praxis der Konkursabwicklung in der Bundesrepublik Deutschland*, Bundesanzeigerverlag.

Hallett, G. (1990), 'West Germany', in A. Graham with A. Seldon (eds.), *Government and Economies in the Post-War World* (Routledge, London).

Macrae, N. (1966), 'The German Lesson', *The Economist*, October 15, 17.

Mayer, C. P. (1988), 'New Issues in Corporate Finance', *European Economic Review*, 32: 1167–83.

— (1990), 'Financial Systems, Corporate Finance and Economic Development', in G. Hubbard (ed.), *Information, Capital Markets and Investment* (National Bureau of Economic Research, Chicago).

— and Alexander, I. (1991), 'The Finance of U.K. Investment', unpub. paper (City University Business School).

Monopolkommission (1978), *II Hauptgutachten 1976/77: Fortschreitende Konzentration bei Grossunternehmen* (Nomos Verlag, Baden Baden).

Perlitz, M. *et al.* (1985), 'Vergleich der Eigenkapitalausstattung deutscher, amerikanischer und britischer Ungternehmen', *Zeitschift für Unternehmens- und Gesellschaftsrecht*, 1: 17–49.

Pfeiffer, H. (1986), 'Grossbanken und Finanzgruppen—Untersuchung uber Personelle Verflechtungen der Grossbanken', *WSI-Mitteilungen*, 39: 473–80.

Prais, S. (1981), *Productivity and Industrial Structure* (Cambridge University Press, Cambridge).

Vittas, D. and Brown, R. (1982), 'Bank Lending and Industrial Investment: A Response to Recent Criticisms', unpub. paper (Banking Information Service).

14

The Role of the German Capital Markets and the Universal Banks, Supervisory Boards, and Interlocking Directorships

ELLEN R. SCHNEIDER-LENNÉ

14.1 INTRODUCTION

Corresponding to the intensive discussion in the United Kingdom on the influence of the capital markets, institutional investors, and banks, on the attitudes of senior management in industry, there is a similar debate being conducted in the Federal Republic of Germany. However, the focus of attention in each country is different. Whereas in the UK there are aspirations which aim at a closer relationship between banking, institutions and industry, hand in hand with healthy measure of long-termism as an antidote to undue short-termism, in Germany there is, primarily, concern about an alleged lack of efficiency in the country's capital markets. In fact, the financial systems in the two countries do vary in several important respects which deserve study.

During a spell spent as a corporate account officer at Deutsche Bank's London Branch from 1975–80, the author experienced at first hand how very differently executives in industry in Great Britain and Germany conceive of themselves and their activities. When British managers describe their companies, they do so in the language of financial analysis, with precise figures on the development of profits, return on investment, the price–earnings ratio, and shareholder value. In Germany the situation is quite different: when one calls on a company, discussion tends to centre on products and turnover, market share, and the number of people on the payroll. Profits seem to be rather a subsidiary issue.

There are numerous indications that managers in each country pursue different goals in several respects or, to be more precise, do, in fact, set their priorities differently. In Britain, the main goal is the maximization of shareholder value, whereas in Germany, directors pursue a number of goals which are longer-term in nature, including *inter alia* the long-term success and viability of the company. It seems that the British system is dominated by the firm intention of shareholders to participate in their company's success as 'instantly' as possible. By contrast, what is found in the German corporate landscape is a broader concern which weighs up the interests of all who are involved in a company's fortunes, i.e. shareholders and employees as well as customers, suppliers, and the relevant sections of the general public. It could be described as a 'consensus model'.

This difference is reflected, among other things, in accounting standards. In the UK such standards are geared primarily to transparency for the shareholder inasmuch as they aim at ensuring as realistic a presentation as possible of the company's financial situation. In Germany, a chief concern is the protection of creditors. The principle governing the valuation of assets, which prescribes the lower of cost or market price, allows companies to create substantial undisclosed reserves which can be mobilized in adverse situations.

It would certainly be interesting to speculate as to the genesis of such wide divergencies in corporate philosophy within the limited confines of Europe; it comes as less of a surprise that such differences should exist between the US and Japan, given the pronounced diversity of their cultural and historical backgrounds. That, however, is a field of enquiry for economic historians or sociologists, but, whatever the reason, mentality is bound to have something to do with it. It may be that Britons feel happier about taking a—calculated—risk and are consequently capable of greater flexibility, whereas Germans tend to cling to the status quo and search for compromises.

These differing mentalities are also reflected in corporate cultures and financing techniques. London is justly proud of the financial engineering skills that have made this city Europe's premier financial centre. The numerous activities in the financial sector which have taken on totally new dimensions in the wake of the globalization and liberalization process of the last twenty years have attracted many young and gifted people. Foreign institutions also find the City attractive. The degree of sophistication and know-how accumulated there is unequalled—at least in Europe.

In Germany, the concept of 'financial engineering' was, until recently, largely unknown. However, our engineers are, typically, 'real' engineers who often play a dominant role in the management of companies. Germany's competitive advantages are still in industry as opposed to finance—in mechanical and electrical engineering, machine tools, or in the car industry. That conclusion, it should be stressed, is not, in any way, meant to question or disparage the technological prowess of the United Kingdom. Many unfortunate developments have been rectified in the last ten years and British companies have meanwhile become leaner and more efficient. The present crisis stems from a cyclical dampener, the consequence of previous overheating; but it is not a structural phenomenon as was the case in the 1960s and 1970s.

The different roles of the financial sector in the two countries are also bound up with the fact that Britain has long had an efficient capital market, a market which has enjoyed continuous evolution and which, naturally, has been the quickest to adopt innovations from the USA. By comparison, the German capital market, for all its soundness, is, relatively speaking, a conservative affair. A market with little innovative potential, it has been slow to introduce new financial products and has only a limited financing function. On the other hand, the German banking system enjoys a good reputation. Foreign and overseas observers focus, above all, upon the German 'universal banks' and frequently overestimate the closeness of their links with German industry. The underlying assumption behind this fascination seems to be that the universal banks do in Germany what the capital market does in the UK.

Is this actually the main difference? Is the strength of the banks in Germany really all that effective and pervasive and the significance of the capital market really so modest?

14.2   RELATIONSHIP BANKING

In Germany, relations between banks and companies are traditionally closer than in the United Kingdom. This has to do with the prevalence of universal banking. If a corporate customer so wishes, he or she can obtain all the banking services he or she needs from one single banking institution—from liquidity management through credits to capital market products. In addition, the banks in Germany have always subscribed to the principle of relationship banking. To a much greater extent than their counterparts in the USA and in the UK—of whom it is said that their philosophy is often one of deal-based banking, i.e. a concentration on individual transactions—the German banks tend to seek a more stable relationship with the customer and vice versa. This, ultimately, can be very much to the long-term benefit of industrial companies. Banks see individual transactions with the customer within the overall context of a comprehensive business relationship. Experience has shown that it pays to come to the aid of a company in temporary financial distress. This is in the banks' interest because it gives them a better prospect of having their endangered loans repaid, but at the same time, and above all, it is in the interest of the companies themselves, their employees, and the community where the company is located.

The 'house bank' principle linked with this philosophy has regained importance recently, but this does not mean that German companies only work with one bank. Most larger-sized firms prefer to co-operate, not only with their main house bank, but will maintain a relationship with a further five to ten core banks as well, and also keep in touch with a whole string of other ancillary banks with whom they transact individual deals. At present, as the business environment becomes more difficult, a close relationship with one's house bank is increasingly perceived as a sensible and prudent strategy. In many cases a firmly established co-operation between bank and customer has proved its worth precisely in such periods of increasing economic difficulty.

Correspondingly we find, on the customer side, a noticeably strong loyalty to one's bank; a company does not change its bank without good reason. This does not, of course, mean that the banks can fleece their customers. In a transparent and highly competitive market with largely homogenous products, banks must continually demonstrate efficiency, especially in the sensitive area of the terms and conditions applied to contractual relationships. The German financial markets have tended to become much more open and thus more competitive over the last twenty years.

The relatively close nature of the bank–customer relationship in Germany has given many outside observers the impression that German banks exercise an inordinate influence on the business activities of German companies. This has led to a recurrent debate in Germany as to the power of the banks. This controversy revives as regularly as the news every summer about the Loch Ness monster having been sighted. One basic remark at the outset: most observers, and particularly those abroad, tend to grossly overestimate the influence of the German universal banks on the domestic economy. One often comes across the erroneous idea that German industry is actually controlled by the big banks or that these banks are to Germany what MITI is to Japan. The facts, however, do not support such extreme contentions. This can readily be seen from the market share of the three largest universal banks in relation to the aggregate balance sheet total of the entire banking sector: in Germany (West) the three major banking groups account for a portion of 14 per cent, whereas the comparable figure for the UK is 18 per cent. (When considering this one has to bear in mind that the UK figure is distorted by the huge international business conducted in London as one of the major financial centres of the world. The UK banks' share in the domestic sterling market is higher at 23 per cent. The German banks' international business is conducted from Luxembourg.) A proportion of only 14 per cent does not exactly accord with a position of dominance over the domestic economy.

It is true, though, that there are more than just borrower–lender relations linking banks and companies. German banks being universal banks, capital markets issues, holdings in industrial companies, supervisory board mandates, and proxy voting rights provide further links.

14.3 BANKS' INDUSTRIAL HOLDINGS

Some observers apparently believe that the universal banks are the main shareholders of German companies. That, of course, is a gross exaggeration, although, admittedly, a long-standing tradition of bank participations in industrial companies does exist in Germany.

How did this situation come about? In Germany the process of industrialization commenced in the second half of the last century, much later than in Britain but with great vigour. At that time, companies in Germany depended on banks for their external financing. One reason for this was that there was a deficiency of savings coupled with the lack of well-developed capital markets. Another contributory factor may have been that Germany did not have a uniform currency or a central bank until Bismarck's Deutsches Reich came into being in 1871. In England, by contrast, the industrial revolution was financed by a broad cross-section of the well-to-do. As a comparable source of finance was non-existent in Germany, the banks had to assume an active role when companies were being founded—both by granting credit *and* injecting equity capital.

Because there was so little capital available, industry was also interested in developing efficient banking institutions as a means to channel savings into investments. Deutsche Bank AG, itself, for instance, was originally formed by banks and industrial companies as a consortium bank in order to participate in the financing of foreign trade. It was this situation which forged, from the very start, a close link between industry, on the one hand, and banks on the other. A relatively close relationship between the two has remained a distinctive feature of the German economy ever since.

Even today, banks still occasionally acquire new equity participations. In most cases this happens if a company is facing financial difficulties. The most prominent case in the 1980s was the crisis at AEG, Germany's second-largest electrical engineering company. At the time of the crisis a large banking syndicate was involved in the rescue operation. One element of the restructuring consisted of transforming loans into equity. Two years ago, Deutsche Bank acting alone, averted the collapse of Klöckner & Co., one of Germany's major trading houses. In both instances, the banks retained their stakes only as long as necessary and then sold their holdings to investors as soon as possible. Deutsche Bank's holdings in Daimler-Benz and Hapag-Lloyd also resulted—at least in part—from similar rescue operations in earlier years.

German banks regard industrial participations as financial investments which help to stabilize their profit base by way of asset diversification. At the same time, participations help to enhance business relations and, in some cases, can be a factor in warding off hostile takeover attempts.

The overall trend in the last decade—and this has gone largely unnoticed by the public eye—has been towards a reduction in banks' industrial holdings. In 1976, the ten largest private banks held 1.3 per cent of the capital of all non-financial public and private limited companies (AGs and GmbHs) in the Federal Republic. By 1986 the percentage had fallen to 0.7 per cent and by the end of August 1989 had dropped further to a mere 0.6 per cent. Disposals related mainly to holdings of more than 25 per cent. Of

Germany's 500 biggest companies, there are only about thirty in which banks hold participations of more than 10 per cent; in one case only is there a stake of over 50 per cent (WestLB/Horten).

One interesting feature is that while the private banks have reduced their industrial holdings, some state-owned banks—which have a share of 35 per cent in total banking assets—have actually stepped up their participations. West-LB in particular has built up a number of important holdings over recent years.

In general, however, the banks' holdings are greatly overrated. German banks do not dominate German business and industry, nor are they by any means the owners of Germany's companies.

It is of importance to note that banks in the Federal Republic are subject to strict legal regulations when it comes to acquiring industrial holdings. The main limiting factor is that relating to equity capital. Pursuant to section 12 of the German Banking Act, a bank's investments in property, buildings, etc., together with its holdings in other banks, and in industrial companies may not exceed the bank's own capital. Within the context of this Act, holdings are defined as participations of more than 10 per cent.

The amount of a bank's own capital therefore represents an effective constraint on new participations—all the more so as holdings in other banks and near banks at home and abroad are included in this category.

European Community banking law, which will take effect in 1993 and will form the framework for a single financial market, expressly allows banks to hold stakes in non-banks. There are no restrictions on holdings in financial companies but industrial participations are limited in two ways: first, no one individual participation may exceed 15 per cent of a bank's equity capital; and second, banks' total industrial holdings may not exceed 60 per cent of equity capital.

An important—and necessary—feature of EC law is that holdings acquired in order to salvage a company with the intention of subsequently disposing of such shares via the Stock Exchange are not included in the computation of these limits.

As regards adoption into national law, it is possible that both national and EC regulations will exist side by side in Germany. This would mean that the stricter regulations of the two would apply. Nevertheless, the new EC regulations are not a major stumbling block for German banks' policies on industrial holdings; in other words, they can conform to them, without drastically changing their policies concerning industrial participations.

14.4 BANKS' SUPERVISORY BOARD MANDATES

In contrast with the UK, in Germany there is a formal division of labour in a company's management. First of all, there is the board of managing direc-

tors which actually runs the company and takes all managerial decisions;
and then there is the supervisory board to monitor and supervise the board
of managing directors.

For that reason members of the board of managing directors may not be
on the supervisory board at the same time—in contrast to the Anglo-
American system. Interlocking directorships are not possible either. For
example, a member of Deutsche Bank's board of managing directors could
not sit on the supervisory board of Daimler-Benz and, at the same time, a
member of Daimler's management board sit on Deutsche Bank's supervisory board. However, one person may hold up to ten supervisory board
mandates. Here, interlocking mandates are possible. It would be possible,
for instance, for a supervisory board member of Daimler-Benz to also be on
Deutsche Bank's supervisory board, even though the speaker of the board
of managing directors at Deutsche Bank, Mr Kopper, is chairman of the
Daimler supervisory board. This mutual interlinking is, for good reasons,
not seen as a problem by the German public. What some people do consider a problem is the alleged over-representation of banks on supervisory
boards. Again, it will be instructive to examine a few figures first. In
Germany's 100 biggest companies, banks hold 9.1 per cent of all supervisory board mandates. Though not an insignificant percentage, the corresponding figure for trade union functionaries is 12.5 per cent and
representatives of other companies hold 25.8 per cent (Table 14.A1).

Under the Co-determination Act, the supervisory boards of larger
German companies are composed of an equal number of shareholder and
employee representatives. In the event of a tie, the chairman—always a
shareholder representative—has a casting vote. In effect this means that the
shareholders' side can always carry through its plans, provided of course
that its representatives on the supervisory board are all agreed.

The figures reveal that the influence exerted by banks via their supervisory board mandates is quite substantial, but by no means excessive. If
banks wield greater authority than other sections of the community, then it
is because of their expertise in financial matters. Large corporations, often
invite representatives of competing banks to join their supervisory board.
At Daimler-Benz, for instance, where Deutsche Bank is the largest shareholder with 28.5 per cent of shares, Germany's other two big commercial
banks are both represented on the supervisory board, although they have
no stake in Daimler.

If the business community had its way, the number of the banks' supervisory board mandates would be higher still. It is simply not possible to fulfil
all wishes expressed in this respect, especially as the burden on the banks
has been growing. In the course of the years, the emphasis of the supervisory board's work has shifted more and more towards advising and counselling the board of managing directors. The rationale of monitoring

companies' management is no longer felt to be just a question of detecting past mistakes, but rather one of preventing them from being made in the first place. 'Consultancy' of this nature presupposes expert knowledge and a comprehensive view—both characteristics which people seem to think bankers possess to an eminent degree.

One last point should be made on this subject. In Germany there is constant debate, not only over the so-called power of the banks, but also as to how effective the supervisory board's control function really is. In some ways, this resembles the current discussion in the UK on the role of non-executive directors. With an average of four meetings per year, even for big companies, it is quite obvious that the influence of supervisory boards on companies' managements is circumscribed. At well-managed joint stock companies, the most important function of the supervisory board is probably its right to appoint the members of the board of managing directors.

14.5 PROXY VOTING RIGHTS

A third area which is characteristic of the German universal banks' relationship with industry is the so-called proxy voting rights. Smaller shareholders often ask the bank to represent them at annual general meetings by way of proxy. The bank acting via proxy must, of course, follow the shareholders' instructions. Proxy voting rights may only be given to one specific credit institution, and only for a maximum of 15 months. During this period the bank will, prior to each Annual General Meeting ask the shareholder to attend the meeting him- or herself and to exercise his or her voting rights. The bank also notifies the shareholder of how it proposes to vote at the AGM, if the shareholder does not give any instructions. The custodian bank must then exercise the voting rights in accordance with those proposals.

Banks in Germany often have to defend themselves against the accusation that under this system many shareholders practically invest the banks with a right to act at their own discretion. It is argued that shareholders lose the necessary interest in the decision-making process since they rely on the banks to make the right decisions based on their expert knowledge of the situation.

This reliance clearly is a compliment to the banks. If meant as a reproach, it would be addressed not to the banks but, if at all, to the shareholders themselves. The banks have often stated that they would also accept and support forms of shareholder representation other than proxy voting rights. However, no other practicable alternative has so far been proposed which would provide an equally successful way of ensuring that small shareholders can cast their votes effectively. This answer was given as a result of detailed investigations conducted by the Banks' Structure Commission, an inquiry which the Government set up after the collapse of the Herstatt Bank in 1974 in order to explore whether the state of the German banking system called for regulatory change.

None the less, it is a sound view that it is absolutely essential and in a company's own interests that as many shareholders as possible actually take part in General Meetings. In the absence of proxy voting rights, companies' managements would be confronted with the problem of unstable and random majorities. This could be perilous at times when the company is the object of a takeover bid. In that sense, this particular arrangement—whatever else can be said of it—does ensure a certain degree of continuity for companies. Furthermore, it should be pointed out that whenever there are momentous or controversial decisions to be taken, banks will expressly seek their customers' instructions on how they should vote, and they will not exercise the voting rights if such instructions are not given.

To sum up, the banks in Germany have quite considerable potential influence on the business world as a result of their participations, supervisory board functions, and proxy voting rights. However, companies are not dominated by the banks, nor is it in the banks' interests to assume responsibility for other firms' business; they would not be able to do this satisfactorily owing to a lack of the necessary expertise in this area. Moreover, the banks—alongside companies, trade and other associations, and unions—are only one factor in an intricate system of checks and balances governing the wide range of business interests. Nor, finally, are the banks themselves a homogeneous block, but compete intensely with each other.

14.6   COMPANY FINANCING

The widely held notion that German banks control German industry is often accompanied by the belief that the banks prevent companies from obtaining finance via the capital market so that they, the banks, can grant them loans instead. Apart from the fact that, in view of the intense competition, a bank can simply not afford to advise its customers to adopt a less than optimal financing structure, an analysis of company financing in Germany and the UK shows that this theory is untenable.

Contrary to popular suppositions, the financing structure of companies in the UK and Germany is similar in many respects, and has become more so particularly over the last few decades. An analysis of financing strategies in the non-financial sector reveals the following results (see Table 14.A2):

• Internal resources are by far the most important source of financing in both countries. If we include all capital investments, that is, investment in fixed assets, financial investments and participations (gross financing), Germany's internal financing ratio of 67 per cent is slightly below that of the UK (74 per cent). If we only count investment in fixed assets (net financing), Germany's ratio increases to over 80 per cent and that of the UK tops 100 per cent.

- Both in Germany and the UK, the stock-market plays a somewhat insignificant role in the financing of the non-financial sector. Its share of gross financing (fixed-asset and financial investments) is only 2.1 per cent in Germany and 4.9 per cent in the UK. This is hardly a significant difference if one considers that a large proportion of share issues in the UK were in connection with takeovers. Between 1982–8, two-fifths of all new issues in the UK were either directly or indirectly related to takeovers. This factor is of little importance in Germany.

It is worth looking at this analysis in a little more detail, distinguishing between large and medium-sized companies. First of all, the *large companies*:

- Compared with the average for all German firms and with that for major British enterprises, this group of German companies, as can be seen from Table 14.A3, finance themselves to a much greater extent via internal resources (almost 90 per cent in gross terms). The large UK firms, by contrast, obtain a relatively large proportion of their financing from outside sources (just under 42 per cent in gross terms). This is partly due to a more generous dividend pay-out ratio which, in the UK is roughly twice as high as in Germany.
- In both countries, medium- and long-term loans are the most important form of *external* financing for fixed capital investment. Incidentally, the fact that British companies obtain an even larger proportion of their capital investment financing in this way (14.1 per cent) than German companies (8.8 per cent) explodes another popular myth.

In the case of *medium-sized companies*, the situation is somewhat different. Although figures for the purposes of comparison are difficult to obtain, surveys—for example in electrical engineering—indicate that medium-sized companies in Germany obtain a greater proportion of their financing from bank loans than their British counterparts. (Possibly this relates to the fact that more medium-sized UK companies are quoted on the Stock Exchange—see below.)

About two-thirds of the bank loans extended to companies in Germany are long-term (Table 14.A4) and such loans are normally granted at a fixed interest rate for the entire life of the loan. By contrast, the maturity structure of bank loans in the UK appears to be exactly the opposite. It is estimated here that approximately two-thirds of loans extended are *short-term*. Moreover, in the case of long-term loans, it is the exception rather than the rule for a fixed interest rate to be agreed for the entire maturity.

14.7   FUNCTION OF THE STOCK-MARKET

The stock-market plays a more important role for UK companies than for German companies, and this applies particularly to small and medium-sized firms. This is obvious if one merely looks at the number of joint stock companies. In the UK there are 1,950 domestic listed companies as opposed to only 650 in Germany. The number of listed German companies did, in fact, decrease steadily in the 1960s and 1970s. Deutsche Bank repeatedly drew attention to the dangers inherent in such a trend. The economic crisis at the beginning of the 1980s, when extremely high interest rates led to a deep recession, underscored these risks.

In the wake of this development, the banks found it easier to convince their customers of the advantages of going public, which led to a gratifying increase in the number of Stock Exchange listings. Since 1983, 150 companies have gone public on the German Stock Exchanges (Fig. 14.A1), among them many small and medium-sized firms.

In addition, many companies took advantage of advantageous share prices in the 1980s to raise capital (Table 14.A5). The aggregate nominal value of listed share capital rose from DM 39.4 bn. in 1980 to DM 67.2 bn. last year, an increase of 70 per cent. Share capital placed by listed companies, which totalled just under DM 4 bn per year between 1979 and 1984, for the following six years rose on average to DM 13 bn. per annum. Despite this considerable share capital increase, the equity ratio of 27 per cent of total assets computed for German joint stock companies is markedly lower than the corresponding figure in the UK (approximately 50 per cent).

An upward trend in share prices on German Stock Exchanges also led to increased turnover. Last year, trading in *domestic* shares on the eight German Stock Exchanges totalled DM 1,620 bn. (UK: DM 920 bn., including SEAQ). That was two and a half times as much as two years previously. In terms of turnover in domestic shares, the German Stock Exchanges retained third place behind Tokyo and New York. The market depth in a number of German blue chips certainly measures up to exacting international expectations. The ratio of share turnover to number of shares, that is, the average turnover per share, is greater in Germany than in the UK. The City, however, is still a long way ahead as far as trade in international equities is concerned.

Despite the progress made to date in Germany, the stock-market still plays a much less significant role in the German economy than it does in other countries. At the end of 1990, market capitalization in Germany was DM 560 bn. (reflecting a price–earnings ratio of 12), whereas in the UK it was more than double this amount at DM 1,260 bn. (price–earnings ratio of 10.4). As a proportion of GNP, it is only 21 per cent in Germany as opposed to 80 per cent in the UK. Measured in terms of the ratio of market capitalization to GNP, the German stock-market ranks not only behind Tokyo and New York, but also after Zürich and Paris, and only just ahead of Madrid.

14.8 PENSION FUNDS

There are a number of structural factors which contribute to the relatively insignificant role of the stock-market in Germany. The first reason is the highly developed German system of providing retirement pensions. The state pension insurance scheme runs on a pay-as-you-go basis, with the result that there is no capital accumulation. The pension level is very high: after forty-five years of paying contributions, the standard pensioner receives around 70 per cent of his last net income as pension. The need for additional private or company superannuation schemes is therefore nowhere near as great as under the American or UK systems. Institutional investors such as life insurance companies or pension funds therefore inevitably play a much more modest role in Germany than in the English-speaking world.

A further institutional peculiarity exists in the approach taken by company retirement pension schemes. In Germany, 60 per cent of the funds earmarked for the payment of company pensions remain in the company as an unfunded long-term liability; that is, they are used to finance general corporate purposes. For the capital market this means less availability of capital compared to the British system, but at the same time less demand for financing, and hence a much-reduced intermediary function for the market.

Notwithstanding the fact that employees' claims are guaranteed by the so-called Pension Guarantee Association in the event of bankruptcy, it is undoubtedly problematic that pension funds are invested within the company. However, it is perhaps admissable to sound a note of caution with regard to certain excesses observed in the systems operating in English-speaking countries. Many observers do not, for example, think it is appropriate for pension funds to try to improve their performance by purchasing high-yield, high-risk paper. Performance competition went so far in the USA that pension funds even invested in junk bonds.

Since pension provisions are at the disposal of German companies on a long-term basis, they are rightly regarded as a reliable financing instrument. In certain respects such provisions in Germany are perceived as fulfilling the function of a substitute for equity; economists have coined the term 'social capital' for these funds. The provisions reported in the balance sheets have now become a substantial financing factor; they amount to approximately DM 200 bn., which is 10 per cent of companies' total liabilities (including shares in circulation).

By contrast, the UK pension funds are of much greater significance than German company retirement schemes. In terms of volume, they are about four times the size of company pension reserves in Germany. They are thus an important element contributing to the importance of institutional investors for the British stock-market. Shareholder structure is, therefore, totally different from that existing in Germany. Whereas institutional investors own 55 per cent of shares in the UK, they hold merely 12 per cent in Germany.

Most pension funds are managed by external managers, like Morgan Grenfell, who are chosen by performance which is measured by external portfolio measurement sources. Trustees do not hesitate to move mandates around based upon very short-term aspects. This is one of the roots of short-termism.

14.9   TAX SYSTEM

A second reason for the relatively modest significance of the German capital market is the tax system. Not only in Germany but also world-wide, external financing is more advantageous, tax-wise, then equity funding. Interest on loans and bonds reduces taxable profit for the assessment of corporate tax. Therefore it is more favourable for a company to borrow funds, for example from a bank, and to pay interest thereon, than to issue shares and pay dividends to shareholders—at any rate if shareholders are to receive the same income as the bank.

There are several additional peculiarities in Germany. Business Capital Tax (*Gewerbekapitalsteuer*), for example, which is levied at municipal level, discriminates against equity capital in favour of debt. Even though long-term liabilities count as capital, they are only taxable by half, whereas capital proper is liable to tax in full.

Another matter of significance at present is the 1 per cent levy on shares issued (*Gesellschaftsteuer*). This will no longer be imposed after 1992. Finally the problem of double taxation through the Wealth Tax should not be underestimated. This tax is levied on a company's assets, and the private investor then pays a second time through the taxation of his financial assets, which naturally include his shareholdings. In addition, there is a built-in tax advantage in owning property as against holding financial assets.

The German Government has announced a small-scale corporate tax reform for 1993; the corporate Wealth Tax burden is to be reduced and the Business Capital Tax is to be abolished. But, given the current majority of the Social Democratic Party in the Bundesrat, Germany's Upper House, this initiative is probably doomed to failure.

The favourable tax treatment afforded to borrowed funds may be a reason why German companies have a high gearing ratio. The share of capital and reserves as a percentage of balance sheet total has sunk steadily since the early 1960s, when it had stood at 30 per cent, to 18 per cent in the early 1980s. Since then it has climbed slightly to 19 per cent. This ratio is somewhat higher for listed joint stock corporations (as mentioned above, 27 per cent) than for sole proprietorships, partnerships, and private limited companies. Moreover, there is a tendency for the ratio to increase with the size of the company. However, the problem remains that equity capital is relatively expensive in Germany and is frequently only increased when it is feared that creditors will be reluctant to provide any further funding owing to poor balance sheet ratios.

Since the German corporate tax system was reformed in 1977, it now—like the present British system—treats dividends paid to the shareholder favourably in so far as a double taxation on profits—affecting the company and the shareholder—is avoided. The shareholder can now claim a tax credit, in his or her annual tax return, in respect of the 36 per cent Corporation Tax already paid by the company on profits distributed and of the 25 per cent Withholding Tax paid on dividends. The outcome is that dividends paid by corporations are taxed at the individual marginal rate of the recipient shareholder.

Corporate tax reform has attempted to make the share a more attractive financing instrument, to encourage joint stock corporations to make more use of the 'pay out/take back principle', and thereby to strengthen the role of the stock-market. In practice, the reform enjoyed little success as evidenced by the relatively low level of dividends paid by German joint stock corporations. German companies tend to regard this procedure as discriminating against retained profits, which, after all, ultimately serve to strengthen the company and its capacity for capital investment.

Reservations about adopting the legal form of the joint stock corporation and in particular the process of 'going public' have their origins also in the German mentality. The backbone of the German economy is its small and medium-sized companies. They are mainly family companies, operating as partnerships or private limited companies. Many of these companies, however, have grown to dimensions which make going public seem an appropriate move. But the owners of such companies often seem disinclined to do so. One reason lies in the public disclosure requirements. In Germany, it is not customary nor acceptable to be required to disclose details of one's income or wealth to the public. Another reason for the reservations against turning companies into joint stock corporations is that there is often a strong aversion to sharing control of the company with outsiders.

Finally, investor behaviour also plays a role. In Germany the problem is not only to interest private investors in the share market; even institutional investors such as insurance companies by no means exploit fully the relatively restricted opportunities open to them for investment in shares.

14.10 BONDS

Neither in Germany nor in the UK do domestic industrial bonds play a notable role in finance. The German bond market is dominated by public sector issues and bond issues by banks refinancing their medium and long-term business. Domestic industrial bonds outstanding come to only DM 3 bn. (0.2 per cent of all domestic bonds outstanding). When a new industrial bond is issued it is likely to be in the form of a convertible bond, or a bond with equity warrants attached. On the whole, companies in a position to issue paper, tend to resort to the Euromarket. Eurobonds have clear advantages, such as lower issuing costs, better pricing, no liability to Business Capital Tax (provided the funds are used abroad), and simpler issuing procedures (no offer prospectus). All in all, there is so much more flexibility here that top-rate companies with access to the Eurobond market will also in future probably continue to go down this route.

14.11 DEREGULATION OVERDUE

A third complex of problems which helps to explain the relative insignificance of the German capital market concerns the backlog in deregulation and innovation. Until the 1980s, the German capital market was relatively strictly regulated, and many well-established financing methods regularly employed abroad, particularly on the Euromarkets, were not permitted. Since the mid-1980s the authorities have been pursuing a policy of step-by-step deregulation.

The first step was the authorization of floating-rate notes, zero bonds, and dual-currency bonds, and later also of Ecu bonds and bonds denominated in Special Drawing Rights. Mandatory registration at the Bundesbank began to be handled far more flexibly and the prescribed minimum maturity of bonds was reduced. Foreign banks domiciled in Germany were allowed to act as lead managers. The most recent significant change was the revoking of Stock Exchange Turnover Tax and the abolition of the need for Finance Ministry permission to issue domestic bonds with effect from the beginning of 1991.

The consequence is that a commercial paper (CP) market has developed astonishingly quickly in Germany. By the end of September, 20 CP programmes had been mounted with a total volume of DM 13 bn, with Deutsche Bank leading the way as sole arranger of 15 of these programmes.

The degree of utilization under the programmes is around 50 per cent; this compares favourably with a ratio of around 35 per cent on the European commercial paper market. In this way, new financing channels are being created, in that substitutes for bank loans are evolving, and investors are being offered alternatives to short-term bank deposits.

But if the aim is to strengthen Germany as an international financial centre, there is still a good deal to be done. Above all, the minimum reserve requirements, which drive international banking business away from Germany, must be abolished. By permitting pure-bred money-market funds, the willingness of the German financial markets to innovate could be bolstered. Furthermore, it is essential that the eight German regional Stock Exchanges should join forces to form an effective stock-market structure.

14.12 SHORT-TERMISM VERSUS LONG-TERMISM

What are the implications of the German corporate finance model *vis-à-vis* the British system? This question obviously has many facets. Advantages may well be seen in both models, depending on the perspective from which they are viewed. Taking the capital market as an efficient instrument for allocating limited capital resources to the best economic use, there is much in favour of the British model. On the other hand, the German system has led to considerable financial stability and high levels of corporate investment.

A big disadvantage of the British model, from a German view, is that, in giving absolute precedence to shareholder value, there is the danger of a preoccupation with short-term corporate performance with the repercussions now being discussed in the UK under the heading of short-termism. To avoid any misunderstandings, the author believes that it is the shareholders who, after all, are the owners of their enterprise and they should, consequently, have strong rights, including the right to a fair dividend and to a satisfactory performance of the share price. However, the maximization of shareholder value can be counter-productive if horizons are set too short-term. This would also, ultimately, put the shareholder in conflict with the responsibility that attaches to ownership.

This may sound strange to those who believe in capitalism in its unadulterated form. Germany, however, practises a so-called social market economy and Article 14 of the German Constitution (*Grundgesetz*) states that 'Ownership involves obligations', and, further, that 'Its [i.e. property's] use should at the same time serve the common good'. We have not fared badly with this principle. The idea can certainly be defended that a company should not be run in a narrow way that takes account only of shareholders' interests over the short-term. The interests of other groups also deserve consideration. This includes its employees, customers, suppliers, and the city or community in which it operates. How else can environmental concerns, for instance, be adequately taken care of?

Naturally, a strategy aimed at the *longer-term* maximization of shareholder value would also take account of these objectives. But the British system, where investors' and analysts' interest focuses heavily on companies' quarterly results and the resultant development of share prices, runs the risk of sinking into short-termism. For company managements there is an—almost—irresistible temptation to avoid measures that might detract from a positive showing, especially since schemes which incorporate incentives, such as management rewards in the form of stock options, encourage the managements' interest in maximizing reported profits. This can impede the readiness to undertake long-term investments and to invest in research and development. Robert Malpas, a former managing director of BP, only recently appealed to British enterprise in the words: 'Look beyond the immediate numbers when considering future investment. Only then will we create the climate of long-termism we all wish to have permeating all sectors of the economy.' Otherwise, it might be added, others will be more successful. At any rate, this explains in part the successes achieved by the Japanese in the USA and Europe.

14.13 CORPORATE GOVERNANCE

The difference between the British and German systems is most apparent in the area of corporate governance, i.e. control over enterprises aimed at ensuring the efficient use of the assets entrusted to them by the proprietors. In the UK, control takes place primarily through the market, on the one hand by investors buying or selling with corresponding repercussions on the company's share price and the scope for raising further capital and, on the other, through actual or potential takeovers. Companies which are perceived as being inefficient soon run the risk of becoming the target of a takeover, which may take the form of a hostile bid. In the UK, the market mechanism of the takeover is much more highly developed than in Germany.

In Germany, too, the number of mergers and acquisitions has increased significantly in recent years—partly as a prelude to the single European market. The number of such transactions has jumped from 1,000 in 1984 to a figure of around 3,000 last year. It is worth noting, incidentally, that, since the end of 1990, the acquisition of former state-owned enterprises in the former East Germany has played an important role here. A significant point, though, is that so far the hostile takeover has been the absolute exception in Germany rather than the rule. In this respect, control through the market is not as pronounced as it is in the UK. But the way a share price moves has, of course, a control function in Germany too. In addition, the banks have a degree of influence on corporate decisions through their supervisory board mandates. Finally, the influence of public opinion—in other words the media—on corporate behaviour should not be underestimated. Here, too, a company's long-term development rather than its short-term performance is in the foreground.

As the market mechanism of corporate takeovers is still underdeveloped, takeover rules in Germany are still at a rudimentary stage. The acquisition of a stake only has to be disclosed from a holding of 25 per cent upwards. There is no threshold from which it becomes compulsory for the buyer to make a public offer for all of the company's shares. To that extent, it is easier in Germany for a buyer, discreetly and unnoticed, to build up a considerable shareholding, something, which may well be to the detriment of the other shareholders. Incidentally, this is a reason why a number of German companies have introduced maximum voting rights which limit the voting power of any one shareholder at shareholders' meetings to a certain percentage—in some cases 5 per cent, in others 10 per cent—of the company's capital. Deutsche Bank has been arguing for some time in favour of disclosure rules applicable to the acquisition of substantial shareholdings similar to those in force in the UK. This would allow German companies to rescind voting right restrictions.

As it is, the effectiveness of these restrictions is open to question. In the Feldmühle/Nobel case, they did not prevent the ultimate takeover by Sweden's Stora, but the instrument proved to be something of a hindrance to Pirelli and friends in the case of the tyre-maker Conti. Effective protection against potential takeovers is certainly provided by the fact that in Germany, in contrast to the UK, the shareholder structure, especially of many small and medium-sized companies whose size would make them ideal takeover targets, is fairly rigid. Many shares are held on a permanent or long-term basis. Institutional investors, who would more naturally have a strong interest in the capital gains potential offered by a takeover bid and who actively manage (i.e. frequently reshuffle) their holdings, play a much more modest role in Germany than in the UK, as already mentioned.

In my opinion, it is not necessarily a disadvantage that the mechanism of corporate takeovers is a less incisive market instrument in Germany than it is in the UK. The large and rising number of corporate link-ups shows that meaningful mergers or takeovers are not excluded in Germany. But we have been spared the excesses of takeover battles such as those witnessed in the USA and Britain. Their outcomes, especially the resultant high indebtedness of the companies involved, some of it financed through high-yield instruments such as junk bonds, are not particularly appealing. Another problem is the practices of corporate raiders who, after taking over a company, strip its assets to make a quick profit. This would be very difficult to perpetrate in Germany and that is something to be grateful for.

However, let there be no misunderstanding: the author is not against takeovers, even unfriendly takeovers, as long as they do not go hand in hand with asset stripping by corporate raiders, or lead to over-indebtedness, or are done for financial gains only; but instead are part of a sound and— dare one say it—longer-term industrial strategy.

14.14 OUTLOOK

In the interest of the future well-being of British and German enterprise, it is much to be hoped that there will be success in combining market efficiency with a longer-term philosophy. Indications that such a development is taking place are already visible. In the UK, banks are now allowed to implement the universal banking model within the framework of their group operations. In Germany, banks are making strenuous efforts to develop the capital market. So, basically, a process of convergence has already begun. The completion of the European internal market, especially the single market for financial services, will accelerate this development. There is growing integration: the big British banks, for instance, have continued to expand their positions in Germany, especially in securities business. The same applies in the opposite direction; German banks have further strengthened their presence in the City.

Deutsche Bank, for instance, took an important step into merchant banking by acquiring the Morgan Grenfell Group. When it decided on the takeover two years ago, the bank was particularly interested in the access that such a move would give it to distinctively Anglo-American banking philosophies, which are a major formative force behind many innovative developments in banking. Deutsche Bank sees Morgan Grenfell as its 'centre of competence' for the areas of corporate finance (especially mergers and acquisitions business), and institutional and international asset management. It wanted this additional competence in order to better defend and develop its leading position at a European level.

The bank has, however, no intention of transferring British financing techniques wholesale to Germany, in the same way as it does not feel it would be right to transfer specifically German techniques *en bloc* in the opposite direction. It would be a mistake to believe that the advantages of either system can be transplanted to the other without adapting them to the new environment. In the UK there is an apt saying that 'all business is local'. This is very pertinent with regard to many important areas of the banking business, indeed, the author believes that for some time to come, the shape of banking in Europe will continue to be moulded by established national customs and practices. Which of the national features survive the adoption of the new harmonized EC banking system will be decided not by the EC Commission, by governments, or by the banks themselves, but by customer satisfaction. And that can only be a good thing.

APPENDIX

Table 14.A1. *Composition of the Supervisory Boards of the 100 largest German enterprises (1988)*

Private banks	104
Other banks	32
Insurance companies	24
Trade union representatives	187
Other employee representatives	542
Representatives from industry and other business enterprises	385
Other shareholder representatives (lawyers, notaries, representatives of shareholder associations etc.)	152
Politicians, civil servants	69
TOTAL	1,495

Source: Federal Association of German Banks

Table 14.A2. *Flow of funds of non-financial corporations in Germany and the UK, 1970–1985*

Gross sources of finance	Germany	UK
	(percentage of total)	
Internal resources	67.1	74.2
New equity	2.1	4.9
Bonds	0.7	0.8
Loans and short-term securities	21.1	23.7
Trade credit	2.2	2.8
Capital transfers	6.7	2.9
Statistical adjustment	0.0	−9.4

Source: Centre for Economic Policy Research

Table 14.A3. *The financing of large firms in Germany and the UK 1982–1988*
(percentage of total)

Gross sources of finance	Germany	UK
Internal resources	89.6	58.2
New equity	8.2	14.3
Medium- and long-term loans	0.6	7.9
Short-term loans	−1.7	1.1
Trade credit	3.3	18.5

Source: Centre for Economic Policy and Research

Table 14.A4. *Maturity structure of bank loans in Germany to enterprises and self-employed persons*

	1980		1990	
	DM bn.	%	DM bn.	%
Short-term	224	31	354	30
Medium-term	59	8	90	7
Long-term	439	61	777	63
TOTAL	722	100	1,241	100

Note: Including bills discounted.
Source: Deutsche Bundesbank.

Table 14.A5. *Summary statistics for the German stock-market* (DM m.)

	New issues*		Listed AGs		Equities turnover		DAX[†]
	Nominal value	Market value	Number	Share capital	Domestic	Foreign	(Average values)
1980	3,702	6,948	459	45,592	27,717	5,159	505.28
1985	3,769	11,009	451	54,133	210,708	26,186	1,022.7
1986	7,360	28,021	649	67,237	1,621,155	35,040	1,718.8

* Only official trading and Regulated Market
[†] German Share Index; end of 1987 = 100
Source: Deutsche Bundesbank, Arbeitsgemeinschaft der deutschen Wertpapierbörsen

Table 14.A6. *Structure of share ownership in Germany* (shares in %)

	1960	1970	1980	1990
Private households	27	28	19	17
Enterprises	44	41	45	42
Public sector	14	11	10	5
Foreigners	6	8	11	14
Banks	6	7	9	10
Insurance companies*	3	4	6	12

* Including pension funds
Source: Deutsche Bundesbank, Monthly Report (October 1991)

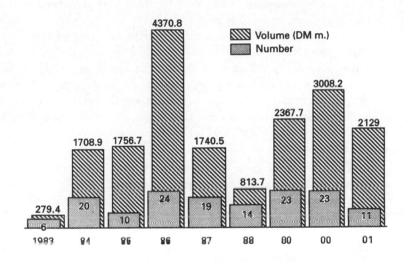

Fig. 14.A1. 'Going-publics' in the Federal Republic of Germany since 1983. *Source*: Deutsche Bank

15

An Overview of the Japanese Financial System

JENNY CORBETT

15.1 INTRODUCTION

Until the late 1970s it had been common to describe the corporate financing system of Japan as characterized by low net worth and heavy reliance on bank finance. As a result there was considerable interest in the question of what allowed Japanese firms to exist with such an apparently high-risk (and yet presumably low-cost) capital structure. This view was challenged as a misunderstanding of Japanese company accounting practices and there have been various attempts to show that Japanese corporate finance does not differ from the standard (i.e. US) pattern.

This chapter examines the evidence on corporate financing patterns from 1970 to 1989 to answer the two questions (1) to what extent is the pattern of Japanese finance really different from other countries and (2) has there been a major restructuring of financing patterns in recent years away from the use of bank finance. The chapter then considers the implications of the statistical evidence for the general view that Japan is a bank-based financial system and considers other aspects of firms' relations with banks.

The chapter concludes that:

- The pattern of finance in Japan differs from that in the UK and Germany but resembles that in some other European economies. The pattern is still broadly characterized as having higher shares of bank finance than the UK and Germany.
- There has been no dramatic change in the aggregate pattern of finance over the 20-year period so that claims that finance in Japan is converging on a UK/US pattern are not supported. Some large firms may have changed in this direction and it would be an interesting question for further research to consider which firms have done so and why.
- Other aspects of the relationship between finance and industry have not changed. The nature of the main bank relationship and corporate group-

This chapter was originally presented as a paper for the NEDO conference on Capital Markets and Company Success in Nov. 1991. I am grateful to the participants for comments. The research on which this paper is based has been funded by the ESRC under its Government-Industry Relations initiative to which I am most grateful. The research also forms part of the Centre for Economic Policy Research Project, *An International Study of the Financing of Industry*. I am indebted to other members of the project—Ian Alexander, Elisabetta Bertero, Jeremy Edwards, Tim Jenkinson, and Colin Mayer—for comments and suggestions.

ings, and the maintenance of interlocking shareholdings do not seem to have changed as far as aggregate data can represent them. Again there is further research needed on the characteristics of those cases in which change has occurred but they are not the majority.

There is much research still needed on the economic effects of these aspects of the financial system but the chapter summarizes the main body of research findings which suggests the following conclusions on the impact of these relationships on corporate performance:

- There is considerable variance in the strength and coherence of the main bank and *keiretsu* (group) relationship across firms and groups.
- A strong main bank relationship makes firms less dependent on internal finance for new investment (supporting the theory that it reduces agency costs associated with outside finance).
- The main bank relationship alone does *not* seem to provide insurance against risk (i.e. profit variability) but does improve the performance during financial distress (supporting the theory that the relationship reduces the cost of distress).
- Membership of a *keiretsu* group *does* seem to provide insurance against risk (i.e. reduces profit variability) although at the cost of lower profit levels.

With respect to the implications of bank relationships for corporate control our own and other research implies:

- Interlocking shareholdings have been used as a means to insulate managers from outside interference. However, it seems plausible that managers will still try to maximize profits in order to have greater resources to divide between internal and external (shareholders') claims (although there is no direct evidence for such a claim).
- Inside (institutional) shareholders have some input into management (via seats on boards) but their impact is limited in normal circumstances
- Banks also have some managerial input (by sending former bank employees as directors of other companies). This input is associated with their role as shareholders rather than with their role simply as lenders.

The chapter is presented in five sections. Section 15.2 presents the conventional view of Japanese companies' financial structure. Section 15.3 uses National Income Accounts and Flow of Funds figures to provide a description of the pattern of company finance from 1970 to 1989. Section 15.4 considers aspects of the main bank relationship, while section 15.5 looks at other features of corporate control, particularly the *keiretsu* relationship and interlocking shareholding. Section 15.6 presents conclusions.

15.2 THE CONVENTIONAL VIEW

Kuroda and Oritani (1980) challenged the conventional view of the 1970s (that Japan was a high-debt, low net-worth system) on the grounds that accounting differences (particularly between Japan and the US) made these comparisons unreliable. They, and others (Wakasugi 1984 and Aoki 1984), used market values of assets to replace book values and recalculated net worth ratios. This procedure naturally results in much higher net worth ratios for Japanese companies because of high rates of inflation in asset values (notably land). Arguing further that US companies use off-balance-sheet finance which should be included with liabilities and should be treated as indirect finance, Kuroda and Oritani conclude that 'the validity of this generally accepted view is very much in doubt'.

Throughout the 1980s, however, the question of the capital structure in Japan has continued to be researched and debated. Aoki (1984), extending the Kuroda–Oritani view, noted a reduced Japan–US differential in debt to equity ratios and a declining trend in both stock and flow measures of debt for Japan. But he also concluded that Japanese debt levels had been higher than could be explained by the standard theory of share price maximization.

By the early 1980s the conventional wisdom about Japanese corporate finance had therefore moved away from the extreme view that the system was unique, to a view in which 'indirect finance can be regarded as a characteristic of Japan's financial system, but . . . the difference with other countries is one of degree, not of kind' (Kosai and Ogino 1984).

More recently commentators have claimed that there is now a significant degree of change in the Japanese pattern of finance which, taken together with the changes in other countries, could be described as a convergence of financing patterns. Borio (1990) shows (see Table 15.1) the figures for gearing ratios from a six-country comparison which are typical of the evidence often presented for the convergence view.

The present conventional wisdom may therefore be summarized as consisting of the following propositions:

- There has been a high level of dependence on bank finance (and an accompanying high debt to equity level) by international standards (this view is often associated with the view that costs of capital are low in Japan because interest rates are low).
- In recent years there has been a change away from bank finance towards equity finance which has resulted in a major shift in debt to equity levels and a move towards US or UK financing patterns (at the same time as there have been increases in debt levels in both those countries associated with leveraged buy-outs, etc.).

Table 15.1 *Ratios of gross debt to total assets and net debt to real assets (market values)*

		1970	1980	1987
Japan	Gross	.86	.65	.59
	Net	.68	.84	.42 (1986)
UK	Gross	.51	.63	.48
	Net	.21	.25	.04
USA	Gross	.45	.50	.51
	Net	.21	.25	.24
Germany	Gross	.72	.81	.77
	Net	.74	.84	.76

Source: Borio (1990), tables 2 and 3

Surprisingly, in spite of the amount of research already done it is still not clear precisely what characterizes the pattern of Japanese corporate finance over time and by international comparison. Without a careful analysis of a range of data sources it is not possible to adjudicate between these views, nor to draw conclusions about whether recent changes in patterns of finance mark a distinct break with the past. For Japan there are several sources of data and careful use of both National Income Accounts data and Ministry of Finance corporate accounting data (from a survey of 20,000 firms) are appropriate for international comparisons. In section 15.3 of this chapter the National Income Accounts data are presented.

15.3 PATTERNS OF FINANCE

This section presents the patterns of finance in some detail and concludes that there are two features which stand out.

* The role of internally generated funds is much higher than that usually recognized but the role of bank lending is considerably more important than in the UK or Germany.
* There has been relatively little change in this pattern in the twenty years since 1970 and claims that there is convergence between the Japanese and Anglo-Saxon (UK/US) systems are exaggerated.

Edwards and Fischer in Chapter 13 of this volume set out the reasons for using flow data rather than the sort of stock data quoted from Borio (1990).[1] They also point out that there is reason to prefer *net* sources of

---

[1] The method has been developed as part of the Centre for Economic Policy's Research Project on *An International Study of the Financing of Industry*. The method is set out in more detail in Mayer (1988; 1990).

Table 15.2. *Gross sources of finance in Japan (% of total sources raised)*

	1970–4	1975–9	1980–4	1985–9	1970–89
Internal	31.2	33.6	49.0	42.9	40.0
Depreciation	25.3	34.0	35.6	29.1	30.5
Saving	5.9	–0.5	13.5	13.8	9.5
Loans	39.7	31.3	35.2	32.7	34.5
Commercial paper	0	0	0	2.6	1.1
From government	3.5	4.1	3.2	1.0	2.5
Bonds	1.6	2.8	3.1	5.9	3.9
Foreign	0	0	1.8	4.5	2.2
Shares	3.1	2.9	3.5	5.1	3.9
Trade credit	22.2	28.0	10.9	9.2	15.6
Other	2.3	1.3	–1.8	4.2	2.1
Foreign	0	0	–4.1	1.3	–0.3

Note: The percentages are weighted shares in the sense that the underlying annual values in each category are summed before dividing by totals i.e.

$$\frac{\Sigma_{t=1}^{n} X_t}{\Sigma_{t=1} S_t}$$

where X_t is each source of finance and S_t is the total sources raised. Values are all calculated at 1989 prices.

Source: EPA, *National Income Accounts*, various years and own calculations.

Table 15.3. *Net sources of finance in Japan (% of new physical investment)*

	1970–74	1975–9	1980–4	1985–9	1970–89
Internal	59.1	70.8	74.6	70.7	69.3
Loans	42.7	33.9	31.7	23.1	30.5
From government	6.7	8.7	4.8	1.6	4.4
Bonds	2.7	2.5	0.6	8.6	4.7
Shares	2.5	3.3	3.6	4.4	3.7
Trade credit	–9.9	–12.2	–8.4	–5.7	–8.1
Other	2.9	1.7	–2.1	–1.1	–0.1

Note: Calculation method as for Table 15.2.

Source: EPA, *National Income Accounts*, various years and own calculations.

finance to *gross* sources as a representation of how new finance has been raised to fund physical investment. The net figures remove the effect of acquisitions of financial assets. There are difficulties about the use of net figures. The value of net sources may be sensitive to the classification of financial assets acquired.[2] More importantly, as Edwards and Fischer note in Chapter 13, aggregate net sources may disguise the importance of a particular type of finance, if some parts of the corporate sector are raising that type of finance while others are acquiring that type of asset (e.g. if some companies are borrowers from banks while others are depositors). For this reason both net and gross sources of finance are shown in Tables 15.2 and 15.3.

The tables makes clear several features of the financing patterns in Japan.

1. *Japan has low gross internal sources of finance.* Internal sources of finance on a gross basis (i.e. as a proportion of total new physical and financial assets acquired) have been fairly low when compared to the UK and Germany (at about 2/3 of the levels reported in Chapter 13) although France is at roughly comparable levels (see Bertero 1990).

2. *It has much higher internal sources on a net basis.* Internal sources of finance are, by definition, higher on a net basis. What is noticeable about the Japanese case is that the proportion now approaches 3/4 to 4/5 of the net levels in the UK and Germany (and 3/4 of the US level reported by Borio). Furthermore, as in other countries, internal finance has been the major source of finance for Japanese firms.

3. *Bonds and shares are a negligible source of funds.* On both a gross and net basis, bonds and shares have been a small source of funding, although in 1985–9 bond issues rose to a sizeable 8.6 per cent. Part of these bond issues were convertibles so that an exact distinction between bond and equity issues is difficult to make.

4. *Loans have consistently been the most important source of external funding and are still relatively high by international standards. They have declined only modestly over 20 years.* On both a gross and net basis, loans (predominantly direct loans from banks) have been the most important source of lending after internal funding. There are two noticeable features here. First, on both a gross and net basis the share of loans is higher than that in Germany and the UK although the difference (an average of 35 per cent gross for Japan compared with 24 per cent for the UK and 18 per cent for Germany) is not startling. The difference with Germany and the UK on a net basis is somewhat greater but comparisons with other European countries (France in particular seems to resemble Japanese proportions according to Borio's (1990) figures) suggest Japan is still not unique.

The second striking feature is the observation of this pattern over time. As noted above, there is a strong perception among practitioners in Japan, and in some academic literature, that there has been a dramatic

[2] For example, whether time deposits should be treated as 'bank assets' and netted out from bank borrowings, and whether purchases of government bonds should be netted out from issues of corporate bonds.

change in the pattern of finance over the 1980s. In Japanese the expression *'ginkoo banare'* ('parting company with the banks') is used to describe the alleged change in corporate finance. Our figures show two patterns which suggest that this is a misperception. The five-yearly averages for loans on a net basis show a steady but not dramatic decline. The underlying data is more complex. The figures for gross loans show no such steady trend even on five-yearly average figures and annual figures (in Figs. 15.1–15.3) make the idea of a steady downward trend quite difficult to support. Part of what the net figures have captured is some volatility in the uses side of corporate flow of funds figures. Although there has been no steady change in the share of bank deposits in total uses of funds the share has been quite volatile and there has been a steady switch between demand deposits and time deposits as market liberalization has made the latter more attractive. In some years there has been a sudden jump in the share of total deposits in the uses of funds (as in 1985 and 1986) which has contributed to greater volatility in net loans than in the gross loan data.

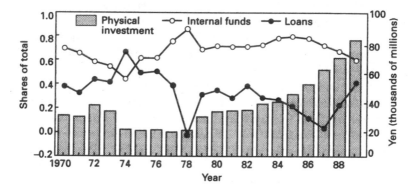

Fig. 15.1. Japanese internal sources and net loans 1970–1989. *Source*: National Income Accounts

We interpret this data to mean that the role of bank finance for funding new physical investment has not significantly declined in Japan. Indeed, since the gross data (bank loans as a share of sources together with the share of bank deposits in uses) provide some indication of the overall level of transactions with the banking sector, it could be argued that there has been very little perceptible change in the interaction between the corporate sector in aggregate and the banking sector.

This is not to say that there has been no change in financing patterns for all firms in Japan. The anecdotal evidence of the change away from bank finance reflects the fact that some, usually large and diversified firms, have

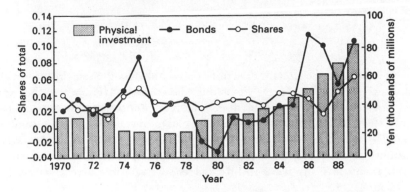

Fig. 15.2. Japanese net bond and net equity finance 1970–1989. *Source*: National Income Accounts

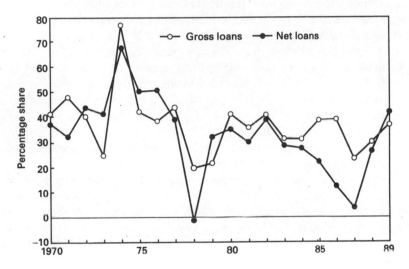

Fig. 15.3. Japanese gross and net loans. *Source*: National Income Accounts

changed their pattern of finance. A more detailed examination of the data by firm size would show that there is some evidence of change in firms with capital of more than 100 million yen but no evidence in firms below that size. It would be a separate, and useful, research exercise to examine why certain firms have changed their patterns while others have not, but that is not the purpose of this chapter.

15.4 MAIN BANK RELATIONSHIPS

15.4.1 *Measurement and Changes in the Relationship*

We suggested in the previous section that bank finance remains relatively important for Japanese firms' financing. Edwards and Fischer in this volume note in the German case that financing proportions do not tell the whole story of the influence of German banks over firms, and the same is true in Japan. It is widely known that in Japan a system of 'main bank' relationships exists. In some respects the relationship is similar to that in Germany but in many ways it differs. Here we consider several aspects of the relationship.

It is important to note that the relationship between a company and its main bank in Japan is both informal and non-exclusive. There is no contract relationship and no legal guarantees are exchanged between firms and main banks. Furthermore, as in Germany, firms will normally borrow from (and hold deposits in) several different banks. It is therefore not entirely straightforward to characterize the main bank relationship. If we take the main bank to be the bank which has the largest share in the total bank loans held by a firm it is common to find that the bank is also a significant shareholder in the firm (although bank holdings are legally restricted to no more than 5 per cent of a firms' equity) and may have sent some former bank employees as top managers (i.e. 'outside' directors) to the borrower firm. Most empirical work on the main bank relationship considers these three aspects to be part of the relationship.

There is no easy source of aggregate information on the main bank relationships of Japanese firms but some empirical research provides a view of the size and changes in the relationship for samples of firms. Hoshi, Kashyap, and Scharfstein (1990) show that for a sample of 125 firms over the period 1978–85 the main bank accounted for an average of 21.9 per cent of the firms' loans and held 4.1 per cent of the equity. Horiuchi and Okazaki (1991) show the time series information for a sample of 38 firms in the electric equipment industry. It is clear that there has been no systematic trend in the ratio of main bank finance over the period 1972 to 1988 with the share at 18.8 per cent at the beginning and 19.6 per cent at the end of the period. Similarly the proportion of equity held by main banks was virtually unchanged from 3.3 per cent in 1972 to 3.8 per cent in 1988.

This picture of no fundamental change in the aggregate size of the relationship is confirmed by Hoshi and Ito (1991) who show the share of loans held by all the financial institutions within a *keiretsu* group in the total borrowing by group member firms (see below for further discussion of group membership). There is considerable variation in the percentages between the major six groups but virtually no change over time between 1978 and

1989 in any single group. It is possible then broadly to characterize the main bank relationship as one in which the main bank provides a stable share of around 20–30 per cent of loans and holds less than 4 per cent equity in the firm.

On the other hand, the relationship of individual firms with the main bank is not necessarily stable. Switches of main banks do occur (Horiuchi, Packer, and Fukuda 1989). Often the switch is from a small, less well-known bank to a leading bank as a firm grows and needs more sophisticated services.

The main bank is also likely to have sent some of its employees as managers to the client firms. On occasion this is associated with managerial reorganizations following financial distress in the client firm but it is common also for the banks to send managers at other times (e.g. when a senior member of the bank staff is passed over for promotion in the bank and it is necessary to find an equivalent status position, or when a bank staff member is nearing retirement). There is some general information available on the number of executives sent by all banks (see below), but it is not straightforward to determine how many are from main banks. Again we rely on the samples presented by other research. Horiuchi and Okazaki (1991) show the time series for their 38 firms[3] varying from 3.1 per cent in 1972 to 2.8 per cent in 1988 and reaching a peak of 5.8 per cent in 1979, a recession year. Apparently the proportions are similar as between main banks and banks in general. Interestingly they note a high correlation between the proportion of directors sent from banks and the equity share held by banks; a correlation which does not exist between any other measures of the bank relationship. As noted below, it is generally true that banks sending directors to firms are shareholders, even if they are not main banks, so that this aspect of the relationship between banks and firms seems to stem from the shareholder relationship rather than the main banking relationship *per se*.

15.4.2 *The Economic Impact of the Bank Relationship*

There has been a considerable amount of theoretical research on the economic impact of the main bank relationship in Japan but relatively little empirical work.

The theory has been concerned with the idea that the main bank either provides some kind of insurance for clients or is able to monitor its client firms more closely than any other creditor or investor. If the latter is true then the 'agency' (and/or asymmetric information) problems associated

---

[3] These proportions show the number of executives sent by the main bank compared to the total number of executives in the firm. It covers both executives who simultaneously hold positions in both organizations and those who have become wholly employed by the receiving company.

with external financing of firms should be reduced. The existence of the main bank relationship should therefore make financing easier in some sense for firms which have it than for firms which do not. There is some debate about what this should mean in terms of measurable economic impact. One could imagine some simple propositions such as that the main bank relationship would: reduce the cost of external finance; increase the availability of long-term finance; increase the proportion of outside finance; lower the variance of bank finance over time (i.e. over periods of tight and loose macroeconomic monetary policy); or lower the variance of bank finance over periods of good and bad performance of firms.

Some recent empirical research helps to fill this gap although it tests a rather limited range of possible effects of main bank relationships. Hoshi, Kashyap, and Scharfstein (1990a; b; 1991a) and Horiuchi and Okazaki (1991) consider whether the main bank relationship eases the internal finance constraint, that is, whether the amount of investment is less constrained by the amount of internal finance available when the firm has a stronger main bank relationship than when the relationship is weaker. The hypothesis is that the strong main bank relationship makes borrowing easier. Hoshi *et al.* (1991b) consider the effect of the relationship on the cost of financial distress. The results are broadly that:

1. Firms with main banks are less sensitive to their internal liquidity in making investments (the constraint is weaker).
2. Firms which reduce their relationships with banks become more liquidity constrained.
3. Firms with bank relationships perform better in financial distress (i.e. they sell and invest more than non-bank-related firms in distress).

These results are consistent with the view that the main bank relationship is able to provide easier access to outside finance and to reduce the cost of distress which might go with higher debt levels. It is suggested that the former is the result of monitoring while the latter may come from the banks' role in co-ordinating other creditors.

To conclude, the main bank relationship consists of three principal parts: a significant share of lending, an equity stake, and some managerial input (seats on the board). The ability to have managerial input is associated with share ownership rather than lending activity alone. There has been relatively little change in the average strength of main bank relationships for those groups of firms for whom information is available over the 1970s and 1980s. The presence of a main bank relationship eases a firm's internal funding constraint and reduces the severity of financial distress.[4]

---

[4] Given that this is true in aggregate there remain interesting, and unanswered questions about why some firms have changed their bank relationships.

15.5 CORPORATE GROUPS, INTERLOCKING SHAREHOLDINGS AND
CORPORATE GOVERNANCE

15.5.1 Keiretsu Groups

The fact that many Japanese firms are linked together in corporate groupings called *keiretsu* is well known. The nature of these groups, their size
and coherence, and their economic impact is much less well known. This
section of the paper considers aspects of group relationships which concern
financing and corporate governance.

There are six large *keiretsu* groups which are well known and account
for a sizeable proportion of the output of the Japanese economy. These
groups are the Mitsui, Mitsubishi, Sumitomo, Fuyo, Daiichi Kangyo, and
Sanwa groups. The first three had their origins in pre-war family-owned
zaibatsu groups which were broken up by the Occupation after the war but
regrouped in loose organizations subsequently. The other three are post-
war groupings with large banks at their centres.

These groups are loosely-structured organizations which are characterized
by a certain amount of trade between members, reliance on finance by the
financial institutions in the group, and regular (monthly) meetings between
the top management of the firms in the group. However, as in the case with
main bank relationships, group relationships are not exclusive and are not
always easy to classify. Many firms will consider themselves to be members
of a group but will not be so closely involved that they are members of the
Presidents' Club (i.e. the monthly meetings of top management). Many
firms which are members of the Club will have extensive relationships with
firms outside the group and may have a main bank which is not the group
bank. Some firms are members of more than one group (including being
members of more than one Presidents' Club).

The publication *Kigyoo Keiretsu Sooran* (Annual Report on Corporate
Groupings) treats about 180 to 190 firms as being core members of the six
big groups and also reports on forty other more loosely structured *kigyoo
shuudan* ('groups'). The six big groups defined this way accounted for 4 per
cent of all employees in Japan in 1989 and 16 per cent of sales. For purposes of research, however, it is usual to consider not only whether a firm
is listed as a member of the Presidents' Club in one year but whether it has
been a stable member of the group. No research uses quite the same
definition as any other.

The key question on corporate groups is what economic effect they have
on corporate behaviour. There have been three specific questions addressed
in the literature on groups:

• Does group membership improve profit performance?

- Does it provide some kind of insurance for group members?
- Does it provide a similar kind of reduction in agency problems as found in the main bank relationship (i.e. making financing of investment easier)?

Some early research (Nakatani 1984) showed the surprising result that group membership actually worsened the profit performance of firms. Group member firms had lower profits on average than non-group firms. At the same time they showed greater stability in profits. The most convincing explanation seems to be that group membership provides some insurance against risk but does so at a cost.

Hoshi *et al.* (1991*a*) address the question of whether group membership has a similar effect to main bank relationships in reducing the severity of the internal financing constraint for investment. They find that this is the case although it is difficult to distinguish how much of the effect is due solely to group membership since almost all group members also have main bank relationships.

Hoshi and Ito (1991*a*; *b*) further examine the group relationship in some detail, developing three measures of group coherence based on the share of group financial institutions' loans in total loans to member firms, on the share of each firms' equity held by group members and on whether group firms supply outside directors to boards of other member firms. These measures show that there is considerable difference in the level of group cohesiveness between the six groups (with Mitsubishi and Sumitomo jointly showing the highest cohesion, Mitsui in the middle and the Fuyo, Sanwa, and DKB groups showing the lowest levels). Separating firms into those which belong to highly cohesive groups and those which do not permits tests of whether more cohesive groups have greater effects on firms' performance. Their results confirm the general results for member versus non-member firms, showing that firms belonging to more cohesive groups have lower but more stable profits and less binding internal cash constraints on investment.

Interestingly Hoshi and Ito demonstrate that over the period 1978 to 1989 their three measures of group coherence show virtually no change within each group.

The conclusions which we draw on the impact of corporate groupings are therefore that: different groups vary in the strength of the relationship, but there has been little change in coherence from 1978 to 1989. Group membership reduces, but stabilizes, profits and membership eases the finance constraint on investment. These conclusions are consistent with the hypothesis that group membership provides insurance against risk and helps to reduce agency problems in capital markets.

15.5.2   *Stable and Interlocking Shareholding*

There are two aspects of the ownership of corporate equity in Japan which bear on the question of corporate control. These are the practices of stable shareholding (*antei kabunushi*) and interlocking shareholding (*kabushiki mochiai*). These two practices may, but do not necessarily, go together.

Stable shareholding refers at one level to the empirical observation that in Japan institutional shareholders have tended to hold equity for long periods and have not been active traders of most of the equity they hold (though they will often hold some shares in special 'trading' accounts). The most actively traded shares are those held by the household sector. Thus, although the broad breakdown of ownership of shares in Japan looks similar to that in the UK (with about three-quarters of shares held by institutions and one-quarter held by households), what is different is the behaviour of the shareholders. As a result it may be true that nearly two-thirds of equity in Japan is held by stable shareholders. This is not the same, however, as an estimate for the proportion of shares held in share interlocks which is much more complicated to estimate.

Sheard (1991: 7) further defines a stable shareholder as a shareholder who:

a) agrees (at least in most contingencies) to waive the exercise of control rights, i.e., holds the shares as a passive, friendly insider, sympathetic to the incumbent management;
b) agrees not to sell the shares to third parties, particularly hostile takeover bidders or bidders trying to accumulate strategic parcels of shares;
c) agrees to consult the firm whose shares are held in the event that it is necessary to dispose of the shares and to give the firm an opportunity to arrange for some or all of the shares to be taken over by another stable shareholder.

'Stable shareholding' thus entails implicit . . . obligations but does not necessarily imply that the shareholder never sells the shares: stability is in a behavioural rather than a literal . . . sense.

These relationships were deliberately set up in the late 1960s and 1970s in response to the opening of capital markets to foreign investors and the fear of an increase in hostile takeover activity. Stable shareholding arrangements are not necessarily linked with interlocking shareholding. The latter refers to the practice of one firm holding shares in a second firm which simultaneously holds shares in the first (A owns shares in B which owns shares in A). The calculation of how much share interlocking exists is tedious and difficult at an aggregate level so that most estimates have looked only at small groups of firms. Sheard (1985) for example, estimates that the Sanwa group (one of the looser groups on the Hoshi–Ito measures) had about 12 per cent intercorporate shareholding while the Mitsubishi and

Sumitomo groups (tighter groups according to Hoshi–Ito) had about 25 per cent.

Stable shareholding arrangements clearly reduce the risk of hostile takeovers for as long as they can be made to last (although there is an obvious incentive problem about these arrangements). Sheard also points out that the stable shareholding and share interlock arrangements are an important complement to the main bank system. By preventing hostile takeover activity they make the monitoring role of banks even more necessary while at the same time the fact that they do prevent takeovers reduces the incentive problem for banks which provide the monitoring.[5]

15.5.3 *Structure and Role of Boards*

The legal structure of companies is similar to the West. The responsibilities of directors of companies appears to be to protect the interests of shareholders by supervising the activities of the firm. Managers and directors are elected by a general meeting of shareholders (although in practice their appointments are merely ratified).

However, the general structure of boards looks slightly different from those in the West. There is usually a president (and sometimes a chairman who is nominally above the president in rank but often not in power), senior executive director(s) (*senmu torishimariyaku*), and other executive directors (*joomu torishimariyaku* and *torishimariyaku*). The board is therefore hierarchically ranked rather than functionally divided, although there may also be functional divisions between executive directors.

What seems to be the most striking difference in Japanese boards is that most of the executive directors will have formerly been middle managers within the company who were promoted from inside. Therefore there is much less distinction between the firm's managers and the board. Executive directors on the board are regarded as having achieved the final level of promotion within the company. This is said to be a reason why the role of the board as a watchdog over management cannot function in the Japanese case.

The role of directors from outside the company is legally the same as that of inside directors and they are not regarded as independent of the company. In fact they will generally come from institutional stakeholders in the company. Banks, in their role as shareholders or as lenders, will play a fairly modest role here while related companies provide the largest number of outside directors. Tables 15.4 and 15.5 show that the current number of outside directors is around 25 per cent in the 2,000-odd companies listed on

---

[5] The incentive problem arises if the bank has undertaken costly monitoring and the firm is then taken over. The new owners may change the bank relationship and the banks' monitoring costs cannot be recovered except within the context of long-term relationships.

Table 15.4. *Outside directors on boards of listed companies by origin 1989 (2037 companies)*

	Total	Outside	From banks	From 6 *keiretsu*	From govt. agencies
Chairman and vice chairman	1,061	412 (38.3%)	65 (6.1%)	n/a	58 (5.5%)
President	2,035	826 (40.6%)	131 (6.4%)	n/a	65 (3.2%)
Total board members	37,899	9,247 (24.4%)	2,050 (5.4%)	4,284 (11.3%)	508 (1.3%)

Source: Tokyo Keizai, *Kigyoo Keiretsu Sooran* (1991)

Table 15.5. *Total outside directors on boards of listed companies 1985–1989*

	1985	1986	1987	1988	1989
No. of companies	1,839	1,888	1,933	1,985	2,037
No. of board members	32,123	33,012	34,203	36,211	37,899
From outside	8,188 (25.5%)	8,073 (24.5%)	8,431 (24.6%)	8,789 (24.3%)	9,247 (24.4%)

Source: As Table 15.4

the Tokyo Stock Exchange and that there has been little change since 1985. Mito (1983), in a survey of the top 200 companies in 1966 and 1976, found slightly over 30 per cent outside directors. In 1976, in Mito's study, 6 per cent of all directors came from banks (5.5 per cent in 1966) while 9.0 per cent came from related companies (7.9 per cent). Of the directors coming from banks 90 per cent came from banks which held shares in the company. Of the total number of directors, 14.3 per cent in 1976 were from institutional shareholders and 4.2 per cent from individual shareholders (in 1966, 12.8 per cent and 4.7 per cent). Apparently there has been little change in the composition of outside directors over the whole period from 1966 to 1989.

It is often noted in Japan that the shareholders' general meeting is not a mechanism for shareholders to influence firms, although it is the case that many fundamental changes to company strategy require a two-thirds majority vote so that control of one-third of voting is enough to block changes. The AGM then is not the mechanism whereby shareholders exercise control.

The majority of directors are promoted from within the firm and the share price performance of the firm does not apparently influence the choice of who is promoted. It is not therefore clear how shareholders can remove or replace poor managers nor how they can force managers to look after their interests. Imai (1989) argues that it is in the interests of managers to pay some attention to the share price of the firm because it signals the reputation and credibility of the firm. Without credibility the firm will not be able to raise external capital for growth (from any source, not only the stock-market) nor will it be able to recruit good, new (potential) managers and directors. Because shareholders understand this, and can themselves influence the share price, they are willing to allow managers to operate without much interference in normal circumstances. Again, this is an area where further research is needed.

15.6 CONCLUSIONS

This chapter has looked at the patterns of corporate finance in Japan and shown that Japan is still more highly bank financed than the UK and Germany, although not more than other European countries. Contrary to popular views there is no evidence of a major change in the pattern of finance for Japanese firms in aggregate over the last twenty years. The pattern of finance and the well-known absence of a market for corporate control (lack of a market-based takeover mechanism) raise the question of how other aspects of the company–bank relationship affect corporate performance and behaviour. Research suggests that main bank relationships and group membership my provide some insurance against risk of financial distress and may solve some agency problems in capital markets thereby allowing greater use of outside finance for investment. There has been little change in the aggregate strength of these relationships over the last ten years. Stable shareholding arrangements and share interlocks are used to reinforce the control of corporations by insiders. The role of banks in the normal management of firms (via seats on boards) is more closely linked with their role as shareholders than with their role as major lenders.

REFERENCES

Aoki, M. (1984), *The Economic Analysis of the Japanese Firm* (North Holland).

Bertero, E. (1990), 'Corporate Finance and the Recent Reforms in the French Financial and Banking System', mimeo, London.

Borio, C. (1990), 'Patterns of Corporate Finance', BIS Economic Papers, No. 27 (Bank for International Settlements, Basle).

Chandler, A., 'Managers, Families and Financiers', in T. Kobayashi and H. Morikawa (eds.), *The Rise of the Managerial Enterprise*, 12th Fuji Business History Conference.

Clark, R. (1979), *The Japanese Company* (Yale University Press).

Horiuchi, A., Packer, F., and Fukuda, S. (1988), 'The Main Bank Relationship', *The Journal of the Japanese and International Economies*, vol. 2, 159–180.

—— and Okazaki, A. (1991), 'Kigyoo no Setsubi Tooshi to Meinbank Kankei', ('Corporate Investment and Main Bank Relationships', in Japanese), working paper, Bank of Japan (Tokyo).

Hoshi, T. and Ito, T. (1991a), 'Measuring Coherence of Japanese Enterprise Groups', mimeo, paper for TCER Finance Conference (Tokyo).

—— —— (1991b), 'Kigyoo Gruupu no Kessokudo no Keisoku to Bunseki', mimeo (Tokyo).

—— Kashyap, A. and Scharfstein, D. (1990a), 'Bank Monitoring and Investment: Evidence from the Changing Structure of Japanese Corporate Banking Relationships', in R. G. Hubbard (ed.), *Asymmetric Information, Corporate Finance and Investment* (Chicago University Press).

—— —— (1990b), 'The Role of Banks in Reducing the Costs of Financial Distress in Japan', *Journal of Financial Economics*, 27: 67–88.

—— —— (1991a), 'Corporate Structure, Liquidity, and Investment: Evidence from Japanese Industrial Groups', *Quarterly Journal of Economics*, 106: 33–60.

Hirata, M. (1985), *Wagakuni Kabushiki Kaisha no Shihai* ('The Control of Japanese Joint Stock Companies', in Japanese) (Chikura Shoboo, Tokyo).

Imai, K. (1989), 'Kigyoo gruupu', in K. Imai and R. Komiya (eds.), *Nihon no Kigyo* (The Japanese Enterprise, in Japanese) (Tokyo University Press).

—— and Komiya, R. (1989), 'Nihonkigyoo no Tokuchoo' ('Features of Japanese Enterprises'), ibid.

Kosai, Y. and Ogino, Y. (1984), *The Contemporary Japanese Economy* (Macmillan, London).

Kuroda, I. and Oritani, Y. (1980), 'A re-examination of the unique features of Japan's corporate financial structure: A comparison of corporate balance sheets in Japan and the United States', *Japanese Economic Studies*, 7: 82–117.

Mayer, C. (1988), 'New Issues in Corporate Finance', *European Economic Review*, 32: 1167–83.

—— (1990), 'Financial Systems, Corporate Finance and Economic Development', in R. G. Hubbard (ed.), *Information, Capital Markets and Investment* (National Bureau of Economic Research, Chicago).

Mito, H. (1983), *Nihon Daikigyoo no Shoyuukoozoo* ('The Ownership Structure of Japanese Large Enterprises', in Japanese) (Bunshindoo, Tokyo).

Nakatani, I. (1984), 'The Economic Role of Financial Corporate Grouping', in M. Aoki (ed.), *The Economic Analysis of the Japanese Firm* (North-Holland).

Okumura, H. (1987), *Nihon no Kabushiki Kaisha* ('Japanese Company', in Japanese) (Toyoo Keizai Shimpoosha).

Ricketts, M. (1987), *The Economics of Business Enterprise: New Approaches to the Firm* (Wheatsheaf).

Sheard, P. (1985), 'Main Banks and Structural Adjustment in Japan', *Pacific Economic Papers*, no. 129 (Australian National University).

—— (1991), 'The Economics of Interlocking Shareholding in Japan', Centre for

Wakasugi, T., Nishina, K., Konya, F., and Tsuchiya, M. (1984), 'Measuring the profitability of the nonfinancial sector in Japan', in D. Holland (ed.), *Measuring Profitability and Capital Costs* (Lexington Books).

Yui, T. (1984), 'The Development of the Organizational Structure of Top Management in Meiji Japan', in K. Nakagawa and H. Morikawa, *Japanese Yearbook on Business History: 1984* (Japan Business History Institute).

16

Role of Japanese Capital Markets: The Effect of Cross-Shareholdings on Corporate Accountability

SEIICHI MASUYAMA

16.1 INTRODUCTION

Cross-shareholdings are an integral part of the unique Japanese corporate system which has grown out of the ruins of the Second World War to become one of the most competitive industrial economies in the world. Cross-shareholdings have also become embodied into Japanese capital markets, now one of the pillars of the global financial system. This unique system is under scrutiny on two fronts. One is on the international front, especially from the USA, where it is asked whether cross-shareholdings restrict competition, trade, and investment. Second, on the domestic front questions are being raised about the distorting effects on capital markets, especially since the boom and bust of the Tokyo stock-market in the 1980s.

This chapter examines first how cross-shareholdings evolved. It finds that they developed originally both to recreate the old business relationships of the pre-war *zaibatsu* and to extend main bank relationships by getting round legislation against monopolies and preventing the existence of holding companies. Cross-shareholding became widespread during the second half of the 1960s due to efforts on the part of companies to create stable shareholders and thus protect themselves from foreign takeovers that were expected to arise from capital liberalization.

Second, the chapter examines statistically the extent of cross-shareholding in Japan and outlines the patterns of the groupings. Third, we look at the major economic issues which arise from the existence of these cross-shareholdings. The high level of efficiency which has been attained by Japanese corporations is attributed by some to cross-shareholdings which are deemed to have freed management from excessive interference by shareholders, and have allowed investment in human resources and the creation of close information networks amongst the groupings of companies. The effect on competition is thought not to have been restrictive, but this issue will continue to come under close scrutiny. The possibility that Japanese corporations pay less attention to the return on equity as a result of cross-shareholdings is relevant to the issue of the effect of cross-shareholdings on competition. There are a number of other issues related to the capital markets. There have been price distortions, not necessarily attributable to cross-shareholding *per se* but due to lax monetary conditions which combined with cross-shareholding to produce a 'corporatization' of the equity market. Another serious issue with regard to capital markets arising from cross-shareholding is the lack of transparency in those markets.

Finally the chapter examines the present condition of the Japanese corporate system and capital markets and finds that both are at a crossroads. It is hoped that the Japanese corporate system will preserve its advantages whilst making itself more transparent and compatible with international norms. More attention should be paid to the return on investment. Capital markets should also become more transparent and conform more to international norms and this process is being aided by a shifting balance in the composition of shareholders with a reduction in cross-shareholding activities and an increase in the number and stake of institutional and individual investors.

16.2   THE DEVELOPMENT OF CROSS-SHAREHOLDINGS IN POST-WAR JAPAN

The development of cross-shareholdings in Japan has been largely a post-war phenomenon arising from three factors: the imposition of a tough anti-monopoly policy by the United States; the practice of lifetime employment in Japan; and the functions of the main banks in Japan. Prior to the war, anti-monopoly laws were loose and holding companies were legal. Japanese industries had become concentrated in the hands of the *zaibatsu* groups, such as Sumitomo, Mitsubishi, and Mitsui. Ownership patterns were vertical and one-way with the *zaibatsu* families and holding companies at their cores.

The defeat of Japan in 1945 forced a complete restructuring of the Japanese industrial system. Victorious America was concerned about the possible revival of the Japanese military–industrial complex and so dissolved the *zaibatsu* and tried to insure against their re-creation through the imposition of tough anti-monopoly laws. The shares held by the *zaibatsu* families and holding companies were distributed, mainly to individual investors, in an attempt to democratize Japanese capital markets. The proportion of shares held by individuals reached about 70 per cent at the end of 1949. The 1947 Anti-monopoly Law prohibited the formation of holding companies (article 9), prohibited non-financial corporations from owning shares in other corporations (article 10(1)), and prevented financial corporations from owning more than 5 per cent of another corporation's shares.

The first wave of cross-shareholdings occurred in the first half of the 1950s. Large Japanese corporations started to revive with the help of various economic and fiscal policies to promote post-war reconstruction and due to the boom created by the Korean War (1950–53). One pattern of grouping emerged in which a large corporation formed a keiretsu or a corporate group, with medium and small corporations under its control and also formed horizontal relationships with other large corporations. In effect these were *zaibatsu* groupings in a new guise. Those which had belonged to the former *zaibatsu* recreated the groups by setting up meetings for the presidents of the companies, merging broken-up trading companies, restoring *zaibatsu* trade marks, and rescuing troubled companies in the former groups.

Cross-shareholdings were used to form bonds between corporations in the group as a substitute for the holding companies which were prohibited by law. These cross-shareholdings were boosted by the relaxation of the anti-monopoly laws in 1949 and in 1953. In 1949 the basic prohibition of non-financial corporations owning other companies' shares under article 10 was amended to being a prohibition only if the shareholding materially damaged competition. The 1953 amendment raised the maximum limit of a financial institution's ownership of another corporation from 5 per cent to 10 per cent; (this has since been reduced back to 5 per cent except in the case of insurance companies). The purpose of the anti-monopoly law shifted from preventing the recreation of the *zaibatsu* to preventing any harmful effects on competition. As well as the former *zaibatsu* groups, other independent corporations also used cross-shareholdings to form groups with the so-called main banks such as Fuji, Sanwa, and Daiichi at their cores. Such groups also involved relationships of *keiretsu-yuushi*, or group priority loans. The main bank system, which was established during the second half of the 1950s when funds were scarce, consisted of a close relationship between the main bank and corporation, leadership by the bank in co-ordinating loans from other banks, and the bank taking responsibility for restructuring and rescuing the corporation in times of financial crisis. These bank groups were forerunners of the new corporate groups established in the mid-1960s (Nakajima 1990 and Nikami 1990).

However the process of forming corporate groupings by means of cross-shareholdings was reversed somewhat in the second half of the 1950s and first half of the 1960s. This period witnessed the fastest economic growth of post-war Japan with rapid technological innovation and industrial restructuring towards heavy industries. This necessitated the reorganization of the corporate groups which were based on old technologies and it undermined the spirit of co-operation by fostering competition amongst companies within the groups over entry into new fields. Furthermore as cross-shareholdings did not raise new finance, corporations found them burdensome when faced by the need for new funds for investment.

The second phase of corporate grouping through cross-shareholding began in the second half of the 1960s and continued into the first half of the 1970s. This wave was triggered by two developments: (1) the disposal of frozen shares held by the Japan Securities Holding Association (JSHI) and the Japan Joint Securities Co. (JJSC); and (2) efforts by corporations to create stable shareholders to protect themselves from much feared foreign takeovers. JSHI and JJSC had been created in 1964 and 1965 to rescue the stock-market from a severe slump (following the boom in investment trusts) by taking over excess stocks arising from the disposal of shareholdings by investment trusts and securities companies. The securities held by JSHI and JJSC amounted to 5 per cent of total existing shares at the end of March 1965. These shares were sold by JSHI and JJSC in the second half of the 1960s and were primarily taken up by banks and insurance companies but many shares were also bought by companies within the same business groups.

With regard to the second spur to cross-shareholding at this time, Japan's joining the OECD in 1964 as a symbol of the completion of the post-war recovery phase, was to result in capital liberalization in five stages between 1967 and 1973. The expectation of this caused great fear of foreign takeovers in the Japanese business community. This prompted frantic efforts by Japanese corporations to create stable shareholders among financial and industrial corporations and to rationalize their operations. Cross-shareholdings were used as a major means of securing stable shareholders. This strategy was also encouraged by the low cost of financing such cross-shareholdings, and was supported by employees. The promotion of stable shareholding was most active between 1965 and 1975, when it is estimated that stable shareholding reached 50 per cent (Okumura 1988). The percentage of shares held by financial institutions other than investment trusts or securities companies increased from 23 per cent to 35 per cent and that held by non-financial corporations increased from 18 per cent to 26 per cent between 1965 and 1975 whereas the percentage held by individuals fell from 45 per cent to 34 per cent (see Table 16.1).

Apart from restoring pre-war industrial groups and establishing bank groups through *keiretsu-yuushi* or priority loans, cross-shareholdings were also used by companies to establish tightly knit networks with suppliers of parts, raw materials, and services. With the development of Japanese production technologies or systems such as 'just-in-time' production, closer relationships were thought to boost efficiency. Lifetime employment played a part in this development. It was confined mainly to large companies and raised those companies' fixed costs relative to smaller companies. Those large companies sought to limit the portion of work done within the company and raise productivity via closer relationships with suppliers and distributors. This also helped smaller companies in creating greater stability in their sales and technological help. As closer relationships entailed larger companies releasing valuable information, and as Japanese contracts were much looser and less specific, so cross-shareholdings formed a means of binding companies to one another.

Table 16.1 *Composition of stock holdings by types of investor (%)*

	A	B	C	D	E	F
1945	53.0	11.2	24.7	—	—	—
1950	61.3	12.6	11.0	—	—	—
1955	53.1	19.5	13.2	4.1	1.8	8.3
1960	46.3	23.1	17.8	7.5	1.4	3.9
1965	44.8	23.4	18.4	5.6	1.8	6.0
1970	39.9	30.9	23.1	1.4	3.2	1.5
1975	33.5	34.5	26.3	1.6	2.6	1.5
1980	29.2	37.3	24.1	1.5	4.0	2.0
1985	25.2	40.9	24.5	1.3	5.7	2.8
1986	23.9	41.7	24.5	1.8	4.7	3.4
1987	23.6	42.2	24.2	2.4	3.6	3.3
1988	22.4	42.5	24.9	3.1	4.0	3.1
1989	22.6	42.3	24.8	3.7	3.9	2.7
1990	23.1	41.6	25.2	3.6	4.2	2.3

Key:
A   Individuals
B   Financial institutions excluding investment trusts
C   Business corporations
D   Investment trusts
E   Foreign corporations and individuals
F   Others

The increase in the degree of cross-shareholding met with some criticism from those in charge of anti-monopoly policy and from the administration of the securities markets and some restrictions were introduced. It was felt that cross-shareholding restricted competition, gave management undue power, impaired the ability to raise finance, and was unfair to other investors, especially individual investors. Measures were taken to control cross-shareholdings in the revision of the Commerce Law in 1981. These included prohibiting a subsidiary from holding its parent company's shares (article 211(2)) and restricting the voting power of an affiliate in the parent company's meetings if the parent company held more than 25 per cent of the affiliate's shares. However, these measures are thought not to have had material effects on the extent of cross-shareholdings especially in ex-*zaibatsu* and bank groups where ownership patterns were in a matrix form and individual ownership of group companies was quite slight (Nakajima 1990).

The process of cross-shareholdings developed its own *raison d'être* and momentum, especially during the relatively lax monetary conditions of the 1980s. The change in equity financing in the second half of the 1970s, from traditional rights issues at par-value or face value, to market price public offerings formed a part of this process. Market price issue rules were modified in October 1976 which encouraged companies to make new issues at market prices. The Japanese economy was slowing down from the high growth of the immediate post-war period and the fall in demand for finance resulted in a period of excess supply of funds in the late 1970s. Slower growth put pressure on firms to cut financing costs. Stable shareholding had tightened demand and supply conditions in the stock-market by reducing the volume of tradable shares. New low-cost financing in the form of equity issues at market price led to a shift away from bank financing to this new source. Companies became more active not only in raising new equity through the stock-market for investment purposes, but also investing more speculatively in the stock-market, and this is thought to have boosted share prices in the 1980s (Okumura 1988; Nikami 1990).

More recently cross-shareholdings have received criticism from the United States. With the intensification of trade and investment friction between the USA and Japan, the USA–Japan Structural Impediments Initiative Talks began in 1989. The US Government requested a discussion of the issue of the keiretsu in relation to cross-shareholdings, alongside other trade and price issues. Furthermore, the attempt by Mr Boone Pickens to purchase a stake and demand participation in the management of Koito, a Toyota group parts manufacturer, heightened awareness of the cross-shareholdings issue.

16.3   THE CURRENT STATE OF CROSS-SHAREHOLDINGS IN JAPAN

It is difficult to calculate statistically the degree of cross-shareholding and its effect on market capitalization and price–earnings ratios, and this is complicated further by there being various definitions. Our first definition of literal cross-shareholdings excludes the shareholdings by life insurance companies, as no equity is owned in return, life insurance companies being mutuals and not stock companies. However, such shareholdings have important effects on control of businesses and barriers to takeover, which will be dealt with below. This preliminary estimate makes cross-shareholding ratios of companies listed on the Tokyo Stock Exchange at end March 1990 about 26 per cent. This omits unreported marginal cross-shareholdings and those with unlisted companies, so the actual ratio is probably slightly higher.

The second approach looks at the degree of control over business transactions, and is important when looking at the effects of competition. From this point of view, cross-shareholdings are looked at in relation to *keiretsu* or corporate groups. There are a number of types of *keiretsu*: (1) the six largest corporate groups (comprising the three ex-*zaibatsu* groups Mitsui, Mitsubishi, and Sumitomo and the three bank groups Fuyo (Fuji), Sanwa, and Daiichi-Kangyo); (2) *keiretsu* organized along vertical lines of produc-

Table 16.2. *Average percentage holding of another company in the group*

End of fiscal year	1977	1981	1985	1987
Average of the ex-*zaibatsu* groups	1.93	2.04	1.76	1.70
Average of the largest bank groups	2.04	1.51	1.39	1.33
Average of the six largest corporate groups	1.99	1.78	1.58	1.52

Notes: Average % holding =

$$\frac{\text{total holdings of group companies' shares by individual companies}}{\text{total number of existing shares within the group}} \times 100$$

Average ownership of a group =

$$\frac{\text{total of average percentage ownership of a group}}{\text{number of corporate groups)}} \times 100$$

Source: Fair Trade Commission Report (1989).

tion (e.g. Toyota, Nissan, and Hitachi); (3) *keiretsu* organized along vertical lines of distribution (e.g. National Store, Toshiba Store, and gas stations). The level of cross-shareholdings in these *keiretsu* groups is not very high. The average percentage holding of another company in the group and the percentage of cross-holdings in the group are shown in Tables 16.2 and 16.3.

The cross-shareholding patterns of the six largest groups as well as those of the bank groups are characterized by a matrix-style ownership of shares, with no single key ultimate shareholder in the group. By contrast, the independent corporate groups such as Toyota, Nissan, Hitachi, and Nippon Steel have radiating patterns of cross-shareholdings from the single key company at the centre of the group. The main shareholders in these groups are financial institutions followed by non-financial companies involved in business relationships, subsidiaries, and affiliated companies. The largest shareholders of such groups do not have cross-shareholding relationships with each other (Nakajima 1990).

The third approach to analysing cross-shareholdings is to look at stable shareholders and focus on their effects as barriers to takeover. Stable shareholders are defined as those who, having over 200,000 shares and direct business relations, have promised to keep the shares for an indefinite period or will inform the company before selling them. In order to prevent takeovers, the targeted level of stable shareholders has been over 50 per cent for individual companies. The following tables (16.4 and 16.5) compare the shareholding structures of listed non-financial corporations and financial institutions in 1985 and 1988. For non-financial corporations,

Table 16.3. *The percentage of cross-shareholdings*

End of fiscal year	1977	1981	1985	1987
The average of 3 ex-*zaibatsu* groups	28.86	32.18	29.41	28.93
The average of 3 bank groups	18.85	18.75	17.39	16.36
The average of the 6 largest groups	23.86	23.86	23.40	22.65

Notes: The percentage of cross shareholdings =

$$\frac{\text{total percentage of shares owned by member companies out of the total number of existing shares of the member companies}}{\text{number of member companies in the group)}} \times 100$$

Member companies of a group are defined as those whose presidents attend group meetings.
Source: Fair Trade Commission Report (1989).

Table 16.4. *Composition of shareholdings in listed non-financial corporations* (100 million shares)

Fiscal year end	1985	1988	Change between 1985–8
Stable shareholders:			
Public sector	28	26	−2 (−7%)
Banks	589	747	158 (41%)
Non-financial corporations	512	622	110 (28%)
Life assurance companies	347	387	40 (10%)
Property companies	116	124	8 (2%)
Sub-total	1,592 (62%)	1,906 (64%)	314 (81%)
Non-stable shareholders:			
Investment trusts	62	137	75 (19%)
Foreigners	169	132	−37 (−9%)
Individuals	709	723	14 (3%)
Securities companies	50	74	24 (6%)
Sub-total	990 (38%)	1,066 (36%)	76 (19%)
TOTAL	2,582 (100%)	2,972 (100%)	390 (100%)

Source: Based on statistics of the National Conference of Securities Exchanges

Table 16.5.   *Composition of shareholdings in listed financial institutions* (100 million shares)

Fiscal year end	1985	1988	Change between 1985–8
Stable shareholders:			
Public sector	1	1	0 (0%)
Banks	117	144	27 (28%)
Non-financial corporations	255	291	36 (38%)
Life assurance companies	83	93	10 (10%)
Property companies	27	31	4 (4%)
Sub-total	483 (80%)	560 (81%)	77 (80%)
Non-stable shareholders:			
Investment trusts	3	11	8 (9%)
Foreigners	14	16	1 (1%)
Individuals	93	99	6 (6%)
Securities companies	50	74	24 (6%)
Sub-total	122 (20%)	141 (18%)	19 (20%)
TOTAL	605 (100%)	701 (100%)	969 (100%)

Source: Based on statistics of the National Conference of Securities Exchanges

stable shareholding accounts for 54 per cent of total shares existing in 1988 and 81 per cent of the net increase in shares between 1985 and 1988. For financial institutions 81 per cent of shares in 1988 were stable and account for 80 per cent of the increase in the period. These proportions are over-estimates in some sense as they include those shares owned by financial institutions for portfolio investment purposes. It is nevertheless felt that most companies have succeeded in attaining a stable shareholder ratio of above 50 per cent forming an effective barrier to takeovers. Stable share-holding, by restricting the supply of and demand for tradeable shares, also has important effects on share prices.

16.4   ECONOMIC ISSUES RELATING TO CROSS-SHAREHOLDING IN JAPAN

Cross-shareholdings have altered the concept of the stock company in Japan. They have freed management substantially from the influence of shareholders. Stable shareholders are selected by and are dependent on management, and cannot therefore play a disciplinary role on corporate management. The availability of low-cost equity finance has also helped to liberate management from the traditional discipline of the main banks. This leaves the main source of disciplinary pressure coming from the need to satisfy employees. This stems partly from the lifetime employment system which tends not to distinguish clearly between management and employees, and forces management to give a high priority to employee satisfaction. Even this source of pressure may not act in the conventional disciplinary sense. Management and employee interests coincide over a number of issues. They will be united against takeovers as the costs of terminating long-term relationships and re-establishing new ones are high, especially if lifetime employment is the norm. Overall, cross-shareholdings create a corporate structure which allows the management much stronger controlling rights than shareholders.

This difference in structure in Japan is consistent with quite distinct corporate behaviour from corporations in the West. It is often pointed out that Japanese companies seek market share rather than profits. The average return on equity of Japanese corporations is low compared with that of American companies. The return on equity (ROE) of the Nomura Research Institute (NRI) 400 in 1990 was 6.9 per cent whilst that of the S&P 500 was 11.6 per cent. This is believed to be because Japanese management is more concerned about job prospects for employees (job security and promotion prospects) which improve directly with market share than about profitability which is the primary concern of shareholders. The main corporate shareholders are not as concerned with profitability as their counterparts in the West, as cross-shareholdings being mutual investment in each others' shares create a tacit agreement to the other company's goals. Dividend payout ratios of Japanese corporations are also low for the same reason and because dividend payments are taxed more heavily than capital gains. The dividend pay-out ratio (calculated as dividend payments divided by post-tax profits) in 1990 of the NRI 400 was 30.8 per cent whilst that of the S&P 500 was 56.7 per cent.

These differences in corporate behaviour raises issues both domestically and abroad, primarily in the US. There are at least four issues connected with cross-shareholdings: impact on economic efficiency; impact on competition; impact on capital markets; and compatibility with the external community.

16.4.1   The Impact of Cross-shareholding on Efficiency

The impact of cross-shareholdings on corporate efficiency is believed to be positive. It is argued that freeing management from the influence of shareholders and from the fear of takeovers has enabled Japanese corporations to invest more heavily in human resources, the most important factor in the successful production of knowledge-intensive goods and services. The corporate networking of the *keiretsu* is also felt to be an effective way of benefitting from a wider access to information.

This school of thought is promoted in particular by Itami (1991) who advocates peoplism in place of capitalism. He uses three criteria in comparing Japanese peoplism to American capitalism: (1) ownership of the company sovereignty); (2) sharing of information and decision making; (3) type of markets. He finds that peoplism is identified with employee sovereignty, the dispersed sharing of information and decision making amongst a wide spectrum of the workforce, and organized markets with an emphasis on long-term economic gains through long-term relationships. On the other hand, capitalism is characterized by stockholder sovereignty, and the concentration of information amongst those in high positions and of exceptional ability. He argues that employee sovereignty makes sense as employees rather than shareholders invest the most important resources and take the greatest risk from their investment. He feels that information rather than money is the most vital resource in the modern technological environment. Under the lifetime employment system, the risk that employees take is greater than that of the shareholders who can withdraw their investment at any time.

Miwa (1991) argues that insulating management from interference by shareholders, investors, and takeovers may be justified in that the accumulation of human resources, which itself is essential to a modern enterprise, demands a freedom to react to continuous change and an increasing need to improve and innovate. Corporate relationships with distribution *keiretsu* and subcontractors require a similar adaptability to changing conditions. The loosely knit network of keiretsu established by cross-shareholdings allows more initiative to be taken by suppliers. It is argued that the alternative structure of internal divisions or subsidiaries under holding companies does not allow for the same degree of initiative and is therefore less efficient. An example of this difference in structure is in the automobile industry. Japanese manufacturers depend more on outside sources than their US and European counterparts. Japanese automobile manufacturers produce internally on average 25 per cent of their value added whilst their US counterparts produce about 50 per cent internally. Japanese manufacturers also use a smaller number of outside suppliers than their American counterparts.

Broadly speaking, the Japanese system of cross-shareholdings does contribute to economic efficiency but there are some concerns. The low rate of return on investment might have led to resources being wasted on uneconomic marginal investment projects. There are also some doubts as to how favourably the practice is viewed by the international community and whether it contributes to the health of capital markets. US criticism has focused on the restrictive impact of the *keiretsu* on competition, trade, and investment. It is claimed for instance that the horizontal and matrix *keiretsu*, which characterize the six largest groups, impede imports into Japan and do not improve efficiency; that the vertical *keiretsu* do not restrict imports to the same extent and do improve efficiency resulting in higher exports; and that the Japanese distribution system as a whole restricts imports.

The Japanese argue that *keiretsu*, organized vertically along production stages, foster close relationships with suppliers, which helps to develop high-quality parts and boost efficiency, and that such relationships whilst being co-operative are also competitive and are not exclusive. For example in the automobile industry, companies without cross-shareholdings also have close business relationships and many companies belong to more than one group. There is, however, an entry barrier, in that joint development work needs to be undertaken first (Ota 1991).

Several factors point to these relationships not being overly restrictive. First, they cover only a fairly limited proportion of the economy. The six largest groups accounted for about 4 per cent of total employment, 13.5 per cent of total assets and 16.2 per cent of total sales in Japan in 1989, according to a survey by Toyota Keizai. According to another survey, the ratio of intra-group transactions accounted for 10 per cent of purchases and 10.5 per cent of sales and the ratio had declined slightly since a similar survey was done in 1981 by the Fair Trade Commission. Secondly, the criteria to enter into these relationships were consistent with promoting efficiency, namely on quality, performance, and price grounds. The Fair Trade Commission report concluded that the six largest groups were loosely knit relationships between independent corporations with such links as meetings between the corporations' presidents, cross-shareholdings and the exchange of directors, and hence very different in form from the pyramid-like structure of the pre-war *zaibatsu*.

16.4.2   *Impact on Competition*

It is too early to conclude whether the *keiretsu* relationship with cross-shareholdings greatly affect competition; discussions are centred on the USA–Japan Structural Impediments Initiative Talks. However, such relationships are exclusive to the extent that they have been organized to engender stability through long-term relationships. They are not as exclusive or anti-competitive as is sometimes thought outside Japan and there are openings to the outside world.

One aspect of the competition issue relates to the cost of capital. It is argued above that Japanese corporations are oriented more to market share than to profitability because they are not constrained by the demands of shareholders for a higher return on equity. This, it is argued, gives an unfair advantage to Japanese corporations at the crucial development stage of strategic new products. The success of Japanese manufacturers in dominating basic semiconductors, for example, is attributed to this by some (Nakatani 1991). Banking is another area which has been cited where Japanese banks have benefited from a lower required rate of return. The recent BIS (Bank for International Settlements) rules on capital adequacy attempt to tackle this issue by forcing banks to raise targeted rates of return to meet the minimum capital ratio. Such arguments are stated too simply but may have an element of truth. It is important that Japanese corporations becoming international in their operations be aware of these views and act to reduce the risk of confrontation.

16.4.3 *Impact on Capital Markets*

Another major issue concerns the impact of cross-shareholdings on price formation in capital markets. There are three points to make. One concerns definition and measurement. The second concerns the impact on demand and supply in the equity market. The third regards fairness to shareholders other than cross-shareholders, such as individual investors and financial institutions.

On the question of definition, theoretically cross-shareholdings should have a neutral effect on share prices and an inflationary effect on price–earnings ratios and market capitalization. Cross-shareholdings are equivalent to buying back own shares. Roughly speaking, the market value of the company's investment in cross-shareholdings needs to be subtracted in order to calculate the price–earnings ratio and market capitalization (Kobayashi 1990). Nomura Research Institute estimates that the price–earnings ratio of listed shares on the Tokyo Stock Exchange at the end of 1990 should be adjusted downward by at least 20 per cent from 46 to 37 and market capitalization adjusted downward by 26.3 per cent, from 458 million yen to 338 trillion yen.

The combination of cross-shareholdings, which restrict the supply of traded shares, with loose monetary policy resulted in an asset inflation centred on property and shares. (Loose monetary policy was attributable to efforts to finance the US deficits, stabilizing global financial markets faced with the Mexican debt problem, and the 1987 crash.) Japanese corporations accumulated excess funds, partly as a result of high share prices which made equity finance relatively cheap. These surplus funds within corporations were used for portfolio investment purposes which contributed to the inflation in share prices. The rising property market also added to the rise in the stock-market, as shares were revalued on the basis of companies' property holdings.

On the issue of fairness to shareholders other than cross-shareholders, it has been noted that Japanese management has paid much less attention to the interests of shareholders than in the USA and Europe and that therefore the return on equity and dividend pay-out ratios have been low. Another related issue is the effect of cross-shareholding in diluting the rights of other shareholders. Since corporate investors acquire the bulk of voting rights through cross-shareholdings at virtually no cost, the voting rights of non-corporate shareholders become impotent. However, the counter-argument is that non-corporate shareholders benefit from cross-shareholdings through increased capital gains resulting from the greater efficiency promoted by cross-shareholding discussed above. Low pay-out ratios have not been considered a problem as the Japanese taxation system favours capital gains over dividend income. It is argued further that non-corporate shareholders are not interested in participation in corporate management and will not worry as long as capital gains persist. There will doubtless be greater scrutiny forthcoming in a weaker market.

Another aspect of the fairness issue is that the predominance of the corporate investors over the non-corporate investors has altered the characteristics of the Japanese market such that its distinct rules are hard for outsiders to understand. This lack of transparency is said to have put off individual and foreign investors. For instance the distortions to price–earnings ratios discussed above make traditional valuations difficult. Table 16.1 shows that individual and foreign holdings declined in the second half of the 1980s.

16.4.4 *Compatibility with the External Community*

The last issue is whether the Japanese corporate system is compatible with those in the USA and Europe, however beneficial it may be domestically. This is increasingly important because the Japanese economy and capital markets now constitute large shares of the global economy and markets. Japanese people feel an inherent vulnerability due to a high degree of economic dependency, lack of military power, and the remoteness of their culture from the mainline of European and American culture. From this perspective, the lack of accountability of the Japanese system to the outside world is a problem.

16.5 JAPANESE CAPITAL MARKETS AT A CROSSROADS

The Japanese system of cross-shareholdings has evolved from the ruins of the Second World War and has contributed to Japanese development partly because cross-shareholding has freed management from interference by shareholders and has enabled corporations to develop a co-operative network. In Japanese eyes this system does not unduly dampen competition nor is it excessively lacking in transparency. But even in Japan, the younger generation has become critical of the general orientation towards corporate life and the corporations themselves are wanting to change. The Japanese system does contribute significantly to the non-Japanese world through its high degree of efficiency with low-cost, high-quality products, and through demonstrating how to transfer technology. However, the system is facing criticism from the external community, especially from America on whom Japan depends heavily both economically and militarily. The Japanese need to admit that their system lacks transparency and is difficult for outsiders to break into. Since Japan derives benefit from and is vulnerable to any malfunctioning in global markets, this lack of understanding poses quite a problem.

Faced with these challenges, the Japanese corporate community must react. Some argue that they should discard their unique system and adopt the Anglo-American system, regarded as the international norm, without questioning its economic efficiency. In legislative terms, this should involve allowing holding companies to exist. This route is neither feasible nor productive. It is not feasible to dismantle the giant Japanese corporate system overnight, although the introduction of holding companies would be possible. It would be counter-productive because the corporate system is playing a constructive role in the global economy and its disruption would have a negative impact on the world economy.

Instead the Japanese corporate community should make the system more open and transparent. Information about cross-shareholding and intergroup transactions should be disclosed as fully as possible. The criteria for selecting long-term suppliers should be fully disclosed and foreigners invited to participate. We are witnessing some embryonic developments in this direction. In addition the greatest efforts should be taken to make Japanese corporate practice as compatible as possible with international norms. Globalization will accelerate this process. Japanese multinationals have been employing local staff abroad and have been delegating decision making to them. To make these multinational organizations a success, transparency and compatibility in the decision-making process are crucial. Since the current system grew out of employee loyalty formed from the experience of poverty-stricken post-war Japan and xenophobia at around the time of capital liberalization, there is probably some excess that could be corrected without removing the advantages of the system. Even without foreign pressure, corporations are changing. Different products and services are being demanded—more unique, information-oriented, quality products and services are replacing low-cost, functional products. Employees are shifting from an emphasis on stability to becoming more creative and are demanding 'creative' management (Murakami 1991).

Japanese corporations should moderate their emphasis on market share and growth and pay more attention to profitability and return on equity. A higher return on equity requires a shift in production towards higher value-added products. The collapse of the Tokyo stock-market is ending an era of relatively cheap equity financing and will put pressure on companies to be more particular about the return on investment. It will also make corporate investors more selective about entering into cross-shareholding relationships. This is already happening with the financial institutions in that the decline in the market has made it harder for banks to fulfil BIS capital ratio requirements. Furthermore, there is pressure from life insurance companies—which can distribute dividend income, but cannot distribute capital gains to policy holders—on corporations to distribute more in the form of dividends. These changes of attitude on the part of corporate investors should work to moderate cross-shareholdings.

Japanese capital markets have affected the desire of corporations to free themselves from shareholder influence and takeover threats and to acquire low-cost equity funding, and thus shift away from their traditional dependence on bank loans. However, the accompanying 'corporatization' of the capital markets has made them less transparent to non-corporate investors, especially individuals. The market boom during the 1980s partly arising from a loose monetary policy has led to many excesses, correcting which will prove quite painful.

Japanese markets need to be more transparent and the securities industry must work hard to recover the trust of clients, especially individuals. The accumulation of vast amounts of personal financial wealth provides a huge potential demand for equity, be it direct or indirect via such vehicles as pension funds, for example. It is estimated that pension fund assets could grow from 160 trillion yen at the beginning of the 1990s to over 300 trillion yen by the end of the decade, whilst personal financial assets could grow from 950 trillion yen to 2000 trillion yen during the same period. It is generally expected that growing investments from pension funds and individuals will gradually replace cross-shareholdings and restore the balance of the equity market (Tanabe 1991). Faced with difficulties in equity financing and the growing trend in securitization, the corporate bond market suddenly started to grow rapidly in 1991. This will pave the way for the development of what has been so far a relatively underdeveloped corporate bond market and needs to be accompanied by improvement in the necessary regulatory infrastructure. Japanese markets will need to move quickly to bridge the gap between their operational norms and those of international markets. The increase in institutionalization will aid this move. With regard to equity financing, investment criteria will focus more on earnings growth and the return to equity and price–earnings ratios that are adjusted to take account of cross-shareholdings.

REFERENCES

Itami, Hiroyuki (1991), 'Peoplism' (a draft version).

Kobayashi, Takao (1990), 'Kabushiki no fandamentaru baryuh' ('The fundamental value of stock') in K. Nishimura and Y. Miwa 'Nihon no Kabuka-chika' ('The prices of Japanese stock and land'), *Tokyo Daigaku Shuppankai*, April.

Miwa, Yoshiro (1991), 'Mochiai wa Yuueki', ('Cross-shareholdings are beneficial'), *Nihon Keizai Shinbun*, 19 August.

Murakami, T., Nishiwaki, T., *et al.* (1991), *Strategy for Creation* (Woodhead Publishing Limited).

Nakajima, Shuzo (1990), 'Kabusiki no mochiai to kigyohoh' ('Cross-shareholdings and corporate laws'), Shoujihoumukennkyuukai.

Nakatani, Iwao (1991), 'Nichibei inbaransu no kihonkozou' ('The fundamental structure of the US-Japan imbalance'), *Chuokouron*, January.

Nikami, Kiyoshi (1990), 'Nihon no shokengaisha keiei' ('Management of Japanese Securities Companies'), *Toyo keizai shinposha*, April.

Nishimura, Kiyohiko and Miwa, Yoshiro (1991), 'Nihon no kabuk chika' ('The stock and land prices'), *Tokyo daigakku shuppankai*, April.

Okumura, Hiroshi (1988), 'Nihon no Kabushikisijou' ('The Japanese Stock Market'), *Dayamondosha*, June.

Ota, Fusae (1991), 'Jidosha mehkak, buhin kaisha kyousouteki kankei' ('Automobile manufacturers have competitive relationships with parts suppliers'), *Nihon Keizai Shinbun*, 10 October.

Tanabe *et al.* (1991), 'Kabu wa Shindaka' ('Is equity dead?'), *Nihon Keizai Shinbun*.

INDEX